SOUTH EASTERN RAILWAY

Adrian Gray, M.A.

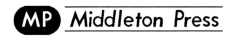

MP *Middleton Press*

1990

For Charles Devereux and Andrew Whitworth

First published November 1990

ISBN 0 906520 85 1

© Copyright A.Gray, 1990

Design - Deborah Goodridge

Published by Middleton Press
        Easebourne Lane
        Midhurst, West Sussex
        GU29 9AZ
        Tel. (0730) 813169

Printed & bound by Biddles Ltd,
        Guildford and Kings Lynn

CONTENTS

CHAPTER				PAGE
	Introduction			5
1.	The Origins of the South Eastern Railway			6
2.	The Opening Stages			11
3.	Years of Turmoil			22
4.	The Watkin Era			37
5.	London Bridge to Redhill -			
	i)	London Bridge to Redhill		53
	ii)	The East London Railway		63
	iii)	The Caterham Branch		65
	iv)	The Tattenham Corner Branch		68
6.	Lines in North Kent -			
	i)	The London & Greenwich Railway		70
	ii)	From Greenwich to Gravesend -		
		North Kent Line and Dartford Loop		72
	iii)	The Bexleyheath Line		87
	iv)	The Gravesend & Rochester		90
	v)	The Chatham Central Branch		96
	vi)	The Hundred of Hoo and Port Victoria		99
7.	The Bricklayers Arms Branch			104
8.	To The West End and The City -			
	i)	Charing Cross and Cannon Street		110
	ii)	The Blackfriars Junction Line		124
9.	The Mid-Kent Line and its Branches -			
	i)	The Mid-Kent Railway		128
	ii)	The Hayes & West Wickham Branch		135
	iii)	The Woodside & South Croydon Joint		137
10.	The Old Main Line from Redhill to Dover			140
11.	The New Main Line and its branches -			
	i)	The New Main Line		157
	ii)	The Bromley Branch		166
	iii)	The Westerham Branch		167
12.	Two Routes to Maidstone -			170
13.	The Reading, Guildford & Reigate			176
14.	Tunbridge Wells & Hastings -			
	i)	Tunbridge Wells & Hastings		192
	ii)	The Bexhill Branch		205
15.	The Rye Line			208
16.	Surrey & Sussex			215
17.	Branch Lines in Central Kent -			
	i)	The Tenterden and Hawkhurst Area		223
	ii)	The Lydd and Dungeness Area		227

18. The Hythe and Elham Branches -
  i) The Hythe & Sandgate Branch 230
  ii) The Hythe & Sandgate Tramway 235
  iii) The Elham Valley Line 236
19. East Kent and Thanet -
  i) The Canterbury & Whitstable Railway 239
  ii) The Canterbury & Thanet Line 243
  iii) The Deal Branch 251
  iv) The Deal & Dover Joint Line 254
20. Across The Channel -
  i) Folkestone Harbour and its Branch 259
  ii) The Development of The Channel Services 265
  iii) The Channel Tunnel 277
21. The Traffic -
  i) The Passengers 283
  ii) Premium Traffic - The Mails and Gold 290
  iii) Goods Traffic 293
22. Working for The South Eastern -
  i) The Staff 297
  ii) The Senior Staff 302
  iii) The Locomotive Department 305
  Sources 309
  Acknowledgements 310
  Index of characters 311
  Index of companies 312
  Index of places 314

DIAGRAMS

North Kent 73
Medway Area 91
Bromley Area 129
Dover Area 156
South Eastern Rly in 1898 Inside back cover
London Area Inside back cover

INTRODUCTION

The South Eastern was a fascinating railway with more than its fair share of strong personalities. It had the glamour of participating in the London to Paris traffic, regularly carrying royalty, international political figures, and celebrities like Charles Dickens. Closer to London, it handled a dense suburban traffic and has etched its own indelible print on the shape of London today - whole areas of the capital's south-eastern suburbs were created through the opportunities opened up by the SER.

Its story contains a large number of famous incidents and events: two very early railways like the lines to Greenwich and Whitstable, a famous accident at Staplehurst, and the celebrated robbery of gold bullion.

In the popular mind the SER is often associated with the "follies" of Sir Edward Watkin, who dominated its affairs for thirty years. It is Watkin who has traditionally been blamed for the weaknesses of the SER, but it is a fascinating part of the South Eastern's story that Watkin actually took over a railway torn apart by factional infighting - other names are as black, if not blacker, than Sir Edward's, for it was others who allowed the SER's deadly rival to gain a foothold in Kent.

Watkin was a visionary, forever dreaming of grandiose schemes for which he was ridiculed. The Channel Tunnel was almost an obsession with him, yet he has been proved right - in terms of the national interest, if not in terms of easy profits. His vision of a national port at the Isle of Grain was also scorned, yet came to pass. The record also shows that he made several attempts to unite the railway companies of southern England, and was generally not the cause of the failure of these attempts. Certainly he did waste shareholders' money on some of his imaginative schemes, but the SER provided an adequate express service and handled its suburban traffic competently, rewarding its investors more abundantly than its rival, the Chatham, could manage.

This book is intended to stand beside the present author's volume on the London, Chatham & Dover Railway, but is a wholly separate work. It is hoped to be able to produce a subsequent work dealing with the South Eastern & Chatham Railways from 1899.

A.G.
Colchester, May 1990.

CHAPTER 1: THE ORIGINS OF THE SOUTH EASTERN RAILWAY

Many of the earliest railway schemes were promoted with the object of developing local commerce or of making profits from heavy goods traffic. In the early 1800s canals and coastal waterways were the best means of transport for heavy goods, but offered a fairly slow service for passengers with the exception of the steamers that plied their trade along the Thames from London to pleasure resorts like Gravesend and Margate.

Kent was especially well served by water transport. Three sides of the County were enclosed by navigable waters and few substantial towns were far from the reach of water transport. Tonbridge was reached by the Medway Navigation and all the towns of northern Kent could boast excellent services for both goods and passengers to the Metropolis.

Attempts to extend the waterway network were largely doomed to failure, since few profitable opportunities remained untapped. One of the few that achieved any form of success was the Medway Navigation, which operated between Maidstone and Tonbridge; in 1835 this Company even planned an extension to Forest Row in East Sussex.

One of these schemes was John Rennie's Weald of Kent Canal, which was proposed in 1812 to link the rivers Medway and Rother. It included a proposal for a tramway to Wye Downs, but was never built.

The idea of using a tramway to extend the reach of a Canal was gradually replaced by the idea of building a tramway, or railway, as an entity in itself. However, as late as 1832 a tramway and roadway was being proposed from the Medway at Penshurst to Tunbridge Wells Common, including a tunnel at Mount Ephraim.[1] By the 1830s, though, such proposals were already seeming archaic. In 1823 William James had proposed a number of railways in the South-east, including one from Strood to Portsmouth via Edenbridge and Horsham. Another substantial proposal to affect Kent was Henry Palmer's 1824-5 Kentish Railway scheme for a railway from Camberwell to Strood, via Eltham and Crayford. It was to have branches to Greenwich, Dartford and Maidstone, although at various times it offered the prospect of rail services to most Kent towns including Dover.[2]

Almost simultaneously, Palmer became involved with The Tunbridge Wells, Snodland and Edenbridge Suspension Railway; this had its origins in the need to provide a more reliable means of transporting goods to Tunbridge Wells, one of the few Kent towns remote from navigable waters. The line was to be built on Palmer's "monorail" principle, running from Spong's Wharf at Snodland. The scheme seems to have fallen foul of local landowners and by January 1826 was despairing enough to abandon any hope of a Parliamentary Bill.

Altogether more ambitious, and the most substantial of the schemes in this first Kentish "Railway Mania", was Thomas Telford's Kentish Railway of 1829. This was a £1,000,000 plan to build a railway from London to Dover along the North Kent route via Gravesend, Chatham and Canterbury. Branches to

Maidstone and Tonbridge, and to Ramsgate and Margate, were to be included. Sadly, this visionary proposal found no Kentish prophets to herald its advent.

Henry Palmer was behind a scheme in 1830 as well, also for a line terminating at Ramsgate. In 1832 he produced an imaginative proposal for a line from the Regent's Canal and the West India Docks, crossing the Thames and the Medway by train ferries, to Canterbury; from there the railway vehicles were to use normal roads to get to the coast. However, this was to be a horse-drawn railway.

The first actual railway to be built in Kent was the Canterbury & Whitstable. This line was the result of Canterbury's frustration at the impossibility of using the River Stour for goods transport and in 1823 William James had proposed a railway instead. However it opened to the public on 4th May 1830, making it easily the first proper railway in Kent.[3]

The South Eastern Railway's history really begins with the London & Greenwich Railway, whose Act of Parliament was passed on 17 May 1833. This was to create a terminus at London Bridge and a short line, almost entirely on brick-built viaduct, to Greenwich. This was the spark that lit the blaze of Kent's second "Railway Mania", and one that was eventually to bear significant results.

The key figures in the London & Greenwich, Colonel Landmann and George Walter, did not intend their line to stop at Greenwich. As early as February 1833 there were reports that the Company intended to go on to Dover while Walter tried to form a London & Gravesend Railway. During 1834 this seems to have also been known as the "New Kent Railroad" and the "Continental Railway Company", before reverting to the plain Gravesend Railway.

Palmer was also active in 1833-4, planning a line for Sir Isaac Goldsmid that was to reach Plumstead via the north side of the Thames due to problems passing through Greenwich.

By March 1834 the *Maidstone Journal* was very excited about the New Kent Railroad, which was to run from Greenwich, via Wouldham, to Cheriton, from where two branches would lead to Dover and Folkestone. Landmann and Green, the Secretary of the London & Greenwich, were heavily involved in promoting the line. However, by October 1834 Walter had decided to restrict himself to a £600,000 plan to extend from Greenwich to Gravesend though the Bill for this had to be withdrawn in 1835 due to vigorous opposition. However the Company did get as far as doing trial borings in Greenwich Park, going as deep as 43 feet without finding water. However, it was the very existence of Greenwich Park and the powerful vested interests of the Royal Observatory which was to frustrate attempts to extend the London & Greenwich line.

Captain John Pringle, formerly of the Royal Engineers, was also active with a number of others, including the architect Decimus Burton, in surveying for a railway from London to Dover during 1834. They chose to avoid the North Kent route, perhaps because of competition from the Thames steamers, though a by-law of the Watermen's Company restricted these to 5mph. They were particularly occupied in searching for a way through the North Downs but after examining the Ravensbourne Valley (via Farnborough and Pratts Bottom) and a Greenhithe to New Hythe line concluded that a route via Godstone was the most satisfactory, since this avoided difficult river crossings and the high ground around Sevenoaks. This brought a London-Dover Railway over twenty miles in the direction of Brighton, and so a Brighton line was added to the scheme. This was the genesis of the South Eastern route, for those involved included many who were highly influential in South Eastern Railway history. Pascoe St. Leger Grenfell, a banker, organised the finance and became the first Chairman of the SER. The solicitor, Fearon, and other backers such as David Salomons and Thomas Tyndall, maintained long connections with the Company. Salomons chaired a number of public meetings, such as the one at Tunbridge Wells in October 1835.

In the days of the hectic promotion of railway schemes, the autumn months often proved crucial. This was the time when promoters prepared their Parliamentary Bills and assessed the state of the opposition, when engineers and directors addressed inquisitive crowds in small country towns, and also when solicitors gleefully contemplated the coming legal battles. By September 1835 Palmer was in the field again helping the South Eastern with a London to Brighton scheme, routed via Godstone and with a branch to Tunbridge Wells. By October 1835 the South Eastern Railway had formally joined the fray with an ambitious scheme for a line from London to Dover via Oxted, and with a "branch" from Oxted to Preston in Sussex, from which a further extension was contemplated to Hove and Shoreham. It intended a branch to Maidstone as well, but felt that Rochester could organise its own service. At the London end it was planning a link to the London & Southampton Railway at Wandsworth.

The London & Greenwich faction had been intending to advance only with a "Greenwich & Gravesend Railway", though it had changed its name to "London & Gravesend Railway" by the time its Bill reached Parliament for the First Reading in February 1836.

Yet by the time the Gravesend Bill reached Parliament, Green and Walter were already concerned that the new schemes would impinge on territory that seemed naturally theirs. In November 1835 they therefore set about promoting the "London & Dover Railway", which was to continue from Gravesend to Ashford, Folkestone and Dover; it would seem that Maidstone was to have a branch from Strood.

As the battle lines were drawn at the end of 1835 there were five main contenders in the field. There was the Greenwich & Gravesend, the extension of the original London & Greenwich, which had sprouted two extensions of its own - the Northfleet and Dover (via Maidstone and Ashford) and the Kent Railway (via Rochester and Sittingbourne to Canterbury, Deal and Dover, with a Ramsgate branch). The Central Kent Railway was the scheme backed by Maidstone since it went via the Darent Valley and Kent's County town to Canterbury and Deal. The latter was an ill-prepared scheme, though it continued to make hopeful applications to Parliament from 1836 to 1842.

The South Eastern Railway, though, was a serious contender and remained in the field. It had the security of strong support from Liverpool and Manchester financial interests, who played an influential role in its progress over the next 30 years. It is notable that in May 1836 it had 112 "local" subscribers who had promised to invest £215,000 - a relatively small part of the total £982,000 subscribed for[4]. It prepared itself for the likely Parliamentary conflict by dropping the planned Brighton line by January 1836, since there were a number of other rival Brighton schemes, and also dropping the Tunbridge Wells branch. Its representatives toured the south-east relentlessly, pouring scorn on their rivals at every opportunity; the problems of the Gravesend & Dover were so great, a Tonbridge meeting was told, that "it was impossible that the plan could ever be acted upon." John Herapath campaigned on behalf of the Greenwich factions, whipping up support in Maidstone by prophesying that the London & Dover (or, more accurately, Northfleet & Dover) via Maidstone would yield a 15% return.

The conflict reached its peak in February-March 1836. Representatives from the rival concerns toured the Kent towns, drumming up support or answering critical questions. Gravesend disliked Landmann's Northfleet & Dover (London & Dover), fearing that its route from Northfleet to Meopham and Maidstone would leave the north Kent town out on a limb; Maidstone, though, was enthusiastic. It received helpful publicity from John Herapath who published the *Railway Magazine*. Maidstone felt that the South Eastern, which would leave it on a branch from Tonbridge, would be "highly injurious". In April 1836 they therefore tried to repromote the "Direct London, Dover & Central Kent Railway" in order to place their town on a through route. Some people opposed any line that had a tunnel: one man believed that lines with a tunnel would never be popular due to the danger of meeting therein a manure train going in the other direction[5]. Kent was experiencing the first Railway Mania, with so many proposals that some wondered what it was in the county that brought in these schemes:

"Like Paddy's potato in a ten-acre field, our railroad virtue....is grown so monstrously large, as to thrust every other good or bad quality over the hedge.[6]*"*

The London & Gravesend Bill came unstuck on its second reading when opposition was led by John Julius Angerstein, who said the line was entirely pointless since the Gravesend steamers already did the job very well, taking about one and a half hours and charging one shilling. The Bill was lost by 177-62.

This defeat left Herapath, Landmann and their acolytes distraught, for the failure of the Gravesend Bill doomed its two offshoots. However Herapath continued campaigning on behalf of the "London & Dover" into March 1836, though he mostly concentrated on denigrating the South Eastern - which he told the people of Rochester was impracticable, badly engineered, circuitous, missed the centres of population and passed through "barren parts". The following month he called the SER "perfectly absurd."

When the South Eastern Railway Bill reached the Committee stage, it came under close scrutiny because of its ambitious plans. There was to be a lengthy embankment from Croydon to Riddlesdown, where there was to be a tunnel with another one close by at Oxted. Peter Sinclair of the Bolton Railway gave evidence as to the suitability of the gradients on this stretch of the line. There were to be three "inclined planes": at Riddlesdown of 1 in 150, south of Oxted at 1 in 100, and at Beachborough of 1 in 100 - all to be worked by "assistant power". Herapath seized on comments that trains would only be able to manage 9mph on these climbs:

"A very un-railway like speed it is true, but perhaps intended for the purpose of affording time to...examine the geological structures of the deep cuttings...and to save the nerves of young ladies from the shock of entering too suddenly the tunnel under Riddlesdown[7]*."*

The four tunnels were to be at Riddlesdown (528 yards), Oxted (2706 yards), and two on the coastal section through the cliffs between Folkestone and Dover - of 1600 and 1040 yards. The idea of taking the line along the cliff face so as to serve both Folkestone and Dover was attributed to Palmer. It was to terminate at Astley Fort near Dover. The estimated cost, not including any branches, was £1,334,649.

The House of Commons Committee under T. Hodges was unimpressed by the Central Kent Railway's poor state of preparation and felt that the Kent Railway - the most northern route - was satisfactory for a London to Ramsgate line but not for a route to Dover.

The South Eastern Railway gained its Act of Parliament on 21 June 1836, with an authorised capital of £1.4m and borrowing powers of £450,000.

This was not the end of the SER's battle. The London & Greenwich faction had regrouped, this time with James Walker as engineer instead of Landmann, but still with the omnipresent George Walter. They took the name of the Kent Railway and, even before the South Eastern had gained its Act, issued a prospectus in May 1836 having amalgamated with the Dover Railway interests the previous month. However the success of the SER's Bill persuaded the Kent Railway to content itself with a North Kent line to Ramsgate. When the Bill for this reached Parliament many unsatisfactory details emerged about Walter's financial methods and he resigned from the London & Greenwich in 1837. Warburton's Parliamentary study of the Kent Railway Bill also revealed some unusual practices; the subscription list, where members of the public signed to show their commitment to the scheme financially, included the name of Herapath's young son, who had promised to subscribe £5,000. This very youthful capitalist was eclipsed by his sister, pledged to subscribe £5,250. Warburton's investigations led to the rejection of the Bill and this left the North Kent route unoccupied, a situation which was to cause problems for the SER a few years later. Herapath was spiteful about Warburton, printing rumours in the hope that his enemy could be smeared; he reported a rumour that Warburton "does not like the ladies, which is so very wicked a calumny - so unlike an Englishman - we cannot believe it[8]."

1.   J.Corley, **The Tunbridge Wells, Snodland & Edenbridge Suspension Railway**, p.17.
2.   R.Thomas, **The London & Greenwich Railway**, p.12.
3.   See Chapter 19.
4.   **Maidstone Journal**, 31 May 1836.
5.   From a letter to **Herapath**, dated 25 April 1836.
6.   Letter to **Herapath's Railway Magazine**, 1836, p.72.
7.   **Herapath**, 1836, p.72.
8.   **Herapath's Railway Magazine**, June 1837.

CHAPTER 2: THE OPENING STAGES

The South Eastern Railway Act was passed on 21 June 1836, the Board having its first official meeting on 2 July. Pascoe St Leger Grenfell became Chairman, but the Board consisted of relatively few who were to see the Company through to maturity; this reflected the problems that were to lie ahead. James Yeats was appointed Secretary.

An immediate problem was that Henry Palmer, whose illness had delayed his Parliamentary evidence, was unable to accept the post of permanent engineer. Palmer told the Board that he claimed responsibility for the Bill's success, having designed "the passage along the cliffs near Dover...to which the success of the Bill is mainly attributable[1]." Palmer was replaced within a few days by William Cubitt at a salary of 1200 guineas per annum, plus seven guineas a day when "out on the line".

Cubitt had already gone to bed one night when the messenger arrived with the good news from the SER; he flung open his bedroom window to find what the caller wanted, had the news shouted to him from the street, then went calmly back to bed[2].

Cubitt began his new job by surveying the route that Pringle and Palmer had laid out. He started by looking at the London end of the line, where problems were immediately apparent. Leaving the London terminus of the London & Greenwich Railway, South Eastern trains were to run over L&GR tracks as far as Corbetts Lane; from there to Croydon they were to use the lines of the London & Croydon Railway, which had been authorised on 12 June 1835 and eventually opened to West Croydon on 5 June 1839. Cubitt disliked the sharp junction between the L&CR and the SER at Croydon, did not approve of the crossings over the turnpike in Croydon itself, and also disliked the 1 in 100 climb to Oxted.

He suggested that the SER should leave the L&CR further north, at Penge Common, pass to the east of Croydon to Riddlesdown and then, after a tunnel near Godstone, rejoin the authorised route at Wellwood Farm near Limpsfield. Cubitt also wanted deviations in the line between Ashford and Dover, largely so as to avoid leaving Folkestone on a branch.

Cubitt was not the only one unhappy with the details of Palmer's plan; there were many complaints from landowners such as Major Leake, whose "pleasure ground" near Oxted was affected by the scheme.

The South Eastern Board had been watching the Parliamentary struggle over London to Brighton routes with great interest and when Robert Stephenson's London & Brighton Railway Bill was thrown out on 2 August 1836 they despatched Cubitt to survey an SER route to Lewes and Brighton, with a branch to Newhaven. This started a lengthy discussion over routes - the intial proposal being to start from a junction at Hurst Green, passing either by West Hoathly or Turner's Hill, then through a tunnel at Clayton or Ditchling to Brighton. On 2 September 1836 a Board member suggested to Cubitt that they should go via Merstham rather than Oxted, but by 9 September Cubitt had already surveyed from the Jolly Sailor in Norwood (later Norwood Junction) to "Bow Beech" (the modern spelling is Bough Beech) in Kent. He was inclined to adopt an intermediate route between the two using "Godstone Pass" - 220 feet lower than the Oxted route and with a tunnel of only one mile.

The Autumn was largely taken up by constant discussion over the choice of route, now influenced by the desire to serve Brighton too. Cubitt had to meet Lord de l'Isle as a deviation around Tonbridge powder mills and to give better crossings of the Medway and a turnpike at Tonbridge would affect Penshurst Park. Lord Strongford declared he had had to abandon plans to build a mansion at Westenhanger because of the railway; he received £1500 compensation in June 1837. Sandling Park was also affected since trains would be visible from the drawing room windows - it is to be assumed that there were then no rich railway enthusiasts willing to pay a premium for such a facility!

By 4 November Cubitt had crystallised his deviation proposals: "Bowbeech" to Tudeley[3], Wellwood Farm to Moor House in Godstone, Moor House to the Jolly Sailor, and the alterations between Dover and Folkestone so that the latter was not left on a branch.

By January 1837 work was ready to start on the trial shafts for Riddlesdown tunnel and the issue of travelling in tunnels was discussed. The length of tunnel on the Oxted route was a major objection so in February the SER borrowed a locomotive from the London & Birmingham Railway for experiments in Primrose Hill tunnel. According to the Minutes, they also had a day of experiments on the Leeds & Selby Railway. As a result, the Board was told that it had been "established satisfactorily that the objections urged against tunnels have no foundation whatever." To support this, Cubitt brought a tunnel "Transit Instrument" from the London & Birmingham, and the Oxted route - with its long tunnels - was back in favour. Work began at Riddlesdown on 11 March 1837[4].

The Act authorising Cubitt's deviations was passed on 3 July 1837. Although this included the significant improvements in the Dover and Folkestone area, more important was probably the London & Brighton Railway's Act of 15 July 1837. This line was to be built according to Rennie's plans and its route

1.   Shakespeare Cliff Tunnel in about 1850.

2. **Foord Viaduct, Folkestone, in the first years of the SER. Note the guards sitting on the carriage roofs.**

southwards from London had much in common with the SER's. Both lines were to share the tracks of the London & Croydon Railway as far as Norwood, and then were to run almost side by side as far as Purley. The Brighton Act therefore contained a clause to allow the two Companies to share a route so as to avoid wasteful duplication, and it allowed the SER to alter its route to have a junction with the Brighton line anywhere north of Earlswood. Powers for such a junction had to be sought within two years and the SER could buy the shared route north of the junction. This rendered work at Riddlesdown useless, so the contractor's equipment was transferred from there to Tonbridge in September 1838; the contractor was paid £100 for this inconvenience.

By September 1837 Cubitt was under instructions to co-operate with Gibbs, the Brighton Railway's engineer, in surveying a junction between the lines. Agreement was reached in January 1838 for a line to Redhill via Merstham; this had the additional advantage of saving the SER a great deal of money at a time when it was encountering problems because of defaulting share subscribers. Of the original 28,000 shares, there were problems with at least 10,000.

The agreement to build a shared line direct to Redhill (as it later became known) gave a strong advantage to the Brighton Company since it was directly on a course for Brighton but far from direct for trains going to Dover. Although the idea is usually credited to politicians, it had been suggested before - but the final decision to go for this route seems to have been motivated by financial concerns above all else. It proved to be a fateful error, for the trek via Redhill merely accentuated the indirect way in which the South Eastern was to serve Kent's major towns; therefore it was a direct cause of later rival schemes.

It was agreed in February 1838 that the Brighton Company would be responsible for the works on the shared section of line south from the Jolly Sailor at Norwood. However the SER was uncertain as to how to link Redhill (sometimes referred to as "Redstone Hill" or "Red Hill") to its original line near Tonbridge and during 1838 was hesitating over alternative routes. In November 1838 it was finally decided to have the junction at "Red Hill" rather than the more northerly Merstham, where local opposition had led to the arrest of Cubitt's son while surveying; this, the "Redstone Junction" line, was authorised on 19 July 1839. Four months later it was agreed that the section of line between Red Hill and Stoat's Nest Farm, near Coulsdon, would be built by the L&BR and then conveyed to the SER on completion at cost plus maintenance. The rest of the line to Norwood was to remain in L&BR hands, according to terms agreed on 25 April 1839, with both companies being allowed toll-free use of each other's section.

This resolved how the SER was to get into Kent, but there had also been a debate over how it was to enter London. In November 1836 it had been proposed that the SER should build an extra line to give better access to the West End, running from the Jolly Sailor to the obelisk in St George's Fields. Another plan suggested a line from the London & Croydon at Penge Common to the obelisk. The obelisk site soon became known as the "Central & West End Terminus", but it remained obstinately on the Surrey side of the Thames.

As early as December 1836 Cubitt was concerned that the SER's access to London depended on two other Companies. He therefore suggested to the SER Board that they take over the London & Croydon Railway which he thought would be a "valuable appendage" to the SER. The Board met their L&C counterparts on 10 December and proposed a union with two L&C directors to join the SER Board, but the L&CR rejected the terms.

In January 1837 the plans for the obelisk line were dropped - but only for a time. They were briefly revived in June 1839, with a plan for a new line from Dartmouth Arms (near Forest Hill) via Peckham to Elephant & Castle; there was also an alternative suggestion for a direct line from Addiscombe Road to Elephant & Castle via Herne Hill, but this would have meant moving the Croydon station.

At the opposite end of the line Cubitt was seeking a good site for the Dover terminus. In August 1836 he had advocated the Military Hospital site but any extension of the line came into conflict with questions of defence. Having the terminus west of the Archcliffe Fort "ditch" was considered unacceptable by the SER since passenger traffic required that the line actually reached Dover rather than expiring at its ramparts. However military authorities were obsessed with the idea that, if the line pierced the defences, hordes of foreign invaders would slaughter the poor citizens of Dover. By January 1837 the issue had become bogged down in talks with several interested parties, including the Dover Harbour trustees who wanted a more inland course. The Board decided to defer the decision.

With all these matters being discussed, progress on the works was slow. Both the selection of the Merstham and Redhill route, and the chronic lack of cash, imposed their own limits. By February 1837 substantial contracts were at last being let, the one for the double Shakespeare tunnels going to Rowland & Hight for £11,707-17-0d. Money was so short, though, that payments to Directors were suspended in June 1837 and their expenses limited to only £1 per meeting! This cash shortage probably explains why the Rowland & Hight contract was not actually signed until December 1837.

This did nothing to help the prospects of one Director, Edmund Halswell, the first in a long line of SER Board members to be struck by scandal. He was removed from the Board of the Kent, Surrey & Sussex Banking Company after allegations of impropriety in paying share deposits. Halswell was then told that it would be helpful if he did not attend SER meetings either.

By March 1838, when Grenfell had moved to Liverpool and been replaced as Chairman by Thomas Tyndale, seven shafts had been sunk down to 100 feet at the Dover tunnels, but work in the area was held up by claims about ownership of land at the base of the cliff. In February 1839 it was decided to build a sea wall to protect the line between Shakespeare and Archcliffe tunnels, using spoil from the tunnels themselves. A fall of chalk at Shakespeare Cliff in February 1839 revealed the "vertebrae of an immense animal", but work was delayed in December 1839 when the contractor at the Dover tunnels abandoned the task.

Relationships with landowners were difficult, especially when men working on the line were caught poaching. Peter Barlow, the engineer in charge of the Tonbridge section, sacked some men for this in October 1839. Four Inspectors of Police were appointed to keep the navvies in order, but another three men had to be appointed in June 1840. However, the navvy's life was also dangerous - at least five men died during the construction of the Dover section. Perhaps to sweeten their toils, the Board decided in October 1840 to build a chapel for the labourers at Folkestone.

However, at least the line was starting to take shape. Once the "Redstone Hill line" was authorised, contractor Tredwell moved his men there from Folkestone Warren. Collis, doing the "Bowbeech" works, even pressed the Union Workhouse into use. However the contractors at Godstone, Parr & Co., were sacked in August 1840 following a row between the partners.

There were still financial problems due to arrears on the various calls for payment. One proprietor, Tyrell, started an action against Tyndale, claiming that the Chairman was responsible for the unsound state of the finances. Eventually he had to withdraw his suit and was loudly hissed at the General Meeting in December 1839. He certainly had cause to be worried however, for arrears on calls had reached £71,092 by 1st October 1839, rising to a peak of £110,455 on 6th April 1840.

One sign of a railway nearing completion was a flood of petitions for stations - Headcorn being the first in with a request. In January 1841 Brenchley, Goudhurst and Horsmonden also petitioned for a station in their district. It was decided to build timber viaducts over the Medway near Tonbridge and to use triangular sectioned sleepers - 9 feet long, 12 inches wide and 6 inches deep. Rails were brought up the Medway to Tonbridge at 7s. per ton, and twelve engines were ordered from Sharp, Roberts at £1455 each; tenders were an extra £275. Decimus Burton was engaged to offer architectural advice to Cubitt.

Bletchingley became the centre of attention in April 1841. An extra watchman had to be employed after a gin rope was severed, then the Board learnt that tunnel work was being done there on Sundays. They decided that this should occur only "in cases of indispensible necessity." In July the Rector of Bletchingley visited the tunnel and "descended several of the Pits"; he was apparently satisfied of the need for Sabbath-breaking.

The first celebration seems to have occurred in April 1841, when workmen were allowed £20 to spend on commemorating the completion of the northern one of the Shakespeare Cliff Tunnels. Not that the financial troubles had passed to issue in a new phase of generosity - for in November 1841 the Chairman, now Joseph Baxendale, lent his own Company £10,000!

The navvies celebrated Christmas 1841 with a riot at Godstone, during which a constable was injured. With opening now imminent J.S.Yeats, the SER Secretary, was appointed Superintendent of the Line. One of his staff soon complained that a contractor in the Ashford district was operating a "tommy shop", to exploit the navvies by charging high prices.

The SER was hoping to start running some trains to Tonbridge in May 1842. Several orders for carriages were placed and timetables were discussed with the Croydon and Brighton railways during April 1842. The Croydon had, of course, been running trains since 5 June 1839 whilst the London & Brighton had opened as far south as Haywards Heath on 12 July 1841. Thus both were in operation well before the SER, emphasising the problems caused by the late start on the "Redstone Junction" line. The SER decided not to stop down trains at Merstham station and several rules were introduced - for example, dogs, smokers and drunks were all banned from the carriages. It was decided to run no trains on Sundays.

Obviously the L&BR had been using the SER portion of the shared route since its opening, having built the Stoat's Nest to Redhill portion itself. The SER was meant to pay for this when it had completed its own line as far as Edenbridge and it set 19 July 1842 as the date when it would pay the L&BR. As the day drew near the SER began to complain of delays in readying it for their use and instead invested the £240,000 they had set aside until the differences could be settled. These events seem to have coincided remarkably with a collapse in the SER share price during August 1842 amidst rumours of a shortage of capital.

The dispute over payment for the Merstham line continued for several years. In June 1843 the Brighton Company Minutes reported that they were expecting £357,410-1-8d, but the SER objected on the grounds that no proper contract had been awarded for the works and alleged overspending of £22,070. They refused to pay £132,465 of the sum due and also rejected outright the gas lights that the L&BR had installed in Merstham tunnel for the convenience of timid passengers; the L&BR never succeeded in palming the gas lights and the works off to the SER, instead providing lights in its carriages from 1 December 1842 and using the redundant apparatus to light Lewes station.

The first part of the SER's line to be constructed by itself was not opened until 26 May 1842 when trains began running through from "Red Hill" (Reigate Junction) to Tonbridge[5]. This involved employing staff to cover the service of four trains each way per day, and those enlisted at Tonbridge included carriage examiners at 30s a week and switchmen at 25s. Journalists were soon investigating the new line and approved of the first class carriages, finding them to provide "a luxury not usually met with on a railway[6]." They were pleased with the results of the Adams bowsprings and noted that the livery was "Wellington brown."

The initial traffic returns were disappointing so it was decided in July 1842 to introduce a Sunday mid-day train; the excuse for this reversal of policy was "public necessity". In fact there was a serious lack of through traffic on the line, a situation which seemed unlikely to improve until the line reached Dover.

The first stations opened were at Red Hill, where the SER opened its own temporary station on the down side of the junction. The L&BR had a quite separate station (originally "Red Hill & Reigate Road") on its own line, also on the down side of the junction and separated from the SER station by an uncomfortable road journey. This state of affairs arose because the two Companies disagreed as to where traffic should be exchanged - the L&BR had decided on Merstham and had provided a substantial station to the south of the village, which they hoped would be paid for by the SER; the SER wanted a junction station just to the north of the junction itself.

Beyond Red Hill, the first SER stations were at Godstone, Edenbridge, Penshurst and Tonbridge. Staff were also employed at Bletchingley to supervise the tunnel. On 31 August 1842 the line was extended to Headcorn, including additional stations at Maidstone Road, Staplehurst, Marden and Headcorn itself. The service was then increased to six trains per day, the fastest journey from London Bridge being in 2 hours 15 minutes.

During the period of the line's construction, the Medway Navigation had an Indian Summer. Goods were brought up by barge to Maidstone, where they were stored in Town Meadow before being collected by SER carts. Baltic fir

3. The Duke of Wellington's personal carriage, which gives an interesting view of luxury travelling conditions in the 1840s. (Wakeman Collection)

was brought in for sleepers and an "immense copper, resembling a steam-engine boiler" set up in a meadow to do the seasoning.

Getting the contractors to abide by the Truck Acts continued to be a problem. Sub-contractor Painter had to be hauled before the Cranbrook magistrates for paying a labourer 5s3d in cash and 4s in a ticket for Ralph's tommy shop. The case was dismissed on a legal technicality. The navvies also suffered from dangerous working practices; two were killed at Marl Pit Hill near Tonbridge when they were riding on a wagon laden with sleepers and the train made a sudden stop - they were crushed as the pile of sleepers collapsed.

Bad feeling was caused between the L&BR and the SER over the failure to settle the issue of Reigate Junction. Both companies had stations at the country side of the junction, but the SER was intent on having a station built just up from the junction. That the public agreed with the SER can be seen from a letter written to the *Maidstone Journal* in June 1841 - by a passenger who tried to travel from Tonbridge to Brighton. He complained bitterly that he was forced to travel nearly a mile[7] between the two stations along a "muddy or dusty road", though only five minutes was allowed in which to make the connection. He went on:

"I cannot conclude without stating that great civility is shown to passengers by those in power at the Reigate (Dover) station, they allow their porters to carry the luggage; but at the Red Hill (Brighton) station, you are obliged to hunt till you find some idle man willing to earn a shilling."

In the SER's view it was wasteful to have two stations, but the L&BR favoured using Merstham as the interchange and keeping separate stations at the junction. No doubt this was motivated by self-interest, since the L&BR station was nearer to the actual town of Reigate and it would lose the advantage if a "joint" station was constructed. The L&BR had also built the Merstham station at Battle Bridge, inconvenient for the villagers there. Having inherited this station, the SER decided it would be a good idea to demolish it in October 1842, but in fact the buildings survived for another 100 years.

The expenses of the Merstham station were cut in April 1843 by removing the sidings and the SER offered to provide a temporary station at the junction with simple platforms, offices and two water cranes; the L&BR rejected this offer. However, by September 1843 the Brighton Company had at last conceded to pressure and a new shared station at "Red Hill" was firmly on the drawing board. The SER took immediate steps to close the unprofitable Merstham station from 1 October, sending its staff to "Reigate Junction" (presumably meaning the new station) and Bletchingley. The Countess of Warwick, who lived nearby at Gatton, disliked this and took out a legal action to force the SER to reopen Merstham from 4 October 1844[8].

The new station at the junction was opened on 15 April 1844 on the site of today's Redhill station and was known as "Reigate", altering to "Reigate Junction" on 4 July 1849 and "Red Hill Junction" in August 1858. Special rules were issued in September 1843 for the switchmen at this important junction, who were instructed to display a "Danger" signal for 5 minutes after the passage of a train and "Caution" for the next five. All Brighton trains were to be signalled "Caution" and limited to 10mph. Dover up trains were to be given priority over Brighton up trains. Not surprisingly, by 1844 the L&BR was complaining of the "detention" of its trains by SER staff at the junction.

All this diverted attention from the main purpose of the SER - to reach Dover, though in August 1842 rumours suggested that it was to abandon the costly Folkestone to Dover section altogether. In November 1842, however, the Board decided to promote the Dover Terminus Bill; this was to extend the line in tunnel beneath Archcliffe Fort to a station which the *Dover Chronicle* prophesied with considerable inaccuracy would be "on a scale of magnitude unequalled in this country." The Board of Ordnance required that the tunnel mouths should be "capable of being closed like the exterior gateways of Fortresses." The Act for the extension was passed in 1843, and allowed for the line to be carried from Shakespeare Cliff towards Dover on a wooden trestle at the top of the beach.

The public opening of the line to Ashford took place on 1 December 1842, but this was preceded on 28 November by a special train. According to one report this was driven by "Benjamin" Cubitt of the SER and Charles Gregory of the L&CR, leaving London Bridge at 9am. The weather was miserable as the train ran over the original portion of the SER, but one journalist recorded that, "The traffic of the last two months has made the old portion firm and there was no longer the vibration which was at first observable." It consisted of one third class carriage and six first class, hauled by *Harold* and taking three and a half hours to reach Ashford. It was reported that, "On the new portion of the line the puffing monster dragging the train excited no small degree of surprise in the rustic inhabitants - and no less consternation among the brute creation." Once on the new portion of line, General Pasley made several requests for stops so that he could inspect the works for the Board of Trade. Cheers greeted the train at Pluckley at 12.05pm and at Ashford, while at the latter a band joined in with the inevitable *See the Conquering Hero Comes*, which one would have thought the ardent clergy of the day would have condemned as blasphemous; the SER was called many things in its time, but messianic was not a common description of a railway.

Many of the original stations were of a simple wooden character rather than the grand structures originally favoured, and did not impress a shareholder named Wicks. It was reported that he complained about the Board's policy in strong, if patriotic, terms:

"As foreigners were likely to use the South Eastern line they ought to honour their country and have becoming stations, not miserable paltry erections and he would submit to a smaller dividend in order to pay for them rather than incur the jeers of foreigners."

Ashford was a large station, though it was provided with the standard wooden buildings loved by the SER; it may well have had two platform lines and two through lines from the beginning.It was the scene of one of the first fatal accidents on the SER when, in May 1843, a guard was killed. He had stepped onto the "running board" of a carriage to look for a passenger's bag when the train started suddenly; his head hit the "sentry box" and he fell under the wheels, suffering decapitation.

Work had started on the Folkestone to Dover section in 1837, notably the tunnelling at Shakespeare Cliff where the chalk was said to be so compact that it needed no lining. On 8 May 1839 work began on the section between Abbot's Cliff Tunnel and the Foord viaduct at Folkestone. Some of this work was in the hands of Grissell, Peto & Betts - names that brought the SER great problems a few years later.

The headings at the Shakespeare Cliff Tunnel had met in October 1839 and it became well-known for the strange tricks the light played in the chalk galleries. The *Kentish Times* reported that "on some occasions a blue light is thrown up, which produces a strange and almost unearthly effect." The northern of the two tunnels was completed in May 1841, putting it well ahead of the Saltwood Tunnel - west of Folkestone - which was not begun by Grissell, Peto & Betts until 1842. In October 1842 there was a navvy riot at Folkestone, with three being arrested.

Parts of this line were exposed to the elements and in October 1841 the *Times* printed a story that heavy seas had seriously damaged the railway. The SER retorted that it had only been a spoil tip that had washed away. On 5 December there was a heavy chalk fall near Dover and a navvy was buried.

The line was opened to Folkestone on 28 June 1843 following the completion of Saltwood Tunnel that June; a gala "dress ball" was held in the town on 5 July to celebrate. The terminus was only a temporary one on the western side of the viaduct and the first official train to cross it ran on 13 November, when a treat was laid on for the navvies, but the public opening was delayed by bad weather. The line was extended across it to the proper Folkestone station on 18 December; the station was known as Folkestone Junction for much of its life. A service of seven daily trains was introduced, the fastest taking 3hrs 5mins to London. A request for a station at Smeeth was not acceded to, and at first there were no intermediate stations between Ashford and Folkestone. However in July 1843 the SER received a request from Hythe, and agreed to build a station between the Bargrave Road bridge and the east end of Saltwood Tunnel if the local authorities would construct road access. In August 1843 the Board decided that Twopenny Bridge, on the Stone Street road, was a better site, but the people of Sandgate disliked it.

On 28 November 1843 the Board decided that the station for Hythe should be called "Westenhanger" and it opened on 7 February 1844; no doubt this had nothing at all to do with the hopes that Joseph Baxendale, the SER Chairman, had of becoming MP for Hythe.

One of the most famous occurrences during the construction of the SER was the huge explosion that took place on 26 January 1843. This was staged near Dover to remove part of the cliff, and was supervised for the Government by General Pasley and Lieutenant Hutchinson.

The reason an explosion of this magnitude was needed at all was Round Down, a massive cliff one hundred yards west of Shakespeare Cliff. As it projected out, William Cubitt had originally intended to tunnel through it, but a series of slumps and falls in Spring 1840 showed Round Down to be treacherous and unstable - the whole mass slumped eight inches.

Even to do the dangerous tunnelling work or dig it out by hand would have cost at least £8,000, but Cubitt's decision to use explosives saved the SER £7,000 according to contemporary claims. Army officers were brought in to do the work at the SER's expense, Lieutenant Hutchinson being an expert on creating simultaneous explosions using electric charges from batteries. He had blown up the wreck of the *Royal George* using this method. For Round Down he amassed 18,000lbs of gunpowder; 55 barrels of it were placed at either end of the cliff and 75 barrels in the middle. Then, while fashionable society watched from boats out at sea, Hutchinson blew the charges. Everyone agreed that the explosion was astonishingly quiet - there was "only a low murmur, lasting hardly more than half a second," the *Athenaeum* reported. A section of cliff 300 feet long, 70 feet thick and 300 feet high slumped forwards and down - 400,000 cubic yards of chalk.

The experiment was such a success that it was tried a number of times more. On 2 March 7,000lbs of explosives were used to blow away the "crown" of Round Down and on 5 May 4,000lbs was exploded in three "mines" at Acre Flat, Dover, removing 30,000 tons of chalk.

In November 1843 the Duke of Wellington inspected the works at Archcliffe. He walked through Shakespeare Cliff tunnels, "admitting the principle and execution of its lancet arches," according to the *Maidstone Journal*. Then he watched another blast at Round Down.

In early December 1843 a chalk fall blocked the line at Abbott's Cliff, causing public alarm about the likely safety of the line once opened. It was the work at Abbott's Cliff that was holding up the line, for the tracks reached there by October 1843 but it was deemed necessary to have another explosion there as late as 17 October; a simultaneous explosion of thirty mines was laid on, but half of them went off too soon, to the disappointment of Directors and their guests who were watching from the steamer, *Sir William Wallace.*

The extravagant designs of Cubitt and Burton for the Dover terminus were rejected due to a shortage of funds and in December 1843 the Board opted to erect an iron roof over some converted buildings - but even then the station contract cost £29,475. By January 1844 the SER was nearly ready for opening, and even decided to employ an interpreter at Dover. The people of Dover voted to treat the Company to a public dinner.

The opening was set for 7 February 1844. A special train left London at 9.30am, stopping at Folkestone for a brief Board meeting, and hauled by *Shakespeare.* The pause at Folkestone gave the *Maidstone Journal* reporter time to enthuse over the Foord viaduct, which he described as being 105 feet high and having 19 arches. When they continued on towards Dover the train passed through Folkestone Warren, causing the reporter to comment that "this portion of the line is exceedingly romantic."

As the train emerged from Shakespeare Cliff tunnel loud cheers were heard, and Archcliffe Fort fired off a salute. The dinner for 300 people was held at Dover theatre, with the SER receiving a suitably dramatic address from Dover Corporation. The South Eastern was referred to as "a Work of great National Importance" and the Mayor told the Directors that "...you have accomplished a great step in forwarding the progress of our National Commerce." For the SER, Joseph Baxendale replied by calling Dover "the highway of Nations."

The SER had created a great railway linking the nation's capital to the chief ferry port for Europe; it was a railway featuring many noble achievements, including one of the most spectacular stretches of line ever built in Britain. In 1844 the Company could afford to feel satisfied, as could Dover, but few of the years that were to follow contained such amity.

1. SER Minutes, 6 July 1836.
2. Samuel Smiles, **Autobiography.**
3. The resultant deviation from the "straight line" across the Weald can still be identified on an O.S. map today.
4. **Herapath's Railway Magazine,** April 1837.
5. The station name was spelt Tunbridge until 1893.
6. **Railway Times,** 28 May 1842.
7. Presumably an exaggeration, unless Hooley Lane has shrunk since the early days of the SER.
8. C.Clinker, **Closed Passenger Stations & Goods Depots.**

CHAPTER 3: YEARS OF TURMOIL

"Why might not whole...public bodies be seized with fits of insanity, as well as individuals? Nothing but this principle, that they are liable to insanity equally at least with private persons, can account for the major part of those transactions of which we read in History." -Bishop J. Butler, d.1752

It is impossible to consider the history of the various SER lines without studying the men who made the decisions, for the SER was always a company that was dominated by strong personalities. Just as Edward Watkin came to be synonymous with the SER in its later years, so James MacGregor was apparently the South Eastern personified in the late 1840s and early 1850s. Yet his reign was a turbulent one, and his management appears to have left the Company impotent in the face of burgeoning competition from the East Kent Railway - an initially benign creature that was transformed into the consuming monster of the London, Chatham & Dover Railway.

As early as 1844 the SER had become a victim of the stockbrokers' fantasies. Some proposed rival schemes to depress SER shares while others used the extensive financial press to talk the share prices alternately up and down so as to make a profit for themselves. As early as January 1844 the *Railway Times* was not optimistic about its prospects:

"The Dover Railway is now a grand football for the speculating gentry; all their force is directed against it, and while keeping up the steam of depreciation, they are quietly buying up the shares in all directions[1]*."*

James MacGregor became prominent in SER affairs during these difficult months of 1844. It was a year of considerable Boardroom change, with Chairman Joseph Baxendale attempting to control the SER's direction. However Baxendale went abroad for a few months in July 1844 and during his absence MacGregor led a revolt by discontented Liverpool shareholders - among whom was Martin Pritchard, an influential figure in MacGregor's career and a fellow director of the Liverpool Commercial Bank. As a Liverpool banker, MacGregor was put forward to criticise Baxendale's conduct in the relationship between the SER and carrying firms like Pickford's.

The Liverpool group's quite reasonable view was that Baxendale's position as chairman of Pickford's had influenced the SER's policy on the carriage of general goods traffic, to the detriment of profits. It was felt that Pickford's had gained a share in handling traffic that the SER should have profited from itself. At the General Meeting in September 1844 MacGregor therefore proposed a motion that the accounts were unsatisfactory and the meeting went on to vote that the SER should become a "general carrier" like other railways. A damaging split was prevented by electing MacGregor to the Board to represent the powerful Liverpool interests; Benjamin Harding of Wadhurst Castle joined the Board at the same time.

Baxendale returned to Britain in December 1844 to find this opposition now encamped in his own Boardroom. The Pickford's issue was discussed immediately. At the Board meeting of 7 January 1845 Pickford's were directed to vacate their privileged station warehouses which they had used for collection and delivery of goods consigned by the SER, causing Baxendale to resign as Chairman, to be replaced by Sir John Kirkland of Pall Mall. On 13 March Richard Davies also resigned from the Board, "in consequence of not being able to concur cordially with some of its recent proceedings." He was replaced by William Fielden, MP.

Kirkland's time as Chairman was brief, for he resigned in September 1845 apparently because the other members of the Board opposed his handling of the dispute with the London & Brighton. James MacGregor was elected Chairman on 4 September. MacGregor seems to have been aware from the start that his position depended on a narrow group of northern supporters, so in December 1845 he brought Randall, a Maidstone banker, onto the Board. This was seen by the *Railway Times* as an attempt to improve his standing with Kent shareholders.

MacGregor's elevation seems to have coincided with a number of key changes among the SER's senior employees. Firstly, Captain Charlewood resigned from the Superintendent's position on 20 September 1845 following severe criticism of the SER's staffing practices by the Board of Trade in the wake of an accident at Penshurst on 28 July. This gave MacGregor the opportunity to become "Managing Director". W. O'Brien resigned as Secretary in October 1845 to take up a job with the Government, and his place was taken by George Herbert at a salary of £350 per annum.

This opened the way for MacGregor to draw a lucrative salary, but his era in charge of the SER was marked by a number of vituperative rows and Boardroom scandals. His attention concentrated initially on the details of the relationship with the Brighton Company; he adopted a pugnacious attitude to the Brighton's backing of the Mid Kent Railway. As the two companies appeared to be preparing for a long struggle, their shareholders met together on 9 March 1847 and passed a motion objecting to ruinous competition; some even wanted amalgamation.

1848 was a difficult year for most railway companies, with revolutions abroad breeding financial uncertainty at home. The SER weathered it tolerably well, though MacGregor was ill during August and the continental traffic was hit by the troubles in France. There were also delays in opening the North Kent line and this caused problems since one of the contractors, John Brogden, was the son of a SER director. Brogden was already in trouble over the timberwork of the Gravesend & Rochester Railway in the Higham tunnel, which he had removed as part of his contract, and kept for his own purposes. Now his work was considered unsatisfactory and on 28 October 1848 the Board voted that his father should be excluded from discussions of the contract. When Brogden Senior objected to this, the Board set up a "Constructive Committee" (to which he was not elected) to get round the problem. The elder Brogden attempted to defend family honour by alleging improper transactions, notably over the handling of a cheque for £10,000.

In January 1849 a group of Manchester shareholders objected to the creation of preference stock, some of them arguing that the Rye line should be abandoned if the SER was short of capital. But at the General Meeting on 8 March, held in the large ballroom of the Bridge House Hotel in London, the first issue to surface was the Brogden Contract.

John Brogden's contract was a quite substantial one for £45,000, his tasks included the building of the bridge under the London & Croydon line for the

North Kent-Bricklayers Arms link as well as work on the Gravesend to Strood line. During the summer of 1848 there had been a number of reports that he was "in trouble", prompted largely by slow work. In fact the Brogden problem soon became eclipsed by more exciting scandals and was left to quietly drag on into a legal battle when the SER refused to pay John Brogden in full. At the court hearing, in January 1851, Brogden claimed £5,000 from the SER on the grounds that the line had been "ready for traffic" on 21 July 1849; he won the case, the SER having argued weakly that the line had not been ready by the agreed date as there had been "a deficiency of chairs."

The issue that arose at the March 1849 meeting that really hit the headlines in the railway press was the astonishing revelation about Viscount Torrington's "golden handshake." Torrington had only been a director of the SER for eighteen months, part of which he spent as Deputy Chairman, when he was appointed Governor of Ceylon early in 1847 and voted a testimonial by the shareholders. He had then gone "shopping" with MacGregor and bought a dinner service for the huge sum of £2800, though the *Railway Times* later put the figure as high as 3000 Guineas[2]. It is worth comparing these figures to the annual salary of the Maidstone stationmaster - £120. Torrington was also treated to a special dinner that Josiah Wilson, a Manchester shareholder, alleged cost £700. This prompted another director, Thomson, to complain that he had been deliberately kept in the dark about financial transactions even though he was on the Finance Committee.[3]

The General Meeting voted to set up a committee to investigate all the allegations, but Thomson complained that the "jury" was hand-picked by MacGregor through his control of proxy votes. In its report, the Committee of Investigation blamed Martin Pritchard, another former Deputy Chairman, for many of the financial irregularities. The shareholders were told of this in May 1849, but tempers began to rise. Pritchard, a Liverpool associate of MacGregor's, alleged that the Chairman himself was well-acquainted with all the deals.

Between May and September the Board was besieged by complaining shareholders. Mr Cunliffe alleged that £107,932 had gone missing from the debit account, that stores had been debited against traffic, and that nothing was allowed for depreciation of the track - in short, the accounts were a lie.

At the September General Meeting Josiah Wilson led the assault with a point about the depreciation of rolling stock. MacGregor acidly retorted that the rolling stock was so well maintained that there **was** no depreciation! Wilson then said that a Mr Smith should be removed from the Board as he had been paralysed by a stroke, though the *Railway Times* thought this was a tasteless remark. Wilson also complained about MacGregor having reduced the train speeds to a paltry 15mph. The meeting coincided with Pritchard's appearance in court for bankruptcy with Pritchard having entered MacGregor as a debtor owing him £1,343. Pritchard alleged that MacGregor had asked him to buy some SER shares for him, but when the price had suddenly dropped MacGregor had refused to pay for them.

MacGregor survived this fiasco but again had to face Wilson's taunts at the March 1850 meeting. Wilson "took up a conspicuous position in front of the Chairman" and quickly won a vote to declare how many shares each person held. After MacGregor had read the Company Report, Wilson launched into a catalogue of complaints. The engines on the Greenwich line had fallen to bits since the line had been laid with stone sleepers originally. Barlow's patent iron track, where the rails were laid on lontitudinal iron sleepers with tierods to maintain the gauge, was a failure and Macgregor, a "complete dictator", did not deserve his £2000 p.a. Wilson was satisfied with the Secretary's remuneration (£600 and a house) but complained about the engineer (£2000), the goods manager (£600 and under notice for corruption), cashier (£400) and accountant (£350).

By this stage the Board was dividing into factions, with MacGregor and James Renshaw leading one side, Thompson the other. Wilson said that the SER was "notorious for the irregularities of its management." Thompson however was outmanoeuvred when MacGregor arranged for the Board to be "slimmed down" to only nine Directors - he was unseated; Wilson denounced this move as illegal.

Many SER shareholders were disappointed that their company paid lower dividends than other concerns. Some saw this as bad management, but it had a number of problems. Firstly, the land costs per mile on the SER by the year 1849-50 were £9,990; the LNWR's were £8,190, the Great Northern's £6,508 and the Great Western's £4,905 in comparison. Parliamentary and legal costs per mile for the SER were £3,825; for the LNWR they were £2,227, the GNR £894 and the GWR £1,517[4]. Thus the SER was burdened from the start by the high cost of achieving construction.

On 14 March 1850 Thomas Carlisle, a shareholder, secured an injunction stopping the payment of any dividends until the Rye line had been completed. This gave Wilson wonderful ammunition for the April meeting, where he was told that "You invariably come here to create a disturbance" - which was true, of course.

At the root of it lay the SER's chronic financial problems. The SER's own position had been made worse by an ill-judged policy of supporting other concerns which themselves were poorly financed. During August Thompson tried unsuccessfully to get another injunction to stop any further payments to the Reading, Guildford & Reigate Railway, which MacGregor had chosen to support through a lease in 1847 despite its lack of commercial promise. James Garrard of the RGR complained that Thompson's move was "vindictiveness", but in September the *Railway Times* commented that the SER's lease of the RGR "guarantees them (the RGR) a dividend much higher than the line is worth at present."

During 1851 the affairs of the SER were in danger of lapsing into uncharacteristic peace until the SER's Engineer, Barlow, and his patent iron sleepers caused trouble. In June 1850 the *Railway Times* had been lukewarm in its review of them, but in March 1851 MacGregor had referred to them as "Barlow's great invention of the permanent sleeper." One of the strongest arguments in their favour was that they lasted longer than wooden sleepers and even then could be sold for scrap value. In MacGregor's view they cut track costs from £45 a mile per annum to only £20.[5] By September 1851 the SER had laid 75 miles of track with iron sleepers.

However at the Board meeting of 29 May 1851 problems with the sleepers at Merstham and elsewhere were reported. Exactly a month later the Board decided to get rid of them and Barlow tendered his resignation. This was refused since the Board wanted him to stay to carry the responsibility, but within a week they had given him notice anyway.

At the end of July Barlow alleged that the whole line north of Merstham (where his iron rails began) was unsafe as well, but the new engineer - Thomas Drane - ridiculed this. Peter Barlow then disappeared from SER affairs, only to turn up in September 1852 involved with a Chatham to Chilham project.

Shareholder George Smith had requested that MacGregor showed less "talent" and more "plodding business habits", but MacGregor's greatest concern seems to have been to strengthen his own political position on the Board. In 1852 he was able to get Henry Rich MP back onto it; Rich had been a Director until July 1846, when he had left to become a Lord of the Treasury. The main cause of argument had now shifted to allegations of "reckless losses" on the RGR, but MacGregor's control of proxies kept him secure. An attempt to cut his salary by half failed and Wilson's claims that the RGR was losing the SER £32,000 per annum were rebuffed.

Perhaps the greatest charge against MacGregor, though, was that he let slip the opportunity in Autumn 1852 to seal an agreement with the promoters of the East Kent Railway which was soon to grow into the SER's deadliest rival. The EKR developed because MacGregor's South Eastern had failed to provide a service to the towns between Rochester and Canterbury which the people of Faversham, in particular, resented. Therefore members of the local gentry such as the Lords Harris and Sondes, decided to promote their own line from Strood to Canterbury. According to several reports, the SER could have struck a deal with the East Kent by guaranteeing 3% on their £600,000 capital. However this chance was let slip, perhaps because MacGregor had already burnt his fingers on a similar deal with the hopeless RGR and feared the reaction of the shareholders to another such commitment.

In May 1853, with the East Kent Bill progressing healthily through Parliament, an East Kent landowner wrote to the *Railway Times*:
"The evil of the obstructive policy of the South Eastern Directors has at length become apparent, for not only have they failed in repelling the invasion of their territory, but they have rejected an offer by which they might have had possession of the new line upon most advantageous terms.[(6)]*"*

Years later, Watkin complained that "the terms were a bagatelle" - that the SER could have bought up its nascent rival for virtually nothing.

For ten years the SER had attempted to pacify the people of the North Kent towns by vague promises and spuriously floated schemes, so that the long-suffering inhabitants of the district had concluded that the only way they would get a railway was if they built one themselves. The SER then found itself unable to control this incipient threat, for at the General Meeting of 17 March 1853 it was voted that no outlay or liability was to be incurred without general approval from the shareholders. This vote was a direct consequence of the breakdown of trust between Board and shareholders and it left the SER unable to respond when the EKR Act was passed on 4 August 1853.

MacGregor came under increasingly personal attack - there were allegations during summer 1853 that he had been involved in improper share dealings during 1847 (probably "buying in" shares to maintain prices), paying dividends out of capital, and that he had misled SER proprietors over the RGR affair. The Reading, Guildford & Reigate, which MacGregor had depicted as a source of great profit and strategic advantage, had become a bottomless pit into which SER funds disappeared without trace.

The charge of the rebels was led by John Hamilton. In the September 1853 meeting he claimed that MacGregor had "packed" the meeting with compliant employees. He also complained that MacGregor had bought off the opposition of G. E. Smith, a glass and crockery manufacturer, by awarding him the lucrative contract to supply the SER's Lord Warden Hotel at Dover. Hamilton also claimed that a very late train from London Bridge ran for MacGregor's personal convenience alone, since it allowed him to get home after late-night Parliamentary sessions. MacGregor retorted that he used his rooms at London Bridge on such occasions.

An interesting sidelight to this affair is MacGregor's career as MP for Deal. It was popularly rumoured that the only advantage the Kent resort gained from this was an extra excursion train!

It would have taken a greater manager than MacGregor to weather these storms and cope with the East Kent as well. George Smith, beneficiary of the pottery contract, said of the SER Board, "I would not trust them to manage any small business, much more so an undertaking such as this." Yet MacGregor's power was clearly waning, for a contest for a seat on the Board in March 1853 was won by an opponent of his, Captain Daniel Warren; the defeated man was James Whatman, an MP from Maidstone, and a member of the famous paper-making family.

One of the factors that divided the Board was whether the SER should pursue an aggressive policy, building new lines, or whether it should enter a period of consolidation. One result of this was that in 1852 the SER had been hesitant in its response to plans for a line from Sydenham to Bromley proposed by the West End of London & Crystal Palace Company; then it had projected a line of its own from Lewisham to Croydon which served only to anger the London, Brighton & South Coast Railway. In October 1853 a new scheme for a Mid-Kent Railway from Lewisham to Bromley emerged, but this divided the Board. Coles Child, Hon. James Byng and Warren objected to it as unprofitable, unlikely to deflect the WEL&CP line, and also unconstitutional since the shareholders had not been consulted. As Lord of the Manor of Bromley, Coles Child was able to portray himself as selfless in opposing a scheme that would have enhanced his property's value. The anti-expansion faction published a pamphlet in January 1854, by which time director Ironside had joined their number.

Committees of shareholders became active in Manchester, London and Liverpool, agreeing to support Matthew Forster, Jonathan Mellor and Sir J. Campbell in the next elections for the Board. MacGregor, clearly the target of this faction, retaliated by declaring a dividend of 4% - the highest since 1848. Campbell was a former ambassador to Persia, the other two were businessmen. Tension built up before the meeting. MacGregor sent out proxy forms, paid for by the SER itself, which were stamped for return and with the name of his chosen candidate - Sir Henry Rich - already filled in. This move was possibly illegal.

Letters then began to appear in the railway press alleging that Coles Child, a wealthy merchant, wasn't being so selfless after all; it was said that the value of his property would be improved a little by the SER's Bromley scheme - but it would be improved a great deal more if the SER scheme was dropped and the WEL&CP one succeeded. This was because the SER's proposed Mid-Kent line passed further from his estate than the rival proposal. Persistent rumours claimed that he stood to gain £60,000.

At the General Meeting of March 1854 MacGregor lost the Chairmanship, and then also resigned as General Manager. He was replaced by Campbell, who was no doubt helped by his nine years as a director of P&O. Matthew Forster and Seymour Teulon were also elected to the Board. A surprise candidate for the Chair was Viscount Torrington, back from Ceylon, and quite prepared to hit out at the conduct of his brother, Hon. James Byng. However it was revealed that Torrington had joined the Board in August 1845 only a day after buying his first twenty shares; perhaps the dinner service counted against him too.

These changes ushered in another phase of spitefulness and rivalry. Campbell, Forster and Teulon alleged that MacGregor had declared a dividend worth £148,674 when there was no provision for paying it. The problem had to be solved by borrowing money at a high rate of interest, or the share price would have dropped sharply. It was alleged that only MacGregor had known the truth of the situation.

MacGregor claimed immediately that Child, Warren and Byng had all seen and signed the accounts. Their defence was that MacGregor did all the financial work and "refused to submit to any interference on our part."

A furious row then broke out over the appointment of Captain R. Barlow as General Manager in April 1854; in this post he replaced MacGregor, having previously been Superintendent of the Line. James Renshaw and MacGregor objected to Captain Barlow on the grounds that he had been responsible for the disastrous appointment of Wyke as stationmaster at Godstone. A truck had been carelessly shunted into the path of an express while Wyke was having his breakfast. In return Wyke blamed MacGregor for an accident at Headcorn, with which he had also been involved! Renshaw pointed out that there had been nineteen applicants for the job that Captain Barlow was given, none of whom had been given a chance. However one of them, G. W. Brown, was subsequently appointed Superintendent of the Line in Barlow's place.

The Board was dividing into two warring factions: the supporters of new lines (notably MacGregor and Renshaw) and their opponents. Two of the latter, Seymour Teulon and Matthew Forster, succeeded in May 1854 in winning a vote 6-2 for the abandonment of the SER extension to Bromley. Ironically events showed that it was the MacGregor expansionists who were the wiser, since within two months the Board were hastily making plans for new surveys when they heard that the "Direct Mid-Kent" was planning a line through the district to Tonbridge.

On 27 June Renshaw published a letter complaining that the SER stores were being bought "of inferior quality and at a higher price than such oats could have been obtained..." Renshaw alleged that this had occurred in 1851 and 1854, with Child being accused. At the subsequent General Meeting George Smith, the pottery maker, accused Child of profiteering and said that another director, Captain Warren, had tried to bribe him into silence.

Renshaw pointed out that he was suggesting an error of judgment, not corruption, but refused to withdraw his claims. The Board then passed the following extraordinary Minute:

"That Mr Renshaw in refusing to withdraw his offensive and intemperate letters to Mr Child acts in a manner irreconcilable with the harmonious action of the Board on which the best interests of the Company depend; and also in a manner inconsistent with those mutual relations of personal courtesy and respect which it

is indispensable to maintain in the intercourse of Gentlemen working together in the fulfilment of a public trust."

The passing of the WEL&CP's Act for its extension into the Bromley district in 1854 put a rival line deep into SER "territory". The Board met on 21 August 1854 to discuss the "policy of the Company" and decided to abandon their own Mid-Kent plans, with Renshaw dissenting. MacGregor then demanded that the following comment was entered in the Minute Book:

"The Majority of the Board have in my mind allowed the interests of the South Eastern Railway Company to become subordinate to other and rival interests."

Tempers were now white-hot and in September 1854 MacGregor used the Minutes in a speech to shareholders which was then leaked to the railway press. The *Railway Times* called this "malign indulgence in personal hostility". In a furiously-argued Board meeting of 14 September, MacGregor's use of the Minutes "for the purpose of opposing and vilifying the policy of a majority of his colleagues" was condemned. The Board then resolved that his conduct was "unbecoming and dishonourable."

Such was the division between the two camps that blind adherence to policy became more important than careful analysis of a changing situation. In October 1854 Forster and Teulon wanted to refuse to even see any group promoting a new line since the SER would not be interested in assisting, but at least this motion was voted down. However, a week later they voted 4-3 not to discuss working the Direct Portsmouth line which was then being promoted. In November Campbell resigned from the Board and was replaced by Byng.

This left a vacant place on the Board which was filled by an invitation to Alexander Beattie. MacGregor and Renshaw, however, favoured Jonathan Mellor; he was one of the Manchester group, a Rochdale millowner with experience as a director of the Oldham, Ashton & Guide Bridge Railway.

On 19 October 1854 the Minutes recorded that George Herbert was retiring from his position of Secretary and that he was awarded £1400 for his "long and faithful service". Thomas Drane, the SER's Engineer, also resigned at the same time.

On 9 November the Board decided to appoint Samuel Smiles as the new Secretary. Matthew Forster was angry that his own favourite candidate, a member of the Reform Club, had not secured the post[7]. Smiles, later to achieve great fame as an author, had been with the Leeds Northern Railway and earlier in 1854 had been transferred to Newcastle when this had been absorbed into the North Eastern Railway. On 11 November he received the good news in a letter from Captain Barlow, but Smiles' friend Robert Stephenson had a warning for him:

"I am very glad to hear of your success, and I trust sincerely it may be permanent, for I fear you will find the South Eastern a very difficult concern to keep in train satisfactorily."[8]

Smiles soon found that Stephenson was right, for having gone to some Board meetings he found that, "It was not so much business as speech-making, that seemed to be the work of the Board." Things were complicated by Forster, the MP for Berwick, setting up a "third party" on the Board.

The Engineer's position was filled by Peter Ashcroft on 23 November; Ashcroft had been Superintendant of the Line on the Eastern Counties Railway and in March 1854 he had been tried for manslaughter following a fatal accident in snow near Thetford - he had been acquitted amidst sensational scenes[9].

The two replacements did not satisfy everyone. Renshaw led demands for Herbert to be reinstated, then teamed up with MacGregor to demand the return of Drane as well. They lost a vote 4-2, but this clearly suggests that both Drane and Herbert were dispensed with as they had been linked with the "wrong" section of the Board.

A few weeks later Renshaw renewed protests about Herbert's "retirement" payment, and also the £1166-13-4d paid to Drane.

Within six months Ashcroft, together with Brown - the Superintendent of the Line - were involved in rumours of fraud which the Board was forced to investigate. Some of the allegations came from William Brown, stationmaster at Bricklayers Arms, who claimed that a bath and rustic chairs had been made for the Superintendent's private use in the SER workshops there. Captain Barlow tried to use the issue to persuade the Board to sack G.Brown, the superintendent [10]. The allegations were found to be untrue - or at least said to be untrue - and the stationmaster was sacked in July 1855.

Yet treatment of staff was surprisingly varied. In July 1857 the Captain of the steamer *Prince Ernest* was reported for being drunk on duty. To the fury of Mellor, the Board voted 6-4 not to sack him, yet the abuse of alcohol was something that many railway companies regarded with the utmost severity.

To return to the main Boardroom struggle, in January 1855 Rich led an expansion plan to fill the space between Lewisham and Tonbridge that was proving so tempting to rivals. Byng kept his temporary control of the Chair over this issue only by using his casting vote. Liverpool shareholders also pressed for an increase in the Directorate from nine to twelve, achieving this at the General Meeting in March.

By this time the events that were to finally remove MacGregor from the SER were already in motion. Rumours reached the railway press in February 1855 that MacGregor had borrowed £40,000 from the contractor Wythes under dubious circumstances. Some claims were also made that the sacking of Peter Barlow was because he objected to these dealings. In February the events surfaced in a legal battle between Wythes and the SER's bankers, one opinion being that MacGregor had got the money from Wythes in December 1852 at a time when he was financially embarrassed due to reckless share dealing.

As if to emphasise the perilous state of the SER, a sudden fall in Mountfield Tunnel in early March closed the Hastings line for months, providing a fitting counterblast to MacGregor's announcement that he would be stepping down from the SER Board due to his own financial position.

At the meeting of the reorganised Board on 22 March 1855, Henry Rich MP became Chairman and Byng dropped down to the Deputy Chairman. Beattie retained a seat on the Board despite being lampooned for a business record liberally dotted with failures, of which the Caterham Railway was the most prominent. Matthew Forster resigned at the end of the month, perhaps tainted by his association with MacGregor.

With the disruptive MacGregor out of the way, and a new Chairman, this seemed to be a new dawn for the SER despite its problems with the Hastings line, but any high hopes the shareholders held were soon dashed once more. In July Rich had to resign the Chair and go abroad due to illness, with Byng stepping in again. According to Smiles, Byng was "an honest and honourable man." The Company's new station in Reading opened on 30 August but on 12 September 1855 it was the scene of a disastrous accident between a light engine and a passenger train with the loss of eight lives. It was due to the incorrect working of the single line from the ticket platform into the new station. This section was meant to be operated on a "one engine in steam" basis, with down trains being run round at the ticket platform and then pushed into the station.

Crossley, the offending train driver, was reported in the press as having given the impression of a man "in a state of mental aberration". He was killed, but subsequent enquiries by the Board and by the Board of Trade revealed a catalogue of mismanagement. Captain Barlow, the SER General Manager, blamed Brown, the Line Superintendent, for cutting the staff allocation at Reading so that there had been no "switchman" on duty; certainly Reading staff were depleted that day - two of them had gone out with an excursion train. However it is also possible that Captain Barlow was seeking to use the issue to continue his quest for personal revenge on Brown[11]; certainly this was the view of Smiles.

The Board felt that both Brown and Barlow were to blame, noting "the absence of that free communication and cordial co-operation between the General Manager and the Superintendent of the Line, which is essential to the satisfactory working and management of the undertaking." However part of the problem, though the Board did not admit it, was a confusion between the two officers over responsibility and seniority and it was all underlined by another accident at a station where staff had been cut - this time at Gravesend on 29 September.

The debate became characteristically bitter. On 11 October Mellor and Kay led a Boardroom vote asking for Barlow's resignation, which passed 5-4. At the same meeting it was declared that Cornelius Eborall, with six years experience on the East Lancashire Railway, was an ideal replacement - he seems to have been Mellor's candidate, for both had Lancashire backgrounds.

Barlow refused to resign and so was sacked on 15 October. It was then found that the SER letter books in his office had been cut up and many parts removed, so the Board instigated legal proceedings against him. The prompt return of four boxes of papers by Captain Barlow's solicitor averted a public blood-letting.

Commenting on these developments, the *Railway Times* pronounced itself pleased that Captain Barlow had been thrown out; it referred to him as "that autocratic officer known as general manager." The Secretary, Samuel Smiles, was, however, "active, diligent and intelligent."

On 1 November the Board heard that Captain Tyler, the Board of Trade Inspector, was displeased with the management of the SER lines, especially at Reading. The Directors even discussed whether they could prevent the BoT publishing Tyler's damning report on the Reading accident - they could not. The Board of Trade's Captain Galton was also very critical of staff discipline. At the same meeting on 1 November the Board confirmed that Eborall had been given the job of General Manager at £1000 per annum plus bonuses. Since his duties also covered those of Brown, the Superintendent resigned in March 1856 and the SER management structure began to appear more logical.

Mellor did not have everything his own way, for in January 1856 the Board voted 5-4 not to pay him travelling expenses from Manchester for the meetings which took place every fortnight.

Eborall was a professional railway manager and brought a new dynamism to the SER, advocating a policy of taking-over dangerous schemes like the

Mid-Kent Direct which was promoting a new route to Tonbridge. However some Directors remained anti-expansionist well into 1857; again notable was Coles Child who opposed a scheme for a line from Whitstable to Herne Bay which was intended to block out an offshoot of the East Kent Railway. In October 1856 there had also been a dispute over whether the SER should have a new line to Dartford - W. G. Thomson, the Deputy Chairman, favoured it, while Gilpin was opposed. However, on 26 October 1857 the name of "Charing Cross" appeared in the Minutes of the SER for the first time - indicative, at last, of a more ambitious policy.

This new policy caused problems for Child as he owned a coal wharf on the Surrey side of the Thames, the position of which made it vital in the SER's scheme to improve its position by building a new line to a terminus in the West End. Jonathan Mellor, assisted by John Hamilton, began a campaign against Child's conduct in the matter. It was said that he wanted £10,000 for the wharf and stood to gain also through being a Director of the Hungerford Bridge Company, which the SER was buying out. Mellor was prepared to accuse Child of extortionate demands, conduct which the *Railway Times* thought "offensive" and "gross." The SER eventually settled on Hungerford Market as the site for their new station; the Market Company's shares were priced low and, Smiles later alleged, one of the SER directors "was able to perform a little manipulation with the depreciated shares...very much to his own advantage." Another claim was that Child owned a wharf at East Greenwich and so was promoting a SER extension from Greenwich to Woolwich which would benefit his property.

John Hamilton was worried that men like Byng and Child held too many directorships and thus could be compromised. An example of this was in 1862 when the Rhymney Iron Company, of which Child was also a Director, tendered for an SER rails contract. Child had to leave the room while the matter was discussed, but the Rhymney Company won the contract on grounds of quality rather than price. However, when the rails were delivered at Strood they were found to be poor and the contract was cancelled.

In February 1861 Child opposed any start on the new City terminus at Cannon Street until more progress had been made on Charing Cross, though the Cannon Street line got its Act in the summer of that year. Mellor campaigned to have Child voted out and replaced by John Barlow, succeeding after a vituperative circular had gone the rounds in March 1862. Captain Warren survived similar attacks even though Hamilton dug up a story that he had "lost his ship" - it was said to have been abandoned by him in an Indian port. Warren explained that his Indiaman *Exmouth* had been badly damaged in a hurricane in 1839, but had not sunk. He also pointed out that he had been decorated by Louis XVIII in 1823 after bravely rescuing French sailors in a Biscay storm.

From September 1855 until March 1866 James Byng retained the Chair and gradually established order, especially once Eborall started to become effective. Smiles' verdict was that Byng was "an honest and honourable man" and that Eborall was a ceaseless worker. In his *Autobiography*, Smiles provides us with a picture of Eborall:

"My dear friend Eborall was always of an anxious turn of mind. He could never get rid of his business. He would take it home with him; take it to bed with him; turn it over and over to the loss of his sleep; and rise up with it in the morning; for it ever burdened his mind. Sometimes when a thing had struck him in the night

that he wished to remember, he would get up, light the gas, and commit it to his memo book."

Smiles, in contrast, was able to enjoy his evenings away from the office and reflect on the comforts a salary of £750 could provide. He liked to play billiards at home but also applied himself to writing and published his biography of George Stephenson in June 1857; it sold 7500 copies in its first year. Its success allowed him to have *Self-Help* published, though he had written this book in 1854; it sold 35,000 copies in two years and made Smiles famous.

In 1861-2 Jonathan Mellor investigated the lifestyles of the SER's main officers after one of them had absconded with £700; he was very pleased with Smiles, who he found "diligent, earnest and indefatigable." He conjured up an image of domestic bliss in the Smiles household:

"Mr Smiles lived in a humble residence in Greenwich, and was sedulously engaged in the evenings in literary pursuits, and in watching over the education of a young family."

However, even the apparently saintly Smiles could run foul of John Hamilton, the SER's agitated shareholder. Early in 1862 Hamilton accused Smiles of having written an article that libelled him, complaining of:

"...an abyss of moral degradation into which a man must have sunk who could wilfully and designedly concoct a mass of villainous misrepresentations."

This period of furious argument was of great significance in the history of the SER for it meant that the Company was divided in its approach to the growing problem of the East Kent Railway. As early as 1855 that Company had been seeking a better route to London than the service the SER provided for it along the North Kent line from Strood; a Bill for a "Western Extension" was rejected by Parliament in 1857 only after a bitter battle. Thus it is curious to see that opposition to any EKR backed schemes was not an automatic policy of the Board; in June 1857 a Board motion to oppose the Herne Bay & Faversham Bill (in reality a branch of the EKR) produced a vote of 5-5 and was carried 7-5 only after the vote of an absent Director and the Chairman had been included.

By October 1857 the SER was negotiating with the EKR but prudently taking steps to secure a merger with the Mid-Kent Railway. However talks with the EKR did not go well and in December one of its proprietors, S. R. Lushington, was deprived of his free pass over the SER! However the EKR presented a new Bill for a line to connect it at Strood with the St. Mary Cray Company and it was the likely success of this that spurred the SER into its massive commitment for a line from London Bridge to Charing Cross. The EKR secured its Act for the line in 1858 and at about the same time the SER was further threatened after stories that the LBSCR was to take over the WEL&CP to Bromley. The East Kent (which renamed itself London, Chatham & Dover in 1859) thereby had a route from Kent, via Strood and Bromley, to Victoria station which opened on 3rd December 1860.

Attempts by the SER to tame the emerging monster of the EKR came far too late and were, of course, the cause of Boardroom unrest. In June 1858 the Board was hoping that the disputed issues between the SER, EKR and WEL&CP could go to Robert Stephenson for arbitration. The Chairman of the House of Lords Committee, the Duke of Devonshire, wanted the two companies "to come to an agreement on the basis that the line from Canterbury to Dover be completed." His Committee regarded the EKR's moribund Canterbury to Dover extension as "of great national importance" since SER access to Dover was rather exposed. On 26 June Rich and Teulon proposed that the SER should try to take over the EKR, against strong opposition but the EKR got its Western Extension Act in July and any chance of a takeover on easy terms had gone; the *Railway Times prediction of 1856 that the SER would be able to buy up its rivals for "an old song" now had no prospect of coming true.*

An interesting interlude occurred in SER affairs in July 1858 when the Lewes Old Bank sued the SER for damages after the SER telegraph system had carried an erroneous report saying that the Bank had "ceased paying." The Bank requested a transfer of funds from the SER to itself to the tune of £2500 on the grounds that the SER had "published a libel", but the case was dismissed in January 1859.

On 15 July 1858 the SER Board met to plan a response to the EKR's success. The meeting unreservedly abandoned the old "anti-expansionist" policy and adopted a five point plan: the improvement of Folkestone Harbour, a new line from Saltwood into Folkestone, a new direct line to Tonbridge, a line from Battersea to New Cross, and the Charing Cross extension.

At the beginning of January 1859 "*The Times*" published a rumour that the SER had reached an agreement to take over the EKR, whose shares immediately rose in value by 25%. Such rumours were common during the struggle between the two companies, many of them having their origins in stockmarket schemes to boost the value of poor stock. The SER continued to consider schemes that could have a useful defensive role against the East Kent - in November 1859, for example, plans for a £20,000 line from Ramsgate to Broadstairs were considered but abandoned after a report from the Ramsgate stationmaster.

From 1 August 1859 the EKR changed its name to the London, Chatham & Dover Railway, a name which was intended to reflect that it was becoming a main-line from London to Dover, rather than a local scheme of a few East Kent landowners. Early in November 1859 Byng, of the SER, received a private letter from Lord Sondes of the LCDR requesting a meeting to discuss arrangements between the two Companies. Byng's background of Kent nobility placed him in a good position for discussions with the aristocratic backers of the LCDR. On 23 November Byng led an SER delegation that included Thomson and Rich in a meeting at the London Tavern with Sondes, Hilton and Edwards of the LCDR. Byng immediately complained that news of the meeting had already been leaked to *The Times*, prejudicing the negotiations. However another meeting was held at the London Tavern on 1 December; the SER formed the opinion that the LCDR was anxious for fusion with the SER with the senior company to assume all its liabilities - involving a substantial debt. The SER more cautiously held out for an "amicable arrangement".

Relations did not remain amicable. In February 1860 a number of leading stockbrokers received an anonymous pamphlet that cast scorn upon the finances of the LCDR. The printer of the pamphlet was subsequently called before the House of Lords Committee and testified that the pamphlet had been produced for a gentleman named Samuel Smiles! The souring of relations was caused largely by the LCDR's Metropolitan Extensions Bill, that became law on 6 August 1860. This gave the LCDR powers for a new and more direct line towards Victoria station, and a new route from Herne Hill across the Thames and into the heart of London. The SER replied swiftly, by announcing that from

1 September 1860 passengers transferring from the LCDR to the SER at Strood would have to rebook.

Although the SER direction had become steadier under Byng's control, he did not always have a smooth ride. On 31 January 1861 he was criticised at the Board meeting for sanctioning the withdrawal of a Dover - Calais day boat against the resolution of the Board. However Byng's control was sufficiently strong for the SER to approach the subject of new lines with care rather than the usual rhetoric. By Autumn 1861 the subject of a direct line to Tonbridge was alive once more and the Company was active in seeking to get the maximum value from its area. In January 1862 it assured the LBSCR that it knew nothing about a Mid Kent Railway scheme for a line from Beckenham to Croydon.

Early 1862 was a period of frantic negotiation between the SER and a number of other companies. It was anxious to gain powers for the new Direct Tonbridge line, but feared opposition from other concerns. Minutes of 13 February indicate that a bargain was struck with the Crays Company, whose short line was an integral part of the LCDR's extension plans although the original intention had been for the SER to work it: the Crays agreed not to oppose the SER's Tonbridge plans in Parliament if the SER did not oppose the LCDR takeover of the Crays. By early March discussions with the LCDR had resulted in an agreement not to oppose each other's lines through the Mid Kent area.

More protracted were the discussions with the Mid Kent Railway, which felt that it would suffer a severe blow if the SER opened a new Tonbridge line running from Lewisham via Sevenoaks. In May 1862 the SER offered to pay the MKR a minimum annual fee based on its traffic receipts before the new line opened.

The SER opposed energetically any other LCDR lines that threatened its region, including all branches planned to the East Kent Coast where the LCDR had even hoped to gain control of Ramsgate Harbour. Shareholder John Hamilton objected, however, to the plan for cutting fares in order to compete with the LCDR in the Canterbury and Ramsgate area. By January 1862 a 1st class ticket to Folkestone was 14s. but one to Canterbury, a similar distance, was only 11s. Hamilton used the issue in his vociferous campaign against Byng and Child, who he felt held too many directorships to serve the SER effectively.

Relations with the LBSCR were no more stable than they were with the LCDR, especially because of the Mid Kent's plans for an extension to Croydon. In October 1862 the SER met Schuster, of the LBSCR, to discuss the situation. Schuster was anxious for a better relationship between the companies so that they could work "in perfect harmony for mutual protection against any common enemy." However there was considerable suspicion between the two concerns, with the LBSCR particularly worried about a plan for a line from Penge to Lewes and Brighton; this evolved into the Beckenham, Lewes and Brighton. The SER disliked the LBSCR's involvement with a line from Leatherhead to Dorking and suspected it of involvement with a plan to extend the South London Railway to Woolwich. Schuster offered to "strangle" the latter scheme.

One major development was the concluding of an informal Continental Traffic Agreement between the SER and the LCDR, set to run from 1 February 1863. This involved the "pooling" of continental traffic receipts on a sliding scale; 1863 receipts were to be divided 68% to the SER and 32% to the LCDR, then to be gradually altered until they were divided evenly in 1872. The Agreement was formalised on 7 September 1855 and was to include all traffic from London which crossed the Channel from any point between Margate and Hastings.

As 1863 drew to a close the final work was being done on the new terminus at Charing Cross which, though nominally owned by an independant Company, was controlled by the SER. In Charing Cross and Cannon Street the SER was to gain two of the best termini in London, and this strengthened position may have contributed to a friendlier attitude between the various railway companies. On 5 November 1863 the SER discussed coming to a permanent arrangement with both the LCDR and the LBSCR, though the LBSCR rejected the idea - but expressed an interest in through bookings to Charing Cross. One possible result of this warmer climate was that in March 1864 the SER and LBSCR reached agreement on the projection of new lines in the West Kent and East Sussex area.

Thus as 1864 drew to a close the SER seemed to be a more stable Company with brighter prospects than it had been for many years. The imminent shortening of its main-line to Tonbridge, together with the improved London termini, suggested a strong position. Yet many of the shareholders, and in particular the northern ones, felt dissatisfied with the SER's performance and management. As early as 1862 some shareholders had suggested that a young railway manager named Edward Watkin had the qualities that the South Eastern needed.

1.   **Railway Times,** 6 January 1844.
2.   **Railway Times,** 1 April 1854.
3.   **Railway Times,** 10 March 1849.
4.   Analysis based on figures given in J.Simmons, **The Railway In England & Wales,** p.44-5.
5.   **Railway Times,** 8 March 1851.
6.   **Railway Times,** 28 May 1853.
7.   Samuel Smiles, **Autobiography.**
8.   **Ibid.**
9.   See H.Paar & A.Gray, **The Life & Times of the Great Eastern Railway.**
10.   **Railway Times,** 15 March 1856.
11.   **Railway Times,** 15 March 1856.

CHAPTER 4: THE WATKIN ERA

On 24 January 1862 the Lancashire shareholders of the South Eastern Railway gathered in the Clarence Hotel, Manchester, to air their grievances about the Company's lack of progress. Jonathan Mellor, a Rochdale industrialist and director of the Oldham, Ashton & Guide Bridge Junction Railway as well as the SER, argued that Coles Child should be voted off the Board. After a lengthy discussion, the meeting voted by twenty to eighteen to support Edward William Watkin as their candidate in the forthcoming elections.

Mellor had wanted Child out for some time and the issue of the Rhymney Rails contract had given him strong ammunition. His choice as replacement was Edward Watkin, who had been born in Salford in 1816 and was the son of a cotton merchant. He was in every way representative of the financial power of the northern counties in the Nineteenth Century. In terms of his involvement with the South Eastern, Watkin probably made his most significant first step in 1845 when he married Mary Briggs, the daughter of Jonathan Mellor; though he could not have known it at the time, this step probably had a considerable impact on Watkin's eventual elevation to the Chairmanship of the SER. Watkin then became Secretary to the Trent Valley Railway in 1845 which was taken over by the LNWR the following year. He then went to Canada and the USA in 1851 before returning to take a senior post with the LNWR.

By 1852 he was earning £1000 per annum and became assistant to the General Manager, Mark Huish. His career had taken a controversial turn in 1854 when he had moved to the Manchester, Sheffield & Lincolnshire Railway, which was a rival of his former employer. As General Manager he was awarded a salary of £1200 with a bonus on traffic increases.

Watkin soon developed an involvement with many other companies and briefly managed the affairs of the *Illustrated London News* after its founder died in a shipping accident in 1860. He took his knowledge of LNWR matters with him when he joined the Board of the Great Western in 1866, having earlier caused considerable controversy during the later 1850s when the Shrewsbury issue caused ill-feeling between the two companies. In 1861 he went to Canada at the request of the Secretary of State for the Colonies to study government reforms and railway developments; while there he overhauled the management of the Grand Trunk Railway but in his absence the MSLR Board had changed many of his policies and Watkin resigned. His activities in Canada won him fame and fortune - he personally made £38,000 out of the Hudson's Bay Company and in 1868 was knighted for his services to Canada. He remained President of the Grand Trunk until 1868.

At the time he was nominated for a post on the Board of the SER he was still in Canada but had also been devoting some of his energies to politics: Watkin topped the poll as Liberal candidate for Yarmouth in 1857, but was then unseated on petition. He had been defeated in the 1859 election too, but was eventually elected for Stockport in 1864, which he held until 1868.

At the SER General Meeting in March 1862 Coles Child was at last unseated, in no small part due to the pamphlet about his activities that Mellor had circulated. However not everything went Mellor's way, for John Barlow was elected to the Board and not Watkin. Child's Wharf, one of the causes of its proprietor's downfall, was eventually bought by the Charing Cross Company for £12,000 in 1863.

The name of Watkin re-emerged in SER affairs in February 1864, by which time he had become Chairman of the Manchester, Sheffield & Lincolnshire following his triumphant return from Canada. He appeared at the General Meeting of the SER but immediately fell foul of John Hamilton, who accused him of not being a shareholder. An advertisement appeared in the *Railway Times* which alleged deceit by Byng and other SER directors over the matter, for which Hamilton was libelled - the Judge threw out the case. Hamilton also attacked Samuel Smiles with the result that "a scene of indescribable confusion ensued."

Hamilton, who held £30,000 of SER stock, was concerned that the SER accounts did not reveal the true position and secured a writ allowing him to inspect the books. Other shareholders were furiously opposed to the Continental Agreement with the LCDR and a vicious attack on the SER Board appeared in a letter to the *Railway Times* in August 1864:

"Such is their mental obliquity, their soulless and stupid apathy,their craven and abject - I had almost said grovelling - subserviency, they richly deserve every injury and wrong their heaven-born masters can inflict upon them."

Some felt that the Continental Agreement meant that the SER was handing over £120,000 every year to a blackmailer in the shape of the LCDR.

During 1865 the mood of the SER seemed to be returning to the daily scandal and recrimination that had characterised the MacGregor days. Things were not improved when the Railway Times claimed that there was "an ugly looking discrepancy" in the accounts for the sale of the steamer *Eugenie* which had been sold to Cunard in 1863 but shortly afterwards turned up as a blockade-runner in the American Civil War. The SER had bought it for £16,660 but then sold it for £18,233 at a time when fast ships were selling at a premium and when the sale of British ships to the Confederacy had become a major political issue. The newspaper pointed the finger at Smiles over the affair, and Smiles sued - he won damages that were insultingly put at one shilling. Another libel case brought by Smiles against Hamilton resulted in the latter having to withdraw his claims and pay Smiles £250.

On 13 October 1864 James Byng, the deputy chairman, had met a number of Manchester shareholders who were keen that one director should retire or be voted out so that Watkin could join the Board.

Watkin finally achieved a seat on the SER Board in January 1865 when Whatman retired; by March 1865 he was already deputy chairman. Watkin was already closely acquainted with several SER directors and sat on the MSLR Board with Mellor and William Fenton. Interestingly he also knew a number of key LCDR figures very well. However in July 1865 Watkin declared that he was too busy to be deputy chairman - there was a General Election and he then went to America until November.

By the start of 1866 Watkin had become very prominent in SER affairs, leading attacks on the LBSCR (which had elected Coles Child a director!) and annoying the Great Western by fly-posting the West Country in an attempt to get passengers to change at Reading and go to London via the RGR line. Though criticised by some for this action, others credited Watkin with a major success when the Great Western agreed for continental passengers to change trains at Reading on to the RGR and for an improvement in junction arrangements. At the same time there was clear evidence that some of the Board wanted to get rid of Seymour Teulon, who had paid out substantial damages to two sisters hurt in a disastrous accident at Blackheath in December 1864 without the agreement of other directors. There was general disenchantment among the shareholders with the Board and Watkin devised a scheme for a ballot to replace four directors at one go, opposed by Rich, Teulon and Thomson. At the resulting fracas in February 1866 John Bibby of Liverpool, John Stuart of Manchester, James Whatman and Teulon won the ballot; Rich and Thomson were voted off.

Watkin was elected Chairman after the General Meeting in March 1866. Byng, the aristocratic guide of recent SER fortunes, stepped aside, but was nonetheless assaulted in typical style by the *Railway Times*:

"The miserable vanity of the disrobed gentleman, like the ruling passion strong in death, evinced itself to the very end of his career. The mean and vulgar flattery by which alone he was kept in position left him not until the curtain had fallen..."

Such bitter words, and to be proved so bizarrely wrong - for a positively ancient Byng returned to chair the South Eastern again in May 1894, having spent much of the intervening period as Deputy Chairman.

Watkin was a man who seemed to court controversy, and such was the breadth of his business interests that he was bound to become involved in failure at some stage. 1866 proved to be a terrible year for the financial markets following the collapse of the banking firm Overend, Gurney & Co. The LCDR itself was taken into Chancery and the Humber Iron Works, of which Watkin was Chairman, went bankrupt too. This led to rumours in December 1866 that the SER's Chairman was also to be declared bankrupt, but he survived - no doubt helped by his £2500 salary from the SER. Watkin later told Lord Redesdale that he had used his own personal fortune to keep the SER afloat through the crisis, "I became responsible for everything I had in the world to the Bankers of the Company," he said.

An immediate result of Watkin taking over was that the Board became far more dynamic in its approach. The agenda and detail of discussion at each Board meeting increased considerably, and Watkin brought a new energy to the Company. One of the first issues he had to tackle was relations with the London & South-Western, which were strained by a SER scheme for a line to Richmond. Archibald Scott, the LSWR Traffic Manager, suggested an amalgamation of all four southern railway companies.

In April 1866 Watkin had a meeting with the LCDR whose Lord Harris had suggested a union of the SER and LCDR to oppose the LBSCR and the LSWR. Cornelius Eborall was directed to discuss a system of joint management with James Staats Forbes of the LCDR, but Watkin was annoyed to find reports of the proceedings in *The Times*. The LCDR was keen to have a junction at Bickley where its line crossed under the new Tonbridge Direct route, which opened in 1868. There were simultaneous talks with the LBSCR where an Amalgamation Bill was considered; the companies agreed to drop various competing lines, notably the London, Lewes & Brighton scheme of the SE/LCD and the LBSCR's Ouse Valley line.

The financial collapse of the LCDR on 12 July 1866, and the stretched position of many other railway companies, put a new perspective on amalgamation deals - the LCDR was in a much weaker position since its debts were said to be monstrous. One immediate consequence of the LCDR's collapse was that Watkin tried to get it to accept a change in the agreement between the two companies. The LCDR had promised to build a network of junctions at Lewisham and was no longer able to; this affected a number of complex issues over running powers in the Greenwich and South London area since there had been the possibility of LCDR running powers over new SER lines to Woolwich.

Samuel Smiles left the SER at this time for a new post as Secretary of the National Provident Institution. The SER gave him plate worth £100, six months salary and he was allowed to keep his free pass for life. The new Secretary was J.A.Chubb on a salary of £700, though he switched to Treasurer in August 1868 and John Shaw became Secretary.

In 1901 R.D.Blumenfield met the elderly Samuel Smiles, and recorded his impressions in a diary. "The old gentleman is more proud of the fact that he was once Secretary to the South Eastern Railway than of his literary efforts," Blumenfield recorded.

With the LCDR incapacitated, Watkin turned his attention back to the LBSCR. The passing of the London, Lewes & Brighton Act did not help but in February 1867 the LBSCR Board approved Heads of Agreement for working arrangements. By May the SER was keen to pursue amalgamation and also hopeful that the LBSCR would take over all traffic on the Redhill line once its new Tonbridge route was open.

In November 1867 the SER decided to drop the LLB scheme altogether and on 28 November agreed to admit the LCDR into the amalgamation talks with the LBSCR. However reports of this again appeared in *The Times*, and Watkin suspected that this was due to someone in the LCDR who stood to gain from stock market manipulation. In February 1868 the SER learnt that the LSWR was not interested in "fusion".

Plans to amalgamate the southern companies were now concrete and advanced. By March 1868 a Bill was well advanced and Watkin hoped that it could be put into effect from 1 January 1869. In April 1868 the LSWR agreed that it would not oppose the amalgamation, but petitions against it were received from the Midland Railway, the LNWR and the Corporations of Brighton and Dover. When the Bill reached the House of Lords in June it came under considerable pressure for the inclusion of clauses to force the reduction of fares, as a result of which the companies withdrew it; there was a powerful fear that amalgamation would create a rapacious monopoly company in south-east England.

Some good things did result from this time of warm relations - an agreement on the division of competing traffic between the SER and LBSCR was fixed by arbitration in December 1868 and included Croydon, Redhill, Dorking, Tunbridge Wells and Hastings. But the collapse of fusion, and the subsequent bitter fighting that broke out, was largely because of Parliament's fear that a monopoly could be created. Hostility was to be the order of the day - once the Amalgamation Bill had been rejected, LBSCR trains were no longer allowed to run through to Cannon Street.

For a time Watkin and Eborall worked together in developing the SER traffic, though Eborall was ill on a number of occasions. Watkin even got into trouble with the Board of Trade in 1873 after complaining that its Inspecting Officer's treatment of Eborall was "insolent". It was the latter who dismissed the idea of a branch to Dungeness and a jetty there in 1869, while the imaginative Watkin sought to increase traffic by allowing ladies to travel at half price when accompanied by a gentleman. The financial situation was still poor but he sought to be energetic where possible; when the need for covered accomodation at Folkestone was discussed in November 1869, the Chairman observed that "We must show our desire to do something even if we actually do little at present." He showed little inclination towards the reckless expenditure for which he is supposed to be infamous - the SER was cautious about branches to Hythe and Dungeness, positively opposed to one serving Tenterden and Appledore. Most of his attention in the 1869-70 period seems to have been directed at improving the situation between Greenwich and Woolwich.

In March 1870 the SER's engineer, Peter Ashcroft, was replaced by Francis Brady on a salary of £1000 per annum.

April 1870 saw the renewal of discussions with the LBSCR and LCDR for a "fusion of interests." The SER and LCDR also looked at joint investment in improving facilities at Calais and Boulogne.

In October 1870 talks about pooling traffic receipts with the LCDR and LBSCR were revived though LBSCR shareholders had disliked the agreement with the SER that had been made in January. However in November Laing, of the LBSCR, advised Watkin that Forbes of the LCDR was cool about the proposal. It seems that talks between the SER and the LBSCR made considerable progress, but fierce opposition in Parliament to a proposed amalgamation of the Lancashire & Yorkshire Railway with the London & North Western during 1871 convinced the SER that amalgamation was unlikely to succeed.

Relations with the LCDR steadily worsened as the smaller company's financial position recovered. Having agreed to pool receipts for continental passenger traffic, the SER was annoyed in September 1872 when Forbes refused a joint tender for the French Mails contract with the result that it was captured by a third party, Delahaute, in November. Competing schemes also began to emerge that Autumn, with the SER planning a new branch from Sevenoaks Weald to Maidstone while the LCDR was behind a scheme for Adisham to Sandwich. In fact the LCDR was in by far the strongest position with new proposals for a Maidstone line and the SER was never able to improve its access to the town. From 1872 Watkin was also Chairman of the Metropolitan Railway, which resulted in an SER attempt to gain a link to that Company via the LCDR's Blackfriars line.

From May 1873 Eborall was forced to have six months off due to illness and this inevitably left Watkin with more day to day control of SER affairs. During the early part of that year it seemed that relations with the LCDR would degenerate still further, but by September the two companies were again corresponding with each other. The SER suggested that the gap between Dover and Deal should be filled in with a joint scheme and that traffic for Crystal Palace should be "divided in a liberal way towards" the LCDR with a new link to New Cross. The talks collapsed by February 1874 with the LCDR feeling more confident as its Maidstone and Holborn Viaduct lines neared completion.

On 19 December 1873 Eborall died after an attack of apoplexy in his office, an event which led to the recasting of SER management. The post of General Manager was abolished, with the work being shared by Watkin and John Shaw, whose salary rose to £1200. Watkin was also still interested in a political career but suffered defeat in the Exeter election having been unseated at Stockport in 1868; however he did have the compensation of being High Sheriff of Cheshire. His son, Alfred Watkin, became "Locomotive Superintendent" in 1874, though he was junior to James Cudworth who was "Locomotive Engineer". The younger Watkin was responsible for the day to day use of the locomotives.

1874 was meant to be a "year of truce" but during Summer 1874 rival schemes proliferated. The LCDR was plotting to get control of the Crystal Palace & South London Railway, while the SER was supporting the Bromley Direct Railway which would give it access to a LCDR stronghold. Sometimes small incidents could cause bad feelings too - the Secretary of the German Embassy wrote to complain that when he arrived at Dover he had been misled into travelling to Hastings via the LCDR and Victoria station instead of the direct SER route! Watkin replied by reviving ideas for using Dungeness as a port and for a Maidstone to Ashford line, signs that his frustration with the LCDR was beginning to result in a policy of building defensive lines whatever the cost. As if he did not have enough to do, Watkin at last secured election as MP for Hythe, a constituency that included Folkestone, in 1874; perhaps this explains the excessive attention the SER Board came to give to matters concerning the Hythe branch and all related issues in the area. The 1874 Parliamentary contest ended with a joint SER and LCDR Act for a Dover and Deal line, but also an Act for the SER-backed Bromley Direct Railway and for a line to Dungeness which was intended to strengthen the SER position in the Channel contest. However the year also saw the opening of the LCDR's direct line to Maidstone, which Watkin reckoned would cost the SER £15,000 a year in lost traffic. A "truce" was agreed on 30 July 1874 but lasted less than a year.

From the early 1870s Watkin became an enthusiastic exponent of a Channel Tunnel in the belief that train ferries could never be a solution to the problem. By January 1872 he was working closely with Sir John Hawkshaw in this, who claimed that a tunnel could be built in ten years for £10million. This affair is perhaps typical of the way in which Watkin tended to become obsessed with great issues in his later years, and thereby lost touch with the small detail of railway management which had been the basis for his career. The Channel Tunnel dominated his political activities as well for though he was at first a Liberal and later a Unionist, he was always a maverick; Lord Radnor said of him that, "No-one (not even himself) knew what his politics were; excepting that he would vote for any one or any thing to get support for his Channel Tunnel." As late as 1893 he was criticised for interfering in an election at Grimsby to support a Radical candidate who happened to be pro-Channel Tunnel. Not all of the SER directors supported the issue and there was considerable debate about investing money in trial borings in March 1875. His interest and concern with the Channel Tunnel was a similarly unrealistic obsession to his 1889 scheme for a massive tower at Wembley Park.

However, the SER was certainly in a stronger position by the mid-1870s than when Watkin had taken over, perhaps because it had not yet begun to waste huge sums in later useless projects like the Chatham branch. T.R.Gourvish has assessed that the SER was producing a gross return on capital in the period

4. The effects of the 1877 landslip near Folkestone, showing a party of SER officials making an inspection. Watkin is second from right. (R.W.Kidner Collection)

1870-4 of 9.29% and in January 1876 Watkin declared a creditable dividend of 7.5%. In December 1876 Watkin told the SER that he was resigning his seat on the MSLR Board due to pressure of work with the SER.

By this time Watkin was a well-known public figure, due to his railway and to his political careers. He achieved further fame, of a kind, by being the subject of a portrait in *Vanity Fair* in 1875. The magazine made a few rather waspish comments about him:

"Even his enemies who assert that he is very unscrupulous, admit that he is very clever...He is now rich enough to require to be well paid for the work he does; he has an adequate idea of his own value; and his wife possesses some imposing diamonds and her husband's fidelity."

Fusion with the LCDR was discussed seriously during early 1875 but broke down when the SER discovered, after reading about it in a newspaper, that the LCDR was starting a Sheerness to Flushing ferry service. This was felt to be in contravention of the Continental Agreement of 1865, especially as it offered a cheaper route to Cologne than the SER's via Ostend. During 1876 there was some pressure from shareholders for "fusion" but that Autumn the SER considered building a line to the Isle of Grain in response to the LCDR's Flushing service. The SER considered using Grain as a ferry terminal for Sheerness but at the meeting of 5 October the Board decided not to press ahead with the scheme in case it annoyed the LCDR. In January 1877 talks with the LCDR reopened once more, with proposals for joint stations at Dover, Margate and Canterbury together with a scheme to "fill up" the space between

Maidstone and Ashford. Profits were to be split 33/67 in favour of the SER after five years. However the complete collapse of the line between Dover and Folkestone after a storm threw the SER into disarray and the LCDR withdrew from negotiations. The climate turned cold once more and powers for compulsory purchase on the Dover & Deal line were allowed to lapse, though Watkin blamed the demands of the landowners.

Watkin himself was soon in more personal trouble. His son, Alfred Mellor Watkin[1], had been appointed in charge of the SER Locomotive Department in succession to Cudworth on a salary of £800. Cudworth had resigned after Edward Watkin had commissioned an outsider, John Ramsbottom, to design a class of new passenger locomotives. On 1 August 1877 Alfred Watkin was elected for Grimsby where one of his father's companies, the MSLR, was influential. The SER had introduced a rule in 1870 that none of its officers was to hold two posts, and some of the Board objected to Alfred Watkin continuing with the Company. The younger Watkin was also a director of the MSLR and the Metropolitan Railway, though under the terms of his contract in March 1877, awarded after the retirement of Cudworth, he was only allowed to act as a director of the Seabrook Estate Company and the Bromley Direct Railway.

Edward Watkin attempted to defend his son in the SER Boardroom and lost a bitter battle by 6-4 in which, significantly, even Mellor voted against him. The *Railway Times* complained that Watkin had "made a good thing out of the South Eastern" and there was much criticism of his running private specials to Hythe at the SER's expense. Alfred Watkin was dismissed at the beginning of September 1877. The affair clearly caused some enmity between Mellor and his erstwhile protegee, for in November 1878 Watkin attempted to embarrass Mellor by raising the question of how he had obtained more SER stock but been slack in paying for it. James Stirling was appointed the new locomotive superintendent in March 1878 after a period with the Glasgow & South Western Railway. Ironically, the Ramsbottom engines proved a comparitive failure.

Meanwhile Watkin had been working hard to improve relations with the two companies whose territory lay beside that of the SER. During the latter part of 1877 he reached an agreement with the LBSCR about lines through the disputed ground of western Surrey and eastern Sussex and then watched as a Bill for the fusion of the SER with the LCDR was prepared once more.

Sadly the Bill ran into considerable local opposition, perhaps exacerbated by ill feeling caused by accusations against both companies of price-fixing in raising their fares in January 1877. Within a few weeks of the failure of the Bill, the SER Board began to discuss seriously the construction of a line along the Hoo Peninsula to Grain in the promotion of which their own engineer was involved. Another Bill in 1877-8 failed because a LCDR meeting rejected it after the collapse of the SER's line between Folkestone and Dover. However Watkin had to face opposition from some of the SER Board in August 1878 over his dealings with the LCDR and LBSCR; Mellor was again among the opposition.

However the SER was a stronger company than the LCDR, which was hampered by a switchback main-line that restricted speeds. Thus in September 1878 it was the LCDR that approached the SER wishing to make a deal on the division of traffic receipts for Bromley and Thanet. The SER, needing to improve its station at Canterbury, briefly considered a joint project there with the LCDR and in November looked at the possibility of having a joint Dover station in connection with the Dover & Deal line.

One of the most consistent criticisms of Watkin's management style has been of his tendency to gather too many directorships so that he could attend to the affairs of no company properly. During July 1878 there were a number of fierce criticisms of him, including a number of complaints that he had handled the capitalisation of floating debentures badly - especially considering he was paid £2500 per annum by the SER. It was felt that his record with the Humber Ironworks, the Erie Railroad and the Hudsons Bay Company was not satisfactory. Many on the South Eastern Board agreed and at a stormy meeting on 27 December 1878 he was censured for his dictatorial attitude by 7-4. It seems that the issue that had precipitated this attack was that Watkin had become Chairman of the East London Railway in addition to the MSLR and the SER. The East London itself had become a very contentious issue in SER affairs, causing strained relations with the LBSCR, and some SER directors felt that the position of the SER in the matter was prejudiced by Watkin's division of interests. Watkin defended himself by arguing that Hawkshaw had advised him to "interfere" in the East London to save it from being used against the SER.

On 9 January 1879 the issue of directorships and each director's stake in the SER was discussed at length. In addition to Watkin, the SER Board included Withers, who was deputy chairman of the MSLR, Hugessen, who was on the Board of the Metropolitan and the East London and Whatman, who sat on the ELR as well. The relative debenture holdings of the directors makes an interesting contrast:

James Byng:	£14,100
Edward Watkin:	£2010
Alexander Beattie:	£9250
John Bibby:	£93,400
Nathan Buckley:	£55,750
Joshua Fielden:	£64,000
Jonathan Mellor:	£28,050
Henry Rawson:	£17,600
Col. Charles Surtees:	£2000
E. Knatchbull-Hugessen:	£2200[2]
James Whatman:	£4530
Richard Withers:	£2200

Thus Watkin is revealed as having a smaller stake in the SER than many of the other directors and naturally they felt that his loyalty was in question. Virtual open war broke out in January 1879 between some of the Board members and the Chairman, with an aggressive circular being sent out to SER shareholders: *"Shall Sir Edward Watkin assume to himself the entire control of your great property? Shall he, as he has put it in his own words, have "supreme authority"?"*

The *Railway Times* believed that the SER Board was divided 8-4 against Watkin and that it was especially annoyed about the Metropolitan Railway's plan to connect into the ELR. Watkin's policy was to secure a connection between the SER and his other Company in the area, the Metropolitan, via the East London line whereas Henry Rawson believed a connection to the ELR at New Cross would mean traffic being siphoned off the SER onto other lines.

The move against Watkin failed, for the shareholders supported his policy of increasing the SER position in London by new lines, including connections on to the East London at New Cross. It was won at the price of a bitter row with Byng and a dispute with Bibby. One MSLR shareholder told Watkin "not to mistake notoriety for fame." Watkin's victory meant that by July 1879 the SER was able to give notice of its intent to share in the working of the East London line, which it was empowered to do by an Act of 1870; the line passed under the Thames at Rotherhithe and gave access to the Great Eastern Railway. Reports in August 1879 that Alfred Watkin MP (who lived at Dunedin Lodge, Folkestone, and was an MP from 1877-80) was to stand for the SER Board and in October that John Shaw was to relinquish his managerial role seemed to confirm Watkin's triumph over the rebels. Both events duly took place.

In fact Watkin had probably already decided his next move - to bring the Metropolitan Railway's capable General Manager, Myles Fenton, to the SER and this was done by moving Shaw back to Secretary on £2000 while Fenton was appointed on £3000. Fenton had been born in 1830 and had joined the Kendal & Windermere Railway at the age of fifteen, then progressing through the East Lancashire, Lancashire & Yorkshire, MSLR and LSWR to the Metropolitan in 1863. Perhaps Watkin realised that if he was to retain his Chairmanship of the SER he had to bring in a railway professional to ease his own burdens.

Watkin was also accused of bribing the Hythe electorate by gifts at the expense of the SER. In July 1880 a shareholder complained about the costly hotel there, saying that "while Sir Edward Watkin enjoyed the music, the South Eastern paid the piper." One hopes that he paid a fair sum when he bought the table from the SER's old Royal Saloon in 1882.

Watkin's attempts to expand the SER in the London area angered the LBSCR. In February 1881 Laing wrote to complain about a SER scheme for access to the Crystal Palace. "Will you let us alone," he wrote to Watkin, "if not it is **war**, and I do not see what there is to discuss." During March 1881 the LBSCR suggested that the Woodside & South Croydon scheme should be a joint project, perhaps hoping to contain the expansionist SER. However Watkin was still hankering after a New Cross to Crystal Palace line in December 1884 though the joint Metropolitan and SER Bill was eventually withdrawn in April 1885. Relations were improved substantially as the two companies came to agree a joint policy over the Oxted line which, curiously, closely followed part of the original line laid out for the SER.

The unlimited power of Watkin is perhaps best seen in his obsession with the Channel Tunnel, whose affairs occupied much of his attention in 1881-2. Watkin had 1000 shares in the company, as did Jonathan Mellor. Even Forbes and the LCDR were interested. SER powers to invest in it were severely limited, however. Even more hopeless was the branch to Port Victoria which opened in 1882; its function was largely to irritate the LCDR by providing a train and ferry service to Sheerness and was also seen as a rival to LCDR activities at the port of Queenborough. The crafty Watkin offered the LCDR free use of the line to Port Victoria in 1882 - in exchange for SER running powers to Faversham! This unequal bargain failed to tempt Forbes. In June 1884 the SER heard that Forbes was prepared to drop the LCDR's Flushing service if the SER withdrew its offer to the Zeeland Company of Port Victoria. The German Government was not pleased to hear this and threatened to transfer its business to Harwich anyway; the SER wrote back to Baron Rothschild to apportion the blame to the LCDR:

"These gentlemen keep the whole of our district in a constant ferment, are perpetually attacking us in Parliament, and are acting throughout, in our opinions, as bad partners."

The SER received the unkind attentions of the press despite the best efforts of Watkin and Fenton. In September 1883 the Board of the SER complained that "...*The Times* continues to pad its columns with twaddling and wearisome correspondence about the unpunctuality of SER trains..." However the following month the Sevenoaks Chamber of Commerce registered its own protests about unpunctuality. In July 1884 a passenger registered a protest of a different sort - he sent the SER a packet of dry rot from SER carriage no.462! A year later *Truth* magazine complained that "third class passengers on the South Eastern are still treated as if they were habitual drunkards, felons or pigs."

1884 was probably one of the worst years for relations between the SER and its neighbours. There was a bitter legal battle with the LBSCR over the use of the "Croydon up line" and the LCDR attempted to gain powers for a line from Kearsney to Folkestone. Opposition to this cost the SER £4000. The LCDR also floated a scheme for a harbour to the north of Deal and opened its line from Maidstone to Ashford.

Watkin's response to the aggressive behaviour of Forbes and the LCDR was a Bill for a branch to Chatham, probably one of his most disastrous schemes. The SER also attempted to alter the rules of the Continental Agreement by an Arbitration Bill, but this was rejected. In late June 1885 there were further rumours of amalgamation between the SER, the LCDR and the LBSCR but a Bill to amalgamate the LCDR and the LBSCR was rejected in January 1886.

The danger for the SER was that it might invest too much in competing with, or trying to keep out, the LCDR and that the quality of its services overall would suffer. In the period 1870-98 the SER's ratio of spending on stock and new lines was 18/100, compared to more secure companies like the North Eastern where the ratio was 80/100[3]. This was bound to effect what the passenger saw - stations, trains and services. On 15 March 1884 *Herapath's Railway Magazine* exposed this weakness is a heavily vitriolic attack:

"The South Eastern Railway is a railway! It is necessary to say so, because some people believe it is a canal, some others a tramway, and the great majority a steam plough in a field. The reason it is a railway is because it is so called by Act of Parliament. The reason it continues to be a railway is on account of the national respect for the majesty of the law.

The SER starts indifferently from Cannon Street or Charing Cross and goes back there again. Sometimes, by mistake, it goes elsewhere. Occasionally it gets to Folkestone, and tries to throw itself into the sea. This is good for Folkestone, because multitudes of philanthropists reside there in order to assist the deed.

The SER is generous to excess. It will always buy old cabs, broken-down omnibuses, or mouldy perambulators from anybody who doesn't care to keep them till next cold weather. A number of these vehicles tied together in a string is called a South Eastern Railway train.

At the end of each train there is a stationary engine. It is because no more of these engines can be procured that there are no railways in China.
The SER is profoundly philosophical. Its time-table is the only instance of the human mind fully defining eternity.

The SER is going in a tunnel to France, and the Government is going to spend twenty millions on fortifications to prevent it ever coming back.

If you want to travel by the SER, you take a ticket and walk.

Generally speaking the SER sought a better working relationship with its neighbours from a position of strength. During the early 1880s its gross return on capital, averaging 10.34%, was more than double that of the LCDR at 5.09%. Its operating ratio, the balance between working expenses and receipts, was improving steadily. Yet the South Eastern Board estimated that they had spent £48,584 on opposing LCDR Bills between 1875 and 1884, to which must be added the cost of lines laid down largely for tactical reasons like the Hundred of Hoo (which had cost £222,568 by May 1885), the Elham line and later the Chatham branch. Most irksome of all, though, was that the long-standing Continental Agreement drained SER revenues into the ever-hungry LCDR wallet.

The Continental Agreement certainly worked in the Chatham Company's favour, but SER attempts to force changes to it achieved little more than inflated legal bills. The attempt to force the LCDR to include the receipts of the Queenborough to Flushing service (estimated by the SER at £99,400) in it failed by early 1886; Forbes had alleged that Eborall had excluded Queenborough from it in 1865 and had told the Committee on the Hundred of Hoo Railway this, though the SER claimed it was untrue.

The SER's most long-running attempt to circumnavigate the Continental Agreement began with a decision in March 1880 to improve Shorncliffe station; the simple idea was to detrain continental passengers there - supposedly outside the boundaries of the Agreement - and thus deprive the "shared pool" of a large part of the SER's continental traffic receipts. The LCDR immediately leapt into battle and in 1881 Justice Kekewich ruled against the SER, which promptly appealed. Traffic at Shorncliffe had increased from £6020 in 1865 to £28,000 in 1883, much of which was due to the continental traffic, but when the LCDR demanded the payment of £62,648 the SER handed over only £6,545. In August 1887 the House of Lords ruled that the SER must pay £45,000 into the fund as Shorncliffe was part of Folkestone. The SER appealed again, but lost the case once more in May 1890 when it was ordered to pay £51,735. The SER then began another legal battle over the amount of interest due.

During the conduct of the Shorncliffe Case, relations between the two companies were acrimonious. The Deal to Dover joint line had opened in 1881, but the SER used it as a weapon against the LCDR, and the LCDR sought to do likewise - most notably by putting in a loop at Kearsney so that it could run Deal to London trains without going via Dover. The SER replied to this by scheming to exclude the LCDR from the use of Deal station, which was wholly SER property. The LCDR applied pressure elsewhere, by opening its own branch to Gravesend in 1886 and starting a fares war to the riverside town in 1887. The SER determined to press ahead with its Rochester and Chatham branch (opened 1891-2) to punish the LCDR, but punished its own finances thereby as well.

Early in 1888 there was pressure for a better working relationship from a number of sources. In January a shareholder named Abbott agitated for a union of the three companies and in February Laing, of the LBSCR, suggested a five year truce. However rumours of fusion talks soon collapsed when it was learnt that the LBSCR had angered the LCDR by trying to get access to its City station at St Paul's; Laing described reports of talks as "premature and unauthorised". The SER was more serious and in March announced that it would withdraw three contentious proposals from its Bill if this would encourage the LBSCR to discuss fusion. The SER was less trusting of the LCDR and offered to advance £100,000 to the little Bexleyheath Railway when it discovered that a Bill was in progress for making a connection from it to the LCDR! It also felt that the LCDR's financial position made it a poor partner for anyone.

Watkin's attention was diverted in early 1888 by the death of his wife. He did not spend long alone, though, for in 1893 he married Ann Ingram, the widow of the founder of *The Illustrated London News*, who was eighty-one at the time. It was a time when a number of deaths changed some of the key personnel in SER circles - Whatman died in 1887 and Beattie on 10 February 1889. Jonathan Mellor died on 9 February 1890; a Colonel John Mellor was elected a director two months later.

Fenton received a knighthood at the end of 1888, leading some publications to assert that he was the first railway manager to be knighted, though this is doubtful. He was also said to have "a winning smile" which had impressed Royalty! He was further elevated by the King of Belgium who made him an "officer of the Order of Leopold" in 1894.

For a time in 1890-1 the SER Board included four lords, though not all the shareholders were impressed. Captain Sharpe complained:

"He was not so sure that a lord was so much believed in these days, because he was generally put forward as a sort of decoy in a bubble company."

Watkin continued to hope that the LCDR could be tempted into giving up the Continental Agreement voluntarily. In June 1888 he offered the LCDR running powers over the Elham Valley line to Folkestone if it would cancel the Agreement, but the LCDR declined the offer; why should it cancel such a great benefit? In 1890 the SER considered whether it could run its steamers from Littlestone, between Hythe and Dungeness, to evade the Continental Agreement having just lost the Shorncliffe Case. Talks about altering the Continental Agreement collapsed in November 1890 with the LCDR refusing to reduce its share below 37%. Watkin visited Littlestone using his special train in 1891.

It is significant that at this time the local Corporations of Kent towns became more active in trying to force better links between the two companies, with Folkestone Corporation lobbying for LCDR running powers from Ashford to Folkestone and Maidstone pressing for a service to link the Maidstone & Ashford line of the LCDR with the SER's Ashford station. The *Railway Times* felt that Folkestone would gain little benefit from having the LCDR there as well - "two blacks will not make a white" and considered "that no sane person would travel" by the LCDR route to Ashford. Fenton complained that negotiations were made more difficult by the "insulting communications which I regret to say are characteristic of..." the LCDR.

The SER and LBSCR went through a period of hostility caused by such issues as the Crystal Palace proposal, the East London Railway, and the legal battle over the Croydon "up" line. Lessons were to be learnt from this, though, for when rumours circulated in early 1887 that the SER was planning an intensive London to Redhill service in competition with the LBSCR, the shares of both companies fell sharply. After this period of ill-will, relations with the LBSCR were handled by the more sensible method of appointing an arbitrator. Henry Oakley of the Great Northern Railway studied the question of the Hastings traffic and the Competitive Traffic Agreement between the two, though when he made his award in 1889 it incurred the wrath of Hastings Corporation. The success of this approach encouraged the use of Oakley as arbitrator over the use of Deal station.

During the first quarter of 1890 rumours of amalgamation between the SER and LCDR again circulated, but they were generally blamed upon the stockbroking firm of Arthur Anderson & Co.; the *Railway Times* believed the rumour to be "the reroasting of the very stalest chestnut." In fact Watkin went so far as to meet Arthur Anderson and told him that the SER was not averse to talks and three representatives from each company discussed the proposals in detail. Watkin had a personal meeting with Forbes at the Charing Cross Hotel on 7 June. In July 1890 Folkestone Corporation made it clear that they were opposed to fusion without terms to protect their town, though Lord Brabourne was in favour. The SER rejected the LCDR terms in November 1890 and in early 1891 the General Meeting voted against amalgamation. The SER's decision to acquire control of the Sheerness Pier tolls in November 1890 can hardly be considered as a friendly gesture to the LCDR. The ruling of the Railway Commissioners in February 1891 that the SER and LCDR must provide "reasonable accommodation" between Maidstone and Ashford (SER) sparked off further angry scenes.

In August 1892 Nathaniel Spens launched a campaign to get the SER and LCDR to amalgamate. By December a draft agreement had actually been prepared on the lines of the 1878 Bill. In January 1893 some SER shareholders also expressed fears that an amalgamation with Watkin's other favourite company, the MSLR, was also a prospect. The *Railway Times* considered the proposed arrangement between the SER and the LCDR to be more "un mariage de convenance" than a love match, especially since the two companies were spending £17,000 each year on legal and Parliamentary fees. Folkestone again, Dover and Tonbridge were prepared to oppose any working agreement or fusion. A Bill for fusion was withdrawn in February 1893 with Watkin blaming the "temper" of Parliament. The improved working relationship between the two companies was, according to the *Railway Times*, due to the fact that SER and LCDR affairs had come more under the control of Fenton and John Morgan, rather than Watkin and Forbes.

Lord Brabourne, the SER deputy chairman, died on 6 February 1893. His interests had included the Metropolitan, the Channel Tunnel and the Madrid & Portugal Direct. This opportunity to bring in fresh faces was ignored, for he was replaced by James Byng, the elderly former Chairman. This change was minor compared to the one that occurred the following year, for on 19 May 1894 Watkin wrote to the SER Board to say that illness had forced him to tender his resignation as Chairman of the SER and that he was also retiring from the MSLR and the Metropolitan Railway. The *Railway Times* commented that "his picturesque personality has loomed large in the railway history of our time." Byng, older than Watkin and a relic of the time when the Kent gentry had controlled Kent railways, replaced him as Chairman with Sir George Russell MP as deputy and then, within two months, Brabourne also died. A Minute of 16 July records a suggestion that Cosmo Bonsor MP should become a director. Fenton, a Liberal Unionist like Watkin had been since 1885, was tipped to become MP for Hythe, but retired as General Manager in 1896.

What was Watkin's achievement? Despite the criticisms, the SER was a better railway than the LCDR in most ways. It had a more secure financial basis, a more efficient operating ratio, and paid better dividends. The record seems to suggest that Watkin was often prepared to discuss fusion with the LCDR or the LBSCR and that it was the political process that stood in the way. Watkin and the SER Board were guilty of some foolish acts, of which the construction of the Hundred of Hoo and the Chatham Central branches are the most notable, and some provocative behaviour - for example, the Sheerness Pier issue. His greatest crime was probably that he attempted to do too much and was concerned with too many companies, thereby getting involved with some highly visible failures - the worst of which was the Wembley Tower, for which plans were drawn up in 1889, construction reaching only the first stage by 1896 with the whole farcical structure being demolished in 1907. Because of his involvement with the Tower, malicious stories were circulated in 1893 that he had bought Mount Snowdon "from which to watch the success or non-success of his manifold enterprises." He actually bought *The Chalet* at Beddgelert and a path to Snowdon's summit was named after him. He was carried to the summit on a bier shortly before he died. He also received much criticism for his obsession with the Channel Tunnel, but this was killed off in 1891 by political enemies like the imperialist Joseph Chamberlain, not for practical or financial reasons. He remained M.P. for Hythe from 1874 until 1895 and was described as having had an "intimate friendship" with Gladstone.

Yet Watkin's SER generally managed to achieve a reasonably constructive relationship with its western neighbour, the LBSCR, with which it managed to resolve the question of the Surrey & Sussex line by a joint project. Watkin personally claimed credit for the abandonment of a SER/LCDR scheme for a line to Brighton in 1889. He could also be autocratic and was much criticised for allowing the French revolutionary, General Boulanger, free use of a train in April 1889.

Watkin was a larger than life character and he gave great opportunities to the railway press, who loved to lampoon his style or the condition of any of his companies. In 1891 the Kaiser of Germany travelled from Port Victoria to London Bridge, and the railway press satirised the SER by reporting that the Kaiser had asked for the plans of London Bridge station - he was so impressed he wanted to copy it in Berlin! In 1888 the *St. James's Gazette* chose the SER's North Kent line as an easy target:

"A Trip on the Flying Watkin"

"It was high noon as I stood on the platform at the Gravesend station. There was a certain sense of bustle and agitation in the air, but nothing sufficient to indicate that "The Flying Watkin" was about to start. The driver of the engine was chatting unconcernedly with an acquaintance; the fireman was quietly mending the connection of one of the valves with a piece of string; the guard had not yet put in an appearance...

The very train itself was an example of that English desire to gratify every idiosyncrasy and to be independent of every hard and fast rule which so favourably distinguishes us from the hide-bound Pedants of the Continent. There were no fewer than fifteen vehicles...and such was the ardent desire of the directors to gratify every taste that of this whole number only two carriages bore the slightest resemblance to each other.

With a cool, collected air characteristic of his profession, the driver puts over his lever and opens the valves. The result is not immediately satisfactory, and I must admit that the effect is somewhat marred by the necessity for reversing the engine and setting back the train before the wheels begin to revolve in the desired direction...

We run through Bexley at high speed. If the platform had been longer, or if our brakes had worked better, we should not have overshot the station and been under the necessity of going back to it....."

In December 1894 a London evening newspaper insisted that the legacy of Watkin still haunted the SER and published a letter attributed to "The Worm That Turns":

"The SER is the worst railway in the world. Its engines are asthmatic, its lamps are trimmed by foolish virgins, its fares are excessive, its carriages let in the snow in winter and are furnaces in summer, its motto is unpunctuality...it enables one to realise the horrors of Dante's Inferno."

The LCDR Act of July 1894 included powers for it to work with the SER from 1 January 1895. The result of this was a general agreement on fare levels that produced some savings for longer distance travellers - perhaps a clever move, since it was the more distant Kent towns that were the main opposition to amalgamation or working union.

Further changes occurred in the higher ranks of the SER when Sir Myles Fenton retired in 1896 and James Byng died on 21 May 1897. Sir George Russell became the new Chairman, but also died on 7 March 1898. Russell had extensive business interests, including Eagle Insurance, the Argentine Great Western Railway and the Mexican Southern. The rapid removal of the older generation created opportunity for Cosmo Bonsor, who succeeded Russell as Chairman and came to dominate the SE&CR. Bonsor was paid £1,200 a year, with A.Gathorne-Hardy as his deputy. Alfred Willis, the former Passenger Manager and solicitor, became General Manager in 1898.

By early June 1898 Bonsor and James Forbes of the LCDR were involved in "informal discussions" about the relationship between their companies.

Further talks were held at Charing Cross in July 1898 following which it was agreed that the two companies would work together from 1 January 1899. All receipts were to be pooled, with the SER taking 59% and the LCDR 41%. Although such an agreement was covered by SER powers of 1893 and the LCDR Act of 1894, it was decided to seek the further authority of Parliament. This Act was passed on 5 August 1899 - eight months after the South Eastern & Chatham Railways Managing Committee had been formed.

Under the new arrangements, the operating functions of both companies were merged into the SE&CR. However, both the SER and LCDR still had separate existences as financial and holding interests, with entirely separate shareholdings; Willis, for example, was made General Manager of the LCDR as well, rather than being appointed to the SE&CR.

1. Born 1846, died 1914; named after Jonathan Mellor.
2. Became Lord.Brabourne in 1880.
3. T.Gourvish, **Performance of British Railway Management after 1860.**

CHAPTER 5: LONDON BRIDGE TO REDHILL

1. London Bridge to Redhill

As has been seen in Chapter Two, the SER did not have its own line into London but depended on the use of tracks belonging to other companies. Between London Bridge station and Corbetts Lane Junction it ran over the route of the London & Greenwich Railway, from there to Norwood Junction (Jolly Sailor) over the tracks of the London & Croydon and from there to Stoat's Nest over the line built by the London & Brighton Railway. Only then did the SER run over lines that it could call its own, though as far as Redhill they were built by the L&BR but transferred to the SER under its Parliamentary powers. This complex state of affairs had great significance in the later development of the SER - it gave rise to the opening of a new terminus at Bricklayers Arms, for example, and had a major long term impact on the concept of railways having their own "territories" in South-East England.

The South Eastern was aware from a very early stage that this dependance on other companies made it strategically weak. As early as December 1836 Cubitt, the engineer, suggested that the SER should take over the L&CR as it "would be a valuable appendage to the SER[1]." Four days later the SER met the L&CR and offered to have two Croydon directors join its Board but terms could not be agreed.

5. London Bridge terminus.

Strategic factors also played a part in the negotiations over the purchase of the Merstham section of line, built by the L&BR but then bought by the SER as described in Chapter Two. When this was discussed in January 1838 the SER was aware that the line could be used as a base for a new route to Portsmouth and told the L&BR that "if a western or a Portsmouth line be made each Company shall have the profits of the traffic equally." However the L&BR disliked the SER's involvement with the Portsmouth scheme and by August there was a general feeling that the Croydon and Greenwich lines would not be able to carry the additional traffic.

The question of the capacity of the line north of Norwood exercised minds in June 1839. The SER felt that London Bridge (where the L&CR had provided a three-track terminus to the north of the L&GR) and its approaches could not handle all the traffic, and for this reason suggested a new station at St George's Fields, near Elephant & Castle. On 13 June Cubitt told the SER Board that there should be an additional viaduct built parallel to the L&GR one for trains off the L&CR route and that the new station being built by the L&CR at London Bridge should become the Greenwich station, and the L&GR's station should become the Croydon one. At the same time Cubitt still thought the best solution was a line from Dartmouth Arms to a new terminus at the obelisk near Elephant & Castle.

On 7 August 1840 the London & Greenwich secured Acts allowing it to widen the line approaching London Bridge and to improve the terminus. The passage of the Bills had been watched by a new joint committee of the SER, L&BR and L&CR, which had been formed in March 1840. Under the new powers the Greenwich was to provide a widening of the existing viaduct from Corbetts Lane by an additional two tracks, to be completed within two years on pain of a £50 per day penalty. The L&GR could charge a fixed toll of 4 1/2d a passenger over this line, though it had hoped for 6d. To avoid the ridiculous situation of trains from the south having to cross over to a station on the north side, the Greenwich agreed to swap stations with the Croydon and to provide additional ground, raised to the same level as the tracks, within 18 months or lose £50 a day.

This Act was the result of lengthy deliberations in Parliament in which safety was a key factor and effectively broke the stranglehold of the Greenwich Company, although it retained the fixed tolls which were so irksome to the other concerns. The three southern companies then proceeded to work together on their own joint station - in August 1840 the SER was expecting this would cost them £60,000 each, though later estimates put the total at £250,000. It also estimated that the L&CR had already spent £108,000 on its own station.

On 24 June 1841 the Joint Committee took over the old Croydon station at London Bridge and by February 1843 controlled the old Greenwich station as well, while the L&GR used a temporary facility. The two extra tracks opened on 10 May 1842, while SER trains from Tonbridge began using it from 26 May. The new "Joint" station was in use from late 1843.

Another area of joint activity that the SER decided to explore was the running of locomotives. On 31 May 1841 it decided to try and set up a joint locomotive department, based at New Cross, with the Croydon Company. It took some time for progress to be made, but agreement was reached at the end of February 1842 and became operative from May. Both companies supported the Joint Locomotive Committee by payments into its funds - for example, the SER paid £15,000 in August 1843. The L&BR joined this working partnership in 1844, and problems then began. In June 1844 the SER complained that the L&BR kept the best engines at Brighton, and never let them venture further north than Redhill. The Brighton retaliated by claiming that the SER changed the names and numbers of the engines around and used "anonymous" engines on the night goods. The SER blamed the poor choice of locomotives for its

6. **The junction between the Croydon and Greenwich lines at the high level, with the lines to Bricklayers Arms below.**

having to apologise to the Duke of Wellington after a poor run in October 1844 and soon afterwards the SER decided to abandon the Joint Locomotive Committee[2].

The SER had to take immediate steps to acquire some engines for itself which, given the locomotive market at the time, proved difficult. It also decided to abandon the workshops at New Cross and to seek a base elsewhere - Ashford was selected. The Joint Commitee was closed down on 31 January 1846, from which date it vacated New Cross workshops. The SER used New Cross under a temporary agreement for a further year.

In May 1842 the SER had agreed to pay the L&CR 1s a passenger for the use of its line, but both companies had difficulties with the Greenwich. The SER wanted to introduce 3rd class on its trains into London Bridge, but the Greenwich refused to abandon the idea of fixed tolls - which were calculated per head, ignoring the class of the passenger. In August 1842 the *Railway Times* reported the Greenwich's refusal to accept 3rd class passengers and in November it reported that many passengers were using New Cross instead to avoid the high fares.

The high fares forced by the L&GR tolls were ruinous to local traffic and the London & Croydon advertised its decision to give up running trains to London Bridge from 25 March 1843. The Board of Trade then intervened but even William Gladstone, the future Prime Minister, could not persuade the L&GR to change its policy and so the L&CR and SER pressed ahead with their plans for a new terminus at Bricklayers Arms. (See Chapter Seven)

It was clear that greater efficiency would result from there being fewer companies. In December 1843 the SER sent Cubitt to inspect the Brighton line with a view to leasing it, and the SER believed the Croydon to be keen on amalgamation. In January 1844 they were prepared to offer to rent the Brighton for £100,000 per year for ten years, but the Brighton rejected the offer, though one result of the talks was that the Brighton joined the Joint Locomotive Committee. By May both the L&BR and the SER were hoping to lease the

Croydon, though after talks the two bigger companies agreed a strategy where the Brighton would seek to lease the Croydon and the SER would seek a similar arrangement with the Greenwich. From 1 January 1845 the SER took over the working of the L&GR while the L&BR took over the L&CR in June 1846 to form the London, Brighton & South Coast Railway.

As has been seen, the SER took possession of 6.5 miles of line between Stoat's Nest and Redhill from the Brighton Company. This included a station at Merstham and also a short branch to Sir William Joliffe's pit nearby. In January 1844 the SER discovered that the latter was in a "dangerous" condition and in September decided to spend £75 improving the gradients on it. The Countess of Warwick, who had forced the reopening of Merstham station in October, threatened to take further action in December 1845 since she felt the station did not comply with the Act of Parliament. In fact the SER had decided in September 1844 to spend £115 on a new Merstham station half a mile to the north, and this seems to have opened during 1845. During March 1845 there were falls of chalk in the cutting and one of the repair workers was killed in a subsequent fall. The SER's refusal to accept the gas-lighting in Merstham Tunnel has already been discussed; much of the equipment was removed by the L&BR but the old gas pipes remained, and in November 1845 the SER decided to attach air pumps to them so that the "policemen" guarding the Tunnel could "whistle" a warning to each other - this cost £80.

The new Reigate Junction station had been built hastily but improvements followed. Its platforms were lengthened and covered in 1845-6 and a footbridge provided.

The line from London Bridge to Reigate (known as Reigate or Reigate Junction until 1858 and then Redhill Junction) was one of the busiest in the country and there were problems with handling the traffic. In January 1845 the SER therefore decided to build a "signal cabin" at Reigate, but there remained problems. In June 1845 a Brighton train left London Bridge at 7.40am followed by a South Eastern one at 8am, but the latter had often caught up the former by the time they reached Reigate. The Brighton train had to be retimed to leave five minutes earlier. In December 1845 there were further disputes with the L&BR about departure times and on 13 July 1846 there was nearly a serious collision at Croydon between a LBSC loco and a SER train.

Further north, the SER had stopped calling at New Cross in 1844 and rejected requests to do so in March 1846. When the L&BR took over the Croydon line, it attempted to use it as a political weapon against the South Eastern; the LBSCR hoped to get the SER to withdraw the Mid Kent scheme in November 1846, but the SER was unwilling to do this while the LBSCR was demanding a perpetual fixed toll on the Croydon line.

The SER, though, was now in possession of all that had been previously controlled by the Greenwich, including the approach lines to London Bridge and the Greenwich's part of the terminus as well as its one third share in the Joint station. When the Croydon had decided to convert its lines to the atmospheric system of propulsion, the SER needed to provide an extra track between Corbetts Lane and London Bridge since steam and atmospheric systems were not compatible. An Act was obtained in 1845 for an extra line on the north side of the viaduct, with one of the southern tracks to become an atmospheric line. However the SER took no immediate steps to build this line, perhaps for financial reasons and perhaps because the future of the atmospheric system was in doubt.

By this stage the SER was pursuing the development of lines in North Kent and extra capacity was plainly needed. It therefore got permission to add two additional tracks on the north side of the viaduct, replacing the 1845 scheme for one additional line, and to enlarge London Bridge. With these additional developments, it was plain that a more rational working arrangement between the two companies needed to be introduced, and agreement was reached with effect from 13 November 1847 though not formally signed until 10 July 1848. The LBSCR was to have toll free access to London Bridge and would gain five acres at Bricklayers Arms for a nominal sum. The SER and trains from the Reading, Guildford & Reigate were to have reciprocal free use of the former Croydon line, but any traffic from later lines built into Sussex would have to pay. The SER was allowed to stop at stations between Croydon and London Bridge and agreed to give up a claim for £25,000 from the LBSCR for a third line which had been allocated to it on the viaduct approaching London Bridge; this became known as the "Croydon up line" and caused much trouble later.

The agreement was also important in that it attempted to reduce wasteful competition by stipulating the "territory" of each company - the SER was not, for example, to promote lines south of its Reigate Junction to Tonbridge line or west of its main Hastings route.

The two extra lines between London Bridge and Corbett's Lane were opened on 24 February 1850, leaving three available for trains to Croydon and Redhill. The most southerly of these, the up Croydon, was not normally used by the SER.

Although the agreement suggests an improvement of the relationship, the reality was very poor on a day to day basis. The SER had grown irritable at what it saw as the failure of the LBSCR locomotives to work satisfactorily and launched a press campaign in July 1847. The *Railway Record* reported the incapacity of the LBSCR engines and said that the SER could get no satisfactory reply to its complaints: "We can only get replies in the shape of quibbles, regrets and wailings..." SER correspondence asserted. The *Railway Times*[3] joined in gleefully, especially when James Walker, the SER's Superintendent, released letters complaining of the "utter indifference" of the LBSCR to complaints. He had told the LBSCR that delays on the SER were caused by "the miserable creeping along of your incapable engines." He also requested that the "mountainous" remains of the defunct atmospheric system be removed before they caused an accident. This was exciting material, and the railway press loved it, but it also reveals that the SER had realised the power of the press and were concerned to improve their own image at the expense of another; the railway journals had considerable impact on share prices.

On 19 May 1847 the LBSCR took about 32,000 passengers to Epsom for the Derby amidst such chaotic scenes that many did not pay their fares. For the following year, the LBSCR asked to borrow 80 carriages from the SER who agreed but refused to accept payment, arguing that this excessive traffic was dangerous.

The SER felt that it had derived some benefits from the agreement with the LBSCR, such as being able to call at Forest Hill and New Cross which it began doing again from about 1 August 1848. However, it also meant that it was outvoted at the meetings of the Joint Station Committee and by November 1848 was preparing to end the arrangement and have its own, separate station. The division of London Bridge into separate stations took place at midnight on 1-2 August 1850 although the *Railway Times* "deplored" the move as liable to hinder

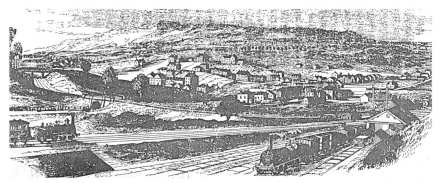

7. The junctions at Redhill in about 1850, with the SER main line in the foreground, the Brighton line on the left and the Reading route in the left background.

amalgamation. The Joint station was then demolished (part of its old iron roof being taken to Bricklayers Arms) and the SER built its own terminus; a new arrival platform opened on 9 December and the main station on 3 January 1851. The SER Board rejected an idea to front the station with a Doric portico.

The last quarter of 1850 saw acrimony over the operation of trains between London Bridge and Redhill, spurred on at least in part by the SER's decision to reduce fares to Redhill in August 1850 but also because of the separate issues of the Mid Kent Railway and the Hastings question. The LBSCR did not approve of changes made to working arrangements and signalling, and complained to the Board of Trade. Colonel Wynne investigated and, in November, suggested some improvements to signalling at Bricklayers Arms Junction and Merstham, but felt overall that the SER's alterations were "consistent with the public safety...calculated to improve the line[4]." Not to be spited, the LBSCR sent the SER a bill for £2-0-7d after damage to a signal and bridge at Forest Hill.

However, by 16 December the two companies had agreed on how to work the line to mutual satisfaction; one result of this was that the SER decided to cease calling at Forest Hill or New Cross.

It was not only the LBSCR who could feel the wrath of the SER - even its own senior employees were not safe. It was the practice in late 1850 to attach carriages from Reading and Reigate Town to up Dover trains for the journey on to London, but this often caused delays to the Dover train. On one occasion the SER Secretary, Herbert, was incensed by the delay and noticed that the Redhill Junction stationmaster, Hastings, was doing nothing about it. When Herbert remonstrated with him, Hastings said that there was nothing that could be done due to the lack of porters. Herbert had Hastings sacked in November, apparently purely on the basis of this incident which suggests a rather harsh approach by the senior SER management.

The track at Merstham was laid with Barlow's iron sleepers and figured in the controversy over his dismissal in 1851. Barlow then alleged that the track north of Merstham was unsafe but the new engineer, Drane, disagreed. Despite this, the Board discussed the bad state of the line between Stoat's Nest and

Redhill in October 1852 and by January 1853 were relaying the down line. In May 1853 the LBSCR complained to the Board of Trade about the line.

Having left the workshops at New Cross and not completed the move to Ashford, the SER lacked a suitable place to do engine repairs and a number were done in the open at Redhill. In June 1851 the Board decided that the sight of engines without their wheels might prove disconcerting to passengers and the staff were instructed to park a row of empty carriages in front of the wheel-less hulks. A new engine shed was built in 1853.

Relations between the SER and LBSCR continued to be variable. In December 1852 the SER was alarmed by rumours of a merger between the LBSCR and the LSWR and in January 1853 suggested a merger to take place in three years. The SER showed some adherence to the 1848 agreement with the LBSCR; after an approach had been made to Forster for it to work the Direct Portsmouth, the SER rejected the plan by 4-3. This vote may have reflected the views of the anti-expansionists on the Board.

In August 1852 a driver of a Tunbridge Wells excursion was fined 42s for ignoring signals at Redhill. An increasing number of staff were being employed there, so twelve extra cottages were built in 1852-3. In January 1853 it was decided to extend the platforms at Merstham to 400 feet and to relay a goods siding there. Merstham was the scene of a collision between a down Reading goods train and a ballast train on 4 March.

Later in March, and perhaps because of this collision, the SER announced new regulations for working the tunnel and station at Merstham. The gas pipes were to be removed and, perhaps, sent to Whitstable Harbour, though for what purpose is unknown. By September 1853 the SER was installing signal wires, presumably with the LBSCR's co-operation, between Redhill and London Bridge. It also complained to the LBSCR that the junction with the Crystal Palace line at Norwood was dangerous, and wanted a viaduct instead to carry the Crystal Palace trains to the down line.

On 21 August 1854 there was a serious accident at Croydon. The 9.40am excursion from Dover had been split into two parts at Ashford for the run to London. The signalman at South Croydon became confused and let a LBSCR ballast train out after the passage of the first excursion with the result that it was hit by the second. Three people were killed and the Board of Trade expressed concern about the lack of liaison between railways. Liabilities for the accident were about £25,000 and in July 1855 a referee stipulated that the LBSC should pay 85% of this and the SER 15%.

In August 1853 the SER obtained an Act for the further enlargement of London Bridge, where the roof was damaged by a snow storm in January 1854.

Rich, one of the leading members of the SER Board, was keen to see the Redhill line sold to the LBSCR in January 1854, though why the LBSCR should want to buy a line that it had free use of and where fair play was overseen by the Board of Trade remains a mystery. On 3 November 1854 the SER and LBSCR agreed to consult on future competing schemes and one result of this was the formation of the LBSC & SE Joint Committee, which began meeting in September 1855; though this did discuss new lines it also talked over issues on the shared route, thereby answering some of the criticisms made by the Board of Trade in the wake of the Croydon accident.

One of the issues that had to be discussed in 1855 was the division of traffic receipts - Redhill and Hastings being the main issues. Hastings was to be divided equally, with the SER to get 60% of the Redhill and Reigate receipts. It also dealt with disputes, such as that in August 1856 over the LBSCR's traffic to Hall's Siding at Merstham. Some results were of great benefit to passengers - from 1 December 1855 Redhill commuters could travel by either companies' trains.

In 1857 the SER decided to rebuild Redhill station, expending about £15,000 in the process and erecting an iron roof supported on columns close to the track with extra platforms being provided as well. It was completed in 1858 with six extra cottages for staff. Merstham was improved in 1860.

The authorisation of the Charing Cross line in 1859 had many implications for London Bridge. In fact the SER had considered enlarging it in 1856, when the possibility of adding extra space on the north side for East Kent Railway trains was discussed. Traffic had risen from 624,000 passengers a year in 1846 to 17.5 million in 1858-9, presumably for all the companies using the station. Parts of the station had to be demolished to create space for the new high level platforms. Improvements there included a new stationmaster's house and new waiting rooms for the down line upper level.

This was the time when the SER felt most under threat from the rapid growth of its rival, the East Kent Railway, into the London, Chatham & Dover. The SER therefore talked closely with the LBSCR about rival projects in July 1858; it was decided that the LBSCR would not seek involvement with any line to the east of Corbett's Lane/Redhill while the SER's West End extension was not to join at any point along this line. A typical clash of interests occurred, though, when both companies wanted to run a 3pm from London Bridge.

The greatest fear that the SER had at this time concerned the LCDR's Metropolitan Extension Bill, but it also feared that, in the event of the LCDR's Bill failing, it would be granted running powers to London Bridge. In October 1862 the SER met with Leo Schuster of the LBSCR to discuss the Croydon traffic, with Schuster keen to work "in perfect harmony for mutual protection against any common enemy." Schuster may have had the LSWR in mind, but he was also worried about the Mid Kent Railway's extension to Croydon. The LBSCR created additional pressure by allowing only passengers with LBSCR-issued tickets to use East Croydon station. During December the talks broadened to cover the fares to Croydon, a LBSCR/LCDR scheme for a line to Greenwich, Dorking, Crystal Palace and even a Birmingham, Brighton & Eastbourne Railway. By 17 December discussion had even covered the possibility of amalgamation, but the LBSCR rejected this. When agreement was reached on 2 March 1864 it covered the key territorial issues including SER expansion in Sussex, and in 1867 the amalgamation issue got as far as a Bill.

Typically, these talks were conducted against a background of bickering. The usual cause of complaint was interference with each others trains and the occasional accident; in November 1862 the 7.55am Dover boat train was hit in the rear at New Cross by the 8am down LBSCR train in icy and foggy conditions - there were no injuries. Such was the Board of Trade's concern about timekeeping and safety that it ordered a return of all late-running between London Bridge and Redhill between 21 and 22 June 1863. Even after this the SER continued to complain that the LBSCR's trains delayed its own, even claiming compensation in August 1865.

The opening of the new main-line to Tonbridge in 1868 altered the SER's attitude to the problematic line via Redhill. Though it continued to run a few main-line trains via the old route, it lost a great deal of its importance. In August 1868 the SER was once more trying to get the LBSCR to take over the line, or at least the traffic, but without success.

Instead there was a further round of talks about the division of traffic in December 1868. The result was the Brighton was to get 75% of the Croydon receipts and 80% of those at Caterham Junction (see below), while the SER would have 80% of the Redhill and Reigate traffic. A revised agreement of 12 January 1870 covered the Caterham traffic, replacing an earlier agreement of 1862, but the SER refused to have its Woodside station (see Chapter 9) included in the Croydon calculation. Such agreements were only ever as effective as the spirit in which they were maintained - thus by June 1870 there was a renewed bout of squabbling over the LBSC traffic to Croydon gas works.

In 1871 catch points were installed to protect the ballast siding at Merstham and in 1872 the level of the down platform there was raised and a new shelter provided. On 22 February 1873 a man was killed half a mile north of Redhill when helping a porter to carry baggage along the track.

In October 1873 Fireman Trindle had to take a week off work after his head had hit one of the iron columns supporting the roof at Redhill station. This was one of a number of such incidents, and in December 1877 the Board of Trade complained about further incidents on 23 October 1876 and 4 October 1877. On 19 March 1889 the conductor on an LBSCR Pullman car was killed by one of the columns. Only in 1895, at a cost of £1,884, did the SER remove the columns.

On 4 December 1856 a Mr Swift was killed at Holmthorpe Crossing, south of Merstham, by the 10.45am Brighton train. At the inquest the jury asked the SER to provide a subway, which the SER were prepared to consider if local people paid half the cost [5].

On 18 July 1877 a LBSC mail train was derailed near Stoat's Nest with a number of injuries. Work was being done on the track at the time and Colonel Yolland, the inspector, blamed both excessive speed and a lack of warning signs.

In 1878 the SER provided an extra platform shelter and a footbridge at Merstham and an extra siding at Redhill. Since the SER's own gas works at Redhill was worn out by 1879 it decided to abandon it and use the local supply instead. A further siding was added there in 1881 and in January 1882 it was felt

8. Reigate Junction Station, looking south.

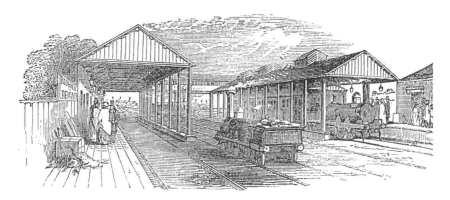

that the station should be "done up in the Spring", with down sidings and a roof over the down platform.

After a short period of relative peace, relations with the LBSCR reached a nadir with the Croydon up controversy which commenced in 1879. This was the third line on the approach to London Bridge which the LBSCR had been using for about thirty years and which the SER now wished to use as well. The SER was hoping to make some improvements, including a new line from Bricklayers Arms that would join onto the Croydon up line and help to relieve the problems caused by shunting traffic from the Blackfriars Junction line into Bricklayers Arms. The LBSCR claimed that, under the 1845 agreement, it had exclusive use of the line even though its signalling and maintenance was done by the SER; when the SER laid in new points, the LBSCR sought legal action.

The daggers were drawn and the SER once more used the press to advantage. It published documents about the line which Laing, of the LBSCR, deemed "offensive". He complained that they "create angry feeling by the most unjust and unfounded personal insinuations." The LBSCR argument that the then engineers of the two companies, Hood and Barlow, had agreed exclusive use by the LBSCR in 1848 when Barlow, whose continued existence seemed a surprise to the LBSCR, came forward and denied it. In March 1884 the Board of Trade sanctioned the SER's use of the line and from 1 January 1885 the SER planned to introduce a more intensive local service to Redhill with stops at Forest Hill and New Cross, both LBSCR stations, but also demanded the right to stop at Norwood; there the LBSCR had opened a new station in 1859 to use as a ticket platform although the SER had continued to use Forest Hill to serve the district at the time.

The affair rumbled on, with the SER stating in 1886 that its trains were delayed because of the "great use" the LBSCR made of the Redhill line. In the week to 18 August 1886 Redhill handled 536 SER and 1,064 LBSCR trains. In April 1887 the *Railway Times* stated that rumours of the SER starting an intensive new service to Redhill had caused the shares of both companies to plummet. After the LBSCR had failed to establish its claim to sole use, Henry Oakley of the Great Northern Railway was appointed to arbitrate on the Croydon up line and the Redhill traffic. Oakley made his award in July 1889 and it favoured the SER, with the LBSCR subsequently paying about £15,000 a year to the SER for the use of the line according to the *Railway Times*.

In the late 1880s the City of London bought Coulsdon Common and needed a station for people to get to it. This was on the SER section of line, and the Company reached agreement with the City to provide a station on 26 July 1888. A footbridge was provided there in May 1889 and the station opened on 1 October, two months later than the SER had hoped[6].

By 1890 the SER was concerned to improve the approaches to London Bridge, reports in January 1891 indicating that it wanted at least one extra line between London Bridge and Corbett's Lane. The problem of capacity was further emphasised by a collision in fog on 6 February 1893, when an up Hastings train hit an empty stock working between Corbetts Lane and Blue Anchor signalbox. £25,600 was spent widening the line past Spa Road and building a new station there and an additional platform was provided on the north side at London Bridge. These improvements apparently resulted in an "immense improvement" in punctuality by September 1894, at a time when one of the signalboxes was said to control 27,000 signal movements per day. In

August 1895 the SER considered a new station for Corbett's Lane and moved on to look at widening from Rotherhithe Road to North Kent East Junction as well - at an estimated cost of £65,700. The programme of improvements on the north side of the route continued until 1901.

In October 1895 a platelayer was killed in Merstham Tunnel, following which it was decided to install extra manholes. A number of extra sidings were provided at Redhill in 1898 and work on installing train describers in signalboxes between there and Couldsdon also commenced. In December 1898 it was decided to build a new signalbox between Redhill and Merstham, but the LBSCR had already created a more fundamental solution to the overcrowding of a busy line by starting work on its Quarry line to by-pass Redhill and Merstham altogether. The line opened to passengers on 1 April 1900.

Perhaps it is typical of this line that one of the last entries in the SER Minute book about it before the creation of the SE&CR records that a new LBSCR timetable had been introduced, causing "considerable unpunctuality" to SER trains; however, the SER concluded, it would take no "retaliatory steps". The Age of Maturity had arrived.

2. The East London Railway

A Company was formed in 1805 to construct a tunnel beneath the River Thames at Rotherhithe but proceeded only fitfully until being at last opened for pedestrians in 1843. During this long gestation period the first stages of the railway revolution had taken place and, as early as January 1840, a correspondent suggested to the *Railway Times* that the tunnel could be used for a connecting line for services between the SER and the London & Blackwall Railway.

All three southern companies wished to have access to the Thames and in 1846 the Croydon company secured an Act for the Thames Junction Railway to a pier near Deptford. By 1851 the SER was interested in using this line itself, but never did so.

In July 1852 the SER received a letter making the suggestion that it should use the Thames Tunnel to make a connection with the East India Dock line on the north bank of the Thames. However no progress was made until the promotion began, in 1864, of an East London Railway to connect the lines of the Great Eastern with those of the LBSCR and SER at their respective New Cross stations. The LBSCR was a keen supporter of this, and denied the SER's accusation that this broke their agreement of 2 March 1864. The ELR Act was passed on 26 May 1865 and included "Railway No.6" to connect with the SER at New Cross, with various links of its system passing beneath the Greenwich, London Bridge and Bricklayers Arms lines. Where the line crossed the SER it was the latter that was charged with doing the works, at the expense of the former; the SER denied claims in June 1869 that the opening of the ELR was delayed by its tardy effort to complete the section beneath the Greenwich viaduct.

By September 1869 the SER was concerned that the ELR had chosen the LBSCR to work it, at least until its junction with the North Kent line was complete. The SER expected to participate in joint working of the line but agreed to the LBSCR being in charge for one year, and the line opened on 7 December 1869.

The ELR then promoted a new Bill to establish the junctions with the SER's North Kent line, which passed on 20 June 1870. This line, to the SER's New Cross station, opened on 1 April 1880.

The East London line caused considerable tension between the SER and the LBSCR, but also caused division on the SER Board. Watkin had become Chairman of the ELR in 1878 on the suggestion of its engineer, Hawkshaw; he was also Chairman of the Metropolitan Railway which, in late 1878, sought an extension to the ELR and running powers over it to New Cross. Two other SER directors, Whatman and Hugessen, were also directors of the ELR and were strongly opposed to this. Rumours circulated saying that the net annual income of the ELR was £12,000, and of this Watkin took £2,000 for his chairman's salary.

In July 1879 the SER gave notice that it intended to share in the working of the ELR under powers granted to it in the ELR's 1870 Act; the SER decided to use its powers to establish the interchange at its New Cross station and to invite the Great Eastern to use it. During August 1879 the SER was planning to begin using the line from 1 September, talking of a service from the East End to Ramsgate. The SER was thwarted in this aim and also failed to get the LBSCR to agree to an "express" service from Whitechapel to Addiscombe. It does seem to have managed to run a few trains through to New Cross (LBSC) at the start of September, for a Board Minute of 18 September indicates that the trains would have to be "taken off" due to LBSC opposition.

On 13 November the SER was hoping to open the line on 20 December, but had to invest £1,200 in new signalling. At about the same time it discussed the through working of coal and other goods with the GER.

At the start of January a temporary agreement was patched up between the GER, SER and LBSCR. This was to result in the setting up of a Liverpool Street to Addiscombe service by the SER, but on 22 January Colonel Yolland refused to sanction the junctions at New Cross (SER).

The service finally commenced on 1 April 1880, with 16 trains per day. In the first three months 78,000 passengers and 2,230 tons of goods were carried between the SER and the GER. The first six months brought 168,000 passengers. Under the Whitechapel Agreement of 28 July 1881 the LBSCR gave up its theoretical sole control of the ELR and a Bill was promoted for the joint leasing of the line by the interested main-line and Metropolitan companies; the East London Joint Committee was formed in 1884. In 1883 the SER considered constructing a new station where the ELR passed beneath its viaduct close to the old Commercial Docks station, but did not proceed.

When the ELR was preparing its Whitechapel extension it enquired if the SER would work it until the joint lease by the ELR Joint Committee began. From 3 March 1884 the SER began a service from Addiscombe Road to Whitechapel St Mary's [7]. However, the SER's opinion was that the Whitechapel extension was a poor line that was too difficult to work, and from 6 October left the working to the Metropolitan and the Metropolitan District. However from 1 July 1885 the SER looked after the maintenance of the ELR.

In October 1884 the ELR decided to reopen the old "low-level" ELR station at New Cross, which had been long disused [8]. The following January the SER and the Metropolitan Railway (or did this simply mean Watkin and Watkin?) looked at the possibility of extending the New Cross service to Crystal Palace.

The possibility continued to exercise the SER until at least 1888. During the later stages of 1886 the LBSCR and GER agreed to run GER trains forward from New Cross (LBSC) to Central Croydon, with effect from 1 February 1887.

It is interesting to compare the SER's experience of the ELR with its experience of the Blackfriars Spur. The latter had superior connections with the main-line companies to the north of London, whereas the East London line produced only limited access to East London and the Metropolitan lines. What is most notable, though, is that the SER's interest in the ELR was matched very closely to Watkin's personal involvement and, as we shall see in Chapter Eight, this was true also of the Blackfriars Spur.

3. The Caterham Branch

At the time of the opening of the Brighton line, there was little population between Croydon and Merstham, but the L&BR opened a small station on their section of line at Godstone Road. The station was unsuccessful and was closed on 30 September 1847. Caterham itself was not a key factor in any of this, nor was it considered in July 1848 when the SER and LBSCR agreed to their division of territory, with land to the east of the Brighton line becoming the SER's.

The first the SER heard of a proposed branch line to Caterham was in August 1853, when local people proposed a line from the old Godstone Road station. This scheme caused confusion over the 1848 Agreement for, though it ran through territory allotted to the SER, its junction was with a line belonging to the LBSCR. The SER decided to withdraw its petition against the line and the Caterham Railway secured its Act on 16 June 1854[9].

In March 1855 the *Railway Times* reported angry scenes among SER shareholders, who felt that the CR would steal traffic from the Westerham district. There was much ill-feeling towards Alexander Beattie, who owned 21 SER shares and was Chairman of the CR; he had also been involved with the LSWR and the North London[10].

During much of 1855 the CR was concerned to settle details of junction and working arrangements; the former had to involve the LBSCR, the latter could also involve the SER. In June 1855 the SER offered to work the CR for two years and and in December stipulated the same terms as had been offered to the Mid Kent Railway but the CR refused them. In January 1856 the CR sought permission from the LBSCR to erect a station at Godstone Road. Talks were held with the contractor, Samuel Morton Peto, to see if he would work the line but he also refused to agree terms. On 10 July the SER even refused to lend stock.

Frustrated, the CR turned to the LBSCR who it found more amenable. The Brighton agreed to stop some trains at the semi-derelict Godstone Road station, whereupon the SER also demanded the right to call there twice a day. At the start of August 1858 the *Railway Times* commented that the opening of the line had been delayed for a year due to "political" reasons. It also felt the proposed fares were "excessive" - it cost more to get to Caterham than it did to Reading. Regular services began on 5 August 1856. There were four trains on weekdays, with two connecting services each being provided by the SER and the LBSCR respectively. There were intermediate stations at Coulsdon (renamed Kenley in October 1856) and Warlingham. Godstone Road was soon renamed Caterham Junction.

Neither the LBSCR nor the SER made any great effort to develop the Caterham traffic - in fact they did the reverse, for the CR felt that they were both trying to stifle it. The CR felt that no proper facilities were given to it and alleged that SER staff even denied its existence, claiming that no trains at all stopped at Caterham Junction. The CR took legal action, but achieved only a ruling that the LBSCR should provide better accomodation at the Junction.

Defeated, the CR offered itself for sale to either Company; the SER was interested in a Mid Kent & South Kent Railway which proposed to link the Mid Kent line with Caterham, but delayed its move, but warned the LBSC in April 1857 not to intervene. The MK & SK Bill was withdrawn in June 1857.

The CR had been worked by stock hired from the LBSCR, but a dispute arose from the CR's slow response to LBSCR demands for payment. The line was nearly closed on 7 May 1857, but escaped the axe when £250 was paid in the nick of time. In its first 11 months the line lost £846.

In fact the Brighton had been talking to the CR about a takeover, offering a paltry £16,000. By May discussions had also included the SER, though there was considerable suspicion between the two main-line companies. The Brighton held the strongest position though, for it could close the line by withdrawing its stock and this it threatened to do in July 1856. Perhaps the LBSCR thought that this would force the CR into bankruptcy and thus make it available at a very low price. When the SER discussed a takeover in October, it found the CR demanding £28,000. The CR felt, though, that its financial position was false - that it should take a share in the revenues that accrued from its passengers using the main line.

The LBSCR withdrew its stock from the CR from 1 January 1857, and the SER installed an engine and two carriages. A further cruel twist of the CR's story then occurred when George Furness, the contractor who had built the line, brought an action for debt and secured possession of the line himself in July 1858. Furness offered it to the SER for £16,000 but the SER, scenting a bargain, said it would go no higher than £12,000.

In October the SER decided that they would purchase the line and continue working it in the meantime. It prepared a Bill to authorise the purchase but met the opposition of the LBSCR; it was felt, though, that the SER takeover of the Caterham could be "paired" with the LBSCR promotion of an Uckfield & Tunbridge Wells line. The LBSCR tried to prevent the SER stopping at Caterham Junction altogether; in the event, a clause was added to the Bill stipulating that the SER was only to stop there to exchange traffic with the branch. The SER and LBSCR agreed formally to this in July 1859. The basic price the SER paid for the CR seems to have been about £14,000, although the total cost of the transaction was recorded afterwards as £15,753. The latter figure may have included a payment to George Drew and Captain Wigsell for their agreement to waive a covenant to stop all trains at Kenley. From 1861 to 1865 Kenley became more or less a "flag station".

The line continued to be a victim of railway politics even after it had become part of the SER. In 1862 a series of letters to *The Times* complained about LBSCR restrictions on passengers using East Croydon station who had SER tickets, and some alleged that the LBSCR there refused to sell tickets to Caterham at all. This was a time of bad relations between the companies, caused partly by the promotion of lines elsewhere. In 1865, for example, the SER considered that an extension of the Caterham line would be a good defence against the Surrey & Sussex line supported by the LBSCR.

On 31 October 1867 the signalbox at "Whiteleaf" was destroyed by fire. In December 1869 the SER received a letter from the famous albino politician, Robert Lowe, who was Chancellor of the Exchequer at the time; he complained about the lack of supervision of the level-crossing at Warlingham, so the SER decided to build a £200 stationmaster's house there so that it could keep a check on the crossing. The following year it decided to provide a lock-up store and porters' room in the goods yard at Caterham. In 1871 catch points were installed to protect two sidings between Kenley and Warlingham but Kenley station had to wait until 1872 before waiting rooms were finally agreed on. New signalboxes were built at Kenley and Warlingham in 1865. A further £565 was spent improving Kenley in 1876.

By 1873 the Caterham Junction station was inadequate as well as, according to Watkin, dirty. It was also dangerous for there was no proper means of crossing the line safely and a passenger was killed there that September. A subway was built in 1874 and further improvements continued up to 1876.

In the mid-1870s the Caterham line became embroiled in much greater things. In September 1873 the SER proposed building a "cheap" line from Caterham to Maidstone via Westerham, but this was only one of several schemes. The South Caterham Railway deposited a Bill for a line from the south end of Caterham Junction station to Upper Caterham. The Caterham & Godstone planned to link the two places of its title and there was also a proposed line from Caterham to Riverhead via Oxted and Westerham.

Of these schemes the Caterham & Godstone Valley was the most resilient, though it was opposed at various stages by the SER and the LBSCR. However in 1877 the SER agreed to work it for 50% of the receipts, having been authorised in July 1876. The promotion of these schemes provoked discussion with the LBSCR about the future of the Caterham line; by January 1879 the SER and LBSCR were considering a joint ownership of it, with an extension to Godstone and new lines between Caterham Junction and Croydon. When the LBSCR discussed taking over the Caterham line itself in 1879, it found SER terms too severe and talks about making it a joint line in 1880 also failed. The Coulsdon & Upper Caterham scheme of 1882 also made no real progress. Ultimately, it was the choice of the Oxted route for a new through line as a joint venture of the SER and LBSCR that doomed Caterham to remain an obscure branch line.

Kenley received some improvements in 1883-4 including a new waiting room and a covered way. The platforms were extended at Warlingham in 1887.

In the late 1880s there were still discussions about the position of the Caterham line, including a branch off the Oxted line to Upper Caterham and an extension of the branch from Caterham to join the main-line south of Coulsdon.

In 1889 the SER began buying land to widen the branch but although Caterham was resignalled in 1893 and a gas works siding installed in 1895, little real progress was made until 1897. The junction with the main-line had to be rebuilt, partly in connection with the opening of a line to Tattenham Corner. During 1898 footbridges were installed at Kenley and Whyteleafe Crossing; the extra platform and a new booking office at Kenley cost £2,072 while the rebuilding of Caterham station cost £3,468. The doubling was completed on 1 January 1900 and included the opening of a new station at Whyteleafe.

4. The Tattenham Corner Branch

In the period before the bankruptcies of 1866 dampened enthusiasm for railway construction, there was a small degree of interest in building railways through the country north of Reigate and south-east of Epsom. When a Banstead & Reigate scheme was projected in 1864 the LBSCR decided not to support it and a Bill for a Reigate & West End Junction line was withdrawn the same year. Only the branch from Sutton to Epsom Downs, opened in 1865, was completed, and this fell within the LBSCR empire.

In the early 1890s Cosmo Bonsor, a man to achieve great significance in SER affairs, was living at Kingswood Warren and found his daily journey to the nearest station, at Banstead, rather time-consuming. In 1891 he became involved in a scheme to promote a line from the main Brighton line up to a point near Tadworth. This steeply-graded line would have been financed largely by Bonsor himself, but it was opposed because it cut the North Park estate in two.

Bonsor revised his plans to support a line along the Chipstead Valley. A Bill was prepared and the line discussed at a meeting held at Burgh Heath, Banstead, in June 1893. Mr W Brown explained that the race traffic would be worth £900 a mile and Fenton appeared to offer SER help in working the line. It was observed that if the SER could not work the line then a 1.5 mile link could be built to the LSWR at Ewell.

The Chipstead Valley company was formed in 1893 to build a line to Tadworth and the Epsom Downs Extension Railway was to extend this to Tattenham Corner and a junction with the Epsom Downs line. Bonsor himself joined the SER Board in 1894, became Deputy Chairman in 1895 and Chairman in 1898. He was thus in a strong position to oversee the relationship between the CVR and the SER, to the annoyance of the LBSCR which disliked the Epsom Downs Extension Bill in 1894 as it included a junction onto the Caterham branch near to Caterham Junction. The LBSCR was responsible for the rebuilding of the junction itself, and in fact Caterham Junction station was replaced by a substantial new Purley station.

The Act for the Chipstead Valley was passed on 27 July 1893 but very little happened until the second half of 1895 [11]. In September the CVR began discussions with Lord Russell who wished to have a terminus at Tadworth Street, whereas the CVR had selected Braggarts Road to avoid the £7,000 cost of crossing Walton Heath. It was decided that if Russell took £7,000 of the Company's shares it would meet his wishes. In October 1895 the Company considered having the line built as a Light Railway, for which a licence would be needed from the Board of Trade.

During 1896 the question of the junctions was discussed further. The SER, which was already providing transportation of materials free, was also prepared to give the land for a junction onto its Caterham line free. However the LBSCR was also widening its line through Caterham Junction (Purley) and the CVR was unsure as to whether it should abandon altogether its powers to connect with the LBSCR. During June it considered whether it should apply for the land to make a direct junction with the LBSCR at Purley and even discussed terms for working by the LBSCR. The Brighton was prepared to offer six trains a day for 45% of the receipts, but would make no commitment.

By this time the junction with the SER had already been installed [12]. The SER, though, thought that the 1 in 60 grades of the line were too steep and offered to lend the £20,000 needed to improve them at a nominal interest rate of 2.5%. In October the SER agreed to include provision in its next Bill to take the line over and complete it. It was built as a single line but with bridges for two tracks at a cost of about £11,000 per mile; the SER estimated in 1897 that doubling the line and improving the grades to 1 in 80 would cost a further £3,000 a mile.

The first section of the line, between Purley and Kingswood, opened on 2 November 1897 but regular services probably began a week later. The line was clearly opened in the usual incomplete state, made worse by the ongoing work to convert it into a double-track. Thus in December 1897 work was in progress installing a down shelter at Chipstead station and building a station at Kingswood & Burgh Heath. Works were also required at Purley, where the SER provided an engine-shed, sidings and staff cottages at its own expense.

In April 1898 the CVR decided to prepare plans for a new station at Smitham Bottom. These were not completed until July 1899 when it was estimated that the passenger station would cost £5,830 and goods sidings £2,760. The station was not opened until 1 January 1904.

The CVR was absorbed into the SER in 1899 [13] and its line was not completed until after the formation of the SE&CR. It opened to Tadworth & Walton-on-the-Hill on 1 July 1900 and to Tattenham Corner on 4 June 1901 for Derby Day.

1.   SER Minutes, 6 December 1836.
2.   SER Minutes, 15 October 1844.
3.   **Railway Times,** 31 July 1847.
4.   **Railway Times,** 19 November 1850.
5.   SER Minutes, 14 December 1876.
6.   H.V.Borley, **Chronology of London Railways.**
7.   SER Minutes, 13 March 1884.
8.   The station, adjacent to the LBSCR station, was in use 1869-1876, then out
        of use until 1884, and closed a second time in 1886.
9.   The Caterham branch has been well-served by historians in J.Spence,
        The Caterham Railway. It is perhaps the best documented of the SER-associated
        branches due to the discussions it aroused in SER, LBSCR and Joint
        Committee Minutes, as well as Caterham Railway sources.
10.   **Railway Times,** 17 March 1855.
11.   Chipstead Valley Railway Minutes record no meeting at all between 19 October 1893
        and 12 August 1895 at which any substantial business was conducted.
12.   CVR Minutes, 26 June 1896.
13.   The SER continued to have a legal existence after the formation of the SE&CR.

CHAPTER SIX: THE NORTH KENT LINE

1. The London & Greenwich Railway

The Kentish Railway first attracted the attention of the public in December 1824, proposing a railway from London to Deptford, Greenwich, Gravesend, Canterbury and Dover[1]. The promoters intended to construct a line to Woolwich in the first instance, being attracted by the high number of road coaches then operating along the route. The line's original engineer was Thomas Telford, but in 1825 he was replaced by Henry Palmer who surveyed a line starting from Bricklayers Arms and running to Rochester; there was to be a branch to Greenwich. The scheme failed to progress further for financial reasons.

The two key figures in the early history of the Greenwich Railway were to be Colonel George Landmann and George Walter. Landmann, who had retired from the Royal Engineers, interested Walter in his scheme for a railway to Greenwich and a meeting took place on 25 November 1831, inaugurating the proceedings of the London & Greenwich Railway. Landmann's most important contribution was perhaps to devise a plan that ran from a point very close to London Bridge, thus making the line a convenient way to reach the City. Despite financial anxieties, the L&GR obtained its Act on 17 May 1833 and almost immediately began talking of an extension to Canterbury or Dover. More importantly, Walter's ingenuity allowed the sale of the remaining shares.

By February 1834 the materials for the line had begun to arrive. Most of it was to be constructed as a viaduct, with the work being done by Hugh McIntosh though attempts to get the young Princess Victoria to inaugurate proceedings were thwarted by illness. Work proceeded rapidly and by January 1835 the bridge over the Surrey Canal had been built, though the ironwork for other bridges caused delays.

One of the L&GR's ideas was that the arches of the viaduct could be rented out. The first was let to a Mr Smith for £30 a year in May 1834 and the following year an attempt was made to let other arches as housing, complete with lighting and cooking by gas. An arch let for this purpose in March 1836 yielded only £20 per year, but there were problems with water; by 1839 only one arch was in use in this way - as a beershop. Others were rented as shops and storehouses.

The first traffic on the line developed before trains were actually running - at Easter 1835 about £50 was collected from people allowed to walk along the viaduct. In June 1835 some trial trips were run using the locomotive *Royal William* near Blue Anchor Road; a mile was accomplished in about four minutes[2]. A number of publicity stunts were organised for the occasion, such as placing a full glass of water on the viaduct as a train passed to show how little vibration there was. Those who stood in the arches beneath found that "the noise was no greater than that which would be occasioned by the passing of a hackney coach."

Further experimental trains were run at Deptford in October, with *Royal William* again being the crowd's favourite. It hauled eight "elegant" carriages and 200 people to the Surrey Canal bridge, where they got out to inspect "the beautiful oblique elliptical arches" over the water.

On 18 January 1836 two of the arches at the Tooley Street end of the line collapsed, but without causing injury. In fact there were occasional scares about the safety of the viaduct, but these were rebutted after an independent inspection by James Walker in 1837; he found little wrong, but disliked the idea of using stone blocks instead of wooden sleepers.

After a derailment in November 1835, trial trips were suspended, but they resumed in January 1836. Rumours soon circulated that the trains had reached 60mph; apparently "there were two numerous parties of ladies in the carriages, who seemed highly delighted."[3]

The actual service commenced on 8 February 1836 between Deptford and Spa Road; takings on the first day were £13, but they soon rose to over £40 and on Whit Monday the line carried about 13,000 passengers. The line adopted right-hand running from its opening until April 1839[4]. The line's first fatal accident took place at Spa Road on 7 March 1836, when Daniel Holmes was run over and a train collided with some carriages[5]. This did little to destroy the attractions of the line - the Prince of Orange enjoyed a footplate ride in May 1836.

In an attempt to boost revenue, the L&GR starting running Sunday trains in June 1836 although they agreed not to do so "during the hours of divine service," the origin of the "Church Interval" in London - a case of one service competing with another. They also rented two pews at St James' Church, Bermondsey, for the benefit of their staff none of whom, presumably, were nonconformists. Sunday trains were stopped in 1839[6].

On 10 October the railway was extended westwards to Bermondsey Street, 300 yards from London Bridge; passengers had to walk the intervening distance on the viaduct. At this stage there were rumours of a large debt to McIntosh and "great embezzlement"[7]. On 14 December the line was formally opened from London Bridge to Deptford by the Lord Mayor. Some 2,000 people attended and over 400 enjoyed dinner. Four special trains performed a "review" before the Lord Mayor, who inspected the workshops at Deptford and the bridge over the Ravensbourne. On the return journey, speeds of 30mph were claimed for his train[8].

However, the L&GR seems to have been an irresistible target for the journalists of London. In December 1836 rumours were being spread about the vast rewards of a close involvement with the L&GR - it was said that the Managing Director and the engineer each received £800 per year, with the secretary earning £500. In March 1837 a hoax story was spread that the L&GR had been seized by its contractor due to a debt of £300,000, but its traffic was steadily improving - earnings were about £135 a day in January 1837, rising to over £200 by March[9]. George Walter ended his connection with the company by resigning from the Board in July 1837, then beginning a legal battle with the L&GR over financial matters.

The public opening of the remainder of the line, as far as a temporary terminus at Church Row, Greenwich, took place on 24 December 1838. The delay in opening this section was due to problems with the machinery for the Ravensbourne lifting bridge. The *Railway Times* noted that new carriages had been ordered - the old ones having acquired a shabby reputation - and that Curtis's switches had been removed due to the threat of carriages going over the parapet of the viaduct. A "spacious terminus" with four tracks and two platforms beneath a "covered way" was opened on 12 April 1840, though not finally completed until 1842.

2. From Greenwich to Gravesend - The North Kent Line

As has been seen from earlier chapters, the London & Greenwich came to have a highly important and strategic role in the history of the South Eastern. Not only did it provide access to London Bridge for the SER and the London & Brighton, but it also became involved with its own plans to extend further into Kent. These were not always welcomed by the SER, but after a period of trials and tribulation the Greenwich line became the basis for a network of lines that helped to create London's south eastern suburbs.

Walter, Landmann and William Green, the L&GR secretary, had plans to extend their line to Gravesend as early as 1833. After flirting with the idea of extending it as far as Dover, they settled to the idea of a Gravesend line and began formal meetings in October 1834. The line proposed to cross Greenwich Park by an ornamental viaduct, apparently ignoring the opposition of the Admiralty which had convinced Palmer and G.P.Bidder, in 1833, that an extension into Kent would have to cross to the north bank of the Thames.

In fact the scheme met considerable opposition in the Greenwich area, and its Bill for the 1835 session was withdrawn. The promoters clearly felt that a tunnel through the Park was less likely to arouse local wrath, and in the latter part of 1835 Landmann conducted experiments to see whether the vibration of trains might upset the Observatory. A new Bill was prepared for the 1836 session for a line to Gravesend, with a 1.5 mile branch into Dartford; it was expected to cost £64,500 but by January 1836 only £10,025 had been subscribed[10]. In February 1836 Colonel Landmann staked out the proposed route across

9. **Northfleet Station, SER, in 1885.**

Evolution of North Kent Lines
(Not all lines and stations shown)

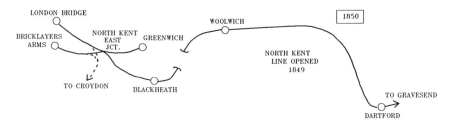

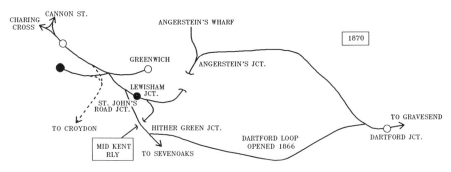

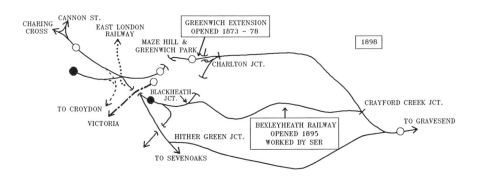

Greenwich Park; he had returned to the idea of a viaduct, though it was planned to have decorative niches in which the busts of past and future naval heroes could be placed. The Bill was rejected on its second reading, its opponents including Angerstein, who took the view that river steamers offered a quite satisfactory service to Gravesend in 1hr 30mins, for only 1s.; Walter chose to oppose the SER Bill anyway since he still hoped that his ideas for a Gravesend line, and a further extension to Dover, would eventually succeed.

Walter continued to campaign for an extension of the Greenwich line into Kent in 1837, using the name of the Kent Railway, and with the support of John Herapath. However he broke his relationship with the L&GR later that year and his interest in extension schemes faded.

The Deptford & Gravesend Railway was proposed by Landmann in March 1838 was a last, and quickly forgotten, attempt[11].

Thus the enthusiasm for railways in the mid-1830s resulted in no direct extension of the L&GR at its country end, but brought only extra traffic to the London Bridge end of the line. One of the last Acts of this period to affect the L&GR was for the Deptford Pier Junction Railway, which was authorised on 21 June 1836; it was abandoned in 1839.

Though the reputation of the L&GR was not exactly spotless, it still attracted big crowds at holiday times. On Easter Monday 1839 it carried 35,000 passengers in 400 trains, earning over £1,000. There were some unusual problems though, such as the footpath near the viaduct being used to shoot at birds; whether this was connected with a shotgun injury to the L&GR's resident engineer, G.M.Miller, in 1842 is unknown.

In November 1839 a train was derailed near the junction with the Croydon line after a post had been left on the track. A navvy working nearby had to jump off the viaduct to avoid being crushed; less fortunate was John Nash, the L&GR conductor, who was caught up in the wreckage. He was taken to Guy's Hospital, but died.

The opening of the Croydon line brought extra traffic for which primitive ideas about signalling were inadequate. On 30 January 1840 an up Greenwich train ran into a down Croydon train at the junction, and was then hit in the rear by a second up Greenwich train which was carrying a party of the Royal Artillery to the Tower. There were a few injuries.

Another accident occurred in March 1841 near the junction. An up train was derailed, and its passengers were told to walk through "dirty streets at night" in order to complete their journey. One of the passengers was an MP and objected to this, so a man with a torch was found to lead them to London Bridge. There they found a down train apparently ready to start, and oblivious of the obstruction further down the line.

Especially at weekends the line carried a high number of pleasure seekers and thus had frequent problems with drunks. Thus in April 1842 two drunks, without tickets, attacked the constable at Greenwich station at about 10pm; they were fined £2 each. Six months later there was a fight at Greenwich station after some drunks had to be pulled out of the carriages three times; this time the fines were £5 each. Perhaps to redress the balance, a L&GR porter was fined £2 in March 1843 for singing obscene songs in a Deptford public house.

In the early 1840s a few schemes to extend the L&GR began to emerge again. One of these, the Imperial Kent Railway of 1840, was another scheme by Walter to extend from Gravesend to Ramsgate. The London & Chatham, proposed in

1841, intended a junction with the L&GR at Deptford. However the position of the L&GR was threatened by a series of disputes with the other companies that used London Bridge, especially when an alternative terminus was opened at Bricklayers Arms in 1844.

With completion of the Bricklayers Arms line imminent, the L&GR found itself, rather surprisingly, in the position of a young lady with a surfeit of suitors from which to choose. The London & Croydon, the South Eastern and the Brighton all made approaches with a view to leasing or amalgamating with the Greenwich in the early months of 1844.

The situation was complicated by a number of schemes for new lines to Gravesend or beyond. Prominent among them was the L&CR's plan for an atmospheric line to Chatham in which I.K.Brunel was said to be interested[12] and there was another scheme for an atmospheric line to Rosherville from Rochester via Cobham. Perhaps fearing the effect on its territory of any of these schemes, the SER Board decided to try to lease the Greenwich line in February 1844.

The L&CR had a scheme for a line from Jolly Sailor to Gravesend while the London, Woolwich & Gravesend Railway intended avoiding the problem of Greenwich Park by starting from a point on the south bank of the Thames opposite the terminus of the London & Blackwall Railway, running thence to Gravesend. The SER was dissatisfied with the terms offered by the L&GR, which wanted a rent of about £50,000 per year[13] and accordingly instructed Robert Stephenson to survey its own line from Bricklayers Arms into North Kent. On 23 July 1844 the SER decided to prepare a Bill for the next session for a line to Gravesend via Lee, Eltham and Crayford. Perhaps this did the trick, for terms with the L&GR - starting at £36,000 and rising to £45,000 per year - were agreed the following month. As a result of this the SER took over the working of the line from the start of 1845, but the agreement to lease the L&GR by the SER had to wait for Parliamentary authority until 21 July 1845.

Having secured control of the L&GR, the SER still felt itself in an exposed position - largely because it served the towns of North Kent so poorly. Charles Vignoles, who had surveyed a line to Chatham in 1840, was again active in promoting the London, Chatham & North Kent Railway by July 1844. This would have passed through Greenwich Park and extended as far as Ramsgate. In September the SER was worried about L&CR plans to extend to Chatham and Canterbury with Brunel as engineer. The situation with the L&CR was made complex by the earlier alliance of the two in promoting a line to avoid the L&GR, but in October 1844 the L&CR at least assured the SER that if its line was successful the part east of Chatham could be controlled by the SER.

Plans for the Parliamentary session of 1845 were deposited in the first week of December 1844, though the SER's North Kent plans were delayed by the illness of the engraver. There were three contenders for the honour of serving North Kent - the SER, with a line to Chilham, the L&CR, and the Vignoles scheme. The L&CR also decided on a line to Ashford which was surveyed by Cubitt, costing him his job with the SER. SER plans included a "duplicate line" between Eltham and Stone, alternative routes via Greenwich Park or Charlton, a 1,430 yard tunnel beneath the fortifications at Chatham, and a branch to Sheerness. On 13 February 1845 the Board of Trade reported in favour of the SER plans but the result of the 1845 session was stalemate - all the schemes were rejected.

During 1845 the SER began to adjust to the business of running the Greenwich line, having absorbed seven drivers and five stationmasters onto its staff. In March 1845 it decided to lengthen the platforms at Spa Road and in September to provide proper platform shelters at Deptford. Traffic in the first year of SER operation amounted to 2,566,187 passengers.

10. **Dartford Station viewed from the east.** (Wakeman Collection)

In December 1845 the SER directors decided to try and buy up the Gravesend & Rochester Railway, discussed below, as part of their scheme to extend through North Kent to Chatham. Robert Stephenson again prepared plans, this time for a line from Deptford Creek to Chilham, but including a loop to serve Blackheath with a tunnel beneath Greenwich Park in order to offer an alternative to those who opposed an extension of the existing line through the middle of Greenwich. Vignoles' committee also presented a Bill for a line to Chilham and Canterbury. The Bills were before the Parliamentary Committee for 33 days, causing much excitement:

"*A large crowd was waiting for the result, two policemen were necessary to control the crowd. When the announcement was made in favour of the South Eastern, a large cheer went up*[14]."

On 3 August 1846 the Act for the North Kent line was passed, authorising an extension to meet the G&R and the taking over of that concern. It was also decided to spend £66,840 on widening parts of the Greenwich line to take the extra traffic.

The new route was to branch off the Greenwich line about 1.5 miles west of Greenwich, at what later became North Kent East Junction. It followed a looping route through Blackheath and then by a tunnel into Charlton, leaving the original Greenwich station as a terminus. Contracts for its construction were issued in the first months of 1847, going to various contractors including Messrs Tredwell and John Brogden; Brogden was awarded the no.3 contract at

£380,255 even though his tender was only the third lowest - a source of later problems.

For the 1847 Parliamentary session a number of rival schemes again emerged. These included a LBSCR plan for a line from New Cross to Maidstone and Canterbury and another independent line to Canterbury. The SER's response was a Bill to extend it from Strood (where the Gravesend & Rochester terminated) to Chilham, and to build another line between Lamb Abbey near Eltham and Dartford, so that fast and slow traffic through North Kent could be run separately. The SER dropped its plan when the others were defeated, a decision which caused bad feelings in the towns east of Strood and contributed to the later rise of the East Kent Railway, especially as local interests had supported the SER against its rivals.

A further delay on the North Kent was caused when Peter Barlow suggested a cheaper route through Woolwich and sought powers to deviate; however a Judge ruled that notice had already been served on property along the original route and that therefore a deviation was out of the question.

Samuel Beazley was appointed architect for the line's stations in November 1848 and the line opened to Gravesend on 30 July 1849. Original stations were opened at Lewisham (renamed Lewisham Junction 1 January 1857), Blackheath, Charlton, Woolwich Dockyard, Abbey Wood, Erith, Dartford, Greenhithe, Northfleet and Gravesend[15]. Woolwich Arsenal station opened on 1 November 1849 and New Cross & Naval School in about October 1850, being renamed New Cross in 1854.

The SER had high hopes for its new line and began a service of fast trains with a first class fare of 7s; presumably traffic was disappointing, for in May 1850 it was decided to stop the trains additionally at Erith, Blackheath and Lewisham. Later the same month it was agreed to run a train to Woolwich every half hour between 7am and 10pm, with trains running on to Gravesend every hour. The line was expected to yield good fruit and potato traffic but it became most notable for passenger traffic: by 1850 it was earning £3,784 per mile per year from this[16].

After the opening, a few minor improvements were made. These included adding a siding at Blackheath in 1850 and straightening the curve near the station there a few months later. In August 1850 it was decided to add an extra "story" to Abbey Wood station.

On 15 July 1850 there was a minor accident in Blackheath Tunnel, following which the Board decided to install the electric telegraph there. However they failed to report the accident to the Board of Trade and were reprimanded for this omission. In September 1850 Henry Clark, who wished to cross the line at Erith with his horse and cart, was fined £2 after assaulting the SER's gatekeeper there.

In November 1850 the SER Board concluded an agreement with John Angerstein for the use of a railway and wharf near Charlton. The following month the SER chairman visited the branch and the proposed new wharf there and a Bill to lease the branch was authorised in 1851. The agreement was to pay Angerstein £450 per annum for the use of his wharf and a toll for the use of the branch[17]. Powers to construct the line were granted to Angerstein himself by Act of April 1851[18]. In July 1851 it was agreed that the branch should be built by Wythes and that Angerstein himself should lay the first stone. The line opened in August 1852, and the following month SER shareholders were told to expect a large increase in coal traffic. At the time of opening the SER was considering extending the line to Blackwall Point, building a 260 foot pier there, and operating ferries across the Thames. By March 1853 cranes were being set up at the original wharf for the colliers to unload and it became an important site of coke ovens, but Angerstein made clear his opposition to the Blackwall Point extension and it was dropped in October 1854. For a time, and at least in 1855, the working of the branch was done on behalf of the SER by Magnus & Sons, but the SER was unhappy with their performance and took it over from 5 March 1856. On 31 October 1888 one of the cranes at the wharf broke a wheel and collapsed, killing a labourer named Smith. Extra wharfage had to be provided to handle increasing traffic in 1890. The SER's lease of the line was renewed in 1853 and 1879, and it was finally purchased in 1898.

The Woolwich local service terminated at Woolwich Arsenal. Therefore, in June 1851, it was decided to complete the turntable and siding at "East Woolwich". The old L&GR workshops at Deptford were adapted as carriage and wagon shops in 1851. Traffic on the Greenwich branch, however, was stagnant and on 1 February 1852 MacGregor reduced the service from every 15 minutes to every 20; this caused protests, and the old level had to be restored from 1 September.

Blackheath station was clearly a temporary affair as first opened, for its final plans were not agreed until March 1852. At this time the SER was also considering a station at New Road, Rotherhithe, and a "barrack" for the emigrant traffic at Gravesend. From 1 September 1852 an additional "early" up train was put on from Gravesend. The following year a stationmaster's house was at last built at Lewisham and extra sidings provided at Abbey Wood and Dartford.

Requests for a station to serve Rotherhithe arrived in the SER offices frequently and in November 1855 it agreed to provide a station to serve the Commercial Dock district. This opened in May 1856 and was called Commercial Dock. Lewisham station was rebuilt in 1856 at a cost of £7,000 as the junction for the Mid-Kent Railway.

In late 1852 the SER showed renewed interest in extending its Greenwich branch through Greenwich Park to join the North Kent line at Woolwich. It then lost interest once more, until prompted into a review of facilities in the area by the East Kent Railway's dissatisfaction with the situation in sending its passengers forward from Strood. In 1855-6 the EKR prepared its own Bill for a route from Dartford to Lewisham, which it thought would be more suitable for main-line traffic than the SER's line via Woolwich. This was dropped in April 1856, but by June the SER was looking at building its own line from Lewisham to Dartford via Eltham and Bexleyheath. The question split the SER Board, but on 9 October 1856 they decided in favour of the idea. The line was expected to cost £250,000 but there were several factors in its favour - a series of accidents had suggested that the North Kent line could not handle its own traffic, let alone that generated by the EKR, while Gravesend traffic had been hit by the Tilbury ferry service.

On 7 December 1855 the 5.26pm from Woolwich had just left New Cross when it was unexpectedly diverted onto the Bricklayers Arms line since the points had been wedged open; when the signalman tried to remove the wedge as the train passed over, some of the carriages were derailed. Richard Beattie, the switchman, was arrested and found to have been using a block of wood to keep the points open instead of doing the work for which he had been assigned. In October 1856 there was an accident in Blackheath Tunnel when two trains ran into each other due to problems with the "self-acting points". The following March a coffee-house keeper won £60 damages from the SER after being injured when a train jerked into motion just as he was getting out of it at Woolwich; he suffered a broken leg.

But the most serious in this run of accidents occurred at Lewisham on 28 June 1857. The 9.15pm up train from Strood stopped just beyond Lewisham station and its guard ran back waving a lamp as a warning. However, the following train from Maidstone hit the rear of the stationary train at about 20mph: the last carriage was crushed, leaving 12 dead, 14 seriously injured and 94 minor injuries. The driver and stoker of the Maidstone train were arrested, but most at fault was signalman Griffiths who had reported a telegraph message that he had not received. The accident badly damaged the reputation of the SER and was also highly expensive because of claims for compensation; by December 1857 awards against the SER totalled £15,933 but they continued beyond that date - in January 1858 a journeyman boot-cleaner was awarded £780, to the disgust of the SER.

During late 1857 the SER was involved in energetic discussions for the improvement of its lines in the district, partly in conjunction with the Mid-Kent Railway. The leading element of the scheme was for a line from Dartford via Sidcup to New Cross, expected to cost £245,000. At Lewisham there was to be a spur onto the North Kent for about £5,000. There were various suggestions from both Fowler (acting for the Mid-Kent) and Ashcroft for branches to Chislehurst; Fowler intended a five mile branch from Bexley, while Ashcroft, supported by the SER, planned a branch from Lamb Abbey. By the time the SER had got as far as depositing its Dartford & New Cross Junction Bill, it included branches to link with the Crays Railway near Chislehurst and also a branch from Eltham to Foots Cray. The SER Bill was intended to defend what it regarded as its territory from the western extension of the East Kent, for which a Bill had been deposited for a line between Strood and St Mary Cray. The contest ended with the victory of the EKR and rejection of the SER proposals.

The EKR's 1858 Act for its western extension meant that, ultimately, the SER North Kent line would cease to handle the through traffic from the EKR and its improvement therefore became less of a priority. Its profits, however, could be improved through encouraging development of the district for housing. In December 1858 the SER reached agreement with a landowner at Plumstead to provide a new station with a similar service as that at Abbey Wood and Erith; this opened on 16 July 1859[19]. On 1 April 1858 the SER discussed a request from Sir Culling Eardley for a station at Belvedere; the SER wanted him to pay and they would provide a train service if at least 50 houses were built within three years. The report to the shareholders in February 1859 mentions a new station at Belvedere, which first appeared in the timetables in March.

The people of Greenwich were growing impatient about the position of their station as a terminus. In January 1858 they began to press for an extension to join the North Kent line at Angerstein's Junction and by November a local scheme known as the Greenwich & Charlton Railway was being discussed, the initial stage of which was to be an extension from Greenwich to Maze Hill. By July 1859 there were two rival committees at work, one of which proposed a line just over two miles long costing £150,000.

The SER showed little interest in the Greenwich question, but in October 1860 revived its concern about a new route from Lewisham to Dartford. Although the idea was soon dropped again, it returned a year later associated with the scheme for a new main-line running direct to Tonbridge via Chislehurst. The Act of 30 June 1862 therefore authorised the line to Tonbridge, with a branch to Dartford leaving it at what was to become Hither Green.

Meanwhile, the SER had to attend to a few problems with the North Kent line. A locomotive firebox exploded at Lewisham Junction on 16 September 1859 and on 11 September 1861 some old buildings and a quantity of sand managed to fall in through a working shaft of Blackheath Tunnel. In June 1862 it was decided to rebuild the wooden Crayford viaduct for £4,500. In August 1863 vandals attempted to derail a train between the two Woolwich stations by placing timbers across the track; apparently the concussion was so great that crockery fell off the shelves in nearby houses[20]. The line still had a few glorious moments - on 7 March 1863 Princess Alexandra travelled from Gravesend to Bricklayers Arms; Gravesend station was decorated for the occasion at the expense of Lord Darnley.

Local people were still pressing for an improvement in Greenwich's railway facilities. In November 1862 it was reported that Smith & Knight had agreed to construct a line, and the SER was asked if they would care to rent it for £9,500 per year. The SER was starting to feel itself under pressure in the district, having been forced to reduce fares due to the cheap LBSCR fares to New Cross(LBSCR) and fears that the LBSCR wanted to build its own line to Greewich and Woolwich. For a few months of 1863 both the LBSCR and the LCDR were planning routes to Greenwich, but by August the former had withdrawn. An agreement was reached between the SER and the LCDR under which the SER was to build a line from Greenwich to Woolwich, over which the LCDR would have running powers, while the SER would be granted running powers over a proposed LCDR line from Greenwich to the South London line

11. **Maze Hill Station in the late 1800s, indicating the urban background of the Greenwich Extension. (R.Thomas Collection)**

and as far as Crystal Palace High Level. Thus by September 1864 the SER was surveying between Greenwich and Woolwich but its Bill was opposed by the Admiralty. The House of Commons Committee adopted a novel solution - they agreed to authorise the two ends of the line, but did not authorise the middle section: the SER had to agree terms with the Admiralty first. It was eventually agreed to pay the Admiralty £8,000[21] in compensation and the Greenwich & Woolwich Act was passed on 16 July 1866, the other sections having been authorised on 5 July 1865.

On 30 January 1864 a woman was killed at Deptford station after she fell off the platform in the course of an argument with another lady. In October 1864 it was decided to enlarge Spa Road station, but nothing seems to have been done until 1866 when a new plan was adopted - the station was to be rebuilt 200 yards further east, at a cost of £12,300, in 1867. Another station improved at this time was New Cross. In contrast, Commercial Dock station had gradually lost traffic following the opening of other stations in the area, and it was closed after 31 December 1866.

On 19 December 1864 the North Kent line experienced its second serious accident. An overloaded ballast train was checked by signals near Blackheath station and came to a halt in the tunnel, where the wet rails on a gradient of 1 in 132 proved too much for the overburdened locomotive. It was decided to split the train so that it could be restarted. The Blackheath stationmaster confused his young signalman, who was in fact a porter standing in for a sick colleague, by interfering with the procedures; as a result, the 2.30pm up Maidstone train was allowed to run ahead and it collided with the rear of the ballast train in the tunnel. Five platelayers and the fireman of the Maidstone train were killed, but the accident could have been far worse had it not been for the wetness of the tunnel, which doused the flames which threatened to engulf the carriages. The 4.20pm down train also managed to stop in the nick of time. Captain Tyler inspected the accident and a Coroner's court found a verdict of manslaughter against the ballast train guard, who should have run back through the tunnel to warn approaching trains of the obstacle ahead. The SER had to pay out less compensation than for the Lewisham disaster, but two sisters received £800 and £1,500 respectively in February 1866. Less seriously, a pile of hay left near the canal bridge at Deptford in May 1860 caught fire and spread to the bridge, causing the suspension of traffic for five hours.

The Dartford loop, via Sidcup, opened on 1 September 1866. A spur onto the Mid Kent line became known as the Ladywell Loop, between Parks Bridge Junction and Ladywell Junction; it was first used in 1865 but came into regular use in 1866. Intermediate stations were at Lee, Eltham (renamed Eltham & Mottingham 1 January 1892), Sidcup, Bexley and Crayford. The line had an important role to play in relieving traffic on the North Kent route via Woolwich, and enabled improvements to be made in the service to Strood and Maidstone. However Dartford station was inadequate for the traffic and in January 1867 it was decided to widen the viaduct there and rebuild the station, making it easier for trains on the North Kent route to terminate there.

The new Spa Road station was proving a success but by 1869 was in a poor condition. It was then provided with an extra staircase to separate "up" and "down" pedestrians. Less happy, though, were the people of Erith and Belvedere who were not pleased with their train service. Goods traffic on the

Dartford loop must also have been disappointing, for in November 1869 it was decided not to build a goods shed at Crayford.

The situation at Greenwich, though, had got worse rather than better. The bankruptcy of the LCDR in 1866 had cast doubts on its ability to build any more new lines, but the SER's decision to construct the Greenwich-Woolwich link had been based on it securing access to other parts of the LCDR. Perhaps the death of LCDR ambitions also influenced the SER into thinking that they could save on the estimated £340,000 cost of the scheme. By April and May 1868 the issue was provoking much discussion in the district, with the SER blaming the high cost of the line on the Observatory (one suggestion being that vibrations could be reduced by laying the sleepers longtitudinally) and Watkin inviting local people to make contributions.

Watkin suggested a cheaper solution - that the line through the Park and the town should be dropped as it was an "abominable" plan, and that a new route round the edge of the Park should be adopted. This, he thought, could be done for £200,000. The problem had to be solved by 1871, for after that the SER would be liable to a penalty of £50 a day for not completing the line. John Angerstein was especially prominent in the calls for completion, but the SER was worried that the closure of the Woolwich Dockyard for shipbuilding on 3 October 1869 had severely damaged the local economy - house rents were reported to have fallen by a third while there were 1,600 empty houses in the district. For local people, of course, this was another reason why a railway was essential, but the SER traffic on the North Kent line had fallen by £3,000 in six months[22].

By November 1869 the SER was clutching at straws, suggesting that a £27,000 spur to connect East Greenwich with the North Kent line at Charlton might be sufficient though the *Railway Times* suggested that a Greenwich to Woolwich tramway scheme might rescue the SER.

Help came from an unusual source - the Post Office. The SER telegraph system was sold to the Post Office for £200,000 late in 1869 and, according to the *Railway Times*, it was decided to use this money to complete the Greenwich line. However, Watkin wanted a new Bill for his deviation route and to extend the time limit on construction for a further seven years. The SER felt that local people would be "satisfied with any line" and proposed to get the advice of French astronomers in dealing with the Observatory. When Parliament threw out much of the SER's plans in March 1870, Watkin took it as a personal insult; he wrote to Lord Redesdale that he had personally saved the SER from bankruptcy in 1866.

There was no alternative but to press ahead with the two ends of the line and leave the central section to Parliament. So by April 1870 work was beginning between Greenwich station and the baths while in May 1870 the contract for the short line between East Greenwich and Charlton was let at £7,883. It also proved possible to buy off the opposition of Angerstein to any deviation by promising to provide a station at Combe Farm Lane - this became Westcombe Park. An agreement to provide the station was signed on 1 February 1871. However the Bill of 1870 was again defeated due to the Admiralty.

Eventually agreement was reached with the Admiralty and an Act to complete the line passed on 25 May 1871; this ran to the north of the Park, a safe distance from the Observatory, but nonetheless the SER had to pay for experiments to see if it would be affected. Progress now became possible and plans for a station at Maze Hill were being prepared by January 1872. The section between East Greenwich and Charlton was finished by October that year and inspected by Captain Tyler; it was opened to a temporary station at "Maize Hill"[23] on 1 January 1873[24]. By this stage there was a renewed threat of a LCDR line to Greenwich. In fact the LCDR did not reach Greenwich until 1 October 1888, terminating close to the SER line but without a connection; in 1898 the Lee Board of Works tried to force the construction of a connection, but it was not provided.

Work on the "gap" had not started by July 1873, perhaps being held up by problems over the land; land costs for the line were at least £160,000 with Aird & Sons doing the contracting, though they were held up by the need to divert 1,700 feet of the southern outfall sewer. The section from Maze Hill to Church Street was reported as being "ready" in June 1875 but an attempt to make an early start with traffic between Greenwich station and Church Street was frustrated by the Board of Trade. Lucas & Aird built a new station for Greenwich which came into use on 31 December 1876[25].

A "lighted" inspection was arranged in January 1877, when a lot of work still remained to be done - including substantial alterations to track levels. The line was inspected again on 23 April 1877, when a turntable at Charlton and interlocking of the Deptford home signals to the lifting bridge there were requested. Completion of the line was then again delayed by a stonemason's strike. It was re-inspected by Major-General Hutchinson on 22 December 1877 and then the opening hurried through for 1 February 1878. The line was used only for local services until 4 March, due to the need for improvements at Deptford, so that most trains terminated at Charlton; the service ran every 20 minutes. With the opening of the line it was decided to change the running lines around between Maze Hill and Charlton to match the unusual pattern on the rest of the Greenwich branch, with a scissors crossing being provided at Charlton to provide normal running beyond there. On 11 May there was an accident at Charlton, which the Board of Trade blamed on poor track layout, poor signalling, and confusion between the two signalboxes; this seems likely to have been a result of the use of the crossing there. This crossing, and a similar one at London Bridge, were the cause of many delays by July 1878.

Despite the excitement, or lack of excitement, at Greenwich, normal life continued on the rest of the North Kent system. In May 1870 a passenger was killed at Spa Road when he got out of a train too soon. The down platform at Gravesend was lengthened in June and in October it was decided to light Eltham station with gas; the latter decision provides us with a vignette of railway economics - the annual cost of lighting a station with candles and oil was £27-10-6d, but gas cost only £17. Near Erith a healthy goods traffic was provided by Beadle's Siding, which was protected by catch points from 1871; in 1888 Beadle added a coal siding near Charlton, presumably for deliveries of coal to the local community. By July 1891 Beadle's Wharf at Erith was handling much of the SER's own coal supplies. Rumours also began to circulate that anyone who passed through Blackheath Tunnel needed protection; the Board of Trade inspected it (having first been refused entry by the District Surveyor) to see if the allegations that it was unsafe were true. They found that parts of the 1,720 yard tunnel were bare chalk and that water fell through the rock onto the trains. When the tunnel was first opened, third class carriages had been provided with corrugated iron roofs to protect the passengers[26].

The Deptford Royal Dockyard closed on 31 March 1869. In 1870 some of the site was bought by a private company who offered the SER 22 acres of it for £100,000. The SER declined the chance, and by November an international cattle market was being projected for the site for which the LBSCR proposed a branch from off their own siding to Deadman's Dock. However the Bill for the cattle market was withdrawn in 1871 but passed the next year; the scheme had failed by November 1875, when another attempt to sell the site to the SER was made. The area was later used for the London County Council meat depot, which had a siding from the LBSCR Deptford Wharf branch.

New waiting rooms were provided at New Cross in 1871, with similar improvements being made at Eltham and Lee in 1872, which also gained a stationmaster's house in 1873. A new turntable was provided at Gravesend so that, from 1 February 1872, the practice of tender-first running could be eliminated on the North Kent line. Plans to open a new station at Rosherville, west of Gravesend, did not bear fruit though some land was bought in 1871. Powers to construct the station were included in the SER Act of 1872.

In October 1872 the War Office approached the SER with a plan for a new line into the "Dockyard" at Woolwich, though of course it was the Arsenal that was to be linked to the outside world; plans for this were completed by November 1873 and the line was constructed for the War Office by the SER in 1875 at a cost of £1,200; traffic probably began the following year. The line was worked by the SER until 1890, after which the Arsenal used its own locomotives; the short system included a swing bridge over a canal[27]. There was also a small amount of traffic into the old Dockyard, which remained in use as a store; it had been connected to the SER since about 1850. Goods traffic to the Arsenal between January and October 1878 amounted to 42,506 tons, so that the SER had to buy extra land to expand its siding facilities.

The arches under the Greenwich viaduct were still in use for a variety of purposes. The dangers of this were brought home to the SER in late 1872 when a boiler beneath one of the arches at Page's Yard exploded. The SER then investigated what went on beneath its trains - and found a number of dangerous activities including the storage of waste paper and nut oil, a varnish works and a fat melting factory at Deptford.

To cope with growing traffic, extra signalboxes were provided between Spa Road and Corbetts Lane and between Blackheath and Lewisham in 1874. Some of the traffic could be quite illustrious - the Tsar of Russia travelled from Gravesend to Windsor via Waterloo on 13 May 1874, and gave some rings to the SER's John Shaw as a memento.

In July 1874 the SER started negotiations with a landowner for a new station at Pope Street, near Eltham. The landowner offered to give the land and £2,000 if a station could be opened by May 1875. The target date was not met, and in February 1878 the Board of Trade refused to allow the station's opening until a bridge and better station accomodation had been provided. It eventually opened on 1 April and the landowner paid £2,300. It was renamed New Eltham & Pope Street on 1 January 1886 and plain New Eltham on 26 September 1927. The Pope Street stationmaster saved the life of a woman who was on the line in May 1878, and was rewarded with £5. Close by, at Sidcup, a ganger was killed by a ballast train on 17 July 1876; it was his first day with the SER and the company paid the funeral expenses.

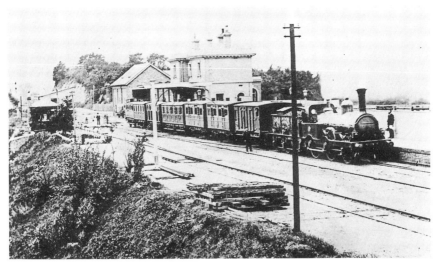

12. **Erith Station in 1876.** (Wakeman Collection)

In September 1874 the Evelyn Estate, which owned land used for market gardens in Deptford, was keen to have a station opened close to North Kent East Junction so that the area could be used for new housing. The SER wanted an acre of land free, close to Rolt Street. However the Evelyn Estate backed out of the plan in May 1876.

The agreement with Angerstein to provide a station at Combe Farm Lane did not produce a station quite as quickly as Angerstein had expected. One of the results of this was that Blackheath people continued to use the Thames steamers to get to work and the SER showed renewed interest in the matter in 1875. In February 1878 it was decided to spend £5,300 on a station there which was opened on 1 May 1879 as Westcombe Park.

With the opening of the Greenwich extension it was decided to remove the Deptford engine shed to Charlton in 1877-8 at a cost of £11,500.

With the growth of residential suburbs, passenger accomodation needed to be steadily improved. Bexley station was improved in 1877 and in 1878 substantial additional passenger accomodation was provided at Erith and Charlton, the former including a footbridge. Woolwich Arsenal gained extra sidings and passenger accomodation in 1878. That January a lunatic woman jumped off the platform there in front of a train; the station Inspector was awarded £20 for his brave but futile attempt to save her.

In April 1878 the Dartford loop was flooded for 1.5 miles between Eltham and Sidcup.

New sidings were provided at Eltham and Maze Hill in November 1878 and a private siding for Messrs. Hepburn at Dartford in 1879. That same year Blackheath station was provided with a new booking office and in 1880 facilities at Lee were expanded.

Swanscombe was becoming a centre of the lime and cement industries. Sidings there were extended in 1879 and in January 1881 the SER signed an agreement to allow a tunnel to be made beneath its line to connect quarries either side of the tracks.

The rebuilding of Deptford station was considered in 1882 but deferred, in the same way that regular pressure for additional stations between Greenwich and London Bridge met with little response until Southwark Park was opened in 1902. There were already a number of stations in the area, notably provided by the East London Railway. The SER did, however, renew the Deptford bridge in 1884.

A highly colourful saga is said to have occurred on the North Kent line on 6 August 1883[28]. The 5.30pm Charing Cross to Gravesend killed a donkey near Greenhithe and then narrowly missed a balloon, which came down across the tracks so that its ropes became entangled in the locomotive.

The character of Plumstead was changing and, as a result of this, the SER was requested to provide more trains for the working class in March 1882. In April 1886 a shunter was killed there and three months later an extra coal siding was added. However it was not a pleasant station and in October 1890 Plumstead Vestry demanded that their "miserable station" be pulled down; the SER decided to spend £2,000 on it, including the provision of a footbridge. The terminal bay on the up side may have dated from this time.

Belvedere received the unusual addition of an experimental footbridge acquired from the Great Western in June 1884 while in 1887 Sidcup received a new up side booking office and platform extensions. Gravesend and Erith received further improvements in 1890, but at the latter station there was a collision on 12 December 1890 between a Tonbridge goods train and the 8.15am from Strood.

Northfleet received new station buildings in 1891 while Eltham and Sidcup were resignalled in 1894. In March of that year Myles Fenton visited Gravesend to discuss the town's station and the possibility of a branch line being built to the Pier; this was never built.

Deptford locomotive shed had in fact continued in use, despite earlier plans to close it entirely. It was antiquated by 1893 and its confined space led to the death of driver Overy, who was crushed between the wall and an engine in November that year. There was also a carriage shed at Rotherhithe Road, where the SER decided to set up its own oil and gas works in 1894 to provide gas supplies for 1,000 carriages.

Another legacy of earlier efforts was the Blackheath Tunnel - on 15 April 1896 it partially subsided, leaving a hollow, 28 feet wide and ten feet deep, where an old excavation shaft had once been.

Goods traffic continued to grow too. Further extensions were made to the chalk sidings near Dartford in 1896 and the London Paper Company there gained a siding in the same year. In 1897 a new asylum was under construction to the south-east of Bexley; a new loop was provided near Crayford to connect with the contractor's railway.

In 1896 work began on widening the line at Dartford station and towards the junction with the Dartford loop, with the provision of an extra track. This gave Dartford a third platform face, easing the problems caused when trains terminated there.

A new signalbox and signals were provided at North Kent West Junction in 1897 and then a Bill was prepared to provide a new loop between the Dartford line and the main-line at Hither Green. A station there had been opened on 1 June 1895; the facilities for the Dartford line included an up through road. The spur from Lee Junction into Hither Green Goods seems to have opened about 1900.

In June 1898 the SER decided to buy the freehold of the Angerstein branch and wharf; this was done by October. There was originally a triangular connection between the branch and the North Kent line, though by 1890 the spur to the east had been closed. The SER maintained its signalling works at the site, however.

The development that was to have the greatest long-term significance for the line was the decision of the SER to use land at Slades Green for its new locomotive depot. By August 1898 it was buying land at Whitehall Crossing, Erith, for this purpose, and it decided to erect 91 houses there for £32,559. The depot did not open until 1900.

3. The Bexleyheath Line

As has been seen, from 1866 the SER came to have two virtually parallel routes between London and Dartford. These two lines helped to open up the district for residential purposes, but property values declined sharply away from the railway. In the late 1870s, land at Blackheath could fetch up to £2,000 an acre, but at Bexleyheath it never exceeded £600[29]. Attempts were made to stimulate development, such as the opening of Pope Street station on the Dartford loop, but it was considered that for the desired large scale residential development a new line would be needed.

A number of local landowners therefore formed a committee to lobby the SER for a line from Blackheath to Dartford via Bexleyheath. They included Thomas Jackson, the owner of Eltham Park, H.W.Bean of Danson Park, Robert Kersey of Brampton Park and Charles Beadle, the coal merchant. The SER's engineer, Francis Brady, studied the question and told the Board that the proposed line would only be of "residential use".

The committee were not discouraged by the SER's lack of interest. The SER made its profits from running trains, but the Bexleyheath committee aimed to make a profit from getting trains to run - for the in their view the rapid increase in property prices would then enable the whole venture to make a handsome return. They therefore turned themselves into the Bexleyheath Railway and, in November 1882, appointed Brady as their engineer - indicating at least tolerance on the part of the SER.

At their second meeting later that month, the BR Board discussed whether they should ask the SER for running powers to New Cross - a request unlikely to meet with approval. Brady suggested that the line start from a junction with the SER at Lee, on the Dartford loop, rather than Blackheath, on the North Kent line.

Despite some concern from the Commons Preservation Society about the threat to Eltham Common, the BR went ahead with a Bill and secured authorisation on 20 August 1883. Then came the real problem - raising money. The very nature of the line - a speculation intended to reap profits through land prices rather than by profits on running trains - restricted the number of people who could possibly have an interest in taking shares to those who owned land in the neighbourhood. In October 1883 the subscription list stood at £33,126, made up of nine shareholders with Jackson having a stake of £11,000[30].

During the succeeding months a furious effort was made to find other investors. Sir Julian Goldsmid agreed to invest £5,000 but one of the shareholders, Colonel Barne, was unable to interest his father. The directors wondered whether Mr Bartholomew could be interested if he was offered a siding. Given that Barne's name was later immortalised in the name of Barnehurst station, one wonders whether sponsorship of stations might have produced better results. On 23 November 1883 the BR's solicitors had to advise the company not to issue shares at a discount.

Although the company had close ties with the SER - it shared a secretary and an engineer, while Colonel Surtees represented the SER on its Board - a dispute arose between the two companies in 1884. The SER decided that it would prefer the junction with the BR to be at Blackheath rather than Lee. The BR had little choice but to agree, so that the section between Lee and Well Hall had to be abandoned in favour of a line from Blackheath.

By December 1884 the line seemed ready to progress, with negotiations with a contracting firm, Lucas & Aird, under way. The provision of stations at Bexleyheath and Pickford Lane was discussed, though first in with a request was Oxford University - which wanted a siding at Bexley for its tenant.

Suddenly, however, disaster struck. The Bills to amend and deviate the line were rejected in the 1885 Parliamentary session and bad feeling between the SER and BR is indicated by the resignations of Shaw, as secretary, and Colonel Surtees. At its meeting of 14 August 1885 the BR Board considered its next step - they decided to reapply for powers to build the line between Well Hall and Blackheath and also to apply for running powers to Charing Cross. The exact relationship with the SER was, apparently, to be kept quiet.

To give the BR Bill a chance of success, it was necessary to avoid opposition from other landowners. A problem was encountered with the St Germans estate, which wanted a better site for a station; in February 1886 the BR Board conceded that a second station might be needed to pacify this opposition. Robert Kersey, however, was prepared to sell land at £300 an acre for a station at Pickford Lane; this sounded generous, but would - of course - benefit Kersey's property enormously. Another station was agreed for Sir H.Barron in March 1886.

By 9 March the BR Bill was progressing through Parliament, but the SER threatened to petition against it. The BR directors, though, were not ignorant of the machinations of railway politics; they threatened to reveal the negotiations that they had had with the SER, perhaps confident that they could always turn to the LCDR if need be.

Although an Act for the line was passed on 25 June 1886 it did not include the desired spur at Blackheath, which had been rejected by the House of Lords after opposition from local landowners, notably the Cator Estate. This was only authorised by Act of 23 August 1887 after a promise to cover over the line through Blackheath Park, a high class residential area.

Once more, though, the SER proved unco-operative by refusing to make any agreement to construct the Bexleyheath line. The BR then considered a link to the LCDR at Farningham Road or Blackheath Hill, with extended running powers[31]. However a draft contract with the SER was agreed by November 1889 though subsequent events perhaps suggested that the SER had been wise in its cautious assessment of Bexleyheath prospects. The SER considered advancing £100,000 at 3% interest to avoid a connection with the LCDR.

The cost of the line, including land, had been estimated at £364,339. It was agreed that William Rigby should be the contractor and he took shares in the company worth £26,980 in part-payment; his contract was worth £173,000. Earlier, Aird had refused to accept a contract with shares in part-payment. To supervise the work, Rigby moved into the "Swiss Cottage" at Blackheath.

By May 1891 matters had got as far as discussing the site of the stations on the land of Colonel Barne and Mr Kersey; the name of "Barnehurst" was adopted for the former in November 1891. Then financial problems resurfaced in February 1892, the Bexleyheath company blaming the SER in being slow paying for its allotted 15,000 shares, which it did not want to do until local contributions had reached £100,000 out of the £226,000 capital. There must be a suspicion that a number of people did their work for the line in return for shares - thus Francis Brady was allotted £2,000 of shares in April 1892. This was a practice championed in the early days of the EKR and LCDR by Samuel Morton Peto, and revealed by the events of 1866 as likely to cause instability.

One of the main works on the line was the "tunnel" through Blackheath Park. Under the Act, 140 yards only of this was to be constructed on the "cut and cover" principle, but in 1893 Rigby caused some controversy by trying to extend this cheap method of creating a tunnel beyond the legal limits. He also caused problems by setting up a tramway with a temporary crossing over Blackheath Park Road. There was a serious slip in the Blackheath cutting on 7 November 1894.

By the middle of 1892 the Bexleyheath Railway was again considering the question of stations - an especially serious matter when a railway was intended to develop property. In June 1892 a goods station at Branston Road in Bexleyheath was suggested. During May 1893 it was proposed that £24,000 should be spent on stations and later that year plans were drawn up for Kidbrooke (sited at Earl Street by decision of 3 October), Welling and Bexleyheath.

Money was still limited, so the BR Board decided to reduce the sum allowed for stations to £19,000, estimating that each station with signals could be done for about £4,500.

At the instigation of the Bexley Local Board it was decided that the name "Bexleyheath" should be used in preference to "Bexley Heath", but a suggestion that Well Hall should be known as "Shooter's Hill" was rejected. Some problems did arise over land issues however, causing one of the directors - Mr Kersey - to take legal action against his own company. In October 1894 there was a "mass trespass", in protest at the blocking of an old footpath.

The line opened on 1 May 1895 with stations at Kidbrooke, Well Hall, Welling, Bexleyheath and Barnehurst. Eltham Park & Shooters Hill did not open until 1 July 1908 and Falconwood until 1 January 1936.

The line was worked by the SER; it was agreed that the SER should receive 60% of gross receipts. It immediately ran into problems typical of a landowners' railway built to encourage development - initial traffic was very low due to the small local population and lack of through traffic. By November 1895 the Board was complaining that its monthly income amounted to between £168 and £216. Income was insufficient to meet even interest repayments, forcing the SER to accept payment at only 50% of gross receipts for the period to the end of 1895 so that the BR could pay its 3% debentures - otherwise bankruptcy would have resulted.

Things got worse - monthly receipts for the BR in January and February 1896 were only £223 even though the SER had claimed a mere 48% of receipts. From 1 April 1896 third class season tickets were introduced, a highly significant move due to the way in which the landowners could try to influence the social tone of the district. In July the BR itself earnt £249 after the SER had claimed the full 60%. This, though, proved to be a false sign of hope - the BR's net income fell again to £207 in November and £189 in December - with the SER accepting only 51% of gross receipts to avoid the bankruptcy of the line.

During 1897 the BR fared little better, its income varying between £215 and £259. The SER itself complained that in the first six months of 1897 it actually lost £200 in working the line, and it was still recording a net loss a year later. After the formation of the SE&CR accounting methods changed, but the gross receipts for the whole line were still only £525 in February 1899.

As a railway, then, the Bexleyheath was a financial disaster. Not until the inter-war period did it begin to develop,by which time the favourable economic climate for house-building with the availability of cheap land at last brought the suburban development that the line needed to prosper.

4. The Gravesend & Rochester

The extension of the SER's North Kent line from Gravesend to Strood had its origin in an Act authorising the Thames & Medway Canal, passed on 16 May 1800. This was a scheme, engineered by Ralph Dodd, for a canal to connect the two rivers of its title, thereby avoiding the lengthy passage around the Hoo Peninsula. The canal was completed from Gravesend to Higham by 1804, but then it remained unfinished. The problem was the chalk ridge that separated Higham from Strood, which Dodd had planned to conquer by a tunnel.

Not until 1819 was an effort made to complete this tunnel, using an astronomer's telescope to keep the working shafts aligned. It was finished on 14 October 1824 and provided with a towpath. However in 1830 a section was opened out near the middle to provide a passing place and resting point, thus converting it into two tunnels, at a cost of £13,000. Higham Tunnel measured 1,531 yards while Strood Tunnel was 1 mile 569 yards.

The canal was not a financial success, since the barges continued to exploit a unique pattern of tides along the Thames and Medway. The first suggestion that it could be converted into a railway seems to have been made in 1836, when a Gravesend & Strood Railway was advertised in the *Maidstone Journal*. In 1840 a Gravesend & Rochester Railway, using the canal tunnel, was reported to be "very popular"(32). On 18 January 1841 the directors of the Thames & Medway met the engineer John Rastrick, who estimated that a single track railway could be built alongside the canal between Gravesend and Strood for £120,000.

The T&M agreed on this plan; because a clause of their original Act authorised the use of "Rollers, Inclined Planes, Railways..." no further Parliamentary sanction was required. Although steps were taken to raise the capital, no work was begun but in 1843-4 a number of rival proposals entered the field, such as the Rosherville & Chatham - dubbed a "monstrous absurdity" by the *Maidstone Journal*.

Thus spurred into action, work on building the railway began in March 1844 in the care of Fox, Henderson & Co. To scotch rumours that the tunnels were

Evolution of Railways
in the Medway Area

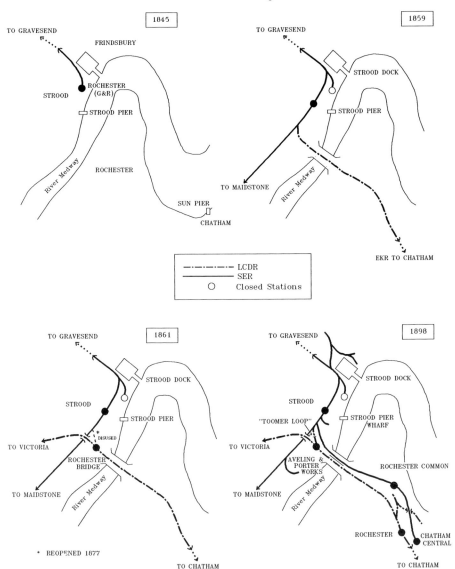

1845

TO GRAVESEND

FRINDSBURY

ROCHESTER
STROOD (G&R)

STROOD PIER

River Medway

ROCHESTER

SUN PIER

CHATHAM

1859

TO GRAVESEND

STROOD DOCK

STROOD PIER

TO MAIDSTONE

River Medway

EKR TO CHATHAM

----·---- LCDR
———————— SER
O Closed Stations

1861

TO GRAVESEND

STROOD DOCK

STROOD

STROOD PIER

TO VICTORIA

* DISUSED

ROCHESTER
BRIDGE

River Medway

TO MAIDSTONE

TO CHATHAM

* REOPENED 1877

1898

TO GRAVESEND

STROOD DOCK

STROOD

"TOOMER LOOP"

STROOD PIER
WHARF

TO VICTORIA

AVELING &
PORTER
WORKS

ROCHESTER COMMON

River Medway

TO MAIDSTONE

ROCHESTER   CHATHAM
               CENTRAL

TO CHATHAM

13. The entrance to the Higham Tunnel, at the Higham end during the short period in which it was both a canal and railway tunnel.
(Railway & Canal Historical Society)

unsafe, tests were held: "The safety of the tunnel was tested by the firing of a loaded cannon in it several times, but no fall was occasioned by the concussion."

Meanwhile, Robert Stephenson had been working with the SER in planning the extension of its system in North Kent, and he seems to have suggested that the two companies should talk to each other. On 1 October 1844 a deputation from the "Gravesend & Rochester Railway" visited the SER and discussed possible SER extensions to Maidstone and Chilham through the tunnels. The SER advised the G&R that it should be built as a double-track, though it was in fact opened as a single line with a passing place at Higham.

Local press reports indicate that trial runs were made on the line on Christmas Day 1844, with crowds rushing out of Frindsbury church to watch. The first train was apparently driven by a man named Faithful Kirkham, and hauled by a locomotive named either *Trafalgar* or *St Vincent*. However the engine's chimney caught the roof of the tunnel, and it had to be shortened by nine inches. On 4 January 1845 General Pasley inspected the line and tested the tunnels by firing blank mortars; he ordered a small amount of brick lining in the tunnel and an extension to the wooden viaduct that carried the line along the south side of the canal through the tunnel.

The opening of the line was further delayed when the contractors took forcible "possession" of the Gravesend terminus on 24 January, alleging non-payment of a debt. The following day the G&R formed an attacking force of their own, who seized control of the Gravesend station once more. At Strood, the contractor's foreman disabled the locomotive by removing a part, which was returned on 29 January after the intervention of the Magistrates.

By the last week of January trains were actually running, with free trips being offered in conjunction with ferry connections between Strood and the Sun Pier, Chatham. Further "experimental" services worked on 8 February, with the official opening taking place two days later. Upwards of 400 passengers began

14. A very early view of Strood, emphasising its isolated position. The picture seems to date from about the time of the opening of the Maidstone extension. (Lens of Sutton)

15. Higham Station in the early 1880s, looking east.

16. Gravesend & Rochester Railway at Strood at the time of first opening. The wooden viaduct for the single track can be seen clearly, but the tunnel portal owes a great deal to artistic licence.

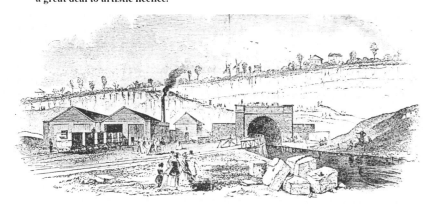

to use the trains each day. *Fraser's Magazine* felt that the G&R fell into the "primitive style of railway travelling." Its staff were unimpressive: "Two full grown policemen and a bevy of boys, dressed up in the left-off garments of a lady's page, constitute the force on duty at the Gravesend station." The reporter was even more worried when he got into the train:

"As soon as you are in they lock the door on your right and leave the door on your left open. We made some inquiries about this...[we] were informed that a whole string of carriage doors had been smashed in the tunnel during the first week that the railway was open. The tunnel, it appears, is very narrow, and several curious travellers had opened the doors in the tunnel, to see what the place was like. The doors were in a moment torn from off their hinges, and the travellers' heads all but torn from their shoulders."

The G&R offered an intensive service of a train most half hours between 7am and 9pm, though with an hourly service at quieter periods of the day. In March 1845, 12,096 passengers were carried with receipts of £377. In May the figure rose to 32,818, perhaps because of improved steamer connections to Chatham. Three Robert Stephenson locomotives were used initially and a fourth, *Van Tromp*, was delivered at Gravesend on 19 March 1845.

The line seems to have been a great success, for by June 1845 an extension into the middle of Gravesend was being considered and an extra engine was being ordered. By Act of 31 July 1845 the company officially changed its name to the Gravesend & Rochester Railway, and was given powers to raise £85,000.

On 4 December 1845 the SER decided to spend up to £310,000 to acquire the line and a deposit was paid on 24 April 1846. The G&R was already a sound concern, having earnt £10,903-0-3d in its first full year up to 23 May 1846, without operating any goods traffic.

The SER Act of 3 August 1846 gave it powers to take over the G&R and to extend the North Kent line to meet it at Gravesend. Robert Stephenson then inspected the line and advised filling in the canal through the tunnel so that it could be converted to double track. Purchase was completed by the payment of £279,000 on 25 September 1846. John Brogden was then awarded a contract to double and improve the line for £48,869-10-0d. To allow this, the line had to be closed from 13 December 1846; work was fairly simple, although a curve of the canal was cut off with a section of new line near the later Hoo Junction.

The line reopened on 23 August 1847 but still used the original terminus at the Gravesend canal basin, which was inconvenient for the Gravesend river piers. The new station was opened on 30 July 1849, when the G&R was connected to the North Kent line, but its old station remained in use for goods.

The station at the Strood end was often known as "Rochester". The SER installed coke ovens at the canal basin there but improvements to the station buildings were delayed while the SER considered an extension to Maidstone. The resiting of the station to the south was eventually forced by the passing of the East Kent Railway Act in 1853, which was to connect with the SER at Strood. The station became important for goods traffic, even though much of the local lime and cement trade went by water so that none of the works except the Strood Canal Dock works had a direct rail connection until 1905; a goods shed was built in 1852 and extra coal sidings in 1853. The other station on the line was at Higham, opened in 1845; a goods shed was provided there in 1853.

Much of the canal itself was left to gradually become derelict. The two basins at each end remained busy, however, and a "measured mile" of the canal was

17. Gravesend & Rochester Railway's Gravesend Terminus.

used for steamboat trials in 1852. In 1855 the SER considered introducing a Bill to permit closure of the canal but it was strongly opposed by local interests.

In 1853 the SER considered opening a station at Milton, just outside Gravesend, on some vacant land that they owned. In August 1870 the people of Denton requested a station, but were refused. Eventually, in July 1906, halts were opened at Denton and at Milton Range.

At Strood, the extension to Maidstone opened on 18 June 1856 and the East Kent Railway on 29 March 1858. A new station to accomodate this traffic opened early in March 1858. A new pier was opened in 1860 in a position close to the new station, from which services operated to Chatham, Upnor and Sheerness. However the coke traffic at the Strood basin declined after 1868, from which date SER engines used coal instead. The SER built some staff cottages at Strood, but without their own water supply; Mr J.Watt was employed to carry water to them, but was sacked in 1884 when mains water was provided.

The smooth interchange of traffic between the SER and LCDR at Strood was disrupted when the latter won approval for its Western Extension line. From 1 September 1860 the SER ended all through booking facilities at Strood, forcing passengers to rebook once they got there.

On 13 July 1861 there was a derailment in the tunnel mouth at Strood, causing the destruction of a guard's van. In March 1862 the 3.10pm from Strood was derailed between Higham and Gravesend, causing the death of the guard; compensation of £500 was paid after allegations that worn out track had not been replaced since the line had opened.

Charles Dickens lived at Gad's Hill Place in Higham until his death in 1870. Visitors often came to see him there and he generally advised them to catch a fast train to Gravesend, then a "fly" to his house, rather than using the slower trains that stopped at Higham. On 14 June 1870 his coffin was loaded onto a special train for the journey to Charing Cross.

In 1898 substantial improvements were made to the Strood station and the SER decided to buy some land "at Higham" for a ballast pit. This was close to the branch that led off to Port Victoria, the site eventually becoming the Hoo Junction marshalling yard. Not until June 1899, however, was £60 spent on "Higham Ballast Pit Siding".

5. The Chatham Central Branch

Although travellers on the Dover road had traditionally crossed the Medway at Rochester, this route was avoided by the SER and no railway crossed the Medway there until the EKR opened between Strood and Rochester on 29 March 1858. The EKR joined the SER at Strood and its traffic was forwarded to London by the North Kent line. Local needs were met by the SER station at Strood and the EKR at Chatham. When the LCDR (as the EKR had become) opened its extension to Swanley and London on 3 December 1860, it opened its own station in Strood at Rochester Bridge. This virtually brought to an end the role of Strood as an interchange.

The SER continued to compete for the Chatham and Rochester traffic by running ferries from the pier at Strood station. This left the LCDR with the upper hand in one of Kent's most populous districts, so on 31 October 1872 the SER discussed extending their own line from Strood to Chatham Dockyard. This would allow direct services between the Woolwich Arsenal and the Navy at Chatham.

The cost of such a line, including a river crossing and expensive urban land, was prohibitive, so the SER pressed instead for running powers into the LCDR station at Chatham. The SER therefore wrote to James Forbes, the LCDR general manager, who confessed to being "surprised" at the suggestion. Running powers had existed for 15 years, he observed, but had never been exercised. The SER Board listened to a report from their solicitor:

"The Solicitor reported he had seen Mr Forbes who seemed very much annoyed at the proceedings of the Company and said that unless they withdrew their application to go into Chatham he should apply to Parliament next year for powers to make a line from Maidstone to Ashford."

The SER wanted to reintroduce a service of 13 trains a day over the defunct connection at Strood, with working to be done by the LCDR. They offered, no doubt in a sarcastic comment on the LCDR's stretched resources, to lend an engine if that company was short of them. The LCDR delayed the position by arguing that Chatham station needed to be improved before such a service could be run, but the SER then revived talk of its own line into Chatham. The LCDR then retorted that the link would be delayed due to plans for rebuilding it having been "lost"; SER Minutes of 9 October 1873 suggest that they had lost their copy too!

There were already legal running powers, but an additional legal technicality was seized upon by the Mayor of Rochester, J.Toomer, in July 1876: the passenger service between Strood and Chatham had been withdrawn without the Board of Trade's permission. Toomer took his case to the Railway Commissioners and in January 1877 they ruled that a service must be restarted by 1 February, with "reasonable" connections at least four times a day. On 14 March 1877 they imposed a penalty for each day the service did not run, charging the LCDR £60 and the SER £15. There seem to have been some problems in rebuilding the link for the service did not start until 2 April 1877, worked by the SER; the line became known as the "Toomer Loop".

This still left the LCDR in control of Chatham and Rochester and the SER, in one of its least inspired moves of the war against the LCDR, decided in 1880 to revive the plans for its own line. The line was authorised on 11 August 1881, no doubt helped by the LCDR's failure to build a station actually in Rochester and protests that its Chatham station could accomodate no increase in the Strood service.

The new SER line was to leave Strood station and run roughly parallel to the Toomer Loop and the LCDR on their north side, terminating at Rochester High Street. There was to be a bridge over the Medway and much of the line had to be on viaduct to "admit of free communication" with the Medway wharves. In 1885 the SER had to buy Foord's Wharf since the line affected it.

The land and works of this new line were costly. In 1884 an extension of time had to be authorised, by which stage the Admiralty had given permission for the Medway bridge to have a fixed span. However work virtually ceased that year in the hope of improved relations with the LCDR, leaving an intermittent service of five up and eight down trains over the Toomer Loop. The SER's best time between London Bridge and Chatham was 100 minutes, compared to the LCDR London timings of 56 minutes.

With renewed hostilities in 1888, the SER applied for permission to complete the line. The LCDR chose to oppose the measure on the grounds that its completion would destroy or damage its new goods shed. Counsel for the

18. The remains of the SER's Chatham Central Station, with the ex-LCDR Line on the viaduct behind. To buy off Rochester's opposition to closure of the ex-SER Line, the SECR agreed to widen the bridge over Rochester High Street seen here. (Author)

LCDR argued that, "...you are welcome to your powers if you will only carry out your works so as not to destroy our [goods] station." With such weak opposition, the SER Bill was passed.

Expenditure on the line after the passing of the second Act totalled £171,329; the Horseley Company built the Medway bridge for £70,245-3-0d, the Strood and Rochester viaducts cost £6,772 and £3,462 respectively, and £5,568 was spent on ironwork for the viaduct over the LCDR's goods yard. Given the additional costs of land and what had been spent in the first attempt at construction, Forbes' estimate of £500,000 for a line less than two miles long seems quite possible. An additional problem was that the line demolished some

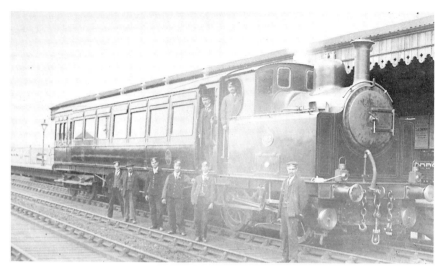

19. A rare picture of Chatham Central, marking the introduction of the "autorail" services. The single platform layout can be seen. (Lens of Sutton)

working class tenements in Rochester and thirty new houses had to be built at the SER's expense.

Whilst work progressed, further extensions were considered. In late 1889 the SER looked at an extension to Hammond's Hill in Chatham, while in 1890 Gillingham requested an extension. All Gillingham got was the transfer of the SER's Strood to Chatham buses to run from the new terminus to New Brompton.

In July 1881 the Board of Trade inspected the line as far as the Rochester Common station. The SER had to promise to set back the iron columns of the roof at Strood to allow six clear feet between them and the platform edge, after which trains began running to Rochester Common on 20 July 1891.

In February 1892 the SER ran a special press train from London to Chatham Central in 53 minutes and the double track line opened to the new terminus on 1 March 1892. It had only one platform, 480 feet long. The name was misleading, for it was not in Chatham, nor was it central to anything except, perhaps, SER ambitions. The LCDR opened their own new station in Rochester on the same day, in a superior location to either of the two SER stations.

The SER took on the LCDR by providing an intensive service of 21 trains a day from Chatham Central to London; the fastest, the 8.30am, reached London Bridge at 9.21am - beating the LCDR's best by nine minutes. Curiously, because of legal obligation, a service also existed between Strood and Rochester Bridge, where it terminated at a short platform on the Toomer Loop. Three trains a day were running in 1893, taking fully one minute for the journey of barely 300 yards. This must qualify as one of the shortest regular passenger workings on a main-line railway, but was still the only way for passengers off the North Kent line to join the LCDR.

The Chatham Central branch had no goods service though there was plenty of military traffic causing the SE&CR to install a "slope" at the terminus in 1904. The elevated nature of the line made the development of goods facilities virtually impossible.

Though the branch survived into SE&CR control, its prospects were never bright once differences between the two companies had been resolved. In 1899 the SECR reached an agreement with Rochester Corporation that there would be no closures, for otherwise the Corporation would have opposed the setting up of the SE&CR Managing Committee. The new spirit of harmony made through workings again possible, including such trains as Cannon Street to New Brompton (later called Gillingham) via Dartford. The fastest train from London became the 4.42pm ex-Cannon Street, which ran to Chatham (LCDR) in 56 minutes, calling at Gravesend and Strood.

The sole purpose of the Chatham Central branch was to wrest traffic from the LCDR. Without that motive, it had little purpose. In 1905 the traffic was handed over to diminutive "railmotors" and in 1906 the SECR reached an agreement with Rochester Corporation that would allow the eventual closure of the line; part of the price of this was widening the former LCDR bridge over Rochester High Street and rebuilding Rochester Bridge station.

Closure came on 30 September 1911 and in 1913 work on demolishing the line's wooden structures began. Meanwhile, all services from Strood were diverted to run over the LCDR to Rochester where the station was rebuilt with two island platforms to handle the extra traffic. The connection between the two routes west of the Medway was removed in 1912.

In fact the Chatham Central branch, perhaps the most clear example of Watkin's folly, came to have a valuable role. Its bridge survived to become the main-line bridge on the ex-LCDR route as well, but that was not an idea that had figured in the railway baron's mind. The greatest follies of the SER's battle against the LCDR were, ironically, both extensions of the North Kent line - one of its best performers; they were the Chatham Central branch and the Hundred of Hoo.

6. The Hundred of Hoo Branch & Port Victoria

The Hoo Peninsula, a narrow tongue of land separating the estuaries of the Thames and Medway rivers, had no attraction to railway promoters in itself, being devoid of any substantial settlements. At its eastern end, the Isle of Grain, it offered a deep water landing place however, and was also only 1.5 miles across the Medway from Sheerness. Its possibilities were realised by Sir Samuel Bentham, who suggested a naval dockyard at the Isle of Grain in 1800.

The idea of building a line along the peninsula to offer a rail and water route to Sheerness in preference to the lengthy LCDR route via Sittingbourne seems to have first occurred in 1856[33]. However, the first substantial attempt was made by the North Kent Extension Railway, which deposited a Bill in November 1864 for a line from Denton to a point opposite Sheerness at Cockle Shell Hard. The proposal avoided costly engineering works by taking a route along the Thames marshes to the north of Cliffe, although there was to be a swing-bridge over the Thames & Medway Canal.

The SER does not seem to have been enthusiastic about the line, but its Act was granted on 6 July 1865. However, as the *Railway Times* later commented, "not a shilling could be extracted from the public in support of this enterprise."

The idea lay dormant until the firm of solicitors who had been behind the North Kent Extension scheme tried to revive it in 1875, perhaps in response to the LCDR's opening of Queenborough near Sheerness as a channel ferry port. Despite earlier lack of interest, the SER engineer, Francis Brady, became involved with a new scheme on a freelance basis, recommending a route through the centre of the peninsula via High Halstow. This idea was discussed by the SER Board on 5 October 1876; they were aware that a jetty at the Isle of Grain could be used in conjunction with one of their smaller Folkestone boats to provide a service to Sheerness, but felt it would be unwise to antagonise the LCDR.

Lacking any support from the SER, the line had to be a local scheme or nothing at all. By March 1878 a number of local landowners were considering a line that would help to develop the trade of the district, with Brady recommending a line only as far east as Sharnal Street at a cost of £72,000. By the time the Bill for the Hundred of Hoo Railway had become law, on 21 July 1879, the plans for it had been extended to Stoke. The ultimate object seems always to have been a deep-water pier on the Isle of Grain, and plans for an extension to there were being prepared by October 1879 when the SER felt that it could guarantee the HoHR £3,000 per year. The Hundred of Hoo Railway Extension Bill was passed on 2 August 1880; the Bill was strongly opposed by

20. **The terminus on the pier at Port Victoria, seen in the SECR era.**
(Lens of Sutton)

the LCDR causing anger among the SER, where it was felt that Forbes had lied in his evidence[34].

The contractor for the line was Furness, who began by putting in a siding at Hoo Junction in March 1880. The extension contract, though, was awarded to T.A.Walker for £33,375-18-1d.

As early as September 1880 the SER began to consider the potential of the new line, suggesting that it could be used for a service to Belgium that would avoid the Continental Agreement's restrictions. It was, perhaps, Watkin himself who suggested that the terminus should be named "Port Victoria", a name first used in January 1881. Later that year the SER looked at the possibility of acquiring nearly 300 acres of land on the Isle of Grain for port development.

The line to Sharnal Street opened on 1 April 1882, by which time the HoHR had been absorbed into the SER[35]. There was one intermediate station, at

Cliffe. In the *Cliffe Parish Almanac*, the Rector of Cliffe warned his parishioners not to let the railway tempt them into becoming a "self-seeking, money-loving, God-forgetting population."

The extension to Port Victoria was built quickly and without the grand facilities at first envisaged; indeed its opening was delayed as Colonel Yolland requested the provision of a turntable there. Only £4,000 was allowed for the buildings and sidings at Grain, and a further £1,900 for a "temporary" hotel - it survived until 1952; all the buildings were wooden.

The extension opened to Port Victoria on 11 September 1882. No doubt the triumph of the SER in opening the new line to Port Victoria was increased by the knowledge that the LCDR's pier at Queenborough had burnt down the previous May. To begin with Port Victoria was used as a terminal for ferries to Sheerness operated by the SER's *Napoleon III*, but it soon proved unsuitable; only in 1890-1 were special vessels, the *Myleta* and *Edward William*, provided at a cost of £7,825 each.

On 6 July 1882 the SER, LCDR, Dutch State Railways and the Zeeland Shipping Company held joint talks. Though the shipping company seemed interested, the SER was worried by LCDR calls for its own line to join the Hoo branch. The following month, with talks deadlocked, the SER still considered whether the Hundred of Hoo line should be doubled; this was estimated to cost £50,000. Watkin thought that the LCDR could have running powers to Port Victoria if the SER were granted something in return - such as access to Faversham via Chatham. This unequal offer found no favour in the LCDR and, with the prospect of heavy traffic receding, the idea of doubling the line was dropped.

The prospects of the line were looking bleak by early 1883. It had not attracted any international steamers, had little local traffic, and depended on what could be extracted out of the LCDR's control of Sheerness. Strange, therefore, that a request for a station at Stoke was refused several times in 1883, but a siding was opened there in 1887. A line with a capital cost of £222,568 was reduced to renting out its "hotel" for a mere £60 a year.

To what use could the line be put? Fenton and Watkin renewed their attempt to get the Zeeland Company to use Port Victoria in 1884 but the terms of the LCDR for the use of Queenborough proved more alluring. Leasing Port Victoria to the Victoria Steamboat Association was considered in May 1888 and later that year a Mr Abernethy was commissioned to produce plans of a great harbour at the site. An Act for this was actually acquired in 1889, perhaps in the hope of attracting the custom of the Navy's new *Ironclads*, but all in vain. In 1890 a SER shareholder suggested it could be employed as a yacht club.

Port Victoria did attract a number of Royal customers as it was free from prying eyes. The Royal yacht, the *Victoria & Albert*, often moored there in connection with Queen Victoria's journeys. Even the Khedive of Egypt used the wooden jetty there and in July 1891 the Kaiser of Germany called there in his yacht, the *Hohenzollern*. From 1891 the SER made a new and more determined effort to capture the Sheerness traffic, using two new steamers from Samuda; it was not a great success, with the winter service being abandoned in 1895, and the atmosphere of the place was typified by the mooring of the redundant *Napoleon III* there.

In 1891-3 repeated efforts were made to interest the Belgian Government in operating an "express" service between Ostend and Port Victoria. The widening and lengthening of the pier was discussed in 1895, but the Belgians proved as reluctant to use Port Victoria as the Dutch.

From 1895 most winter services terminated at Sharnal Street and no trains ran to Port Victoria at all at that time of year. It has been estimated that the line was losing about £15,000 a year by this date[36].

In January 1897 the SER decided to encourage the use of the pier for pleasure traffic. Inspection revealed that some of its piles needed replacing, and a further £16,239 was invested in strengthening the structure which also allowed it to take the larger vessels by then being used by various Royal travellers. For summer 1898 a Port Victoria and Margate pleasure cruise used the pier but little effort was made to develop the line's local traffic potential - a station at Stoke was again refused in October 1897.

In February 1898 the SER reached an agreement with the Royal Corinthian Yacht Club to build a clubhouse at Port Victoria, which opened in 1899 and continued in use until 1914. The SER was paid £133 by the Yacht Club for this purpose.

Although it had its origins in local desires to improve agriculture, the Hundred of Hoo line was eventually built because it offered the SER a chance of seizing an advantage over the LCDR in the struggle for the continental traffic. Because the line failed to do this so spectacularly, it can be cited as an example of the legendary Watkin profligacy - yet it cannot be denied that Port Victoria was an excellent site for a port. Watkin's error was in seeing it as a passenger port, for since 1950 the site has become an important deep-sea oil terminal and, at the time of writing, there are proposals to use it as a container terminal. In many ways, also, it was no worse a site than the Great Eastern turned to advantage at Parkeston Quay in Essex, and it was potentially far better than the LCDR's confined position at Queenborough. A failure in Watkin's day, Port Victoria achieved success only 70 years after its initial opening. As with his other infamous failure, the Channel Tunnel, the idea was right but the timing wrong; ironic, then, that the branch to Grain should eventually play a part in the construction of the Channel Tunnel in the 1980s and 1990s.[37]

1. R.H.G.Thomas, **The London & Greenwich Railway,** p.12. This is a highly detailed account of the L&GR and is to be recommended as a model of railway history.
2. **Maidstone Journal,** 16 June 1835.
3. **Ibid,** 2 February 1836.
4. Right-hand running was again used from 1850 for Greenwich line trains.
5. Thomas, p.53.
6. **Railway Times,** 28 September 1839.
7. **Herapath's Railway Magazine,** October 1836.
8. **The Times,** 15 December 1836; the **Maidstone Journal** made the speed claim, though **The Times** thought 20mph more likely.
9. **Herapath,** March 1837.
10. **Maidstone Journal,** January 1836. The **Journal** seems to have made a mistake, for the line was more likely to cost £660,000.
11. Thomas, p.108
12. **Railway Times,** 13 January 1844.
13. SER Minutes, 11 June 1844.
14. **Maidstone Journal,** 12 May 1846.

15. H.V.Borley, **Chronology of London Railways,** gives simply "1849" for Abbey Wood as does R.H.Clark, **Southern Region Record,** for Northfleet.
16. **Railway Times,** 16 March 1850.
17. SER Report, January 1851.
18. See article by J.N.Young in **Railway Magazine,** October 1973.
19. For this and the date of Belvedere, see Borley.
20. **Railway Times,** 15 August 1863.
21. SER Minutes, 26 March 1874.
22. **Railway Times,** 28 August 1869.
23. This is the spelling used for the first few references in SER sources.
24. SER Minutes, 2 January 1873. Dates given in the Minutes <u>after</u> the event are usually reliable, but Thomas, **L&GR,** gives 11 January.
25. SER Minutes, 11 January 1877.
26. **Ibid**, 22 June 1871.
27. For a full description see article in Journal of the **Railway & Canal Historical Society,** March 1982, p.71. The author gives 1876 as the opening of the SER connection.
28. Bradley gives the story in detail but Kidner, **The North Kent Line,** suggests that the whole story is a fabrication.
29. E.Course, **The Bexleyheath Line.**
30. Bexley Heath Railway Minutes, 23 October 1883.
31. **Ibid,** 27 September 1887.
32. **Railway Times,** 7 August 1840.
33. SER Minutes, 28 August 1856.
34. SER Minutes, 12 August 1880.
35. Authorised 11 August 1881.
36. P.Bagwell in **Journal of Transport History,** 1955.
37. V. Mitchell and K. Smith, **Branch Line to Allhallows** 1989.

CHAPTER 7: THE BRICKLAYERS ARMS BRANCH

As has been seen from the failed quest for a route to the "Obelisk" in St George's Fields, the South Eastern directors recognised at an early stage the value of a terminus convenient for the West End. Their desire for a "West End terminus" was strengthened by a feeling that London Bridge was cramped and inconvenient, so that as early as May 1841 the shareholders were informed that the South Eastern - in concert with the London & Croydon - was hoping to buy land at Bricklayers Arms.[1]

For a while plans lay moribund, but in September 1842 the Board were once more discussing a "Kent Road" scheme with the Croydon Company. At this stage they expected it to be a joint line and to include a goods station since London Bridge was too restricted to handle this type of traffic. Initial ideas for a line as far as Grange Road were soon replaced by a longer one to Bricklayers Arms and by early December 1842 the SER had bought 23 acres there for £35,000 and its plans were expected to meet "warm opposition".[2]

Such opposition was most likely to come from the SER's erstwhile partners and landlords on the London Bridge route. Certainly the Board had realised that a "West End" terminus would have the added advantage of placing the SER in a stronger position when negotiating with the Greenwich Company over tolls. At the General Meeting in December 1842 the Board reported that their decision to press ahead with a Bill for the line to Bricklayers Arms was partly inspired by the London & Greenwich's refusal to accept the SER's 3rd Class traffic. Thus all SER 3rd Class passengers were having to join and leave its services at New Cross - a situation which would be rectified by a new line to Bricklayers Arms. The line was estimated at £200,000 but by late December the SER felt less certain about the L&CR's commitment to the project while the Brighton was not interested.

In early February 1843 the SER felt that the Brighton was becoming more interested and negotiations had begun with the Croydon to give it a share in the management of the Bricklayers Arms line in exchange for subscribing one-third of the capital. However it is significant that the Board of Trade then became involved in the arguments over the Greenwich Company's tolls: by March the SER was prepared to abandon the Bricklayers Arms line altogether if sufficient space for both their passenger and goods traffics was provided at London Bridge[3]. On 11 March William Gladstone, the Vice-President of the Board of Trade, met some of the Greenwich directors in an attempt to persuade them to alter their attitude to the tolls, but even he failed[4]; therefore the SER and the L&CR pressed ahead with the scheme and the SER's Act of 1843 authorised it to raise an extra £177,000 to pay for its share of the line. The branch was authorised by Act of 4 July 1843. Miraculously, the South Eastern heard from the Greenwich early in August 1843 - they wanted to discuss access to the new station.

Construction of the line was very rapid since much of it was built on a wooden viaduct, with the work done by Grissell & Peto. As early as March 1844 the South Eastern had decided on the train service for the new station - there would be five per day with three on Sundays and 3rd Class carriages would cease running to London Bridge.

Lewis Cubitt, later to achieve greater fame with his design for the buildings at King's Cross, was employed to design buildings at Bricklayers Arms that would create the correctly impressive appearance needed for a "West End" terminus[5]. Less impressive was the construction work - on 11 April 1844 about 200ft of the station roof fell in and two men were killed, one more dying later. However, this did not delay the opening of the station which took place on 1 May 1844 from which time the SER ceased to use New Cross. The station buildings at Bricklayers Arms cost £89,000. In contrast the signalling for the main-line junction cost a mere £150. The engineer of the London & Croydon Railway, C.H.Gregory, installed an elevated platform at the junction from which to control points and signals, though this may have been introduced before the branch was open; it has been seen as the first actual signalbox[6].

The London & Croydon was pressing for a line to be laid into the new terminus for use by its atmospheric trains during May 1844, and also for the terminus to be opened up for use by Brighton trains. As no tolls had to be paid to the Greenwich, fares to the new terminus were cheaper. The new station therefore had an almost immediate effect in that the Greenwich Company gave in to pressure over its tolls system and agreed to the Croydon's proposals in July 1844: the inevitable result of that was that the Croydon at first started running more trains to London Bridge again (thus giving an equal service to both stations), at the beginning of March 1845 reduced the Bricklayers Arms service to only two per day, and finally gave up running passenger trains to Bricklayers Arms altogether after 31 March 1845.

It is clear that Bricklayers Arms was a complete failure as a passenger terminus. As early as 6 July 1844 the *Railway Times* was ridiculing it, reporting that the takings per week were as low as £507. The SER Directors had to consider what to do with the station and in September 1844 received a suggestion from the Croydon that they should extend the line from Bricklayers Arms to join the London & South Western Railway at Waterloo. Indeed, by the early months of 1845 the SER was considering starting its North Kent line from a point between Hungerford and Waterloo Bridges, running from there to Bricklayers Arms, and then to North Kent. Perhaps because of this the SER agreed to buy out the L&CR's share in the branch and station in 1845 - it paid £82,877[7]. The SER was also aware that Bricklayers Arms could be used as a locomotive depot in place of New Cross.

A lively incident occurred on the branch on 10 December 1844 when the locomotive *Forester* suffered a firebox explosion whilst on the wooden viaduct section. The blast damaged the viaduct so badly that the locomotive fell through it onto the ground below and two men were killed. Faulty safety valves were blamed.

In October 1846 the future role of Bricklayers Arms was beginning to clarify - for it was agreed that the LBSCR would use the station for its goods traffic whilst Messrs Hoof were contracted to build a SER engine shed there for £4935. The South Eastern attempted to accomodate Brighton goods traffic on the

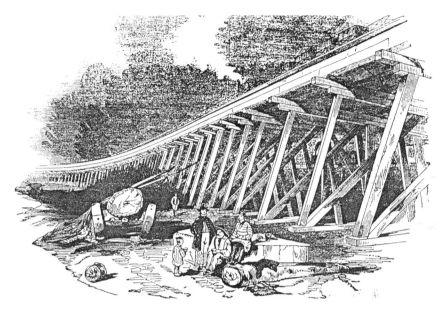

21. The approaches to Bricklayers Arms.

cheap - within a month the LBSC was complaining about having to unload goods traffic at passenger platforms.

The idea of starting the North Kent line at or near Hungerford Bridge did not reach fruition until the Charing Cross scheme several years later, but the SER was actively expanding its North Kent network. The original junction for the Bricklayers Arms branch had been deliberately sited so that up trains would not have to use London & Greenwich tracks beyond the L&C/L&G junction at Corbetts Lane, but the new North Kent route was to leave the Greenwich route further east at North Kent East Junction. In December 1846 the SER therefore decided to include powers for a new Bricklayers Arms Junction line to connect its station directly to the North Kent route, with an original estimate of the cost at £55,000. Much of the work on this line was done by John Brogden, the contractor who provoked a boardroom row; it included a bridge under the main-line. The line opened from North Kent West Junction to Surrey Canal Junction on 1 September 1849, with both passenger (an intensive service every 15 minutes) and goods trains using it. An exchange platform at this junction seems to have opened on 1 September as well[8]. The Board envisaged the use of "light engines" for the connecting service; in January 1848 they had ordered the construction of one in the workshops at Bricklayers Arms - it had to be capable of carrying seven passengers and parcels "on the machine".

Clearly the idea of running North Kent trains into Bricklayers Arms was unsuccessful, for by May 1850 the Board was discussing whether connecting trains should be run to link the "West End" terminus with the North Kent trains. It was felt that a new station could be opened at New Cross (on the North Kent line, opened in 1850) or at "Bricklayers Arms Junction" - the latter suggestion presumably being an error, for this point was on the old Croydon line. This would seem to explain the opening of New Cross & Naval School station, probably on 1 October 1850 and replacing the exchange platform at Surrey Canal Junction which closed the previous day[9]. This station provided a better service for residents of the district, though some North Kent trains continued to have connections to Bricklayers Arms from New Cross & Naval School, probably until 1852.

Less satisfactory still was the construction of the station; on 28 August 1850 part of it "tumbled down"[10] after being hit by a train. The *Annual Register* recorded that the whole roof collapsed into the space between its retaining walls, "leaving nothing but the broken gas-lamps and the bare walls on either side of the station." In October 1851 the SER decided to convert much of the wooden viaduct on the branch into an embankment, and this seems to have been done by September 1852.

The attempts to revive Bricklayers Arms passenger traffic with North Kent passengers was a failure. The service was reduced in March 1850 and from 31 January 1852 the station lost all regular passenger services[11], though it was occasionally used for excursions thereafter and infrequent Royal journeys until Charing Cross was opened. Queen Victoria used Bricklayers Arms for a journey to Tunbridge Wells on 23 June 1849 and it was used for a few Royal occasions thereafter, generally in connection with sailings to or from Gravesend. Princess Alexandra of Denmark used it in March 1863.

By this time the LBSCR had a growing presence on the Bricklayers Arms branch, having opened its own goods depot on the north side of the line at Willow Walk in July 1849. The SER had given the LBSCR five acres there in exchange for running powers over the "Croydon up line" which ran from Norwood Junction to Corbetts Lane and which was later to cause controversy. The Willow Walk goods station was enlarged in 1854-5 while the SER was left to use the actual Bricklayers Arms site on its own though there was a serious fire there in 1857.

22. The exterior of the Bricklayers Arms terminus in 1845.

The SER continued to increase its facilities at the site as goods traffic grew. New hop and grain warehouses were built in 1860, the goods station being especially convenient for serving the merchants of Borough who traditionally handled such Kent produce. Also in 1860, £2000 was spent on new sidings, £3777 on an engine shed and £400 on a turntable. Not all problems were solved though - an accident at Commercial Dock station in July 1860 was blamed on the muddy water from Bricklayers Arms causing poor steaming.

In 1865 the SER began a scheme to improve access to Bricklayers Arms so that it could be used as a carriage depot, involving many empty stock movements on the branch; this cost about £18,000. However Bricklayers Arms was a poor choice for a carriage depot since access to it was poor from all three SER London stations and involved reversal, so in 1874 the Board conceived a bold plan to convert the whole site into a goods station and dispense with the carriage depot function altogether. Carriages could be dealt with in the triangle between the North Kent and Greenwich lines, it was believed. This decision was probably spurred on by the SER's belief that vast new freight flows would begin once the Blackfriars Junction line had been opened, connecting it to the Great Northern and Midland Railways.

Extra land was bought and the carriage sheds converted into goods accomodation. Level crossings on the line were replaced with bridges. The new flow of goods traffic from the north began in 1877 and soon caused problems because, as with the coaching stock, reversal was necessary to get onto the branch at Bricklayers Arms Junction. In July 1878 the LBSCR complained that the shunting that took place on the main line was "a great risk to the safe working of passenger traffic."

On 5 August there was an accident at Bricklayers Arms Junction which the Board of Trade inspector, Colonel Yolland, blamed on the lack of effective signalling. Three days later the SER met the LBSCR to discuss providing alternative goods accomodation on the main-line just south of Corbetts Lane. The possibility of moving all the goods accomodation to St Johns was also considered.

However there were other issues which influenced the situation at Bricklayers Arms. Early in September there were lengthy discussions about the SER position in South London, which were stimulated by the London & North Western's interest in a line to join it at Clapham, via Brixton, to the SER. A number of suggestions were then put forward by men such as Watkin and Hawkshaw; one was for a direct line from the Blackfriars Junction line to Bricklayers Arms, or from Charing Cross and Cannon Street to the former "West End" terminus. A clear intention here was to use the station for both goods and coaching stock purposes. A third idea was for a "relief line" from Corbetts Lane into Bricklayers Arms to get rid of the need for reversal. It was also felt that the locomotive depot could be moved back to New Cross.

Improvements were, in fact, very piecemeal. The branch was widened at the crossing of the Rotherhithe Canal and a new bridge for St James' Road constructed for £14,070. But by the time the Midland Railway added its goods services to those of the Great Northern coming in from the Blackfriars Junction line, on 1 April 1879, little else had been achieved.

In January 1882 the SER drew up plans to connect the Bricklayers Arms branch with the Croydon up line at Corbetts Lane and at the same time entertained ideas once more of extending from Bricklayers Arms towards

Charing Cross and Cannon Street. The Corbetts Lane proposal was at first withdrawn on the request of the LBSCR but then revived in 1884; an Act was obtained on 31 July 1885 but no work done.

The branch was left to continue in more or less the same condition, though much of its work was eventually taken over by the yards developed at Hither Green. In 1897 the SER decided to invest a further £6000 in extending the goods sheds at Bricklayers Arms. All the wagon turntables in the main goods sheds needed replacing and the chance of rearranging the lines was taken. At the end of 1898 it was decided to install electric lights throughout the depot, with the cost expected to reach £25,000.

1.   SER General Meeting Report, 31 May 1841.
2.   **Maidstone Journal,** 6 December 1842. J.Howard-Turner, p.194, gives 26 acres.
3.   SER Minutes, 7 March 1843.
4.   R.H.G.Thomas, **The London & Greenwich Railway,** p.146.
5.   J.Howard-Turner, p.196, refers to William Tite in connection with these buildings. A.A.Jackson, **London's Termini,** refers only to Cubitt.
6.   J.Howard-Turner, p.199.
7.   **Railway Times,** 27 March 1847.
8.   According to research by R.Fellowes, sent to the author by R.W.Kidner.
9.   J.E.Connor & B.L.Halford, **Forgotten Stations of Greater London,** refers to a station at North Kent Junction as closing 1 October 1850.
10.   The complaint of a shareholder, September 1850.
11.   SER Minutes, 22 & 27 January 1852.

CHAPTER 8: TO THE WEST END AND THE CITY

1. Charing Cross and Cannon Street

As has been seen in previous chapters, the SER realised very early in its career that London Bridge was not the solution to all its terminal problems in the Metropolis. In September 1835 it had considered a link to the LSWR and as early as 1836 it had given serious consideration to a line to St George's Fields and on 1 May 1844 a line to a supposed West End terminus had opened to Bricklayers Arms; previous to this, in 1842, New Cross had been advertised as the station for the West End! At the General Meeting of its shareholders in February 1845, much was made of the plan for a line to a "great terminal station opposite to Hungerford Market." This was part of a much wider proposal for a line to serve the whole North Kent district, and extending as far east as Chilham, for which a Bill had been deposited in December 1844.

However this SER proposal was one of several rival schemes for the district which went before the Board of Trade. The SER offered various benefits for its scheme, including an extension from Bricklayers Arms to Hungerford Bridge, but although the Board of Trade reported in favour of the SER scheme it was rejected on standing orders.

The South Eastern did not abandon hope, and the following Parliamentary session brought forward a Bill for a line from Waterloo Bridge to Bricklayers Arms, designed by Robert Stephenson. This Bill was rejected in 1846; all the SER could do to increase its representation in the West End was, in August 1846, to rent a house at Regent Circus[1] as a parcels and information office.

With the decline in competitive schemes after the Railway Mania, the SER lost interest in an extension to serve the West End and instead was content to invest capital in improving London Bridge station. Regent Circus continued to act as the western outpost, in the care of a clerk earning £100 per annum.

In February 1849 the SER decided to take a house in Cheapside as a booking office for its City customers, a reflection that it was aware of the isolation of London Bridge even from the City. Yet probably the most crucial factor in the SER's attitude to extensions within London was its acceptance, in 1852, that Bricklayers Arms was a failure as a station for the West End. From then on the construction of new lines was more likely, though the SER was resolutely cautious - refusing, for example, an invitation to join in a "circular line" to connect the main London termini in October 1852.

In 1854 the question of improving the railway position in London became much more critical and a number of proposals were made, including one by the Westminster Terminus Railway. This was authorised in 1854, for a station at Horseferry Road. In July 1855 the *Railway Times* reported that the SER supported the idea of a line from Norwood to Clapham (the West End of London & Crystal Palace) to take advantage of this and wanted a clause in the Bill allowing it to invest.

The London & South Western Railway wrote to the SER in February 1856 and offered the use of their own station at Waterloo, which had opened in 1848. Teulon rejected this on behalf of the SER, arguing that new road schemes would make extensions unnecessary. Another offer followed in October 1856, when the WELCP offered the use of its own terminus at Battersea on the same conditions as those offered to the LBSCR.

No doubt one of the factors behind the WELCP's offer was the need to ensure high levels of traffic on lines built - at considerable expense - through urban areas. At this time the SER still had a number of opponents to expansion in its midst, and in June 1857 Kay and Child were vigorously opposing any talk of better access to the West End. Nonetheless, as the summer of 1857 came to an end the SER was increasingly drawn into discussion of just such an issue; it discussed the West End in September, then in October it discussed Ashcroft's plan for a line from New Cross to Battersea. It was at the latter meeting, 26 October, that the name of Charing Cross was first recorded in the Minutes. A week later the SER decided that it was not interested in the plan by the Victoria Station & Pimlico Railway, an associate of the LBSCR, for an extension of the WELCP line across the river from Battersea into Pimlico. The scheme was again discussed by the SER in December, when it was considered as a possible factor in the promotion of a Beckenham & Brighton line. The VSPR received its Act of Parliament in 1858.

Some of the more progressive elements within the SER took a more positive approach and, guided chiefly by Samuel Smiles, began to promote a separate company that would extend a line from London Bridge to the site of the Hungerford Market on the western bank of the Thames. This scheme was to include a connection with the LSWR at Waterloo and intermediate stations at Blackfriars Road and close to London Bridge. The SER's surveyor and law clerk were also involved in the promotion.

The delays of the anti-expansionist phase had already created the damage, so that by early 1858 the SER Board was becoming aware of the threat posed by the East Kent Railway. In March 1858 they read a full report by their own engineer on the Charing Cross scheme, which was then estimated at £1.2m including land. It was expected to include £75,000 to alter London Bridge, £111,000 for a four-track viaduct from Wellington Street to the Thames, £208,000 for a bridge across the river and £112,653 for the terminus - for which a choice of sites at Northumberland House, Craven Street and Hungerford Street were being considered.

On 14 June the SER learnt that the LSWR was not interested in making Charing Cross a joint station, though it was prepared to alter Waterloo station - but ten days later the SER learnt that it had changed its mind.

Such was the SER's worry about the EKR that it now seemed anxious to maintain as many opportunities as possible. In July 1858 it discussed the proposed New Cross to Battersea line again, then it began negotiations with both the WELCP and the VSP for the running of between six and eight trains a day at mileage rates or 6d a passenger. The following month the SER calculated that if it carried 100,000 passengers to Victoria, it would have to pay £14,950 in expenses and tolls. Watkin was involved in these discussions during October.

During November the SER held talks with the South London Railway, whose proposed line from London Bridge and Spa Road to Victoria would have been of use for some SER services, but SER powers to use Victoria were omitted from its own Bill. On 12 November the SER took part in talks with the LSWR and the LNWR over the West & South London Junction Railway, in which the other two companies had agreed to invest £100,000 each.

Any extension of the SER to the west of the LBSCR would have infringed the territorial agreement of 10 July 1848 between the two concerns, so the most realistic prospect for the SER remained the Charing Cross scheme. The main problem with this was always likely to be the cost of land, though in November 1858 the *Railway Times* did try to ease the fears of the wealthy by commenting that it would run through the "poorest districts" with stations at Blackfriars and Southwark Bridge Road. On 8 December Teulon suggested that the SER should subscribe £200,000 towards it.

An engineer closely involved with the Charing Cross scheme was John Hawkshaw and his report on the plan was discussed by the SER on 22 December 1858, by which time the Bill for the line was well advanced in readiness for the ensuing Parliamentary session. He reported that Hungerford Market had been agreed as the site for the terminus; the station was to occupy a space 700 feet long, while a width of 150 feet would allow sufficient room for both the SER and the LSWR. He estimated the cost of land at £450,000 and the works at £360,000. Joseph Locke had estimated the bridge across the Thames at £90,000, but Hawkshaw observed that the Hungerford footbridge had cost £150,000. The SER felt that the allowance of £80,000 for the station was too little, and noted that the LSWR was not interested. Nonetheless, the SER decided to subscribe £300,000 to the undertaking with the right to have three representatives on the Board.

The first minuted meeting of the London Bridge & Charing Cross (the "London Bridge" was soon dropped) was held on 4 January 1859 - before the passing of its Act. Its directors, on which the SER representation was recorded as four by the *Railway Times*, included many with SER connections. Lord Alfred Paget was a SER shareholder whilst those who were current, past or future SER directors included Whatman, Byng, Teulon, Thomson and Mellor. Hawkshaw was also on the Board, along with Charles Villiers. Discussions included whether the contractor Wythes should be awarded the contract since he was prepared to subscribe.

The Charing Cross Railway was different from much of the SER in that it was a purely urban line and land costs formed a much larger part of its committments than was normal. On 4 January its Board decided that it would pay a maximum of £157,000 for Hungerford Market, but on 16 February reported that it had agreed on £235,000. The *Railway Times,* 25 January 1862, reported the payment of £50,000 and a further £110,000 had been paid by August 1862. Its line was to replace the Hungerford suspension bridge, so the Board decided to offer a maximum of £30,000 for the bridge plus £50,000 or possibly £60,000 for the right to charge tolls; in February it reported that £125,000 had been agreed.

Under these circumstances, a *Railway Times* report on 5 February that the scheme would cost only £800,000 seems rather a low assessment, though it did also say that the LSWR had renewed interest though it still petitioned against the Bill. More serious was the opposition of the LBSCR, for which powers to use the line were originally to have been included but were removed in February 1859, and the Brighton company was unable to prevent the Bill passing through the Commons in April. SER Minutes of 7 July suggest that the SER bought off LBSCR opposition by promising not to seek running powers for itself to Portsmouth!

The Parliamentary passage of the Bill was unusually complex due to the number of vested interests involved, all marshalled by the experienced Railway committee member, Lord Redesdale. One of the problems was that the planned line passed very close to the north wing of St Thomas' Hospital and so in April 1859 the Charing Cross company offered its governors £20,000. This was rejected since the north wing would be "rendered totally unfit for patients" - the governors wanted an entirely new site.

Lord Redesdale's work resulted in a a number of changes being made to the Bill in March 1859. He required that the name of the company be changed from London Bridge & Charing Cross to plain Charing Cross, that the powers for other companies to subscribe should be limited to £300,000 for the SER and £100,000 for the LSWR, that the signals at London Bridge should be in the SER's control, those at Waterloo in the charge of the LSWR and the remainder controlled by the CCR itself. The Act was passed on 8 August 1859.

23. Cannon Street soon after opening. Note the pedestrian walkway on the west and a rather high number of workers on the track. (E.Course Collection)

By the time the Act was passed the LSWR's attitude had become lukewarm again, though on 2 August the CCR learnt that the LSWR wished to have spare land kept at the terminus for its future use. Two weeks later Hawkshaw reported that an extra £60,000 would be needed to make the Thames bridge four tracks instead of two; this was reduced by persuading Wythes, the contractor, to take 25% of the excess in shares. Wythes' contract included the construction of stations at Charing Cross and Blackfriars. SER connections were increased in December when Samuel Smiles became the CCR's secretary.

Even the Charing Cross line was not to give the SER an invincible lead over its spendthrift and energetic rival, the LCDR, for the rival concern promoted a Bill in 1859-60 for a line via Blackfriars to Ludgate on the edge of the City, extending to join the Metropolitan Railway near Farringdon. This was to cross over the Charing Cross line and the CCR noticed in February 1860 that the planned bridge would only allow for two tracks on the CCR route. Despite strenuous opposition, the LCDR's City line was authorised in August 1860.

Under this pressure, the CCR was pushed forward with uncharacteristic speed. However, its £800,000 capital was proving a problem, with the SER taking £300,000, Wythes £126,000 and other shareholders (most of whom were also interested in the SER) £53,400 only. Work on taking down the suspension bridge had begun by February 1860, with the CCR hoping it could sell the materials for use at Clifton, near Bristol. Byng, wearing two hats as a director of the SER and the CCR, led negotiations with himself as to whether the CCR should be absorbed by the SER. SER shareholders learnt that:

"It is most undesirable, looking at the probable future value of the Railway and terminus....that it should be in any way controlled or influenced by independent, or it may be hostile, interests...[2]"

Thus by March 1860 the CCR had offered the SER terms of 5% on capital value, with CCR stock available at £110 per £100 share. Significantly, there was a lot of opposition to this deal within the SER - led by Rich and Kay; the Board decided to delay any purchase until the resolution of the Parliamentary contest with the LCDR.

The financial situation of the CCR was anything but sound, especially as land problems continued. Coles Child, a director of the Hungerford Bridge Company, owned a coal wharf on the south side of the River for which he wanted £10,000 - provoking a lively row in the process; the issue was resolved in his favour in September though in 1863 the railway press reported that he had received £12,000. By the end of March 1860 the *Railway Times*, always on the look out for a sensation, was putting the latest claim by the governors of St Thomas' Hospital at £750,000 for the whole site. Despite all this, work on the bridge was well under way by April and the CCR obtained the land of an old hat factory cheaply. An Act of 23 July fixed an agreement between the CCR and the Hungerford Market.

During May 1860 Lord Chandos of the LNWR contacted the CCR about a possible link between Charing Cross and Euston.

Work on the piers of the bridge advanced well during the summer, reaching forty feet into the river bed by August. Work in raising money was less successful, with £355,000 still unsubscribed.

Despite the unhealthy state of the CCR, the SER was driven ever forward by the competition of the LCDR. Once the latter had secured powers for a line into the City, the SER was always likely to be drawn into a further effort itself. Hawkshaw submitted a plan to the CCR directors on 25 October 1860, arguing that a short branch to Cannon Street would allow the SER to gain a traffic that the LCDR never could - people who wished to travel between the City and the West End. With the proposed line, Hawkshaw stated, such a journey could be made in five or six minutes and would avoid the crowded roads. The branch, about 800 yards long, was then discussed by the SER and a City Terminus Bill prepared.

To be an attractive proposition, this short line would have to operate a frequent service, and that posed problems of congestion for the Charing Cross line itself. During January and February 1861 there was therefore much discussion of widening the line. Hawkshaw's suggestion was that the line should be four tracks from Charing Cross, over the bridge to Belvedere Road just west of Waterloo; also that a third track should be provided for the City local service from there to Red Cross Street, where the City branch would diverge, at a cost of £30,000 for works and £40,000 for land. The SER General Meeting that February also heard of these plans, though with an additional proposal to widen the terminus at a cost of £55,000.

Hawkshaw had also suggested that the scheme could be funded by selling hotel rights at Charing Cross for £100,000. This proved to be highly optimistic, as subsequent negotiations with Edward Middleton Barry, the architect, showed. On 28 February 1861 the CCR hoped to get £80,000 for leasing a hotel to Barry, but he only offered £70,000 which was rejected. By May 1862 the CCR was looking for takers at £50,000!

The clash with St Thomas' Hospital rumbled on until, in March 1861, the Board of Trade appointed Mr Stewart as arbitrator. In December 1861 he reported that the maximum to be paid by the CCR for the whole of the site should be £296,000; although only a very small proportion of the land was required for the railway, it was likely that the rest could be sold for redevelopment. However St Thomas' would not allow its land to be taken over until 26 July 1862. The SER was able to sell most of the unwanted land for £170,000 in 1865.

During 1862 the Charing Cross scheme continued to cause political disturbances within SER circles. The Mid Kent Railway wanted running powers, in the summer General Meeting of the SER shareholders complained that £650,000 of SER money had been absorbed in the Charing Cross line and £250,000 in the City line. During the autumn the SER considered a Bill for amalgamation but there were fears that if a Bill was deposited other companies could use it to force access.

On 9 August 1862 the Charing Cross Company began to receive its first income, for from that date it began to collect the tolls on the footbridge across the Thames. Its staff there included a chief collector on 27s 6d a week, four other collectors on 25s and a sweeper on 18s. The bridge was kept in use until the footways of the new railway bridge were ready, then its materials were removed for the Clifton Bridge Company which had paid £5,000 for them. From 28 August the CCR also began to collect the pier tolls at Hungerford. In November the bridge and pier staff were provided with mops, tools and brooms by the SER Stores Department, while work on repairing the landing stage got under way. For the Duke of Wellington's funeral in 1863 the CCR charged a 1d toll on the bridge. It had to be closed for a time each year to maintain the legal right to charge a toll; this was done on the night of 10 March 1863.

Various questions now needed to be resolved. Where were the intermediate stations to be? The idea of having one just west of London Bridge was made impracticable by the Cannon Street branch, but there had been requests for stations in Bridge Street and Southwark Bridge Road. Ground in Villiers Street was being cleared in November for the foundations of a hotel, to be run by a new company called the Charing Cross Hotel Company. During December

Barry submitted plans for the hotel and booking offices and it was arranged that Lucas would build them.

In December 1862 the position of the CCR was examined in the railway press. Work on the bridge was well advanced, with six 154ft spans and three 100ft, using two of the masonry piers from Brunel's old bridge. There were to be four tracks across the river and a footway either side, widening to seven tracks on the station approach. The footpaths were producing an annual income of £4,000 by March 1864. The *Railway Times* was concerned about the CCR finances, claiming that £1,356,000 had been raised when £1,926,000 was needed and it blamed Hawkshaw for poor estimates. The SER had to lend a further £100,000 in March 1863.

The construction of the new line affected London Bridge station. The LBSCR complained in December 1862 about a new approach road being built to help develop the former hospital site, while in January 1863 the SER decided to vacate its old offices, which were to be demolished, and move to Cannon Street. In the meanwhile it was to use four houses in St Thomas Street.

The CCR complained of slow work by the iron contractor, Cochrane, in April 1863 at which time the old bridge was being removed. By June it was alleging "culpable negligence" by the ironwork contractor, though Wythes blamed Ashcroft for getting in the way! Work was further delayed by a dispute in the iron industry.

At Charing Cross there were to be six platform lines and a 164ft span roof above. The booking offices were to be built into the lower floor of the hotel, but there had been a delay in getting this started. During October 1863 Lucas agreed to put up a temporary covering over these offices so that the line could open as early as possible.

Saxby & Farmer were appointed to install the signals for £6,740 and by 5 November the connections between the CCR and the SER at London Bridge were complete. The link with the LSWR had apparently been "tested" the previous month.

On 1 December 1863 a trial trip over the line was made, with a tour of its facilities. This seems to have given rise to a report in the *Annual Register* that the line opened that day, and the *Bromley Record* stated that it opened on 2 December. Captain Tyler of the Board of Trade tested the bridge in late December and made a full inspection on 30 December, recommending some minor changes and thus preventing the hoped-for opening on 1 January 1866. Work continued so much that the Home Office complained about work being done on a Sunday, 3 January 1864, and Tyler reinspected it the following day.

In fact the line opened with the departure of the 7.10am Charing Cross to Greenwich on 11 January 1864 but for Greenwich and Mid Kent trains only, using temporary platforms at Villiers Street, with an intermediate station at Blackfriars and new through high level platforms at London Bridge on the site of the old L&CR station; there was an immediate complaint from the LSWR that the spur from its Waterloo station to the CCR at Waterloo Junction had not also been opened. *The Times* felt that it had been a mistake to entrust Hawkshaw with the architectural embellishments to the various bridges which were "the ugliest ever yet put up" while that crossing the approach road to London Bridge was "the ugliest viaduct of all." On 10 February the LSWR told the SER that it was prepared to wait for the link to be opened - presumably there was not a lot to be gained until the City branch was completed. The

Charing Cross line proved attractive almost immediately, carrying 119,829 passengers in its first 21 days - an annual rate of 2,200,000. To make the station even more of a feature, the CCR decided in February 1864 to spend £1,600 erecting a supposed replica of an Eleanor Cross, designed by E.M.Barry, outside the terminus.

A whole clutch of related Bills were being proposed. In August 1863 the CCR, SER, LNWR, GNR and MR had met to discuss a line from Charing Cross to the northern termini at a cost of about £2,000,000. There was also a plan to join the GWR at Hammersmith with a line via South Kensington. By April 1864 Hawkshaw's proposed Hampstead, Tottenham & Charing Cross Junction was being supported by the LNWR and SER, though the CCR was opposed to the suggested link to the Metropolitan District Railway at Embankment. The CCR was opposed to the Metropolitan District Bill as well. An Act for Hawkshaw's line from Hampstead Road to Charing Cross was passed on 25 July 1864 as the North Western & Charing Cross Railway but abandoned in 1868 with the SER left to pay the legal costs; it was a victim of the 1866 financial crisis.

From 1 May 1864 the main SER services began to use the Charing Cross line, the SER having ordered six tank and four tender locos to help with the extra traffic; the delay in opening for main-line traffic was due to the slow work on the station roof.In May 1864 the new line carried 296,537 passengers though the SER was concerned about the sharp curves near London Bridge and wanted guide rails fitted. In June 1864 it persuaded the CCR to spend £50,000 on buying land for locomotive sidings at Stoney Street.

The Charing Cross Railway was absorbed into the SER from 1 September 1864.

As has been seen, the Charing Cross company had decided to build a line to a terminus in the City. The City Terminus Bill was prepared late in 1860, with an estimated cost of £525,000 for a line of about 900 yards. The Act was passed on 28 June 1861 with permission for the SER to subscribe £250,000 of the £525,000 capital. An attempt to get the LSWR to invest failed. Some shareholders, though, doubted whether the idea of running frequent trains to connect the City and the West End would be profitable, but in December 1862 the SER decided to move its offices to Unity Buildings in Cannon Street at a cost of £100,000. In September 1863 it was decided to build an hotel at Cannon Street as well but within a few months the Cannon Street - Charing Cross service seemed threatened by the promotion of the Metropolitan District Railway along the Embankment.

There were some delays over the plans for the bridge on the City line, but by September 1864 the side walls and roof at Cannon Street were progressing well - though Cochrane was again in trouble for slow work with the bridge and roof iron. However Cochrane blamed the delays on several changes to the plans and was partially right to do so - there had originally been an intention for the bridge to be "fan-shaped" at the City end and then it had been decided to add pedestrian walkways on the Hungerford bridge pattern to raise extra revenue. The SER hoped to have the line completed to Thames Street by May 1865.

Though the City line was expensive, it did not have the severe land problems that the Charing Cross line had faced. £300 had to be spent on removing bodies from a graveyard and the cost of the walls, roof and booking offices at Cannon Street was £84,000. The SER also decided to press ahead with the locomotive depot at Stoney Street on the Southwark side, costing £25,000 for land and £30,000 for the works.

By January 1865 the SER was beginning to assess the potential of its new property. It was anxious to talk to the LSWR about using both new stations but a proposed line from Cannon Street to Kingston and Richmond, in which the SER and the LCDR were both interested and which was to be worked by the SER, upset the LSWR. News in January 1866 that three SER representatives were to join the Board of this concern soured relations further though in March Watkin offered to abandon it if the LSWR would drop a scheme for a line to Mitcham and Croydon from Wimbledon. The LSWR protested its innocence; of the schemes associated with the SER, the Kennington, Clapham & Brixton was rejected by Parliament and the City, Kingston & Richmond was withdrawn.

Looking for finance elsewhere in 1865, the SER felt that over £3,000 could be gained per annum by renting the 147 arches on the Charing Cross line. A third line was being put down on the parts of the Charing Cross line which would also handle Cannon Street traffic. A further Act was obtained to raise an extra £500,000 but the cost of the City and West End lines was proving exorbitant: by August 1865 £2,560,134 had been spent on the land and £1,217,016 on the actual works. To this can be added further incidental costs, such as the £16,000 spent on seven bogie tank engines for the Charing Cross to Cannon Street service.

Ironically the opening of Cannon Street was delayed by the works for the Metropolitan District Railway, which passed beneath the station forecourt. When Colonel Yolland inspected the line in June 1866 he postponed opening for at least one month and the SER decided to set a date of 1 September, with the Duke of Edinburgh performing an opening ceremony on 7 August.

The Cannon Street terminus and the two spurs from London Bridge and Charing Cross opened on 1 September amidst a howl of disapproval. *The Times* felt that there were too many signals for the men to control, citing 67 levers in one box, while *The Engineer* reported that 108 changes of points or signals were needed in a peak hour; the *Railway Times* commented that "Never has ignorance been more patent, never extravagance more profound" and quoted the cost of the London extensions at £4,100,000. The main cause of the difficulties seems to have been that the plan to work virtually all trains into and out of Cannon Street, with relatively few going directly from Charing Cross to London Bridge, caused a large number of conflicting movements. Both spurs into Cannon Street had three tracks (the direct Charing Cross to London Bridge section had two), with only one available for down trains to handle the local shuttle trains and the main-line workings. Hawkshaw made a hasty study of the problems and blamed the signals, the track, the points and insufficient training of the signalmen.

The signalling had been installed by Saxby & Farmer, using interlocking of points and signals. The signalbox spanned the tracks at the station throat, "a glass house surmounted by four tall poles, from either side of which project semaphore arms to the number of twenty-four." In this place, "two stalwart men can work, whose time is entirely occupied in looking through the glass sides of their cell, and in pulling this way or pushing that way some of the levers which are arranged before them[3]."

By February 1867 Cannon Street was being used by 162,000 passengers per month with just under half of its passenger services being comprised of Cannon Street to Charing Cross shuttles. In August it was stated that passengers for the

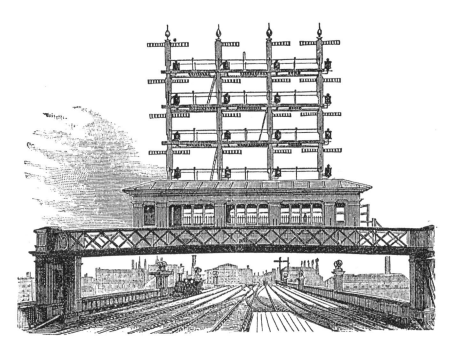

24. Cannon Street Station signals.

past six months had been 931,000 just on the local service, but Watkin reported that he had found wealthy gentlemen such as MPs travelling second class. Despite these figures, the SER was worried by bus competition; fares of 9d first class and 3d third class were undercut by road competition.

The LSWR had shown more positive interest in Cannon Street than in Charing Cross. Its first attempt to get closer to the City had resulted in an agreement with the SER in June 1865 for trains from Willesden, via Kensington, to London Bridge. This was put on as an experiment from 6 July 1865, using the connection at Waterloo, and each company had to give 3 months notice if it wanted to stop the service. By September 1867 the SER was discontented with the small returns from this service having diverted it into Cannon Street from 1 February; a service of 24 trains a day produced only £1,800 revenue for the SER over six months from 1 April 1867[4]. Watkin became increasingly irritated at this service, finding that of 325 trains only seven had run on time and blaming the "wretched arrangements" of the LSWR; between Waterloo and Cannon Street the trains were hauled by SER engines which, with the LSWR and LNWR locos used on other parts of the journey, made for a very expensive mode of operation. Watkin's solution was simple - the through services could stop from 30 November 1867 and the SER would build a station at Waterloo for passengers to make their own transfer. The service was, he said in November, losing the SER £1,500 a year. In fact the service was truncated at Waterloo from 1 January 1868 with outside observers commenting that the SER wanted to keep the LSWR out of Cannon Street in case of a LBSCR/SER merger.

Due to financial uncertainty the SER had postponed construction of its new station near Waterloo but it began in May 1868 after the LSWR had threatened legal action, citing clause 36 of the 1859 Charing Cross Act which stipulated

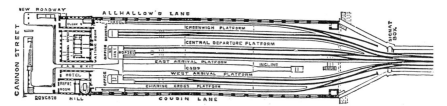

Plan of Cannon Street Station.

that the line was not to open without the Waterloo junction line - but it was prepared to have a new station instead. Initial estimates were for a cost of £10,000 but the SER hoped to save on this by using some parts from the nearby Blackfriars station - but not so many parts that that station could no longer be used. Here was a theme from the early days of the SER being repeated under the frugal guidance of Watkin. Yet Watkin achieved neither of his hopes, for the new Waterloo Junction opened on 1 January 1869 at a cost of £14,290 and replaced the Blackfriars station, which was last used on the previous day. The connection between the LSWR and SER at Waterloo remained in existence but saw no further regular use.

With such intensive services over the London extension lines, accidents were inevitable - such as a collision in fog outside Cannon Street during December 1867, involving an up Greenwich and one of the Willesden to Cannon Street trains. Fog from the Thames was a problem, as was misreading of signals; the latter caused a collision at Cannon Street West Junction on 2 November 1868. More serious was an outbreak of fire at Charing Cross station in February 1868, causing £4,000 damage to the roof and the Customs House. As a result the engineer was instructed to provide foot access to the roof and hoses there to fight any subsequent fires.

The Charing Cross to Cannon Street shuttle service did not prove to be the great success that had been anticipated. In August 1868 the Board commented on the fact that an accident to one of the trains on a foggy day at Charing Cross had cost them £500 in medical fees and damages, yet the takings on that day had only been £88. The future of the service was threatened by the extension of the Metropolitan District Railway, which opened from South Kensington to Westminster in December 1868, and was in the process of extending along the north side of the Thames to Blackfriars and Mansion House. In February 1869 Watkin suggested that the MDR should join on to the SER at Charing Cross and use its tracks to run to the Tower via Cannon Street. This suggestion met with a cool response. The SER could think of nothing other than to increase the fares on the shuttle from March 1869 - an admission of defeat, since the buses were already much cheaper. A small quantity of additional traffic was brought in from 2 September 1867 to 31 July 1868 by the running of two daily through trains from Cannon Street to Brighton; these were a result of friendly talks with the LBSCR, but were the first victims of a sudden freeze in the relationship. The Metropolitan District reached Blackfriars on 30 May 1870 and Mansion House on 3 July 1871; its Cannon Street station opened on 6 October 1884.

Hotels had been built at both termini. The Charing Cross Hotel opened on 15 May 1865, with 250 bedrooms. The City Terminus Hotel Company opened its premises at Cannon Street in May 1867. Both hotels were the work of E.M. Barry, but the City one was unprofitable and by February 1870 £47,274 in debt.

In order to avoid its closure the SER decided to take over the holding company at a cost of £201,500; this was achieved in 1872 though delayed for a brief time by the objections of a single shareholder.

Minor improvements continued to be made. In 1869 a room for the Post Office was provided at Cannon Street and an extra waiting-room at Charing Cross; steel rails were laid down on the Charing Cross route. There was an accident at Borough Market Junction on 28 July 1869 and on 16 July 1870 Porter Cuthbert was killed at Cannon Street; £260 was collected for his family and, perhaps insensitively, invested in SER stock - clearly company loyalty was expected to continue even beyond the grave. More serious was the accident at Stoney Street Junction on 28 March 1872; Hastings and Margate trains collided when the latter ran past signals, with 17 people injured.

During 1870 and 1871 schemes to extend the connections of the City and West End lines reappeared. The most important and complex of these, the Blackfriars Junction line, is dealt with below; the other, the Euston, St Pancras & Charing Cross, was to allow the SER to work its traffic through the middle of London in a shallow tunnel to Kentish Town. This scheme was renamed the London Central Railway in July 1871 when it obtained its Act, but never attracted sufficient investment to proceed further. In 1871 there was also a scheme for a pneumatic railway from Charing Cross to Broad Street, at a depth of 60 feet.

In the second half of 1872 traffic on the shuttle service showed an encouraging increase, up 17,000 on the previous period. The energetic Watkin had also seen an opportunity to develop the traffic by forming a liaison with another of his concerns, the Metropolitan Railway. He suggested a link from Cannon Street on to the Metropolitan Railway near the Bank with a train service being run to Finsbury Park from Cannon Street. This would have duplicated the Blackfriars Junction proposal, at considerably more cost, so it was dropped. But other opportunities presented themselves and in 1873-4 the SER threw itself wholeheartedly into seeking running powers and a junction with the Crystal Palace & South London Junction Railway. The SER engineer, Brady, had a scheme for new junctions between this erstwhile LCDR ally and the SER, but the LBSCR was also in the game and for a few months of 1873-4 there was a tripartite struggle for the soul of this small company. Watkin played the game in his usual way, offering to divide the traffic to Crystal Palace "on liberal terms" with the LCDR, then threatening to build a line to Chatham, then offering to withdraw the Chatham scheme if the LCDR would co-operate.

The footway on the west side of the Cannon Street bridge had been opened to the public for a 1/2d toll, but by November 1873 the SER was concerned that it was unprofitable. The facility was closed in 1877.

The string of accidents continued. A series of signalling errors caused minor accidents at Cannon Street in October and November 1873; in a busy signalbox it was too easy to make a mistake - on one occasion lever 47 was pulled instead of lever 48. On 11 May 1874 the train fitted with experimental Westinghouse brakes and used on North Kent services did its reputation no good by colliding with the buffers at Charing Cross. On 4 September 1875 the 10.35 Charing Cross to Hastings via Cannon Street was derailed at Cannon Street when the overworked signalman changed the points too soon, derailing the last few carriages. Perhaps the saddest of these accidents involved the elderly SER director, Captain Warren. On 15 January 1877 he was seen walking along the junction line between the SER and LSWR at Waterloo, "in deep thought". Oblivious to his surroundings, he was struck by an empty stock train and run over; his umbrella was cut in two, but, still alive, he was carried to the stationmaster. He died on 27 January, one of the few instances of a railway director being killed by a train.

By late 1874 little substantial progress had been made with the Blackfriars Junction line and the SER became involved in discussions with the LNWR and GNR about better links between north and south. The London Central Railway was abandoned by an Act of 1874 and the LNWR did not think a suggested new link between Clapham and Chislehurst would suffice. The LNWR wanted a connection via the Metropolitan Railway as agreed in June 1866, and was prepared to grant running powers to Willesden via a new link from Edgware Road. Such schemes would take time, so in April 1875 it was decided to run a service from the LNWR at Willesden, via Kensington and the West London Railway, to New Croydon and this began on 1 May in the charge of the LBSCR. From 1 July the LNWR also had through services to Waterloo and through booking to the SER was established. The SER also wanted a through goods train from Willesden to Waterloo and on to its own tracks there. The opening of the Blackfriars Junction line from 1 June 1878 reduced the significance of these fanciful schemes.

Watkin's restless energy now started looking into ways of improving the London extensions. In July 1874 he suggested removing the old platforms at Blackfriars and using the space to accommodate empty stock, thus saving having to take the carriages to Bricklayers Arms. However a Bill to allow widening of the SER at Blackfriars was lost in May 1876.

When the Prince of Wales left for India in autumn 1875 he departed from Charing Cross. The SER issued tickets to spectators to avoid a crush, but the Prince brought 160 friends to see him off and there was a serious danger caused by overcrowding.

The following year a new signalbox and signals were installed at Charing Cross for £1,600. Despite this there was an accident there in January 1877, causing Captain Tyler of the Board of Trade to complain that shunting and "train" signals should be interlocked.

The LNWR continued to press for better connections across London even after the Blackfriars Junction line had been opened. In August 1878 it gave the SER a fright by proposing a new line from Clapham Junction to Herne Hill and Orpington and also suggested a line from Bricklayers Arms to Clapham, though this was soon dropped as too costly with the SER suggesting a line from Blackfriars to Bricklayers Arms.

By September 1878 Watkin had created an alternative - a new line from Charing Cross and Cannon Street to Bricklayers Arms with a link to the LNWR via Waterloo and Clapham. The contractors Lucas & Aird also promoted a scheme for Waterloo to New Cross in 1878-9, but this was dropped. In February 1879 Watkin was still hoping for a deal with the LNWR to provide better SER access to Clapham Junction, but it was not forthcoming; although the SER got an Act for a new approach to Charing Cross from Old Kent Road, in 1882, no more new lines were built.

Whatever proposals were made, the same factor always emerged - money. To build or widen lines in the centre of London was hideously expensive and took a long time to complete. In January 1881 the SER decided that an extra track was needed between Belvedere Road and Waterloo where the line crossed over the LCDR and by August 1881 was actively buying up land to allow widening at Charing Cross - £29,596 was spent on land in Northumberland Avenue. What was not wanted, given the goods traffic now flowing in off the Blackfriars Junction line, was more stations, so a request to reopen Blackfriars Road station in April 1881 was rejected. Hopefully improvements were not set back too far by the theft of £100 from the Charing Cross booking office in August 1881.

By February 1881 the SER was involved in a policy to acquire the control of the Charing Cross Hotel by buying out the shareholders. It felt that the Hotel needed "more efficient management" and at the end of 1881 set the seal on this new relationship by having Myles Fenton installed as Chairman of the Hotel company.

At the end of 1881 a Bill was deposited to allow the addition of three more tracks on the Charing Cross bridge and to widen both extension lines in connection with the proposed line from Old Kent Road to Charing Cross. Both the new line and the widenings were authorised in 1882. The widenings would affect the station at Waterloo Junction and at first the LSWR suggested that a new station should be built in a position more directly opposite the LSWR's. The SER did not like this, so in May 1883 the LSWR suggested a gangway, sloping at 1 in 28, between the two stations. The idea of having empty stock sidings at the old Blackfriars Road was also reopened.

Cochrane was given the contract for the new bridge, at £137,000 and the first cylinder was sunk in September 1884. The *Railway Times* commented that this took place "with - of course - much ceremony and feasting." This was completed in 1887, giving six running lines and an engine road across the River Thames; on the opposite bank, at Belvedere Road, one extra track was added in 1888 at a cost of £5,000.

On 25 February 1884 there was an attempted "dynamite outrage" at Charing Cross by Irish Fenians but, unlike a similar incident at Victoria the same month, there was no actual explosion.

By the end of 1884 Watkin had two more plans to increase SER traffic in central London. The first of these was for a new line from New Cross to the Crystal Palace, with a connection at the London end on to the Circle line to provide a new through route for commuters. The Crystal Palace Company, the Metropolitan Railway and the SER promoted a Bill for this but it was withdrawn in April 1885. His other idea was for a revival of the 1874 Charing Cross to Euston scheme but this foundered on details of the financing of the scheme, to which both the SER and the LNWR were to contribute. Although a connecting line between Baker Street and Charing Cross was briefly considered in 1891 in connection with the extension of the Manchester, Sheffield & Lincolnshire Railway to London, and a branch from Corbetts Lane to Waterloo, no further action was taken. After this there was no option for the SER other than to make the best of the Blackfriars Junction line.

An unusual accident occurred at Cannon Street on 7 August 1886 when a horse bolted into the waiting room causing injuries to two or three people.

By the late 1880s SER finances were in a modestly comfortable state and improvements could be considered - especially with the dropping of proposals for expensive new lines. In September 1885 work on widening the Cannon Street line and bridge was under way, again with Cochrane. The bridge was widened to ten tracks, but was not ready for use until 13 February 1892.

Such investment was needed because of the poor punctuality of the trains. In January 1890 services to Charing Cross were only 60.7% punctual, with Cannon Street at 63%. Minor alterations, such as giving all London area signalboxes telephones in 1888-9, could only improve things slightly. Heavy capital expenditure was unavoidable, such as that spent on the Cannon Street bridge, and the widening at London Bridge which necessitated rebuilding the main-line platforms with a new up through road in 1893-4 at a cost of over £10,000.

On 22 April 1893 two new signalboxes were opened at Cannon Street with new signals following the completion of works associated with the new bridge. Yet when a Royal Wedding took place on 6 July traffic was badly disrupted, trains taking 17 mins to travel from Charing Cross to London Bridge via Cannon Street. Problems were re-emphasised by a collision at Cannon Street no.2 signalbox on 22 February 1894 between an up Hastings and a down Dover train.

Although Salomons suggested that the Cannon Street problem could be solved by a "circular railway", the SER decided in October 1894 that it needed to install a second down line between Stoney Street Junction and Borough Market Junction, making four tracks in all, at a cost of £28,837. The bridge over Borough High Street, known as "Hawkshaw's Coffin", was also replaced. This was completed in 1896, ignoring requests from Borough Market for their own station on it.

In August 1895 the SER decided to adopt a similar tactic between Belvedere Road and Metropolitan Junction, where an extra down road was expected to cost £91,580. In fact costs for this seem likely to have exceeded the estimate quite considerably - in the first half of 1897 £62,509 was spent on the project. During 1898 a new up platform was provided at Waterloo Junction and a new bridge over Waterloo Road. The new line was not ready for use until 2 June 1901.

In April 1896 Sir David Salomons suggested that the old locomotive from the Canterbury & Whitstable Railway, *Invicta*, should be exhibited at Charing Cross and talked of buying it himself. Less cultural, but more useful, was the provision of underground toilets at Charing Cross in 1897. On 20 July 1897 there was an accident at Borough Market Junction involving an up special from Chatham and the 10.03 from Maidstone, which had 16 vehicles; there were five injuries.

The LSWR improved its own connections with the City by the opening of the Waterloo & City tube railway on 8 August 1898; this more than halved the local traffic between Waterloo and Cannon Street and contributed to the eventual virtual abandonment of the practice of running Charing Cross to Cannon Street services.

2. The Blackfriars Junction Line

As has been seen, the LCDR pursued a policy of investing heavily in the London area to strengthen its position against its rival. As part of this it planned a City extension which opened from Elephant & Castle to Blackfriars, just south of the Thames, on 1 June 1864, and across the River to Little Earl Street on 21

December. This line passed over the SER's Charing Cross line close to its Blackfriars Road station, but there was no physical connection. The LCDR completed its line by extensions to Ludgate Hill (1 June 1865) and to a junction with the Metropolitan Railway at West Street Junction near Farringdon (1 January 1866).

This route gave the LCDR the advantage of a direct physical connection with the Metropolitan Railway, with its access to northern lines like the GNR and MR. In 1871 the SER therefore proposed the construction of an east to north spur at Blackfriars with running powers for itself over the LCDR to West Street Junction. During a period of warmer relations, the LCDR was prepared to assent to this if the line was used for "non-competitive" traffic only. Forbes of the LCDR wrote to Eborall about it in May 1871:

"Of course neither you nor we can contemplate that the junction should be made use of against the Chatham & Dover Company in respect to traffic passing on to other Railways."

Forbes' hope seems naive in the extreme, given past experiences, but he insisted only that the junction between the new SER Blackfriars Junction line and the LCDR should be controlled by the LCDR. A Bill was deposited in autumn 1871 with the SER to have running powers over the Metropolitan as well as to the Midland and Great Northern lines. The LCDR opposed the line early in 1872 on the grounds that its traffic would cause disruption but was unable to prevent authorisation.

The SER's attention was then diverted by other proposals, such as a connection with the Metropolitan via Cannon Street, and the Blackfriars Junction idea lay dormant until a new Act to extend the time limit on powers had to be obtained in 1874. This only allowed a further 18 months, so the SER began to arrange tenders straight away. Aird was awarded the contract in February 1875, with a fee of £37,927 providing he finished the work in five months. Talks then began with the LNWR about providing a service over the Metropolitan Railway and then via St John's Wood and the Hampstead Junction line to Willesden.

Aird was unable to complete the line within the time limit as there were delays in gaining control of property on the line, though by May 1876 the SER Board was expecting to be able to open one track "soon". The 2 September edition of the *Railway Times* recorded that the line had been completed, although there had been problems with sinking the foundations of the arches 30 feet into muddy ground; the majority of this line was formed of twelve arches at a maximum of 50 feet high and sharply curved.

However relations between the SER and LCDR had deteriorated sharply in the period since the line had been authorised, and in November 1876 the LCDR objected to the line being opened at all, using the grounds of safety as its reason. Since the LCDR controlled the junction between the new line and its own route, the SER was in a difficult situation - and remained so. Attempts to persuade the LCDR to allow the running of a night goods train through to the Metropolitan Railway in March 1877 met with further rejection; even a successful inspection by the Board of Trade on 23 July did not result in opening.

By the latter stages of 1877 the two companies had patched up their latest quarrel and an amalgamation Bill was being proposed. Interestingly, a report appeared in the *Railway Times* in October that the Blackfriars Junction line was intended "solely" for Midland Railway goods traffic: was this a rumour started to ease LCDR fears? In December 1877 the SER decided not to press for the opening of the line while amalgamation was a prospect.

Amalgamation was a failure once more and the Blackfriars Junction line opened on 1 June 1878; its capital cost was £91,395, making it one of the most expensive sections of track on the SER. Initially six trains a day were run from Woolwich Arsenal to the Great Northern Railway, using GNR stock and locomotives since the SER itself had no suitable motive power. The LCDR refused to allow passengers for the SER to board at Ludgate Hill or Snow Hill, allowing southbound trains to set down only. The SER clearly felt that success was immediate, for by 13 June it had decided to increase the service up to a maximum of twelve trains per day, noting that the service to the LNWR via the West London line was a comparative failure.

The SER was also keen to use the line for goods and two services a day began running from the GNR to Bricklayers Arms from 18 June, with a third conditional train running from 18 July. This was important to the SER as in the year up to 30 May 1878 the LCDR had carried £124,658 worth of SER exchange freight traffic via its own Blackfriars line to Beckenham, for which the LCDR had been paid £8440.

The LBSCR disliked the new goods services, complaining that between 18 June and 29 June its own trains to London Bridge had been delayed 13 times. On 5 August there was an accident at Bricklayers Arms Junction between two SER light engines and a LBSCR excursion. This prompted complaints from the Board of Trade about the working of traffic at Bricklayers Arms, for the goods trains from Blackfriars Junction had to reverse there to gain access to the SER's goods station; a connecting line between Blackfriars Junction and Bricklayers Arms remained talk only.

Despite these problems, Allport of the Midland Railway expressed an interest in getting a goods service started. In September 1878 the SER told him that it might consider running a train for the MR between the hours of 10pm and 5.30am. Allport inspected the line in October and then began negotiations with the LCDR.

The Midland did not have running powers over the line while the SER had no condensing engines to work the route. In December 1878 the Great Northern and the Midland offered to lend it some engines and brake vans to help with the service. Clearly the SER was reluctant to invest in working the line until it saw whether it would be profitable: from 18 July 1878 to 31 January 1879 it handled 25,577 tons of goods, with gross earnings for the SER at £4098. The Midland goods service began on 1 April 1879.

The passenger service was proving as problematic as the goods. In its first three months it carried 17,974 ordinary passengers, and a further 2972 excursionists and troops. This produced a loss for the SER of £128 and withdrawal of the passenger service was seriously considered.

Gross earnings from passengers in September 1878 were £7521, falling to £6314 the following month. From 1 July to 31 December 1878 44,497 people were carried with the SER's share of receipts at £1,102-10s; sadly the SER's costs were £1,684-17-6d[5].

By supporting a service between the northern and south-eastern suburbs, the SER was attempting to induce new habits in the population; it took a long time to build up new patterns of travel and, by running the trains to Woolwich, the SER and GNR had chosen to serve some of the poorer and less mobile citizens in its territory. Only 4265 people used the trains in February 1879 and the service continued to lose money. In February 1880 the SER decided to withdraw the service unless the GNR could be persuaded to take it over, which they could not. It was proposed to end the service on 31 March, then an extension to 31 August was decided on.

Having shown such a lack of faith in the service, the SER made a characteristic change of policy and on 29 April 1880 decided to buy three locomotives at £2,045 each from the Metropolitan to help with the service. As a result, the SER took over the running of the service from the GNR on 1 August 1880. These engines maintained the bulk of the service until the SER's own Q class tank engines were ready; they were then sold back to the Metropolitan in 1883-4 for £1,900 each.

From this point onwards the future of the line became more assured and by July 1881 was handling a growing coal traffic as well. The SER's change of heart on the line seems illogical, until its political position is considered; during 1880 Watkin was hoping to steal a large number of commuters away from the LCDR by gaining access to Crystal Palace and the same year the SER began running trains through the East London route to Liverpool Street. Watkin, as a controlling influence in SER and Metropolitan circles, may have seen the chance to control the centre of London.

In 1887 there were negotiations with the Metropolitan about running SER trains via Baker Street to Rickmansworth. By January 1890 ambition had stretched further, with consideration being given to the use of the Aylesbury & Buckingham Railway. The SER was fully aware of the progress through Parliament of the Manchester, Sheffield & Lincolnshire Railway's London extension; Watkin was chairman of this Company and agreement for through rates was reached on 18 January 1890. The MSLR offered the prospect of more traffic on a line that was handling about £160,000 worth of business in 1890. Under these circumstances, one can see that the tiny Blackfriars Junction line had a major role to play in the plans of the ambitious Watkin, who dreamt of a railway empire stretching from Manchester to the Channel and beyond.

1.   Now known as Oxford Circus.
2.   SER Report, January 1860.
3.   F.S.Williams, **Our Iron Roads.**
4.   SER Minutes, 31 October 1867.
5.   SER Minutes, 9 January 1879.

CHAPTER 9: THE MID-KENT RAILWAY AND ITS BRANCHES

1. The Mid-Kent Railway

The opening of the SER via Croydon and the termination of the L&GR at Greenwich left a large area of countryside to the south-east of London without railway services. Though the area was not densely populated, it included a few small towns such as Beckenham and Bromley. During the years of the Railway Mania, there were a number of schemes proposed to fill this void.

One of the first was a scheme proposed in 1843-4 by George Walter, for an extension from the Greenwich line to Croydon. However there was then a rash of proposals for longer distance lines to serve other parts of Kent. To defend itself against "invasion" by other companies, the SER proposed a new direct route to Tonbridge in 1845 but in October 1846 a Mid-Kent Railway was proposed to build a line from Lewisham (on the proposed North Kent line) to Tonbridge, with branches to Bromley and Maidstone, that had better gradients and tunnels than the SER's.

The SER was especially worried about the LBSCR's involvement in what it saw as aggressive schemes[1]. The SER therefore became embroiled in the question of building a new route through north-west Kent to Croydon largely as a counter-measure to the challenges of its opponents. In October 1846 the SER was discussing a line from Lewisham to Bromley and to Croydon, which it estimated would cost £180,000. On 8 January 1847 MacGregor of the SER met representatives of the LBSCR and threatened to build this line if the LBSCR would not allow the SER to take control of the Mid-Kent Railway.

The SER was aware of some lessons to be learnt from this. Firstly, that its devious main-line via Redhill left it open to new, more direct proposals deep into Kent. Secondly, that some towns nearer London, like Bromley, were likely to attract proposals.

With the collapse of the Railway Mania these issues lay dormant for a while, though the SER did discuss a Mid-Kent scheme in 1850 and a line to Bromley in 1851.

During 1852 the SER developed a more positive interest in the issue, causing the LBSCR to write and complain about a scheme for a line to Bromley and Croydon in June 1852. The SER was cautious in admitting its interest in the scheme, but interested it was and in October it met the LBSCR to discuss the issue; finding "more indifference than...expected," the SER decided to press ahead[2]. In fact they even suggested to the LBSCR that the project could be a joint one, but the LBSCR was absorbed in discussions over amalgamation with the LSWR.

The threat of an amalgamation between these two rival companies may have spurred the SER's interest in the MKR scheme, for an alternative route to Croydon that would also help in the SER's defence would clearly be valuable.

Evolution of lines in the Bromley area.

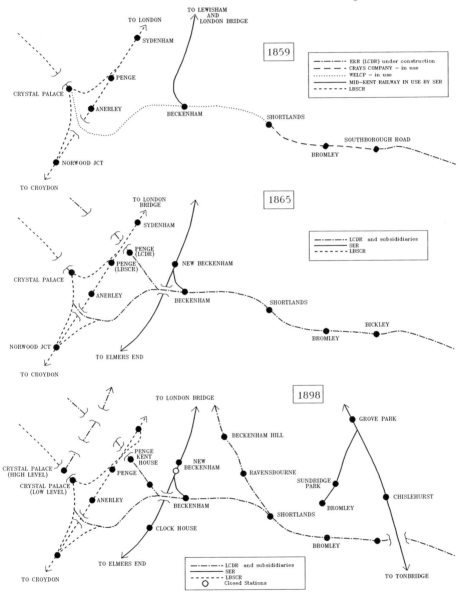

1859

—·—·—	EKR (LCDR) under construction
— — —	CRAYS COMPANY – in use
··········	WELCP – in use
————	MID-KENT RAILWAY IN USE BY SER
- - - - -	LBSCR

1865

—·—·—	LCDR and subsidiaries
————	SER
- - - - -	LBSCR

1898

—·—·—	LCDR and subsidiaries
————	SER
- - - - -	LBSCR
O	Closed Stations

It was possibly also worried about the promotion of a West End of London & Crystal Palace Railway.

In January 1853 the SER offered to abandon its Bill for the MKR line if the LSWR and LBSCR dropped their amalgamation proposals, but receiving no encouragement it began buying land from the Cator Estate, although there were difficulties when Mr Cator, of Clock House near Beckenham, opposed Sunday traffic. By March 1853 the amalgamation proposals had collapsed and the LBSCR was keen to share in a joint scheme, so the SER withdrew its MKR Bill. The WEL&CP Bill continued, and it was authorised on 4 August 1853 to build a line as far east as the LBSCR at Norwood.

This left the SER dangerously exposed and, when some of the Board proposed a line from Lewisham to Bromley, it caused violent disagreement within the Company as has been seen in Chapter Three. The line was estimated to cost about £136,000 but the shareholders had voted not to expend any more on capital projects. At the same time rival Bills were being prepared for a Sydenham & Farnborough line, a West Kent & Crystal Palace line, and for an extension of the WEL&CP from Norwood to Bromley (the "Farnborough extension"). The latter was supported by the LBSCR who, the SER understood, had guaranteed its promoters a return of £8,000 per annum on their extension.

Amidst stormy scenes, which were more to do with internal politics than with the economics of individual schemes, the SER decided on 18 May 1854 to withdraw its own Mid-Kent Bill for a line to Bromley and not even to oppose the WEL&CP. Both the Sydenham & Farnborough and the WEL&CP ran into problems in Committee in June 1854, but the WEL&CP Bill was recommitted and its Act was passed.

Disputes within the SER reached their peak in August 1854 when the "policy" of the company was discussed. It was decided to abandon the Mid-Kent proposals, though MacGregor and Renshaw objected to this.

The one hope for MacGregor and Renshaw was that local interests could be persuaded to promote a line that the SER could then work. This tactic was discussed in July 1854; in November the SER agreed that they would like such a scheme, but would not support it by paying the Parliamentary expenses. During December the *Railway Times* printed a story that the SER was considering financing a MKR scheme by selling its Redhill line to the LBSCR[3]; this may have been a result of confusion over the scheme to build a new and direct line to Tonbridge.

The actual scheme was known as the Mid-Kent & North Kent Junction, and proposed to connect the North Kent line at Lewisham with the WEL&CP at Beckenham at a cost of about £80,000. Beattie, who was on the Board of both the MK and the SE, argued that a line was inevitable and that therefore it was in the best interests of the SER that a friendly line should be constructed. The SER's counsel advised that opposition to its Bill was "hopeless" and on 21 May 1855 the SER agreed to work the line for 50% of receipts. The Mid-Kent Act was passed on 28 July 1855.

No doubt some of the SER directors hoped that this was the end of the matter and the Manchester shareholders were keen to see no further involvement. Yet further promotions continued, including one for an extension of the Mid-Kent eastwards, from the point now known as Shortlands which was the terminus of the WEL&CP, through Bromley to St Mary Cray. Eborall advised that the SER should gain control of this scheme, but it affected property owned by Coles

Child, the SER director, and provoked a further storm on the Board. The Act for the line was passed on 21 July 1856 but the new company, the Mid-Kent (Bromley to St Mary Cray), refused terms for a deal with the SER since by October 1856 it was considering an extension of its own to Tonbridge. It was also angry at the SER's promotion of a scheme for a line from Lewisham to Dartford.

One can see the influence of Eborall, the professional railway manager, in the next stage of the saga. It was clear that the WEL&CP was the greatest danger to the SER in the area since it offered an alternative route to a new West End terminus. In October 1856 the SER therefore held talks with the WEL&CP with a view to taking over the section of it between Beckenham and Norwood, with the additional possibility of running through to the West End terminus. Yet the SER was not very adept at concluding deals of this sort (note also its failure to agree a deal with the EKR), for it was still struggling with the St Mary Cray line, where terms had first been laid out on 10 April 1856; this was to be for a single line, but with bridges for a double, to be worked by the SER for 50%. Behind this lay complex political factors, for the "Crays" company had achieved greater significance in that the East Kent Railway was planning an extension from Strood to join it. By using the Crays and the WEL&CP, the EKR would have access to London without having to rely on the SER, but its Bill was rejected in 1857 leaving the Crays in an unsatisfactory position. The SER suspected that the LBSCR was involved in this scheming.

On 1 January 1857 the Mid-Kent line from Lewisham Junction to Beckenham Junction opened for traffic. The Company was also hoping for an extension to Croydon, but to appease the LBSCR the SER agreed not to support this. A new station was built at Lewisham to handle the traffic. The line had a number of problems in its construction, notably due to problems with flooding; in October 1857 trains had to be suspended for a while after heavy rain caused the washing away of some of the banks.

The SER was aware that the East Kent's Bill had been defeated in 1857 only after a fierce struggle and that a new Bill would be deposited for the 1857-8 session. During October 1857 it even discussed the desperate tactic of taking over the Crays line and extending it to Cuxton, near Strood, itself.

The SER was also committed to proceeding with a direct line from Lewisham to Tonbridge, which would cross the Crays line near Chislehurst. In November 1857 the SER met the company to discuss putting in a junction at Chislehurst and a "relief line". The SER also wanted the Crays company to abandon the two miles on from there to St Mary Cray and to use the money to double the line between Chislehurst (Bickley on the later LCDR line) and Bromley. On 4 November Heads of Agreement were reached - that the Crays should be leased to the SER, doubled to Chislehurst and abandoned beyond, and that the company would not support any rival scheme.

Meanwhile the Mid-Kent Railway was also active, proposing a line to Fair Field, Croydon, and negotiating with the LBSCR for a junction. On 1 April 1858 they agreed on a junction at Norwood. The WEL&CP extension opened from Norwood to Beckenham and Bromley on 3 March 1858. Bromley was renamed Shortlands on 1 July.

On 23 July 1858 the EKR secured an Act for its western extension to St Mary Cray and the right to take over the powers of the Crays company to construct the line between there and Bickley. The Act also stipulated that the Crays line between Bickley and Bromley was to be doubled within a year to prevent obstruction. The EKR changed its name to London, Chatham & Dover Railway from 1 August 1859 to reflect its new status.

The SER began operating services over the Shortlands to Southborough Road (renamed Bickley in 1860) section on 5 July 1858. It was a single line operated on the "one engine in steam" principle. The Crays had reached an agreement with the EKR about doubling its line on 30 June 1858 and the work was completed by June 1859. The situation where the SER had control, for a period of ten years, of one of the key parts of the LCDR's route was bound to cause trouble and in March 1861 the LCDR began to promote its own route parallel to the Crays line. When this was authorised on 6 August 1861 the SER admitted defeat. The Mid-Kent Railway Leasing & Transfer Act of 1862 allowed the Crays line to be taken over by the LCDR between Shortlands and Bickley, which it was with effect from 1 September 1863.

The SER was also concerned to resolve the position of the WEL&CP and the attitude of the LBSCR to lines in the area. In July 1858 it had negotiated terms with the WEL&CP for use of the line between Beckenham and Shortlands in connection with the Crays service, but it was concerned that the LBSCR would try to lease the line and discussed whether the extension could become SER.

Also worrying was the possibility that the MKR itself could fall into the grasp of the LBSCR. As has been seen, the MKR and LBSCR had discussed building a connecting line between Beckenham and Norwood in April 1858 and agreement had been reached. The LBSCR could build a spur at Norwood to allow running from Croydon onto the eastbound WEL&CP while the MKR could construct a spur at Beckenham allowing through running from the WEL&CP onto the Mid-Kent line. The SER was aware that relations between it and the MKR were not as good as they could have been: in January 1859 the MKR had refused to contribute to Lewisham Junction station and in February there was another dispute over the cost of distant signals for the junction. To complicate matters further, the EKR was also proposing a line from Beckenham to join the LBSCR line to London Bridge at Sydenham.

The Beckenham & Sydenham Junction plan seems to have embarrassed the LBSCR because it included a clause compelling the LBSCR to forward EKR traffic to London Bridge and Bricklayers Arms; Schuster told the SER that the LBSCR would oppose it and, should it succeed, all receipts from EKR traffic would be handed over to the SER. The two companies worked out a deal whereby the SER would not oppose the LBSCR's spur at Norwood in return for which the LBSCR would not oppose the Charing Cross Bill. WEL&CP attempts to get running powers over the MKR were withdrawn and, in the event, the Beckenham & Sydenham was rejected by the House of Commons. All went well except the SER was annoyed when the LBSCR opposed the MKR Bill for a spur onto the WELCP at Beckenham, thus depriving it of the access to Croydon it had been seeking since late 1857. By an Act of 23 July 1860 the LCDR was authorised to purchase the section of the WEL&CP between Norwood and Shortlands.

A review of the position of the MKR at the start of 1861 would not have been encouraging. Largely a victim of railway politics, its major sources of traffic were being stolen from it and its attempts to win new traffic - by a new spur giving access to Croydon - had been frustrated. In August 1861 Captain Edwards, its chairman, reported that even the traffic between Lewisham and Crystal Palace had been reduced. The only cheer was strictly temporary - the construction of the LCDR brought an increase in freight revenues as materials were brought in from Angerstein's Wharf.

The MKR decided that the only way to survive was to fight. In January 1862 the SER received a hurt letter from the LBSCR, complaining that the MKR was promoting a line from Beckenham to Croydon. In fact the MKR, now with W. Wilkinson in charge, had changed its tactics; it had abandoned hope of getting to Croydon with the co-operation of the LBSCR and now was planning an entirely independent line via Shirley to Addiscombe. The SER was not as innocent of this as it would have the LBSCR believe, for it had agreed with the LCDR not to oppose that company's takeover of the Crays line in exchange for no opposition to the Mid-Kent extension to Croydon, whereas LBSCR proposals were roundly opposed. Here we see the SER playing a much more successful tactical game, considerably superior to the feeble efforts that had allowed the LCDR to grow into a major challenger.

The Mid-Kent's Addiscombe extension was authorised on 17 July 1862, with additional capital of £40,000. Smith & Knight were the contractors. Here was an interesting example of a railway being promoted by property interests. Wilkinson, its chairman, was also the deputy chairman of the National Land Company which had been buying property in the area including an estate at Beckenham. Charles Gilpin, chairman of the National Land Company, was a director of the SER.

Horrified at this threat to the lucrative Croydon traffic, the LBSCR began to promote the idea of a new station at Central Croydon to which the MKR replied late in 1862 with a proposed extension to Croydon High Street opposite the Town Hall. When this was rejected in 1863 the MKR proposed an extension to join its line with the Caterham branch at a cost of £78,750.

During May 1863 the possibility of the SER buying the MKR was discussed in the railway press, with claims being made that the line was actually being worked at a loss at the time. Coles Child opposed amalgamation. Agreement between the two companies was reached on 1 July 1863 and was authorised by Acts of 1864 and 1866 following lengthy deliberations over methods of payment. A figure of about £120,000 had been agreed but arbitrators (including Captain Huish of the LNWR) awarded £116,800 of SER stock to the MKR shareholders in 1866, giving the MKR proprietors a guaranteed return of 7.25% per annum.

Opening to Addiscombe was delayed by bad weather but the line finally opened on 1 April 1864 from New Beckenham Junction to Croydon (Addiscombe Road). A station was opened at the junction, New Beckenham, and there was one intermediate station at Elmers End. It was agreed to charge the same rates to Addiscombe as the LBSC charged to East Croydon and to further pacify the LBSCR the SER offered to drop MKR plans for lines to the centre of Croydon and to join the Caterham branch. The SER decided in June 1864 that it should invest £15,900 in new carriages for the line, to be similar to those being provided for the Charing Cross to Greenwich service; 30 composites, 10 3rd class and 10 3rd brakes were agreed on.

In 1865 plans for an extension from Addiscombe to the Caterham line and even Stoat's Nest were brought forward, but a Croydon & Caterham Bill was lost on 13 June 1866 due to defects in the plans. Further defective plans were discovered in November 1867 when the Croydon Board of Health found that the road bridge at Woodside had gradients of 1 in 20 instead of the agreed 1 in 30.

From 1870 there were a number of questions about stations that had to be settled. On 6 January 1870 the SER considered the need for better accomodation at New Beckenham, where a new station slightly further north had been opened in about 1868, though no formal discussion of this is recorded in SER sources. £140 was spent on a new siding there in 1874.

In August 1870 the SER considered a new station for the Woodside area and Stroud Green racecourse, but deferred the decision. Local people, however, were prepared to offer £1,500 for a station at Burnt Ash Lane and this money was received by the SER in April 1871. It seems to have opened, named Woodside, in the latter half of 1871. A new signalbox was provided at Woodside in 1877. Coal sidings were added in 1878.

The station at Beckenham Junction (renamed from Beckenham on 1 April 1864) was jointly owned by the SER and LCDR. In April 1871 the SER received complaints from local people that the shunting of manure wagons in a siding was a considerable nuisance, but the SER said that this offensive traffic belonged to the LCDR. In July 1875 it felt that the station needed a new up siding and better accomodation, costing £340. After complaints about the station's dangerous condition, it was inspected by Colonel Yolland in January 1876. There were further complaints to the Board of Trade in 1879 but it was not until the Beckenham Local Board brought an action before the Railway Commissioners in 1890 that progress was made. A booking-office was provided on the SER side, the MKR siding set back and the platform widened and in 1892 it was decided to replace the level crossing with a bridge.

In January 1873 the commuters of Addiscombe complained that the trains were too slow and in October that year their colleagues at Elmers End complained that the platforms were poor, there was no footbridge and no shelter on the up side; the SER provided a footbridge at the crossing in 1882.

There was bad flooding on the line over 11 and 12 April 1878. Close to the junction at Lewisham and at Ladywell the line was closed by water.

At Lower Sydenham (opened 1 January 1857) a new coal siding was provided in 1878 at the expense of the Crystal Palace Gas Company. Traffic was received from wharves at Erith.

In July 1878 the SER received a request to provide a station at Beckenham Road, but the issue was ignored until May 1889 when it was decided to build a station for £3,873. At first it was intended to call this Penge Road, but the idea of calling it Clock House was accepted in June 1889. It opened on 1 May 1890, as recorded in the minutes that day.

There were problems at New Beckenham with level crossings and complaints from the Board of Trade. In November 1884 the SER decided to include provision in its next Bill for a bridge but the issue made no further progress until May 1890 when the SER decided to stop up Lennard Road and Park Road, replacing them with a new bridge to the south. This was not done immediately, for in July 1896 the SER was still discussing replacing the crossing with a bridge and building a new station. In July 1898 this was estimated at £8,800 in total, so the work had still not been done by the end of the SER's independent existence.

Minor improvements were made at Catford Bridge (opened 1 January 1857) in 1891-3, including the widening of the platforms. In 1896 some improvements were made to Addiscombe Road, including the provision of a new roof, in connection with the planned service via the East London line. Remodelling of the station was completed in 1899.

2. The Hayes & West Wickham Branch

The Hayes area was first affected by lines that were planned to pass through it to other destinations, such as the Beckenham, Lewes & Brighton scheme of 1862. The West Kent Railway of 1864 was a LCDR offshoot, for a line from Penge to West Wickham and Hayes with spurs and branches to Oxted and Westerham[4]. This was followed by a less ambitious scheme the following year, for a branch off the LCDR near Bromley to Hayes and Farnborough.

In November 1865 a Bill for a West Wickham & Bromley Railway was supported by the SER, but this was a bad time for the promotion of railways due to the financial uncertainties of 1866 and the scheme failed to achieve lasting results. Another attempt was led by Edward Wilson in 1876, for a line from Beckenham to Eden Park, West Wickham, Addington and Oxted.

The SER was spurred into action by an attempt in 1879 by the LCDR, which sought to build a line to Little Wickham and Hayes[5], which it cost the SER £2,000 to oppose. A Bill for a West Wickham & Hayes Railway, branching off the Addiscombe line near Elmers End, was presented in 1879 and with the support of the SER received its Act in July 1880. It had powers to raise £85,000 in £10 shares. Several local landowners were interested, including Sir John Lennard and Charles Goodhart.

Compared to earlier attempts to promote lines in this area, it was an uncontroversial scheme and deeply attached to the SER. The apparently indefatigable Alexander Beattie was its chairman while Watkin's son, Alfred Mellor Watkin, was on the Board. It had the services of the SER's engineer, Francis Brady. A draft agreement with the SER was prepared in September 1881.

Negotiations were begun with the contractors Lucas & Aird, who at first offered to build the line for £69,283 but reduced their contract to £65,000 after the SER agreed to supply the rails; it did this at cost price in June 1881.

In December 1880 the site of Hayes station was discussed but there were some delays in getting the work started due to problems acquiring land. At West Wickham a beer house, *The Leather Bottle*, and four cottages had to be bought for £1,650 while extra land had to be acquired for a fork at Elmers End. It was agreed to extend the time limit on Lucas & Aird's contract to 1 December 1881.

By April 1881 Brady was working on the station plans. It was decided that the bridge and house at Wickham Green should be in matching brick. The following month a slight diversion at Hayes was agreed and the plans for a station hotel at West Wickham; the Hayes extension was for a short line on a 1 in 80 gradient beneath the public road and up to the edge of Hayes Common with two sidings, according to the WW&HR minutes of 21 July. Early plans of the station area do suggest that preparations were made for this extension, since the line turned to the south-east as it approached the site of the terminus, taking up an alignment that would have taken it nearer the Common and leaving a levelled site to the north vacant. This may reflect early hopes that the line would become popular with Londoners seeking a day out in the fresh air. However,

25. West Wickham Station at about the time of opening. (E.Course Collection)

SER minutes of May 1881 suggest another reason for a deviation - that a change of alignment would allow the line to be extended to Westerham.

The station plans for West Wickham and Eden Park were agreed in June, but at Eden Park the line passed close to a large property known as Elderslie and the railway had had to buy this. The platform there was not to be closer than 70 yards to the house but in August 1881 it was found that the proposed down platform would be on an 18 foot high embankment with a view over the property. Anxious that its resale value should not be diminished, the WW&HR decided to build the platform nearer to Eden Park bridge than originally planned. There were further discussions over the Eden Park up platform in October and in February 1882 the position of the signalbox was also questioned. It was decided to plant shrubs on the bank as a screen and, in April, to move the signalbox to the end of the down platform.

An Act passed on 11 August 1881 authorised the taking over of the WW&HR by the SER upon its completion.

In December 1881 the company began to consider the building of houses for the stationmasters and hoped that they could open the line in two months. The signalling of the line was only begun in late December 1881 and included interlocking of points and signals. It cost £310-15-0d at Hayes, £183-10-0d at Eden Park and £231-0-0d at West Wickham.

Work on providing staff accomodation was very slow, despite the earlier intention to provide stationmasters' houses. It was decided in April 1882 to provide a stationmaster's house and six cottages at Eden Park and at Hayes it was felt that the stationmaster could have a house between the station and the turntable. At West Wickham the staff had to temporarily use the cottages next to *The Leather Bottle*.

General Hutchinson inspected the line on 23 May 1882 and it was opened on 29 May. The first train was hauled by locomotive No. 238. However, a full service did not commence until 1 June[6].

At the final meeting of the WW&HR directors, there were a number of complaints. The subway at Eden Park let in water and the shrubs on the bank were a failure. The West Wickham platform had been left with a very poor surface - a layer of dust one-inch deep that blew into the booking-office. In March 1885 the SER estimated the capital cost of the line at £162,315. It was briefly threatened by a Hayes & Farnborough scheme, off the LCDR, in 1895.

The line was not an immediate success and was slow to develop commuter traffic. The map of the station in 1898 shows few new houses in the vicinity - Station Road having barely half a dozen new properties.

3. The Woodside & South Croydon Joint Railway

As has been seen, the successful promotion of a Mid-Kent Railway line to Addiscombe resulted also in the suggestion that the line could be extended to join the Caterham branch. The 1864 plan for a Croydon & Caterham Junction included a branch to Westerham and was expected to cost £180,000 and a 1866 Bill for an extension of the MKR to Caterham Junction was rejected.

On 6 July 1865 an Act for the LBSCR-supported Surrey & Sussex Junction Railway had seemed to give the SER's rival control of the district to the south-east of Croydon but the scheme petered out in 1869 with only a substantial loss to its backers and some deserted earthworks to show for it. It was the authorisation of the Croydon, Oxted & East Grinstead Railway in 1878 (see Chapter 16) that caused the revival of schemes to extend the Mid-Kent for, at Selsdon, it passed within a few miles of the MKR.

The Woodside & South Croydon Railway, a little over two miles long, was promoted largely by local interests to connect the MKR at Woodside with the CO&EGR at Selsdon, itself very close to the CO&EGR's junction with the Brighton line near South Croydon. The company's Act was passed in 1880 and estimated the line to cost about £40,000 a mile. The Act allowed both the LBSCR and the SER to participate in the running of the line. There were very clear reasons for the SER to do so since it would provide access onto the CO&EGR from the MKR, but the grounds for the LBSCR participating were less clear - it was unlikely to bring that company any substantial new traffic; perhaps its participation was motivated largely by a tactical desire to watch the SER.

On 3 March 1881 the W&SCR learnt that the LBSCR would be joining the SER in the scheme. Within a fortnight the two main-line companies had concluded a deal and on 31 March the SER received a proposal from the LBSCR that the line become a joint project. The SER Act of 1882 allowed the W&SCR to become a joint scheme from 10 August 1882, converting it into the Woodside & South Croydon Joint Committee.

Meanwhile the detailed planning of the line was under way. As early as 13 March 1881 the engineer was looking at the possibility of building a station in Croydon at the junction of Ashburton Road and Upper Addiscombe Road - this became Bingham Road.

In June the contract for the line was let to Joseph Firbank for £68,934. However there were problems with the Whitgift Hospital Estate, which wanted a tunnel. It was decided in December 1882 to include two short tunnels on the line. The plans for a station at "Combe Lane" had been prepared; however, there

were delays over the station at the southern end since a proposed deviation of
the line so that it joined the CO&EGR further south was being prepared. This
deviation was authorised in the LBSCR's 1882 Act but the LBSCR then showed
reluctance in acting on it.

By June 1883 the work on stations was making good progress with a subway
being constructed at Coombe Lane. Buildings there and at "Selsdon Road" were
to be of the same style as those on the East Grinstead line while in October it
was decided that the buildings at the latter should be suitable for use as a "fork
station". More difficult was the civil engineering - problems with earthslips and
slurry were being experienced by March 1883 and in early August were
sufficiently serious to force the Joint Committee to buy more land. Later the
same month there were further slips between the tunnels. By February 1884 the
contractor, Firbank, was experiencing financial difficulties due to the continual
problems[7]; in May 1884 it was decided to solve the problem by extending the
tunnels to try and hold up the wet ground between them.

The laying in of the junction at Selsdon started in October 1883 and the site
was inspected by General Hutchinson in February 1884 in preparation for the
opening of the Oxted line. Sidings to the goods yard there were put in in October
1884.

It was not until October 1884 that the line seemed ready for opening, the
difficult ground having made a severe task out of a short line. However, the
Board of Trade refused to sanction the line on first inspection due to the need
for a footbridge and down platform shelter at Woodside. In the second

26. On the Woodside & S. Croydon Joint Line in about 1902, with an SECR train
passing Coombe Lane.   (R.Thomas Collection)

inspection in early November, there were still problems at Woodside - a siding
was too close to the main-line and the signals, while the platforms had steps
rather than ramps at the ends. There were similar problems with the platforms
at Selsdon Road while there was also a general lack of catch points.

Delays continued into 1885. Although the Croydon & Oxted Joint
Committee spent £4,200 preparing Selsdon Road by May 1885, the SER had
still not got Woodside to a good enough state for opening. The line finally
opened on 10 August with new, and joint, stations at Coombe Lane and Selsdon

Road although Woodside remained a SER station; Bingham Road did not open until 1906.

The line proved financially disastrous for there was too little suburban traffic to justify its upkeep and the only other purpose it had was to allow SER trains access onto the Oxted line without passing through Croydon - but only after a slow journey along the Mid-Kent line. From the start it was worked only by the SER though both it and the LBSCR shared the loss on the revenue account - £250 each in the first year. However the SER was dissatisfied with this and felt that the LBSCR should also share in the loss it sustained on mileage costs. In January 1887 the Joint Committee decided that the SER should work the line until 31 January, then the LBSCR should work through to Woodside until 30 June 1888.

There was so little traffic on the line that the Joint Committee had little to discuss. In August 1888 they agreed to provide extra cattle pens at Selsdon Road, but there was no more to say.

The only issue to exercise intellectual faculties was who should carry the burden of working the line. It was eventually agreed that from 1 July 1889 the companies should work the local service each in alternate years.

The traffic figures for the half-year to 30 June 1889 provide an interesting picture of the situation. Traffic revenue was £356-13s-0d, but expenses came to £694-17s-0d. 48 first class passengers generated revenue of a princely £0-9s-7d, while there were also 259 second class and 8,767 third class.

Perhaps the Joint Committee was encouraged by the opening of an Anglo-American oil depot at Selsdon Road in 1894, but in April 1895 serious consideration was given to actually closing the line since the SER and LBSCR believed they were losing £1,000 a year each. This could not be done, however, for legal reasons, so the line continued its miserable existence until the First World War provided an opportunity to suspend its services. One brief glimmer of hope came in 1896 when the reported profit for six months was £154-11s-0d - to be shared between two companies.

The Woodside & South Croydon is a rare example of a line within 20 miles of central London that contrived to make a net loss even on its working for much of the 1890s. It could never hope to make a realistic return on its capital investment, which was estimated at £85,980 in 1885. Whereas the SER has often been accused of squandering resources in its battle against the LCDR, here was an example of the SER and the LBSCR each investing in a hopeless line purely to influence the activities of the other.

1.   SER Minutes, October-November 1846.
2.   SER Minutes, 21 October 1852.
3.   **Railway Times,** 16 December 1854.
4.   T.Woodman, **The Railway to Hayes.**
5.   Hayes played an early part in the Railway Revolution since Thomas Worsdell, who helped design for the first carriage for the Liverpool & Manchester Railway, was born there in 1788.
6.   T.Woodman, **The Railways to Hayes,** p.22.
7.   Woodside & S.Croydon Minutes, 27 February 1884.

CHAPTER 10: THE OLD MAIN-LINE FROM REDHILL TO DOVER

As has been seen in Chapter Two, the South Eastern opened its main-line from Reigate Junction to Dover in stages between 1842 and 1844. Although this hardly provided the most direct of routes from London to Dover, much of the line east of Reigate Junction was straight and very modestly graded, though it had substantial intermediate settlements at only Tonbridge, Ashford and Folkestone with the majority of Kent's largest towns being sited further north.

One of the first problems the line encountered was criminal activity, for the railway train soon attracted undesirable attentions. In November 1842 *The Times* reported that an SER train had been attacked with an air gun near Tonbridge and that a missile had been shot clean through the window of a first class compartment and out the other side. The *Railway Times*[1] denounced this story as untrue, but in February 1844 a more definite criminal act led to ten days Hard Labour for Thomas Latter after he had thrown stones at a train near Penshurst.

On 11 November 1843 the locomotive *Beult* was derailed at Tudeley because its driver failed to slow when track repairs were taking place.

As was common with many railways, the line had been opened with many of its facilities incomplete; the Company waited to see how traffic would develop before choosing where to invest. Thus the line had opened between Ashford and Folkestone on 28 June 1843, but it included no intermediate stations. The following month the *Railway Times* reported that Baxendale, the SER Chairman, had promised to provide a station for Hythe and Sandgate[2]. This opened as Westenhanger & Hythe on 7 February 1844, the day the line was extended from Folkestone to Dover.

In the months after the full opening of the line, further facilities were added. In June 1844 the SER decided to provide new sidings at Penshurst, Edenbridge and Godstone and the next month it decided to establish coke ovens at Folkestone Warren; it was then normal for railway locomotives to run on coke rather than coal. Plans for station buildings at Folkestone and Dover were also being drawn up in July 1844. However in January 1845 the Board learnt that the cost of "moving" Folkestone station was £290, which hardly suggests a permanent solution to the problem.

Dover had originally been provided with a temporary building made largely out of tarpaulin, which was later re-used - and rejected - at Maidstone. During 1844 Lewis Cubitt had been working on designs for an impressive terminus building at Dover, and in September 1844 he reported that he wanted raised skylights to allow fumes to escape. But then the SER lost interest in such a project and instead, from June 1845, began to pursue the subject of a hotel. By August 1845 they were discussing having a hotel with a tower that could be used by a look-out, and within the next three months land was being acquired. A jetty and sea-wall was needed to protect the site and the building of this progressed during late 1845 with stone brought from Merstham cutting. It was also decided

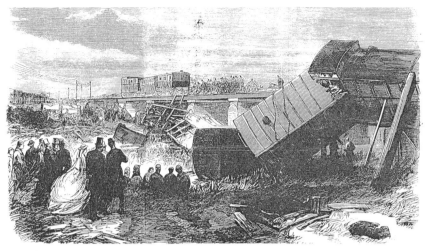

27.   The scene of the Staplehurst disaster.   Charles Dickens was travelling in one of the carriages that remained on the viaduct.

to glaze the Dover station on the seaward side to protect passengers using the departure platform. Goods facilities at Dover included the provision of a shed and cranes at the west end in 1844-5.

In September 1844 the Company continued its interest in hostelries of one class or another by deciding to build an inn at Westenhanger station, though nearby Smeeth was refused a station in November. In October two locomotives collided in Bletchingley Tunnel with one man being hurt. Also hurt was the pride of Tonbridge's stationmaster when he was sacked in November 1844 because of the "ill manner" in which he ran the station.

There were a few early problems with the works on the line. In December 1844 there was a chalk fall in Shakespeare Cliff Tunnel, not all of which had been lined. In January 1846 the sea encroached on the line between Shakespeare and Archcliffe Tunnels.

With the authorisation of a line from Ashford to Canterbury, Ramsgate and Margate, Ashford began to attain greater eminence. In February 1845 Barlow was directed to build an engine shed there and by July both this and a coke works were nearly completed.[3]

As traffic developed during Summer 1845, the SER began to adjust its capacity to the required levels. In April 1845 Folkestone platforms were widened and Westenhanger was chosen to receive a goods shed. In September it was decided that main-line platforms should be lengthened at all stations and that an engine shed should be built in Dover near to Archcliffe Fort. At the end of the year it was decided to have a lime works at Folkestone Warren. Even with light levels of traffic, the SER ran into problems. This was to be expected, since few staff would have had any substantial experience of railway work - even at senior management levels. On 28 July 1845 a Dover to London train left Tonbridge without a rear lamp. When this was realised, locomotive no.103 was sent out after it with the lamp[4]. Unfortunately the main train stopped at Penshurst, where no.103 ran into its rear at about 40mph. The Board of Trade criticised staff practices very severely and this led to the resignation of Captain Charlewood, the Line Superintendent, in September.

During 1845, a footbridge was tried at Tonbridge station and proved successful, so further footbridges were installed at Reigate, Paddock Wood, Ashford and Folkestone for £150 each during 1846. It was felt that Staplehurst was a key location for the hop traffic, so the SER decided to spend £500 on a hop shed there in time for the 1846 harvest.

Paddock Wood station had been left in an incomplete state and in December 1846 it was decided to complete it; it had been the junction for the Maidstone branch since September 1844. £1,000 was to be spent putting up permanent buildings which were completed by Spring 1848, for the stationmaster was told to be ready to move in that March. Charles Dickens chose Paddock Wood as the setting for the death of Carker in *Dombey & Son*, written in 1846-7. Returning from France and needing to "branch off to his place of destination", Carker found:

"*...a retired spot, on the borders of a little wood. Only one house, newly-built or altered for the purpose, stood there, surrounded by its neat garden; the small town that was nearest was some miles away.*"

After dinner at the tavern, Carker returned to the station, "wondering when another Devil would come by." He watched a South Eastern express pass by:

"*A trembling of the ground, and quick vibration in the ears; a distant shriek; a dull light advancing, quickly changed to two red eyes, and a fierce fire, dropping glowing coals; an irresistible bearing on of a great roaring and dilating mass; a high wind, and a rattle - another come and gone, and he holding to a gate, as if to save himself!*

...He loitered about the station,waiting until one should stay to call there; and when one did, and was detached for water, he stood parallel with it, watching its heavy wheels and brazen front, and thinking what a cruel power and might it had. Ugh! To see the great wheels slowly turning, and to think of being run down and crushed!"

Carker had a troubled night at the tavern, emerging to catch an early morning train, which was due soon after the express had passed through. But as he paced the wooden platform, he saw suddenly the face of his enemy, and stumbled onto the track:

"*He heard a shout - another - saw the face change from its vindictive passion to a faint sickness and terror - felt the earth tremble - knew in a moment that the rush was come - uttered a shriek - looked round - saw the red eyes, bleared and dim, in the daylight, close upon him - was beaten down, caught up, and whirled away upon a jagged mill, that spun him round and round, and struck him limb from limb, and licked his stream of life up with its fiery heat, and cast his mutilated fragments in the air.*

When the traveller, who had been recognised, recovered from a swoon, he saw them bringing from a distance something covered, that lay heavy and still, upon a board, between four men, and saw that others drove some dogs away that sniffed upon the road, and soaked his blood up, with a train of ashes[5]. "

Within two weeks of the opening of the Canterbury line on 6 February 1846, the SER decided that Ashford station needed to be enlarged and rebuilt on a much grander scale. Much of this extensive work was done in 1848-9 and then in April 1851 it was felt that the platforms needed lengthening although the engine shed was in the way. The rebuilding of the station to allow it to handle the traffic for the Canterbury and Hastings lines was reported as having cost

£267,433 by March 1853, though this figure presumably included the cost of improving the works as well.

On 24 January 1846 the bridge between Penshurst and Tonbridge collapsed into the River Medway during a flood. In the middle of the night a train ran off the end of the line and into the river. Driver Charles Dolby was cut between the engine and tender and "almost cut in two[6]" but the fireman, his brother, succeeded in dragging him out and swimming to the bank. However Dolby was already dead.

In May 1847 the Board seems to have embarked on a review of the station facilities between Ashford and Folkestone that caused some bad feeling locally. It began with considering whether Westenhanger & Hythe station should be moved to a different site, causing immediate objections. Smeeth, Sellindge and Bargrave were possible alternatives. In the event the Board decided to add a new station at Smeeth, but though tenders were discussed in September 1847 there was little further done until complaints began to arrive in March 1848. In May 1850 it was ordered that plans for a station, cottage and coal siding at Smeeth should be prepared, but then there was a further delay because the SER wanted the land to be given free. Dr Knatchbull, of the Hugessen family, was prepared to comply, but in June 1851 he objected to the SER's conditions. The station at Smeeth finally opened in October 1852.

The possibility of siting a station at Poundhill near Bletchingley was discussed in June 1847 as well. Tenders were opened in September and it was estimated that the station would cost £772. In November the Board debated whether the Godstone station should be closed and its traffic moved to Poundhill, which was convenient for both Godstone and Bletchingley. Nothing further was done about Poundhill and it would seem that Godstone station was left in a neglected condition, for in September 1850 there were complaints about its poor state. A further request from the Bletchingley area for a station at Poundhill in 1855 was also refused

The question of a station between Redhill and Godstone arose again in 1883

28. Tonbridge, SER, 1870.

at the instigation of Henry Edwards MP, a local landowner. On 26 April the SER approved a plan for a station at or near Mid Street, where there was already a siding. Construction of a station at Nutfield was under way by September, but on 25 October the new owner of a nearby estate wanted its name changed to

King's Mill. The station probably opened on 1 January 1884[7]. A stationmaster's house was added in 1885 for £450.

Fortunately some minor improvements were made. In March 1848 it was decided to build staff cottages at all the stations between Ashford and Tonbridge and in August it was decided to widen the platforms at Penshurst, which also received an inn and platform awnings in 1848-9. Platform awnings were installed at Paddock Wood as well and this station received a footbridge in 1850 so presumably the one approved by the Board in 1846 had never been installed.

Yet one of the least well furnished stations on the whole line was the terminus at Dover; in April 1848 there were reports that both the station and the goods shed were in a poor state. The Board had been considering building a hotel for some time, and by May 1847 had even decided on its name - The Lord Warden Hotel. Not until May 1851 was a tender to build it, by Kelk for £19,500, agreed on; the design was by Beazley. Money that should perhaps have been spent on the terminus was diverted into the building of this hotel.

Attention turned to Folkestone in 1851. Longer platforms were provided at the station and a carriage shed was built at "Folkestone Upper", the station that became known as Folkestone Junction and later Folkestone East. In April 1853 it was decided that all local goods for Folkestone should be handled at the "Upper" station instead of at the Harbour. Further west, the wooden bridges over the Medway between Penshurst and Tonbridge were causing worries and urgent repairs were ordered in December 1851, though it was not until 1861 that a new iron bridge was erected across the Medway west of Tonbridge for £2,300.

In 1850 the SER discovered a new way of making money by introducing the running of excursions to illegal prize-fights held beside its tracks. On 24 September 1850 one was run from London to watch Joe "The Spider" Hailes v. Jem Madden and Bob Wade v. Aaron Jones. The train stopped near Edenbridge, specially chosen to be near the border of several counties in the hope of avoiding the strong arm of the law. Steps were cut in the embankment so that the passengers could get down it and walk to the fight scene several hundred yards away. Spider won the first fight and Jones the second. On 27 October another fight was held at Edenbridge, but this time it was interrupted by the authorities and the train went back towards Redhill, where the fighting resumed until terminated by the onset of darkness.

Between 1851 and 1854 the SER had an unfortunate succession of accidents on this line. In May 1851 the down line was out of use for three days near Staplehurst after a derailment. On 1 April 1852 a London Bridge to Dover train was derailed at Edenbridge at 15mph when the locomotive ashpan struck the transverse rails that linked to a wagon turntable. These wagon turntables allowed trucks to be shunted individually and often had associated pieces of track running at angles across the main-line. Their rails were often two inches higher than those of the main-line and this was the third incident of a similar nature. On 30 July there was an accident at Headcorn, as a result of which the driver of the up tidal express and the stationmaster of Edenbridge were suspended. Then on 31 January 1853 there was a derailment between Penshurst and Edenbridge. However the accident that caused the greatest trouble occurred in late Spring 1854. A down express started from Redhill after the "line clear" signal had been received from Godstone. At Godstone the

29. "Folkestone Junction change for Folkestone Harbour". An eastward view towards the tunnel.

stationmaster was having his breakfast and did not realise that the porters had shunted a truck onto the line, with which the express promptly collided. It emerged that the Godstone stationmaster was the same one who had been blamed for the accident at Headcorn the previous July and he had been transferred to Godstone by Captain Barlow, the Line Superintendent, without MacGregor's support. Captain Barlow resigned in April 1854.

Distant signals were installed in 1852 at all the stations between Merstham and Dover. Freight traffic was gradually developing as well and in December 1852 it was agreed that the Pluckley stationmaster could act as an agent for the Southwark Manure Company, who sent horse manure from the streets of London down to Kent for use by the farmers. The Medway Navigation had "coal viaducts" for its traffic at Godstone and Edenbridge; these were replaced with conventional sidings in 1853 with the SER charging an annual rental of £10[8]. More illustrious traffic came to the line in March 1855 when Emperor Napoleon III paid a state visit to Britain; his train stopped at "Tunbridge Junction" (renamed January 1852) and he got out to talk to workmen there.

The line across the Weald included four timber bridges across the Medway and its tributaries. These were rebuilt in cast iron during 1855-6. Extensive rebuilding was also needed at Dover after a hurricane destroyed much of the sea wall in February 1856. A storm the following autumn was so bad that the sea encroached on to the station platforms and £4,000 had to be spent reinforcing the sea defences. £1,000 was spent on new groynes at Dover in April 1858.

Extra goods facilities were provided with a siding for the cattle market at Ashford in 1856 and £1,250 was spent on sidings for military traffic to Shorncliffe Camp, just east of Folkestone, the same year. On 21 February 1857 a Dover to London Bridge train derailed on the approach to Headcorn; the inspector found that the track was 14 years old.

At Dover the Admiralty had begun the construction of a new pier, a little east of the SER's station, in October 1847. It was first used by a channel steamer, the *Princess Alice*, on 19 June 1851. In December 1858 the SER proposed that a connecting line should be built to run on to the Admiralty Pier which, they observed in March 1859, should "go through the pilot house," which had been built only 15 years previously. The SER paid the Admiralty £5 for part of the foreshore in June 1859 so that it could build the extension line, but SER Minutes and Reports do not record the precise date when the line opened[9]. However it was ready for opening to passengers by early November 1861, for the Board of Trade refused to sanction it until a 3ft 6ins gap had been provided either side of the track for public safety.

The SER's rival, the LCDR, began building its own spur on to the Pier in 1864. The Pier retained the name of Admiralty Pier even after the Dover Harbour Board had taken over the area in 1861. In June 1864 the SER was told that £300 per year would be required for the use of the Pier and in July it was informed of the regulations for working it - the LCDR line opened on 21 December 1864[10], so these regulations were obviously prepared for the use of the Pier by two rivals. Regulations included the exclusion of the public from the Pier at least ten minutes before a train was due, the SER was to use the west spur onto the Pier and the platform at the north end while the LCDR was to use the easterly spur and the platform at the south end. LCDR trains were to be allowed to run onto the Pier first unless they were late; SER trains would be the first to depart. In July 1864 the SER Board noted that its extra staff costs on the Pier were £385 per year.

By October 1860 the SER was charging an annual rental of £1,600 to the proprietor of the Lord Warden Hotel. Clearly it was very popular, for extra sleeping rooms were provided in the roofing over the main station and the SER spent £297 connecting these rooms to the actual hotel by a bridge. In October 1861 the tenant asked for an extra storey of rooms over the station.

On 19 April 1861 the Edenbridge stationmaster, Gray, found an iron bar placed on the track with the obvious intent to derail a train. Almost as inexcusable was the behaviour of driver Swan, who was sacked in September 1863 for racing his goods train against a farmer's cart near Paddock Wood.

In January 1863 the rebuilding of Ashford station was discussed and £15,000 was estimated to cover the costs, £900 having already been spent to allow trains to be "shunted off the main line" and widen the through routes. Work seems to have been completed in 1865 with the wooden buildings being replaced by a red brick structure. Two additional platforms were provided.

Many locomotives had now become coal-burners and in 1862 the SER decided to give up coke making at Folkestone Upper. A new station was opened at Shorncliffe Camp on 1 November 1863, but it was renamed Shorncliffe Camp & Sandgate on 1 December. A house for the stationmaster was built in 1864.

One of the most infamous events in the history of the SER occurred on 9 June 1865 when an accident near Staplehurst killed ten people and seriously injured another forty. The timber baulks on the bridge over the River Beult were being renewed and the work had nearly been completed; foreman John Benge calculated that the last work could be done between the 2.51pm up and 4.51pm down trains and part of the up track was removed. Unfortunately he misread the timetable and did not correctly allow for the timing of the up tidal express, which ran at different times according to the Channel tides. The express, hauled by a Cudworth "A" class no.199, approached the scene at 50 mph; the driver saw the flag man stationed 150 yards[11] from the bridge, but only managed to slow to about 15mph before the train reached the bridge.

A passenger described feeling "two terrible jolts and in an instant afterwards, from bright sunshine all became darkness ...and chaos." One of the iron girders snapped and, though the engine succeeded in crossing the bridge with the first three vehicles, eight carriages were plunged into the mud and water beneath. There were numerous eye witness reports of the scenes that ensued:

"Through the broken sides and shattered windows were to be seen protruding human legs, and arms, and heads, and from every one of them was to be heard the piercing cry of human suffering...Some who survived were smothered in the liquid mud in which they were embedded.[12]*"*

Another witness observed that:

"The groans of the dying and wounded, the shrieks of frantic ladies and the shrill cries of young children, rising from the wreck of the train and mingling with the hissing of the steam from the engine, were awful in the extreme."

Among the passengers in the last carriage, which did not go over the edge of the bridge, was Charles Dickens. Though he was recognised at the scene by some of the passengers, his presence was not immediately known to the SER. Indeed Samuel Smiles, the SER Secretary, did not know about it until some time later. Perhaps Dickens did not want publicity at the time, for he was returning from Paris with his young mistress. Having calmed the two ladies in his compartment, Dickens got out to view the scene:

"Fortunately I got out with great caution and stood upon the step. Looking down I saw the bridge gone and nothing below me but the line of rail. The two guards (one with his face cut) were running up and down on the down side of the bridge (which was not torn up) quite wildly. I called out to them: "Look at me. Do stop an instant and look at me, and tell me whether you don't know me." One of them answered: "We know you very well, Mr Dickens." "Then," I said, "my good fellow, for God's sake give me your key and I'll empty this carriage." We did it quite safely, by means of a plank or two, and when it was done I saw all the rest of the train, except the two baggage vans, down in the stream. I got into the carriage again for my brandy flask, took off my travelling hat for a basin, climbed down the brickwork and filled my hat with water.

Suddenly I came across a staggering man covered with blood, with such a frightful cut across his skull that I couldn't bear to look at him. I poured some water over his face and gave him some to drink, then gave him some brandy, and laid him down in the grass, and he said: "I am gone" and died afterwards. Then I stumbled on a lady on her back against a pollard tree, with the blood streaming over her face (which was lead colour). I asked her if she could swallow a little brandy and she just nodded, and I gave her some and left her for somebody else. The next time I passed her she was dead. No imagination can conceive the ruin of the carriages, or the extraordinary weights under which people were lying, or the complications into which they were twisted among iron and wood, and mud and water."

The disaster had a great personal impact on Dickens, who was a sensitive man. In particular, the horror of trying to help people who literally died in his arms was something from which he never fully recovered.

A disaster such as this had both human and economic consequences. First of all there were the tragic deaths and reports described how a honeymoon couple had both died while one woman had been choked to death by the wreckage in front of the eyes of her helpless husband. There were also likely to be economic consequences for the SER, both in terms of compensation payments and bad publicity. Eborall rushed to the scene by special engine, to do what he could to help and to find out under what circumstances the accident had occurred.

Benge was arrested and charged with culpable negligence in causing the death of Mrs Condliff. He was the foreman platelayer, aged 33 and "very illiterate". The legal process examined how far Benge had conformed to the SER's regulations and it discovered that he had placed the look-out too close to the bridge and equipped the man with too few detonators. The guard on the train had not spotted the look-out's flag until it was too late to stop the train by applying the carriage brakes. Benge and the district inspector, Gallimore, were found guilty, but Benge's prison term was only nine months and this reflected the Judge's feelings that he had been unqualified for the heavy responsibility he had been given. This, of course, was a heavy criticism of the SER itself.

The accident seems to have cost the SER over £70,000 in compensation alone. By 28 June 1866 all but two cases had been settled and £61,815 had been paid out; the remaining two were expected to cost about £15,000.

Despite this terrible accident, the SER was capable of carrying heavy traffic in perfect safety. For the Volunteer Review at Dover in 1867 it shared with the LCDR in bringing 135,000 men and their supplies to the town without mishap.

Problems were beginning to emerge on the section of line through Folkestone Warren and along the cliffs. In March 1869 there was a serious slip caused by the sea encroaching and this affected sixteen coastguard houses worth £16,000. Though the slip did not effect the SER's property directly it was concerned and made a contribution for new groynes. The line at Dover was also badly exposed and the sea often broke over the wall, affecting the spur to Admiralty Pier in particular. There was a row in May 1869 over whether the SER or its tenant should pay for repairs to the stucco of the Lord Warden Hotel which had been damaged by spray. Further inland, there was a slip at Bletchingley Tunnel on 16 December 1869 after heavy rain.

The status of the "Old Main Line" was altered by the opening of the new and more direct line to Tonbridge in 1868. From 1 June most principal expresses used the shorter route, though local trains and a few of the Dover to London trains did still use the old route between Redhill and Tonbridge. The original wooden station on the east side of the bridge, once described as "a commodious and extensive structure," was replaced by a brick building on the west side. By 1871 the railway employed 140 people in the town[13].

Minor improvements at this time included the extension of the platforms at Folkestone Junction in 1869. This station had started life as Folkestone and then became Folkestone Old in July 1849, been renamed Folkestone Junction in January 1852, became Folkestone Junction (Shorncliffe) in September 1858, reverted to Folkestone Junction in November 1863. This instability continued later into the era, for in April 1884 it became Folkestone again and then in June 1897 was renamed Folkestone Junction for the third time.

In May 1870 the SER's Engineer, Francis Brady, suggested that water troughs on the main-line would allow it to speed up the express services. A report in June indicated that it would cost £2,161 to install troughs at Tonbridge and £2,100 at Staplehurst; it would also cost £25 to convert each tender to pick up water. Eborall disliked the idea, which he felt was an expensive way to save five minutes on a journey to Ramsgate.

Refreshment rooms were provided at a number of stations on the line. In 1869 tenants of them at Ashford and Tonbridge were paying an annual rental of £250 while those at Folkestone and Dover were held by the tenant of the Lord *Warden Hotel.* In May 1871 the tenant of the rooms at Redhill complained that the rent had gone up from £100 to £250, yet the opening of the direct Tonbridge line had seriously reduced his takings. For once the SER acted charitably and reduced the rent to £125.

In the early 1870s traffic began to grow slowly again after the economic uncertainties of the mid to late 1860s. Safety improvements also began to be made. In 1871 catch points were installed at the Warren siding near Folkestone and at Mid Street Siding, between Redhill and Godstone. An extra signalbox was provided to protect the goods yard at Redhill, which also gained an extra siding for 25 trucks for £250.

More substantially, in 1872 the SER began another plan to improve the station and works at Ashford. This included £8,500 spent on a new carriage construction shed in 1872.

In February 1872 Watkin and Eborall produced a report on the facilities of the line. They were concerned that the engine shed at Tonbridge only had an inside capacity for six locomotives with room for another 12 outside; they recommended a shed for 20 locos and this was provided, together with a carriage repair shed, for £4,500. At Ashford they approved the extensions to the works and to the school. Shorncliffe they found had been built very economically but now needed improvement - it was to get roofing over the platforms, the platforms were to be extended and the signalbox was to be moved to a better site. Folkestone Junction station was replanned in 1873, with a new signalbox being installed at the down end to supervise the points on to the Harbour branch; this cost £500.

On 24 February 1873 a porter was killed at Tonbridge station when he had tried to put the lamps into the carriages. He climbed up onto the roof but fell off as the train moved. Snow had made the surface slippery. He was run over by the tender and three carriages.

The policy of judicious improvements continued. Redhill shed was judged worthy of an extension to accommodate a further six locos in June 1873 but a request for a station at Nutfield that August was rejected, though once again the Board considered moving Godstone station. Later in 1873 Tonbridge got a covered coke stage and Smeeth had its platforms extended. In 1874 the people of the Paddock Wood area pressurised the SER for extra sidings and a weighbridge.

On 10 October 1884 a branch had been opened to Hythe and Sandgate. No station had been provided at the junction and this led to rather unsatisfactory working arrangements. In October 1874 the SER therefore considered spending £3,050 on providing new bay platforms at Ashford for the Hythe trains, and some extra sidings as well. However the following month it was decided to spend £620 on a new siding for Westenhanger so that Hythe trains did not have to travel as far as Ashford to interchange traffic. A new goods shed was provided at nearby Shorncliffe in 1875 for the military traffic.

During October 1875 the SER learnt that there was strong support in Folkestone for a station to serve the west end of the town. The original Folkestone station, at the Junction, was too far east while Shorncliffe Camp

30. The sharp curve between the SER's Dover Station and Admiralty Pier. The proximity of the line to the beach and to the Lord Warden Hotel is evident.

(known as Shorncliffe & Sandgate from 1863 to 1874 and later renamed Folkestone West in 1962) was too far in the opposite direction. The SER had hoped to improve access to Folkestone by extending its Hythe and Sandgate line along the seafront to the Harbour, but this was bitterly opposed by the Earl of Radnor, the landowner.

There seemed no easy solution to this problem so it was left to fester for a while. Instead the SER was faced with many problems in Dover when a severe storm on 14 November 1875 caused much damage to its facilities. The groynes in front of the Lord Warden Hotel were wrecked, much of the station roof collapsed and the tracks were flooded. The Admiralty Pier signalbox "disappeared" and its telegraph instrument was later found in the Inner Harbour.

The storm of 1875 was but a warning of worse to come, for the gales of 1 January 1877 had an even more catastrophic effect. Though the defence works built in 1874 stood up well to the test, the Dover goods shed was wrecked, the line from Dover station onto the Pier was undermined, tracks in the station yard were damaged by flood water and the basement of the Hotel was inundated.

Heavy rain continued and on 12 January part of the Martello Tunnel collapsed. Both tracks were buried under the rubble and trains had to be diverted over the LCDR via Beckenham or Strood. Two men were buried in the chalk and lost their lives. Repair work was done by Lucas & Aird at a cost of nearly £20,000. A single line was opened again on 12 March and both tracks came back into operation on 30 May. The LCDR charged the SER £2,957 for the use of its lines during the crisis.

Watkin made a personal inspection of the scene. He watched as the summits of the chalk cliffs were cut back by excavations and explosions to prevent further collapses. The chance was also taken to include extra sidings and "wharfs" between Folkestone and Dover. The SER reckoned in July that the total cost of the storm and flood damage was £36,159; this included £16,644 spent on Martello Tunnel and £15,477 on the Warren.

As a result of his visit Watkin suggested that a third line be laid in from Folkestone Junction to the Dover side of Martello Tunnel at a cost of about £40,000 for 1 mile 25 chains. In September SER interest turned more towards the construction of a deviation between the two towns to avoid the more troublesome areas, at a cost estimated at £70,000[14].

Elsewhere, extra sidings were provided at Smeeth and Redhill in 1876. A great success was the Pluckley brick traffic, for a new siding was installed early in 1877 and had to be extended by September. There was a collision at Tonbridge on 28 May 1878 when a Dover to Charing Cross train hit a light engine. A small signalbox was installed at Archcliffe Tunnel in 1878 -it cost a modest £35.

In July 1878 a subway was installed at Shorncliffe Camp station but the main developments there followed a decision in March 1880 to improve the station considerably. This was because the SER was increasingly irked by the unfair division of traffic that it believed took place within the legally binding Continental Agreement[15]. The LCDR was able to get around the Agreement's restrictions using ports such as Queenborough, but all the SER's Folkestone continental receipts had to be paid into the joint pool. The SER therefore decided to persuade passengers to use Shorncliffe instead, believing that the station would come outside the restrictions of the Agreement. On 1 February 1881 the SER opened a new station at Shorncliffe, 150 yards from its predecessor. Unfortunately the SER lost the subsequent legal battle and the main raison d'etre of Shorncliffe disappeared. There was an accident at the old Shorncliffe station on 10 October 1878 when a fireman was changing the headlamp on a passenger train and fell off; he lost both legs and was awarded £20 compensation.

The military camp at Shorncliffe was still poorly served for, despite various proposals, no branch had been built to it. In April 1882 the SER began to consider the question once more and within a month had begun buying land for the branch. 10,920 tons of stores were being sent to the Camp in a year, including 4,000 tons of forage, but early in 1883 the War Office decided not to support a branch and it was dropped.

31. Ashford Station on 12th May 1891, looking west.

On 17 April 1879 part of the up platform roof collapsed at Ashford station. Even less excusable was the behaviour of Henry Taylor; he was given ten years penal servitude in 1881 for putting a sleeper on the line near Paddock Wood.

Another development in 1883 was £600 spent on platform shelters at Tonbridge, where the platforms were also extended the following year. The following year the Paddock Wood to Ashford section was resignalled.

In January 1884 the SER discussed the provision of an extra station between Shorncliffe and Folkestone Junction. Two months later it decided to allow £3,000 for the scheme and Minutes of 14 August 1884 record a decision to open Cheriton Arch station on 18 August. In June 1886 Rev A. Hall-Hall suggested that the station should be renamed Radnor Park and the SER said that it would do this when supplies of the "Cheriton Arch" tickets had been exhausted. It is pleasing to note this careful husbanding of shareholders' money! The change of name took place that September.

Further west, the SER was concerned about the LCDR's arrival in Ashford following the opening of its Maidstone & Ashford line on 1 July. The SER suffered a loss of traffic at Ashford but decided not to reduce its fares. The LCDR line was meant to include a connection to the SER at Ashford and also a spur to the SER in Maidstone, though the latter was to be built by the SER. This was to allow through running between the two systems. On 24 July the LCDR began construction of the spur at Ashford, but in a very desultory fashion.

During 1885 the SER bought land for a siding at Great Chart, which opened in 1887, and began to consider moving Westenhanger station to the junction with the Hythe and Sandgate branch, a point to be known as Sandling Park. There were several objections to this in May 1885 but the town of Hythe supported the idea. So the SER decided on a £4,000 plan for "Sandling Park Junction"[16] and began negotiations with a local landowner, Colonel Deedes. In January 1887 it decided to include a footbridge and in September agreed plans for a stationmaster's house for £403. At the same time it decided to call the station "Westenhanger for Saltwood," intending to close Westenhanger station entirely. However in November it decided to keep Westenhanger open for goods and the following month backtracked entirely. Sandling Junction opened on 1 January 1888, though the Board referred to it habitually as "Sandling Park."

An interesting side issue over this station was a row that broke out with Col Deedes. Under the agreement with him, the SER was only meant to build a one-storey station house, but it had built a two-storey. Deedes objected, demanding free travel from the station to London for eight years as compensation. He was refused. More grateful was Hythe Council, which sent a letter of thanks in January 1888.

In April 1886 the SER was excited by reports that coal had been found near Tonbridge and in the no. 2 shaft of the Channel Tunnel workings at Shakespeare Cliff. This offered the prospect of a great boost to goods traffic on the line, though in fact its output was disappointing.

Also during 1886 a new siding was laid in on the down side at Paddock Wood with the intention of reducing the amount of shunting made across the main-line between the wagon turntables. For the summer of 1886 the SER opened a station which they claimed was "temporary" at the Warren near Folkestone. They built a bridge across the line and put in a gate to encourage picnic traffic, to the annoyance of Lord Radnor who owned the land nearby. It seems most likely that the station came into use about 1 July and that Radnor's threat of legal action over trespass caused its rapid closure[17].

Growing traffic and faster trains forced the SER to redesign its signalling provision. Having already installed interlocking over much of the line in 1884, it decided in 1887 that a number of new signalboxes were needed as well. New boxes were needed to break up the sections between Paddock Wood and Marden, Headcorn and Pluckley, and "Sandling Park" and Shorncliffe. It was also felt that with the opening of Sandling's station, another box might be needed between Smeeth and Westenhanger. "Advance signals" were to be installed from Grove Park to Shorncliffe and the platforms at Smeeth were to be lengthened. A new carriage siding was added at Tonbridge in 1888.

The SER's decision to increase fares to Shorncliffe in January 1888 precipitated a major argument that caused the Company considerable political damage. Feeling in Folkestone was already running against the SER and many began to demand a more effective local service between Sandling Junction, Shorncliffe and the other Folkestone stations. A handbill published by Folkestone Corporation demanded a reduction in fares, express stops at Shorncliffe, a better service to Radnor Park, a weekday express to reach London before 10am and cheap excursions. More seriously, it demanded the exercise of LCDR running powers from Ashford to Folkestone, and SER running powers from Ashford to Maidstone. Four months later Maidstone Corporation joined the argument, demanding that LCDR Maidstone & Ashford line trains should run into the SER's Ashford station. The SER blamed the impasse on the "insulting communications" sent by the LCDR, pleaded that the Continental Agreement impoverished it so much that it could afford no improvements, but agreed to put on an hourly local service between Sandling Junction and Dover. With the opening of a new line from Folkestone to Canterbury in prospect, it also decided in October 1888 to build a station at the junction near Cheriton and to rename Shorncliffe Camp plain Shorncliffe; the Radnor Park name (formerly Cheriton Arch) had now been "adopted"[18].

The response was not so positive at all places. In January 1889 a suggestion for a station east of Ashford at Willesborough was rejected but by March land was being bought for the station at Cheriton. The express service to Sandling Junction was improved in 1889 to encourage development of the Seabrook Estate, in which the SER held an interest. A review of facilities at Folkestone Junction suggested that both goods and passenger accomodation was largely unchanged since opening and investment was much needed; £2,250 was spent on it in 1890-1, including a new goods shed.

Another issue at Folkestone was the bridge across the road at Radnor Park which had caused the station to get its first name of Cheriton Arch. This caused road traffic problems and there was much pressure to have the bridge improved. In 1886 the bridge had been surveyed as there was a plan to build a new direct branch to the Harbour, which would have involved changes to the levels of the main-line to take the branch underneath it. Until that was built the SER planned to put in timber decking at a cost of £2,500.

The simple question of a bridge then began to become very complicated. The Folkestone Borough Engineer asked for a bridge with 80 feet span, estimated to cost £4,000. In February 1890 Lord Radnor offered to contribute a miserly £50 if the span was 60 feet wide rather than 40 feet; the SER said it was no concern of their's, but they would contribute £500. Folkestone itself wanted a better road but was also aware that Radnor Park station was a great success; it is "every day more popular for the central traffic," they pointed out. Protracted negotiations then followed: by December 1891 it had been established that a girder bridge would cost £5,719, of which the SER was prepared to give £750, Folkestone Corporation £2,750 and Lord Radnor £750. Eventually the SER agreed to contribute a further £100.

On 14 October 1889 a porter was killed at Folkestone Junction; he was crushed while coupling up a passenger train. Later that year platforms were lengthened at Staplehurst and extra platform covering provided at Sandling Junction. Requests for a better local service between Redhill and Tonbridge were largely ignored, as was a request in July 1890 for a station at Sellindge.

Maidstone Corporation had been less satisfied than Folkestone in its dealings with the two railways. It decided to go to the Railway Commissioners in order to force through running beyond Ashford. When the case was heard in January 1891 the SER said that it could not run to Maidstone as it had no powers to run into the LCDR station there, it having been expected that it would build a spur to its own Maidstone station. The LCDR had been denied access to Ashford (SER) due to "congestion". The Commissioners ordered that "reasonable accommodation" should be provided and work to complete the short spur between the two lines at Ashford had to begin.

From 1 November 1881 the spur was opened and in December it was decided to run five through trains on weekdays and two on Sundays through to Ashford (SER) over a spur of 51 chains, of which 31 belonged to the SER. Trains were to be collected by SER locos at the LCDR junction.

During 1890 there was renewed interest in a branch to Shorncliffe Camp but no progress was made.

In 1891 £150 a siding was installed between Folkestone and Dover with a view to developing coal traffic. Watkin got so excited about this that he even took the "Channel Tunnel" coal to a General Meeting of the SER. On 22 March 1890 oil had been found as well, 1,180 feet down at Shakespeare Cliff. Work on the colliery shafts began in March 1893.

Improvements during 1892 included an expansion of facilities at Paddock Wood, £760 spent on sidings at Redhill, a new up siding west of Ashford station, £300 on down side waiting rooms at Radnor Park, and the resignalling of Godstone and Penshurst. Twenty staff cottages were approved for Aycliffe Farm near Dover. Less welcome in Dover was fire, which struck the station on 5 May 1892. It started in the lamp room and was spread by a strong wind to engulf the offices and refreshment rooms. Soldiers from the nearby barracks and the Lord Warden Hotel's fire-engine were sent to help but the fire ended with "the whole station in ruins." Telegraph wires were brought down so traffic had to be halted. Considering Dover was meant to be a major station, it is interesting that the insurance company paid only £1,900.

On 2 March 1893 the SER agreed to a proposal from the Tonbridge Local Board that the name of the station in their town, Tunbridge Junction, should become Tonbridge Junction. This took effect from about the end of April. Also proposed for renaming was Radnor Park, but in June 1893 Watkin personally prevented it from being changed to Folkestone Central. The change was delayed until 1 June 1895, a final sign of Watkin's loss of power.

The steady growth of goods traffic meant more sidings were needed in 1893. A siding at Headcorn cost £340, Staplehurst gained a siding and cattle dock, and £1,100 was spent at Tonbridge on sidings. Not all rural traffic was welcomed by everybody however - in February 1894 the SER received complaints about the "nuisance" caused by the manure traffic at Marden. A house was built for the Dover stationmaster at Aycliffe for £600 in 1894. No doubt the poor man needed this shelter, for there was a collision at his station on 7 November 1893 and it caused part of the roof to collapse.

Folkestone Central was a poor station, hardly equipped for its role as the main station for the people of the town. In October 1895 the SER decided to improve it, aiming to spend £5,000 on a new up bay which could be used to attach Folkestone portions to up Dover trains with an equivalent bay on the down side; platforms were also to be widened. The Board was not amused when it discovered, after the work had been completed in 1896, that the final cost was £10,158 - a considerable overspend. The service at Folkestone was improved from 1 July 1897 by the addition of a 8.55am up train to Cannon Street, arriving at 10.30am. A balancing working was provided in the 4.30pm ex-Charing Cross/4.40pm ex-Cannon Street, running with portions to Sandgate and Folkestone Central. The platforms at the Central station were roofed over in 1897.

More modest Penshurst received platform coverings worth a cheap £250 in 1895 and in 1896 a siding was provided between Nutfield and Godstone for Williams & Co.'s brickworks, close to Crowhurst Public Siding.

In April 1896 problems were encountered with the sea encroaching near the Warren and in November there was a land slip near Martello Tunnel. As a result of this part of the Tunnel was opened out in 1897 at a cost of £6,568. In October the SER introduced a Bill to allow a deviation between Folkestone and Abbot's Cliff for the colliery works, which also forced the laying down of extra sidings at Dover in 1898.

Also in October 1897 the SER began buying land as part of a longer term scheme to improve Tonbridge station. Less fortunate were the people of Leigh, west of Tonbridge, who were refused a station in September 1898.

In 1897-8 humble Marden station was remodelled including new "station lines" and buildings for about £3,000. Three months later goods and breakdown sidings were added at Ashford and in 1898 extensive work was carried out at Folkestone Junction to build new goods facilities in the triangle of lines at a cost of £5,500. Though Central had become the main passenger station, Junction remained the base for freight activities. A siding was added at Shorncliffe in 1898 for the Folkestone Electric Company.

In March 1898 the SER decided to encourage the Race traffic at Westenhanger by giving prize money (a common practice among railway companies) and improving the station. The down side was extended and the whole area resignalled.

The SER era on the main-line ended with a bang rather than a whimper, certainly at Ashford where there was a collision on 8 April 1898. An excursion train from Folkestone to London was standing at the up platform when it was hit in the rear by loco no.250, and then hit again by no.246! There were 26 injuries.

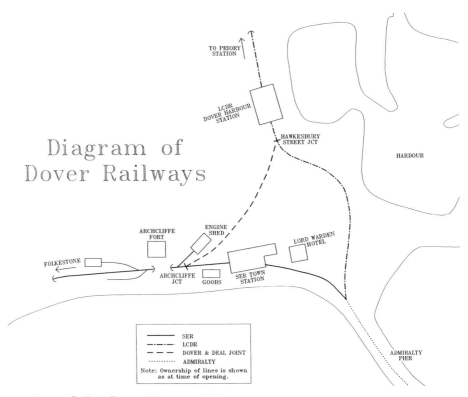

Diagram of Dover Railways

TO PRIORY STATION

LCDR DOVER HARBOUR STATION

HAWKESBURY STREET JCT

HARBOUR

ARCHCLIFFE FORT

ENGINE SHED

LORD WARDEN HOTEL

FOLKESTONE

ARCHCLIFFE JCT

GOODS

SER TOWN STATION

ADMIRALTY PIER

————— SER
—·—·— LCDR
— — — DOVER & DEAL JOINT
·········· ADMIRALTY
Note: Ownership of lines is shown
as at time of opening.

1.   **Railway Times,** 5 November 1842.
2.   **Railway Times,** 22 July 1843.
3.   For a full account of the growth of Ashford as a railway town, see G.Turner, **Ashford - The Coming of The Railway.**
4.   D.L.Bradley, **The Locomotive History of the SER.**
5.   C.Dickens, **Dombey & Son,** Oxford Illustrated Edition, pps.777-9..
6.   **Illustrated London News,** 1846, p.53.
7.   Date given as scheduled opening on a poster of September 1883.
8.   The navigational connection survived in the naming of the Godstone siding as Heasman's Wharf (information from R.W.Kidner).
9.   A.Hasenson, **History of Dover Harbour,** pps.126-7, gives opening as late October 1860 but indicates that the track on the pier had to be relaid almost immediately; this may refer to us for goods only as there was no BoT inspection. See also Chapter 20.
10.   Hasenson gives 30 August 1864.
11.   There are a number of conflicting reports about the precise distance of the flag man from the bridge. 500 and 550 yards have also been given.
12.   **Illustrated London News,** 17 June 1865.
13.   A.G.E.Jones, **When The Railway Came To Tonbridge.**
14.   SER Minutes, 29 September 1877; the figure seems too low for a major realignment of the route.
15.   See Chapter 4.
16.   SER Minutes, 26 August 1886.
17.   SER Minutes, 15 July 1886.
18.   SER Minutes, 18 October 1888.

CHAPTER 11: THE NEW MAIN LINE AND ITS BRANCHES

1. The New Main Line

As has been seen, the SER opened its main-line on a rather circuitous route to Dover that ran via Croydon and Redhill, opening it in stages between 1841 and 1844. This was an unsatisfactory route, because it avoided the populous towns of North Kent and also left the SER exposed to any rival line which would have little difficulty in selecting a shorter way of reaching Dover.

These problems became clear as the Railway Mania gathered momentum and the SER was forced to consider shortening its own line to improve its position against intruders. In the Autumn of 1844, for example, the London & Croydon prepared a Bill for a line from Sydenham to Ashford with branches to Tonbridge and Canterbury for which Joseph Cubitt was the engineer; this act of "unqualified hostility", as the SER saw it, cost Cubitt his job with them and Barlow replaced him. By early November the SER was surveying its own direct line to Tonbridge from off of its North Kent line, a procedure which caused such fury in the L&CR that it threatened to publish correspondence between the two companies.

By January 1845 the SER had already invited Samuel Morton Peto to build the "Direct Tonbridge" line and a Bill was before Parliament. The chosen route was from Eltham, on the North Kent route, to Shoreham, Otford and Ightham, then branching into two forks going to Tonbridge and Paddock Wood. Later,

32.   A Class B 4-4-0 passing Chislehurst.   (Wakeman Collection)

though, Lewisham seems to have become the favoured starting point. However the 1844-5 Parliamentary contest ended with stalemate, for no new schemes were authorised into Mid-Kent.

One of the rivals in the 1844-5 session was the Central Kent Railway, backed largely by Maidstone interests and favouring a line very similar to the SER's. In November 1845 the two parties began talks and in January 1846 Robert Stephenson suggested that the SER should consider a line from the Surrey Canal, via Bromley and Ightham, to Maidstone and Ashford.

Maidstone was a powerful magnet for prospective lines and its peculiarly poor position on the SER enticed hostile proposals for the district. Thus a Mid Kent scheme of late 1846 proposed a line from Lewisham to Tonbridge, but included branches to Bromley, Maidstone and Sevenoaks. As described in Chapter Nine, the SER saw various Mid Kent Railway schemes as a means of keeping the LBSCR out of Kent. However the 1846 session ended with no significant lines being authorised into central Kent, not even the SER's new plan for a line direct to Chart near Ashford. By December 1846 it was anticipating spending £700,000 on a line from the Mid Kent Railway to Tonbridge, and a further £300,000 on a branch to Maidstone from Ightham.

As 1847 began the contest was becoming bitter. The SER had a Bill for a line from Lewisham to Tonbridge with branches serving Sevenoaks, Maidstone and Paddock Wood. The LBSCR was supporting the Kent Railway, an "atmospheric" scheme, for a line from New Cross to Bromley, Otford, Sevenoaks and Tonbridge, with a branch to Maidstone and continuing to Canterbury. According to H. G. Lewin, this scheme's "only chance of success lay in the prejudice of the inhabitants of towns like Maidstone and Canterbury against the company already serving them."

The 1847 session resulted in a moral, if not an actual, victory for the SER. The LBSCR proposals were rejected out of hand but time prevented much progress on the SER proposals. It was clear, however, that a Direct Tonbridge line, from Lewisham to Tonbridge and including a loop from Eltham to Dartford and a spur from Hadlow to Paddock Wood, had a good chance of success if brought forward again the following session.

In fact the SER did not push forward with the idea due to a downturn in financial confidence, followed by a period of Boardroom division. There was an 1851 scheme for a West Kent Railway from Lewisham to Tonbridge, but without result.

Only when hostile interests again began to show an ambition to capture central Kent did the SER return to the issue of a direct line to Tonbridge. In June 1854 the SER was worried that a Mid Kent Railway scheme for a line to Tonbridge could be captured by a rival, and Drane was sent out to survey the shortest possible route. More worrying still was the plan of the West End of London & Crystal Palace Railway, which in late 1854 was planning to extend its line via Bromley to Maidstone and also to Tonbridge.

On the SER Board Rich led the pressure for positive action, favouring SER support for a proposal called the Direct South Eastern, which wanted the SER to work it if authorised. The extent of ostrich-like behaviour on the SER Board can be gathered by the fact that in January 1855 they voted 4-3 against supporting the Direct South Eastern. The DSE was still active in June 1855, but then faded from view; the following year the Marquis of Camden was leading

33. The Hastings Car Train, with its distinctively-roofed carriages, passing Halsted & Knockholt Station. (Wakeman Collection)

the promotion of a Mid Kent & Tonbridge scheme, which aimed to join the SER at Paddock Wood with a branch to Tonbridge.

By late 1856 the SER was worried that a minor company which formed a short extension of the WEL&CP line, the Mid Kent (Bromley & St Mary Cray) Railway, planned a line from t. St Mary Cray to Tonbridge. The following May there were also plans for a line from Dartford to Tonbridge via Otford and Ightham. It was clear that the SER would have to build new lines to make the district safe, especially as it was becoming more concerned too about the role of the fledgling East Kent Railway in the area for this Company was actively seeking a "Western extension" towards St Mary Cray.

The result was that in late 1857 the SER began discussions with its ally, the Mid Kent (quite separate from the MK (B&SMC) about an extension to Tonbridge. By December agreement had been reached to extend the MKR via Chislehurst to Tonbridge, and to build a new SER line from Lewisham to meet it at Chislehurst.

1858 was the year in which the SER paid the penalty of its anti-expansion years. On 23 July the East Kent gained an Act for its Western extension and the LBSCR was on the verge of taking over the WEL&CP. The SER's response was to dust off the 1854 plans for Lewisham to Tonbridge, though there was also a local proposal for a line to Sevenoaks via Westerham.

Expansionism still caused disagreement on the SER Board and in October 1858 the plan for a "Central Kent" line to Tonbridge was only approved by six votes to three, Teulon being among the opponents.

Another local scheme was the Sevenoaks Railway, formed to build a line from the town to join the Western extension of the EKR at Swanley. Its directors included a number of men closely involved with the EKR such as Charles Lushington and Charles Hilton. Despite opposition from the SER, an Act was obtained on 1 August 1859; by 1861 the Company was planning an extension to Maidstone - sure proof that delays by the SER would bring intruders into the area.

In the summer of 1861 an SER director, Thomson, led pressure for the revival of Direct Tonbridge plans and in September surveys began once again. By October a grandiose £1million plan had been formulated - for a line direct to Tonbridge with a branch for Greenwich and Dartford. Estimates for the line had risen to £1.15m by January 1862, largely because of the high cost of making a tunnel at Sevenoaks which was expected to reach £60 per yard.

The promotion of a new main-line caused problems with the SER's friends and enemies alike. The Mid Kent (Bromley & St Mary Cray) threatened to be a bitter opponent, but a deal was struck whereby the Crays Company would not oppose the SER Bill if the SER did not oppose a takeover of the Crays by the London, Chatham & Dover (renamed from EKR on 1 August 1859). Potentially more difficult was the opposition of an erstwhile ally - the Mid-Kent, which feared loss of traffic; the SER promised to pay the company a minimum fee for the use of its line based on receipts before the opening of the new Tonbridge line.

Also threatening was the posture of the LCDR and its ally, the Sevenoaks, which in late 1861 had been planning extensions to Maidstone and Tonbridge itself. A costly legal battle seemed likely, but in February 1862 a round of negotiations took place. The Sevenoaks Company hoped that the SER could be persuaded to drop its own Direct Tonbridge line and use part of the Sevenoaks Railway's track, branching off from its proposed Maidstone extension at Ightham. This did not appeal to the SER but fairly even terms were eventually agreed: the LCDR and Sevenoaks agreed to drop their scheme for a line to Tonbridge of their own and they would not oppose the SER's, while the SER agreed to give up its use and control of the St Mary Cray Company from 1 September 1863, not to oppose the LCDR's take over of it[1], to allow interchange between the lines at Sevenoaks and not to oppose the Sevenoaks Company's Maidstone extension. The result of all this was that the Sevenoaks

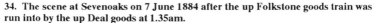

34. The scene at Sevenoaks on 7 June 1884 after the up Folkstone goods train was run into by the up Deal goods at 1.35am.

Railway's line to Maidstone was authorised on 17 July and the SE's new main line on 30 August 1862.

For once the SER pressed ahead with the construction of a new line with all speed, conscious that any delay would help the LCDR to gain a stronger hold on the market. In September 1862 the Board inspected the line between "North Kent Junction and Lewisham Road" and concluded that it would be impossible to make the necessary alterations to this part of the line without disturbing North Kent traffic; they therefore decided that the work there should be done by the SER itself under the direction of its engineer, Peter Ashcroft.

On 9 October the Board met to consider the letting of contracts. The Dartford branch, of 9.5 miles, was to form one contract, Loam Pit Vale to the north end of "Polehill" Tunnel a second (11.5m) and "Polehill" to Tonbridge (12m) a third. It was felt that work should begin first at Sevenoaks Tunnel and that the work between North Kent East Junction and Lewisham should be done by the SER[2]. Also to be done by the SER was the rebuilding of the station and junction at Tonbridge; Tonbridge station was to be redesigned so that trains from Hastings did not need to back out onto the main-line.

Both main-line contracts went to John Jay in March 1863 for £600,000. The Dartford contract was awarded to Rennie, Logan & Matthews for £72,396. Work began quickly after that and a tin chapel was put up in Sevenoaks for the navvies; the SER gave £50 to support the cause.

Once again, though, the SER had problems with its contractors, Jay becoming financially embarrassed so that by September 1864 the SER was complaining of slow progress on the works. The line was very difficult to build due to the geology of the area, which featured greensand, chalk and clay, with substantial quantities of water being trapped underground and causing great problems with tunnelling in particular. Two men were killed while undercutting chalk at Lewisham in the late summer of 1864.

Landowners did not help the line's progress. The tunnel at Elmstead was intended to be only 293 feet long, but extensions were forced by the pressure of a Mr Scott. The contractors were not allowed to cross his land to get to the site and the tunnel had to be constructed without the use of shafts. In January 1865 the completion of this Tunnel (referred to as "Sundridge Park Tunnel") was marked with a dinner for two hundred guests being held in it, catering provided by the staff of the London Bridge refreshment rooms. The keystone arch was laid by Ashcroft.

Jay's bankruptcy forced the SER to take over the work itself, but by March 1865 the line was reported as being nearly ready as far as Bickley and the Board considered putting in a temporary station there. In May the opening as far as Chislehurst was delayed by a month and there was some criticism of the contract with Jay by shareholders since he had been more or less invited to tender for the line. The line opened to Chislehurst & Bickley Park on 1 July 1865, this station being renamed plain Chislehurst on 1 September 1866. There were no other new stations.

The works south of Chislehurst were very considerable, including an 80 feet high embankment at Orpington that caused great difficulty from slipping, a short tunnel at Chelsfield, and two long tunnels at Polhill (1 mile 851 yards) and Sevenoaks (1 mile 1,693 yards). In January 1867 work on drawing up the plans for the new stations began but hopes for an opening on 1 March 1867 were abandoned due to bad weather. The SER informed the Board of Trade that they wished to open the line on 1 June instead, but the Board of Trade found much that was unsatisfactory. The embankment at Chislehurst did not reach the temporary station, there was at least another two months work to be done at Chelsfield, and the Sevenoaks to Tonbridge section needed another three months of effort at least.

The failure of Jay had been well-covered in the railway press and other journals whipped up fears that the line had been badly built. It was said that there had been, and continued to be, many slips, that unsatisfactory chalk ballast had been used, and it was strongly implied that Jay had compromised safety in rushing to finish the works before 1 August 1865 - after which he had faced a penalty of £300 per day.

A major landowner in the Chislehurst district was a railway contractor named Wythes who had bought Bickley Park. In December 1867 he discussed the provision of a permanent station at Chislehurst with the SER under an agreement of January 1864, but the SER was very hesitant and Wythes threatened to use the courts to get a station or delay the opening of the line. Wythes was attempting to develop Chislehurst for housing and eventually Watkin met him personally in February 1868; Watkin agreed to provide a siding for ten trucks, to move the station to a better site, and to provide a road to the station. The opening of the second Chislehurst station is usually stated to be 2 March 1868[3], but this would have involved very rapid construction and the first station was certainly used on that date. The new station was eventually opened at a site on Summer Hill Road, itself partly built by Wythes and offering an easier gradient than Chislehurst Hill[4]; no doubt the site reflected Wythes' development plans for the district.

The line opened in a rather spasmodic way. From 3 February 1868 it began to be used for four goods trains per day, opened to passengers as far as Sevenoaks on 2 March and for local trains only as far as Tonbridge Junction on 1 May. The expresses did not begin using the line until 1 June and this cautious proceeding shows that the SER itself had some concern over the stability of the works. Some continental trains may have used the line before 1 June but without altered schedules, perhaps because the state of the works did not allow for higher speeds. The Dartford loop, which left the main-line at what is now Hither Green, opened on 1 August 1866. Intermediate stations were opened at Orpington, Chelsfield, Dunton Green & Riverhead and Sevenoaks on 2 March. One intermediate station south of Sevenoaks, Hildenborough, opened on 1 May.

While the line was being opened, stories about its safety continued to circulate. The *Railway Times* unwisely printed some anonymous letters and Ashcroft, the SER engineer, sued. He won an apology in December 1868.

The station at Chelsfield had been erected as part of an agreement with a local landowner, Waring. However its position on a hill made it inconvenient for local people and as early as December 1868 there were protests. By February 1869 they had taken their campaign as far as raising a subscription for a new station near *The Wheatsheaf*, with the Vicar of Knockholt joining the campaign in May. In April 1870 the SER received an offer of a £1,000 loan towards the station. A year later the SER looked at the cost of a station and found that for passengers only it would cost £3,500 and a further £4,000 if goods facilities were included. This seemed too much but in August it seemed possible that a landowner might provide £5,000. Watkin and Eborall toured the line in

February 1872 and felt that the SER would provide £1,000 if the locals paid the rest, but by April only £2,000 had been raised. Only by July 1875 was the SER prepared to proceed with a £3,000 subsidy from landowners. It opened on 1 May 1876 as Halstead for Knockholt - the end of a lengthy saga!

Part of the agreement between the SER and LCDR over the new line had been for a connection between the former Sevenoaks Railway (renamed Sevenoaks, Maidstone & Tonbridge) at Bat & Ball and the SER at Tubs Hill, but this had been delayed by the financial problems of the SMTR. In March 1869 the Board of Trade refused to authorise this link until a turntable was provided at the SER station, so the SER decided to move one from Chislehurst. The link, known as the Sevenoaks Junction line, opened on 1 August and cost £13,462. In April the SER station had been renamed Sevenoaks.

The SER and the SMTR had agreed on a level of fares to Sevenoaks which caused uproar in the district. In May 1869 the SER therefore decided to reduce fares, the first class single to London being cut by 1s to 6s; this was done in

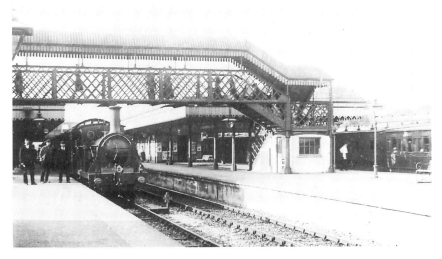

35. Grove Park, SECR.

consultation with the LCDR. In August Watkin admitted that the Sevenoaks fares were "excessive"; they were kept high so as to avoid having to reduce fares to other parts of Kent after the opening of the shorter line.

The station at Hildenborough lacked any goods facilities and in March 1870 the SER was asked to provide them by a landowner. It refused, the Minutes recording that this was because the landowner had forced a high price for his land and demanded excessive compensation when the line had been built. In January 1871 local people requested a proper passenger and goods station, but a plan for a £600 goods siding was deferred in October.

The normally obscure station at Chislehurst achieved greater fame in 1871 when the family of the deposed French Emperor, Napoleon III, moved into nearby Camden Place. For a time Napoleon was a held prisoner by the Germans, but on 20 March 1871 stationmaster Lord received a telegraph message that he had arrived in England and rushed to the Place with the news.

A special train was laid on to take ex-Empress Eugenie to Dover to meet him - a sure indication of Watkin's political favours. On 3 April Queen Victoria herself visited Chislehurst by train, but she found Camden Place overheated and did not become a regular caller!

A station at Grove Park was opened on 1 November 1871 as a result of a deal with a landowner, Mr Pond, who paid the SER £1,511-19-8d. Opening had been slightly delayed when the Board of Trade insisted on platform accomodation on the down side and a clock visible to the line. The same month saw an up side shelter at Chislehurst and the supply of gas to Hither Green signalbox authorised.

On 20 February 1872 Watkin and Eborall toured the line to see how its traffic was developing and to authorise new facilities accordingly. They felt that new stations were required at upper Lewisham and Hither Green Junction though, as stated earlier, they felt that a Knockholt station depended on local support. Chislehurst was to get an up carriage siding and the up shelter previously agreed on. Orpington was to get an up side while Sevenoaks needed a goods shed, crane and siding. It was felt that Tonbridge could be supplied with water brought out of Sevenoaks Tunnel. In May the Tonbridge Water Company offered £100 a year for water from the Tunnel. By 1876 the water was being used for locos at Tonbridge and also at Hildenborough and Sevenoaks stations.

These plans were soon put into effect. By April plans for Chislehurst, at £880, had been agreed; Upper Lewisham station and provision for empty carriage stock was estimated at £4,860. This station, St Johns, opened on 1 June 1873 but did not satisfy all at Lewisham since there were requests for a station at High Street. The SER considered the issue in March 1873 but realised that this site would be only 682 yards from Ladywell and 1,276 from Lewisham station. In November 1873 a station at Court Hill was considered. The SER thought that Hither Green Junction was the best site, but no station was built there until 1895.

During the Parliamentary session of 1872-3 the SER aimed to use the new main-line as a starting point for a direct route to Maidstone and Nettlestead from Hildenborough. It had doubts about the costs of this though, and by February 1873 was seeking a short connection onto the SMTR's line from Dunton Green with running powers to Maidstone. In 1875 the idea resurfaced with a plan for a 1.5 mile line to the SMTR at Otford. The idea was still alive in 1877 when it caused bad feeling between the SMTR and the LCDR.

Chislehurst was gradually gaining more importance, gathering a longer siding on the down side and a stationmaster's house in 1874. Dunton Green gained a coal siding the following year.

On 13 November 1876 a porter was killed at St Johns when he tried to cross over the tracks by walking across the buffers of some carriages.

There were further minor improvements in 1877, including a trial iron bridge at Hildenborough station and a new signalbox between Halstead and Dunton Green to reduce delays.

Most activity centred around Grove Park, which became a junction from 1 January 1878 with the opening of the branch to Bromley. The SER had prepared for this by installing a footbridge and buying three acres of land for marshalling sidings. More land was needed in 1879.

Two cottages were provided in the goods yard at Chislehurst for staff in 1878 and extra sidings at Sevenoaks. Extra signalboxes were provided between Tonbridge and Hildenborough in 1878-9.

During 1878-9 the LCDR promoted a Sevenoaks and Knockholt line, which the SER spent £1,367 opposing; it sent the Bill to the LCDR since it felt that the scheme betrayed their agreement, but there is no record of the LCDR having paid! At the same time the SMTR was encouraging the SER to build a junction line from Dunton Green in the hope that the SER would then back a SMTR extension from Maidstone to Ashford.

With a branch line being built to Westerham, the SER decided in July 1880 to rebuild Dunton Green station in a style fit for a junction. The branch opened on 7 July 1881 but obviously there were problems with passengers changing trains, for in December 1882 it was decided to build a subway to replace crossings over the main-line and the branch.

Early in 1882 the campaign in Lewisham for another station was renewed with petitions and public meetings, the people asking for connections between main-line and local services. In August the SER found that a station at Hither Green Junction would cost £9,500 but, despite a further request being received in November 1883, once more nothing was done. The cause of bad feeling was that Lewisham station was served by North Kent and Mid Kent line trains only, so that the people of this substantial town had to go to St Johns for main-line trains. Even the expenditure of nearly £2,000 on improvements to the station buildings at Lewisham Junction in 1888 could not ease the annoyance felt locally.

On 7 June 1884 the 10pm Folkestone to Bricklayers Arms goods was hit in the rear by the 6pm Deal to Bricklayers Arms at Sevenoaks while taking water, due to negligent work by the Hildenborough signalman. The driver and fireman of the Deal train were killed and the SER had to pay out £4,608 in compensation to the owners of damaged goods.

During the mid-1880s relations between the SER and LCDR went into one of their periodic black phases, resulting in the promotion of a number of schemes apparently designed largely to annoy each other. These included a line from Ightham to Hadlow and Tonbridge and a scheme called the Shortlands & Knockholt, which the SER assumed was a LCDR stooge. The SER Bill of 1884-5 included powers to widen the line from Surrey Canal Junction to Hither Green, but this was not done for another twenty years.

The LCDR had been using its Sevenoaks Junction line an drunning into the SER's Sevenoaks station and paying £1,000 a year for the privilege. The agreement under which it operated the service was set to run out on 30 June 1885. The LCDR continued the service for another year but then a dispute arose over the non-payment of the fees and the LCDR stopped running passenger trains from 1 July 1886 (noted in SER Minutes, 15 July), although a single daily freight continued to shuffle apologetically to the SER station and back again. In February 1887 the SER offered to buy the line, but the LCDR was unresponsive. It remained closed to passengers until 1 January 1899, when the SE&CR came into existence. The SER station went through a variety of name changes, but from 1869 it normally included the appendage "(Tub's Hill)" to distinguish it from the LCDR at Bat & Ball.

In 1891 the favourite issue of a station at Hither Green resurfaced and by Summer 1892 plans for it were actually well-advanced. Construction work was in progress during 1894 and the station opened on 1 June 1895; the buildings themselves cost £1,524 but considerably more was spent on associated works. Other stations received only minor improvements during this time, with Grove

Park getting new waiting rooms in 1892 and there was an extension to the down platform at Chislehurst in 1895. In June 1895 a down boat train split a tyre when passing Dunton Green.

In October 1897 the SER began preparing a Bill for widening the line between St Johns and Orpington, though in fact four tracks were never extended through to the latter town due to the heavy works on its approaches. At the same time the SER had also identified Hither Green as an ideal site for new marshalling yards and began buying land in 1897. Preparations for the arrival of the contractor to build the yard in early 1898 included the installation of new signalboxes - two permanent (with 70 levers and 57 levers) and one temporary to cover the contractor's siding (15 levers). The contractor was Rigby, who was also employed to do the St Johns to Orpington widening.

On 21 March 1898 a very serious accident occurred at St Johns. The 7.45am up from Tonbridge was standing at the up home signal when it was hit in the rear by the 7am up from Hastings. The day was very foggy and the Hastings train only ran at that particular time on Mondays. Three people were killed instantly and over twenty passengers injured. The St Johns signalman admitted liability but the jury at the inquest recommended that the box there should always have at least two men on duty. The SER Board felt that installing "train waiting treadles" would be helpful at such a busy location.

On 1 April 1898 a platelayer was killed at Hildenborough and on 24 June another was killed in Sevenoaks Tunnel. In July the Board decided to buy land at Halstead for chalk ballast and in November it was decided to resignal Sevenoaks Junction in time for the new fast Hastings service which was to start on 1 January 1899; this cost £380.

The new main-line was the last trunk route built by the SER and was built at considerable cost through difficult countryside that was sparsely populated. Its potential as a catalyst for development was shown rapidly in the numerous discussions with landowners and local people about the development of stations at various points. The railway certainly helped to create Chislehurst, Orpington and Sevenoaks as commuter settlements, yet at stations like Knockholt and Dunton Green it had relatively little impact.

2. The Bromley Branch

The first railways in the Bromley area were built by the Mid-Kent company and by the West End of London & Crystal Palace. Neither gave a particularly direct route to the City, with the West End being far more accessible at least until the LCDR reached an arm across the Thames to the fringes of the City in 1864. This inconvenience lay behind an idea for a Bromley Railway in 1863, but although a deputation spoke with the SER no line was built.

In November 1872 a private scheme for a line from Grove Park to Cage Field, Bromley, appeared, but it was dropped the next month. A year later another scheme appeared under the name of Bromley Direct Railway and the LCDR demanded that the SER should oppose it as a territorial infringement. The SER refused to, citing the LCDR's involvement with a Crystal Palace scheme as provocation, and the Act for the line was passed on 16 July 1874. That September the SER gave consideration to buying the Company out and in January 1875 was prepared to give the promoter £3,500 for his expenses. However progress was very slow and further Acts had to be obtained in 1876 and 1877 for an extension of time and for extra capital. There were a number of disputes over land and one landowner at Bromley wrote to the SER to complain that "I cannot offer myself up as a generous victim at the South Eastern Railway Company shrine.[5]"

During the summer of 1876 the SER agreed to help in the construction and to operate the line; the price of this was that the Chairman, Mr W. Starling, was replaced by Beattie and Alfred Watkin was also on the Board. Brady, the SER engineer, was to advise on construction and suggested that money could be saved by using iron rails instead of steel. In November 1876 it was agreed to set aside £6,000 for the Bromley station.

Lucas & Aird won the contract to build the line for £39,500, to be completed by 1 August 1877 - with an extra £500 if it could be finished by 1 July. Neither deadline was met[6].

In July 1877 the Bromley Company was engaged in negotiations with a local landowner, Mr Scott; the Railway had agreed to build a station at Plaistow for him, but there was a dispute as to which side of the road it should be on. In November Scott enquired whether the station should be known as Sundridge Park or Plaistow; in fact it was opened as Plaistow and became Sundridge Park from 1 July 1894. The subject of a goods shed at Bromley and an engine shed at Grove Park was also debated.

Forbes of the LCDR showed close interest in the line and late in 1877 arranged a meeting to deal with the issue. The SER was plainly worried that the BDR's financial problems would give the LCDR a chance to gain a stake in it, and therefore loaned it a total of £16,000 in November and December 1877. The line was opened on 1 January 1878 with the one intermediate station.

The line was opened in a very incomplete state, especially for goods traffic. In February 1878 it was decided to excavate some ground for goods sidings at Bromley and to use the spoil to build an embankment at Grove Park for sidings and a shed. In August a further £400 was agreed to be spent extending the Bromley goods sidings.

In 1878 the SER prepared a Bill to absorb the BDR, offering 4.5% guaranteed SER stock in exchange for BDR stock. This seemed a generous offer, for traffic on the line was not encouraging; in its first six months passenger receipts were £319-10-9d ordinary and £83-15-9d "periodicals", with merchandise only £12-6-4d. However the SER could not risk the line falling into hostile hands and the BDR was absorbed into the SER from 21 July 1879. In 1885 its capital cost was estimated at £78,327.

It would be exciting to record the subsequent life of the branch as full of incident, but this was not to be. Indeed the only moment that diverged from the monotony of life on the branch was caused, rather surprisingly, by an SER decision in October 1887 to equip the good people of Bromley with a new siding. This siding destroyed an ancient footpath leading to Plaistow and sparked off a demonstration by 200 local people in December!

The name of Plaistow station was changed to Sundridge Park as a result of local requests; no doubt it improved house prices.

3. The Westerham Branch

There were several attempts to open a railway to Westerham before one finally arrived in 1881, though perhaps the word "attempts" should be used with caution for there is always the possibility that such lines were promoted to keep others out, rather than from any serious intention of bringing benefit to a small Kent town.

Thus during October 1863 the SER was considering a scheme for a line from Riverhead to Westerham, costing £59,375 for 4.75miles. At the same time there was also the possibility of the town being served by an extension of the Croydon & Caterham scheme, altogether a more grandiose project at £180,000. In fact the Act that was obtained in 1864 was for the branch off of the SER's new main-line, with capital set at £68,000.

Nothing further was done until talk of a new scheme reached SER ears in January 1866. They therefore introduced a Bill into Parliament to extend the time limit on their original powers, but although a further Act was obtained the financial climate was unpromising.

The issue lay dormant until September 1869, when the SER threatened to introduce a Bill for the abandonment of its powers unless local people were prepared to pay for a single line. The SER proceeded with a Bill for a further time extension, but including powers to transfer the whole scheme to local interests; this received its Act on 2 August 1870, but almost immediately the SER pleaded that the Franco-Prussian War made any further progress unthinkable! During this era one local man, Mr Tipping MP of Brasted Park, made himself some enemies by supporting the SER in its attempt to abandon the line; he was a director of the London & North Western Railway. George Wardle, another local landowner, complained that the SER's help was worth "next to nothing."

36. Dunton Green, SECR.

By November 1870 SER efforts had progressed as far as trying to get land cheaply, then - nothing. Westerham talked of getting a branch off one or other of the fanciful competitive schemes talked about in the early 1870s, but realistic progress seemed to depend on local pressure.

In May 1873 a deputation from the town visited the SER Board and later in the year the SER let it be known that it was planning a "cheap line" from Caterham to Maidstone via Westerham, though this was soon trimmed back to Riverhead.

In the Autumn of 1875 local people began to prepare their own scheme and a Bill was put forward for a railway from Dunton Green to Westerham and an extension from there to join the Croydon & Oxted route (which was incomplete) at Oxted. In February 1876 the SER agreed to work the Dunton Green to Oxted section but it threatened to oppose the whole project unless the Oxted extension was withdrawn; this was agreed to in March 1876. The Westerham Valley Railway received its Act on 24 July 1876, for the branch as far as Westerham only.

Once again very little happened. In February 1877 the SER and the WVR were discussing terms for working - would the SER guarantee £2,750 per annum? By April 1878 the SER was considering working it for 50% of receipts, with a minimum of £2,750 and agreement was finally signed on 25 June 1879. The cutting of the first sod, and the obligatory banquet, took place on 1 October was reported in the *Railway Times* of 4 October; no doubt the decision to get started was related to the discussion of schemes to link Otford and Dunton Green.

Some difficulties were experienced with poor weather during construction but by May 1881 the line was expected to open on 1 July. In fact the ceremonial opening and dinner took place on 6 July and the public opening the following day, a condition being that all trains had to stop at Brasted.

By an Act of Parliament of 11 August 1881 the WVR was absorbed by the SER. In September 1881 the SER agreed to contribute £100 towards the construction of a road to Brasted station. Brasted did not get a stationmaster's house until 1883, costing £560.

There was some debate as to whether Sundridge should get a station. In July 1882 one was estimated to cost a considerable £3,200, but in May 1883 it was felt that one could be provided for £695. But nothing emerged until the SECR opened Chevening Halt in 1906.

Despite the difficult country to the north and west of Westerham, the SER still worried about possible invasions from that direction. In 1885 it petitioned against the Westerham & Oxted Railway but its branch, of which the capital cost was then £75,574, remained inviolate.

Incidents were few, though there were complaints in 1897 that the station and yard at Westerham were often flooded.

1. SER Minutes, 13 February 1862.
2. This was to allow the SER to keep a tight control on any disruption to services already running in the area.
3. H.Borley, **Chronology of London Railways.**
4. D.McCall, **Patchwork of the History of Chislehurst.**
5. SER Minutes, 9 March 1876.
6. Bromley Direct Railway Minutes, 5 January 1877.

CHAPTER 12: TWO ROUTES TO MAIDSTONE

As has been seen, the SER main-line was authorised in 1836 to follow a route passing south of Maidstone, which a local paper felt was a "serious injury to the town." Insult was added to injury when the Medway Navigation was used to ferry construction materials for the SER through the town.

The town was first served by Maidstone Road station, opened at Paddock Wood on 31 August 1842, and considered of too little significance to have a stationmaster, being in the care of a clerk paid £100 per annum. This station did little to pacify local interests, with a branch from Staplehurst being proposed in August that year. However progress became more certain on 7 February 1843 when the SER agreed to construct a branch if the people of the town would subscribe £20,000 towards it.

An Act for the line was passed in June 1843 despite opposition from Lord Gainsborough. Robert Stephenson was appointed surveyor and E. L. Betts the contractor. Powers for additional capital amounted to £149,300. Stephenson was instructed to survey for a single line with enough space to allow for a second track, being paid £2,200 for the work.

Opposition to the line came from the Upper Medway Navigation Company which had its own rail connection from Maidstone Road to a coal wharf near Tonbridge; a single track line with three passing places, it opened on 1 May 1844[1]. The plan was to work its own coal trains to points on the SER system. In February 1845 the Navigation ordered a steam engine to replace its horses;

37. An example of the rowdy scenes that occurred when hop-pickers travelled by train.

a shed for it and a house for its driver had been built at Maidstone Road. A second engine was ordered, the first arriving in April with the SER charging £8 for bringing it from London[2]. However the SER refused to allow the engines to operate coal trains over its tracks to the "coal wharves" that the Navigation was setting up at various stations, although it was prepared to allow restricted operation between Tonbridge and Paddock Wood. For a time one of the engines was lent to Messrs Hoof, the contractors building the Tunbridge Wells branch. The Navigation's railway was deprived of its raison d'etre by the SER's intransigence and closed on 17 April 1847. Sadly for the SER, other rivals did not prove so easy to defeat.

Work on the SER's Maidstone branch had commenced in January 1844, coinciding with a shortage of funds. It was decided to spend only £500 on stations for the line instead of the £18,700 originally anticipated. Wateringbury had to make do with an old building being adapted while, at Lewis Cubitt's suggestion, the old wood and tarpaulin structure from Dover was moved to Maidstone. East Farleigh and Yalding stations were also provided economically.

The tarpaulin roof at Maidstone predictably fell foul of the Board of Trade so that passenger traffic was delayed although the line was in use for hop traffic during early September 1844. Free passenger trips took place on 24 September and at a celebratory dinner Stephenson provided "green tea punch" which he had brewed himself. From the same day Maidstone Road was renamed Paddock Wood.

The line opened on 25 September with a special from Bricklayers Arms and prophecies that "greater moral benefits are likely to accrue to the benighted villagers of Mid-Kent." The cost of the line seems to have been £190,461.

On 23 January 1845 the Board voted to build permanent stations on the line; at Maidstone, Stationmaster Kennett had been forced to work in a "large tent" and only the engines had a proper building. However, in April 1845 the SER refused to build a station at Beltring Crossing to serve East Peckham, or to move Yalding station there. Doubling was completed by Grissell & Peto in May 1846 at a cost of £43,560, though this included the building of gatekeepers' cottages. In an attempt to develop traffic, some unusual services were run - Maidstone to Tunbridge Wells being attempted from 1845 until May 1850.

Although work on Maidstone station advanced to include a new platform and carriage shed, those at Yalding and East Farleigh were not improved until at least 1852, until which time the platforms there were only two feet wide. Since the line was not entirely popular because of its devious route, proposals for better routes continued to be put forward. In 1845 a "Maidstone & London Direct" received some attention and in 1847 local people welcomed a LBSCR plan for a New Cross to Maidstone and Canterbury line.

The opening of the North Kent line through to Strood offered the SER the chance of a better route to Maidstone, but it was dilatory in seizing the chance. A line down the Medway Valley, crossing the river at Cuxton, had been surveyed by Gibbs in 1841 while in 1843 Locke had planned a single line from Gravesend to Maidstone. In 1844 the SER had Robert Stephenson survey from Maidstone to "Rochester" (as it liked to call Strood) but the scheme was rejected by Parliament in 1846 and 1847. After this, the SER lost interest.

In 1851 Edward Betts, who lived locally at Preston Hall, led a deputation to the SER with the result that plans were prepared for 1852. The contractor

38. A gathering of hop-pickers at Paddock Wood. (E.Course Collection)

39. A view of Cuxton in about 1910 - before the M2 Viaduct disturbed the tranquility of the Medway scenery.

40. The simple station at Tovil in about 1910. (Lens of Sutton)

Wythes was appointed to do the work for £151,983, the SER's sudden enthusiasm being prompted by fear of rival concerns exploiting a genuine need. The Act was passed on 4 August 1853 for a line from Strood to Maidstone, but the Admiralty's refusal to sanction a bridge below Allington Lock forced the line to the west of Maidstone town centre.

When the line opened on 18 June 1856 most of its facilities were still incomplete. The new station which replaced the old Maidstone terminus was only finished in 1858 and not until April 1858 did the SER decide to spend £8000 on completing the stations at Cuxton (where Lord Darnley gave the land), Snodland and Aylesford. These stations, though, were built in an engaging mock-Tudor style.

Maidstone was now on a loop of the SER running from the North Kent line to join the main-line at Paddock Wood. The line traversed much of the hop-growing district and from 1856 the SER began to run special trains for the less wealthy of London to go and work at hop-picking. The earliest specials offered fares of 2s6d from Bricklayers Arms to any station between Maidstone and Tonbridge. One witness claims that the first train was booked to leave at 6am and consisted of a row of cattle trucks, apparently filled by 4am. The trains soon became notorious for violence and drunkeness. In 1863 the Mayor of Maidstone's wife was assaulted by an Irish hop-picker at Maidstone station but the traffic was profitable - in 1865 the SER carried 11,090 hop-pickers into Kent.

The SER's position in Maidstone, though, was far from secure. On 17 July 1862 the Sevenoaks, Maidstone & Tunbridge was authorised to extend from Otford to Maidstone, with the clear intention of giving the LCDR influence in Kent's County town. However, completion of the line was delayed by the bankruptcy of the SMTR and it was eventually opened on 1 June 1874 by the LCDR. From that date the SER's two lines became merely secondary routes.

The SER had tried to keep the SMTR out by proposing various "cut-off" lines to Maidstone from Hildenborough in 1872-3 and also a link between the SER and the SMTR from Dunton Green to Otford. Other SER suggestions included Maidstone to Pluckley and Maidstone to Headcorn, the latter perhaps a response to an 1871 "tram" scheme for Maidstone-Headcorn-Tenterden. All these failed, as did the 1875 scheme for a Sevenoaks to Maidstone line.

At Strood, Messrs. Aveling set up their works between the SER Maidstone line and the River Medway in 1861. The site, south of the LCDR, provided much traffic for the SER once the firm had become Aveling & Porter in 1862. From 1866 the works became famous for making small industrial locomotives.

Between Strood and Maidstone the SER passed close to a number of cement works which had previously relied on water transport. Most of these had their own internal rail systems and were connected to the SER only gradually. Weekes' works at Lower Halling was connected by 1883 whilst the Boormann & Lee works at Halling was connected as early as 1871, if not before. The growth of Halling as an industrial centre was not matched by provision for its passengers; in 1865 the SER refused a station there, though one was finally opened on 1 March 1890. The Townshend Hook paper mill at Snodland had a siding south of the station by 1880; there was also a large goods shed there, the traffic including receipt of old rags from London. A stone quarry at Allington had rail connections by 1861, when stone from it was taken to pave the ground outside Dover's Lord Warden Hotel. The SER serviced this considerable traffic by operating "roundabout" goods trains from Bricklayers Arms via Gravesend,

41. Snodland Station looking north in about 1910. The large goods shed on the
right handled traffic for Townshend-Hook. (Lens of Sutton)

Maidstone and Tonbridge back to London. Local goods trains also ran between
Strood and Tonbridge.

The LCDR's Maidstone station was centrally located, so the SER spent £500
on a new station close to the point where the two routes crossed. This opened
on 1 July 1874 as Maidstone Barracks, with waiting rooms and toilets being
added in 1876. A number of sidings developed nearby, including a stone siding
and carriage sidings in 1877; in 1889 a carriage siding had to be removed to
allow more goods sidings.

The hop-picking traffic increased steadily; in 1880, for example, 18,902 were
carried down to Kent and 22,607 returned on the special trains - the discrepancy
being due to some hop-pickers using normal service trains. Stations like East
Farleigh were crowded for the return journeys, often with heavy drinking taking
place; the hop-pickers refused to queue politely outside, preferring to "block
themselves into an immovable mass in the interior, until a sufficient number of
tickets has been issued to fill the approaching train." A visitor to this station in
1874 described how one man was so drunk that he fell off the platform in front
of an advancing train and had to be rescued by a policeman.

At Maidstone a special ticket office was erected in the goods yard and the
railway staff barricaded themselves inside for the duration of the shift. £80 of
tickets could be sold in half an hour, though many tried to travel illegally. Stories
were told of people who died on the homeward journey, the corpse being
stripped of everything of value. Violence was common - one woman hit another
with a salt cellar. Matters were also complicated by the large amounts of
luggage, and even furniture, that the hop-pickers carried with them.

In 1877 the Loose Valley Railway was formed to build a line from Tovil,
across the Medway, towards Loose. At first the SER was cool about the scheme
but in 1879 it studied the potential and discovered that heavy paper traffic could
result. In April 1880 work started on the Medway bridge and the SER opened
a station on the "main" line at Tovil on 1 January 1884. An extension to Boughton
was considered in 1881.

The branch to a goods station at the Loose Valley paper mills (known as
Tovil Siding) seems to have opened in 1886 following protests by local firms
about slow progress - four firms agreed to pay a rental of £150 p.a. Plans to
extend the line to Loose never bore fruit. In 1884 the SER had begun to buy
land for an extension via Sutton Valence to Headcorn and in December 1885

arranged for the LVR, which had a capital of £31,730, to amalgamate with the Lydd Railway. However high land prices prevented extensions of any length and by an Act of 1888 the SER took over LVR powers.

An agreement of November 1889 for a guaranteed rental of £60 p.a. resulted in a short extension to Tovil Mill but any extension beyond that would have forced demolition of the mill. After 1893 the SER abandoned plans to extend the line though they did instal a goods shed at Tovil in 1896.

On 1 July 1884 the LCDR opened its line from Maidstone to Ashford. This was a territory the SER had failed to exploit although an independent scheme in 1866 had got as far as an Act of Parliament and asking the SER for help before it folded. In 1870 the SER had considered lending £100,000 to a Maidstone & Ashford Company chaired by Lord Romney, which had planned a Maidstone to Pluckley line. In 1876 the SER had proposed a line to Chilham.

The SER considered a line to connect with the Maidstone & Ashford at Turkey Mill, but this would have passed through a central area of Maidstone and so was abandoned due to cost. This left the SER with running powers over the LCDR to Ashford but with no way of exploiting them, while at Ashford the LCDR maintained its own station and ran no trains into Ashford (SER). Maidstone Corporation instituted legal proceedings in 1890-1 to force a connecting service between the two Companies; from 1 November 1891 some LCDR trains began to run into the SER's Ashford station.

During the 1880s and 1890s the SER made many minor improvements to the line. Snodland received a footbridge in 1883 and in 1884 £3,000 was spent improving Maidstone station, to which a refreshment room was added in 1885. In 1886 platforms were lengthened at East Farleigh and Yalding to obviate "pulling up". Aylesford got its footbridge in 1888.

The firm of Hilton, Anderson & Co. operated a thriving cement works at Halling, depending on water transport. In 1888 they gave land and £1,700 to the SER for a siding into the works. They then enquired about a passenger station, but the SER asked for £2,400 to which the cement company objected. However, in 1889 the SER provided a footbridge across the line at Halling and on 1 March 1890 opened a passenger station there.

In 1893 Yalding station was burnt down and £820 was spent on new timber buildings with massive brick chimneys. The insurance value of the old station was £313.

Further sidings were added at Halling in 1894, Maidstone Barracks in 1895 and Snodland in 1896. In 1897 the SER began an £18,500 campaign to improve Maidstone station after complaints from the Corporation. Rebuilding included new luggage lifts, roofs and a luggage footbridge, following which the station was renamed Maidstone West in July 1899 under SE&CR control.

As a postscript, in 1905 the Headcorn & Maidstone Junction Light Railway was authorised to fill the gap south-east of Maidstone, with a line via Sutton Valence including a tunnel at Hayle Mill. It was never built.

1.   D.L.Bradley, **Locomotive History of the SER**, p.63. C.Hadfield, **The Canals of S. & S.E. England**, p.75, refers only to a tramroad "between Tonbridge wharf and the railway line there."

2.   H.W.Paar, **An Early Locomotive Mystery,** Journal of the Stephenson Locomotive Society, June 1959.

CHAPTER 13: THE READING, GUILDFORD & REIGATE

"The way of a fool seems right to him, but a wise man listens to advice." Proverbs 12.15

During the first era of the South Eastern Railway, and up to the demise of MacGregor, it was as frequently abused for its involvement with the Reading, Guildford & Reigate Railway as for any other reason. The RGR had finances almost as ruinous as the SER's reputation at the time; the SER's involvement with it was a clear case of strategic concerns outweighing economic realities.

One of the most curious aspects of the SER's involvement with a line to Reading is that it became involved in the whole saga through a desire to reach entirely different places. Thus we find that at the start of 1838 the SER was discussing a line to Portsmouth with the London & Brighton, with profits to be shared. However by 23 February the SER was talking with a rival Portsmouth company, the Direct London & Portsmouth, which it also fell out with by August 1838.

Both these abortive schemes accustomed the SER to looking further west, though its interest then lay dormant until 1844 when a rush of Railway Mania schemes forced its attention back to the area. In September 1844 the Brighton Company wrote to the SER suggesting a joint involvement in a branch from Redhill to Reigate and Dorking. The Direct London to Portsmouth line was also planned through the area with support from the London & Croydon, and included a branch from Capel to Reigate.

The SER was keen to become involved with the Brighton in the Reigate and Dorking line, but by November press reports indicate that the Brighton had become concerned that the line could become a basis for the SER to invade Sussex. The Brighton pressed on alone with its plans, but offered the SER use of the line if its Act was passed. The L&BR was not pleased to learn, in April, that the London & Croydon also had plans for extending its proposed Epsom atmospheric line to Dorking.

The 1844-5 session produced no results, but by the late summer of 1845 there were more contenders. Leading the pack was the Direct London & Portsmouth, proposing a line from Epsom to Dorking, Godalming and Havant for Portsmouth. Charles Vignoles proposed a Dorking, Brighton & Arundel atmospheric line, also starting from Epsom. The DLPR did gain an Act in June 1846, but its "parent company", the L&CR, was absorbed into the London & Brighton which already had a line to Portsmouth and so no further progress was made.

An extra complication was caused because parties now began to propose lines to run more or less parallel with the North Downs to connect the South Eastern at Redhill with other railways to the north and west. These schemes hoped to profit from connecting the north and west with the south and the coast. Thus in August 1845 the grandiosely-named Birmingham, Southampton, Brighton & Dover Junction announced its plans for a line from Watford to

42. The fight between Sayers and Heenan near Farnborough on 17 April 1860, with one of the SER excursions in the background.

Reigate via Weybridge. Others in the field included the Watford & Reigate and the Reading & Reigate; by November 1845 there was also a Tring & Reigate. Some of these planned to connect the SER with the London & North Western at Watford or Tring, others to connect only with the Great Western; it was perhaps unfortunate for the long-term transport needs of the country that the former did not succeed.

The most significant proposal was for the Reading, Guildford & Reigate Railway. Led by Frederick Mangles, a Guildford banker, this scheme was unusual for its time in that it actually did propose to connect all the places in its title. At the start of September 1845 it was proposing to spend £800,000 on its main-line and further sums on branches to connect Farnham, Alton and Godalming with its system[1]. On 11 September 1845 D.Mangles, the M.P. for Guildford, gave up the Chair to David Salomons, a well-known financier, but the scheme continued to call itself "Mangles' line" to reduce confusion with the rival proposals. Henry Rich was also on the committee.

By 14 October £53,157 had been invested in the RGR and Francis Giles had been directed to make haste with the surveys. In January 1846 the committee received his estimates of £709,248 for constructing the main-line and £33,778 for the branch. It was proposed to share the route of the Direct London & Portsmouth between Dorking and Gomshall.

Mangles and Salomons realised that one of the main obstacles to their success was that they were hardly alone in the field. Instead of leaving matters to an expensive legal battle before the Parliamentary committees, they very sensibly embarked on a policy of negotiation with the rival groups. In November 1845 they began talks with the Bristol & Dover Direct Junction Railway and the following month with the Reading & Reigate. They hoped to remove the latter from the field by paying off its £3,000 expenses and persuading its supporters to take £5,000 in the RGRR[2]. Supporters of the R&R included David Mocatta, the architect. On 26 January 1846 the RGRR was able to publish an announcement of the amalgamation of rival interests.

Yet other rivals still existed, in the more powerful form of the SER and LBSCR. There was a possibility that a dispute with these two companies over the Dorking to Reigate Junction section would cause the loss of the RGRR's Bill. Although the SER was promoting its own branch from Reigate Junction to Dorking, it made a serious offer to the RGRR in March 1846, being prepared to work that line and pay the RGRR 4.5% on capital and half the profits. During the same month it was agreed with the Direct London & Portsmouth that on the shared section of route there should be a track for the RGRR's conventional trains as well as for the DLPR's atmospheric ones. The SER's own Dorking Bill was thrown out in May 1846 and the LBSCR's followed soon afterwards.

Further west, there was an area of conflict with the London & South Western Railway, which was promoting its own branch from Guildford to Alton via Ash and had gained an Act in 1845 for a branch from Guildford to Godalming. The RGRR proposed using the latter between Shalford and Guildford, continuing then over the LSWR Alton branch as far as Ash. In March 1846 the RGRR reached agreement with the LSWR, with the latter to build the section from Guildford to Ash and the RGRR to pay 35% of its gross receipts over LSWR tracks.

The RGRR obtained its Act on 16 July 1846, with a capital of £800,000. It inherited a curious situation, for between Dorking and Gomshall it was to use about four miles of the DLPR route, and between Shalford and Ash run over two different branches of the LSWR. The LSWR obtained an Act for its Guildford to Alton branch on the same date, and this required it to complete the line within two years so that the RGRR could use it. The RGRR had the powers to build the Dorking to Gomshall section if the DLPR was too slow.

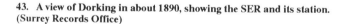

43. A view of Dorking in about 1890, showing the SER and its station.
(Surrey Records Office)

Pressure for the provision of stations began even before the Act was passed. Sandhurst College requested a station at Blackwater as early as March 1846, while in August Dorking let it be known that a station to the east of the church would be very helpful.

On 14 October 1846 the RGRR Board discussed whether they should lease their line to the SER. There were already signs that they were concerned about the financial position - at the same meeting they decided to abandon the "downward" one of the double junctions onto the LSWR at Farnborough, saving £3,000. The SER approached the issue carefully, aware that the RGRR's Act stipulated that its western end had to be opened first which would put the SER in a poor position. At the end of November the SER considered that it had two options - to lease the whole line or just the portion between Reigate Junction and Dorking. The two parties met on 21 January 1847, the RGR amending its terms from 4.5% to 5.5%. Agreement was reached with Salomons leading the RGRR; it was decided that MacGregor and Pritchard should represent the SER on the Reading Board, joining Smale who was already on both. The SER began shouldering some of the Reading's expenses - such as the £300 a year office costs.

During late 1846 and the first half of 1847, the RGRR worked on revising its plans for a new Deviations Bill. The junction at Ash needed some alteration to the levels and also the meeting with the proposed DLPR between Gomshall and Albury needed altering, as well as an alteration to the powers allowing the RGRR to begin immediate construction of the shared section; the *Railway Times* thought that the LSWR and LBSCR were conspiring to use the DLPR to delay the RGRR[3]. The new Act was passed on 22 July 1847.

A careful study was made of the arrangements at the Reading end, where the RGRR met the broad-gauge Great Western Railway. In November 1846 it was suggested that the best plan was to widen the GWR embankment by 35 feet so that the two lines could run alongside each other, but the GWR wanted a promise not to seek access across or beyond its own line. In April 1847 Stephenson warned against this policy, arguing that building the station on the same level as the GWR and sharing its approach road would weaken the RGRR's position since it was "a competing line from Reading to London.[4]" He recommended stopping short of the GWR's station and at a lower level. At the same time the SER suggested that the junction should be built at Farnborough to allow through running of London to Reading trains via the LSWR, although the LSWR was already planning its own extension from Richmond to Wokingham; the RGR retaliated by threatening its own line to Staines. Here was the start of folly, for the Reading line had not been conceived of as a competitive route from Reading to London yet this role was to be thrust upon it; at the same time, its fortune as a linking route between principal companies depended on the maintaining of good relations with them all - especially with the GWR.

The first sod of the new line was cut on 20 August, expenses for the occasion being limited to £200[5]. The ceremony took place in a field near Broome Park, Betchworth. The dignitaries came in a procession of coaches from Reigate station and were "cheered most lustily" by assembled navvies[6]. The ceremonial silver spade was wielded by David Salomons, with a supporting cast of a mahogany wheelbarrow emblazoned with his own coat of arms. When James MacGregor took his turn with the barrow, he overturned it. Contract No.1

covered Farnborough to Reading (awarded to William Jackson) while No.2 was for Reigate Junction to Dorking; the contractor for the latter was George Wythes, a local man. Work on the Mole viaduct began in October.

Francis Giles, the original engineer, had died in March 1847 and his place was taken for a while by Robert Stephenson, who made the telling alteration at Reading. The work was taken over by Peter Barlow, probably in October or November 1847, who disagreed strongly with Stephenson's policy at Reading, warning that "as an extension to compete with the Great Western I believe the necessary expenditure will never be rendered desirable[7]." Barlow continued to voice his protests on this issue in March 1848, arguing for a station at the "upper level". Barlow was wise whereas the policy adopted under Stephenson's influence was foolhardy and ill-conceived.

One piece of good news came in 1848 when it became clear that the DLPR was to abandon its powers for the Gomshall and Dorking section. A contract for the remaining section between Shalford Junction (often called Guildford Junction in RGRR papers) and Dorking was awarded to Charles Henfrey in May 1848.

44. Westcott intermediate signalbox near Dorking in about 1880.

Now more optimistic, the RGRR began to consider the details of opening the line. In September 1848 there were discussions with the LSWR engineer, Joseph Locke, about a station at the junction with the Farnham and Alton branch - the RGRR referred to it as Wyke, but Barlow was dubious over its prospects. Brockham residents sent a request for a station and in October the RGR debated the relative merits of having a station at Shere Heath or Gomshall. It was also decided to reduce the span of the bridge over the Basingstoke Canal near Ash Vale from 40 feet to 24 feet; £117 compensation would have to be paid to the Canal, but £400 would be saved. It was also felt that money could be saved at Shalford by having level crossings instead of bridges. The extent of financial concerns can be judged by Barlow's suggestion in October 1848 that £23,000 could be saved by having only a single line between Dorking and Farnborough.

The RGRR did allow some of its funds to be used for philanthropic purposes. £200 was given for a Parish school at Sandhurst and £7 was given to the widow of a navvy killed by a fall of sandstone at Shere on 15 November 1848.

The RGRR was unimpressed by the LSWR's dilatory progress with its Farnham and Alton line, for which the latter had to seek a time extension. The RGRR was also annoyed to learn in March 1849 that the LSWR's Ash station would not be at the junction, thus making exchange of traffic difficult. At the start of April it was decided to build the Reading station mostly of wood, with only the central building of brick so that a second storey could be placed on top of it if needed later. Wokingham and Blackwater were to have similar buildings, but Farnborough was to be only temporary. Barlow didn't like the site of the Dorking station, since it was on a gradient and would make the working of goods traffic difficult.

During April 1849 there were further discussions with the LSWR about the use of Farnborough as a junction and interchange; the LSWR agreed to stop some trains at Frimley, but not expresses, providing the RGR paid for the station. The RGR also wanted to run Reading line trains into the LSWR's Farnborough station to connect with its up expresses. The issue of the Farnborough junctions was resolved by an Act of 26 June 1849 which authorised a junction facing towards London rather than Southampton, but the concept of a joint LSWR/SER London to Reading service was never popular with the LSWR. In 1855 a number of Hampshire people produced a petition to try to force the SER and LSWR to provide a connection between their two Farnborough stations, but this was never done.

The section from Reigate Junction to Dorking was the first to be ready for opening, but the RGRR Act bound it to open the western end of the line first. Therefore, on 4 July 1849, it opened two unconnected parts of the line - Reigate Junction to Dorking, and Reading to Farnborough. On 20 August the section from Farnborough to Ash Junction was opened, from where trains ran to Guildford over the LSWR. The same day the line between Dorking and Shalford opened in rudimentary fashion - Gomshall & Shere Heath had only temporary sheds for the passengers and hastily erected platforms only 50 feet long; Minutes of September 1852 indicate a decision to change the station name to Gomshall & Shere. No goods facilities were provided at many of the stations until at least 1850. The intervening section of LSWR track, from Shalford Junction into Guildford, was delayed when the roof of St Catherine's Tunnel collapsed but it opened on 15 October and was then promptly closed again by the Board of Trade from 22 to 24 October.

The basic cost of the line was £611,408-14s-5d - a very considerable sum. However the abandoning of the Direct London & Portsmouth meant that the RGRR had to foot the bill for Gomshall to Dorking, which it had been hoping to pass to the now defunct concern. This came to a further £92,437, or so the RGRR estimated in February 1850, on top of which the SER required £25,000 for its work in building the stations[8].

A few minor adjustments soon had to be made to the sparse train service; from 1 May 1850 the 12.30 up train called additionally at Wokingham, though with so few towns on the line one must wonder as to why it missed the place out in the first instance. Later that month the 6.30pm down train was extended to Guildford, by which time the LSWR was already complaining about the low fares. On 24 May the SER decided to close the station at "Shere Heath" (ie

Gomshall), though it survived to be listed in the Minutes as an active station on 8 July.

The opening of a station at "Sandhurst Road" had been considered in May 1850 and the following month a request had been made for a screen in front of the line at Sandhurst. Requests for the station continued for many months until, in February 1852, the SER decided to open one "on the cheapest possible terms." A siding was also provided there for a Mr Gibson and the station opened on 4 May 1852, as recorded in the SER Minutes of 13 May. The station was a disaster - "wholly unremunerative" - and closed on 31 December 1852. In a way it came to be a symbol of the fortunes of the RGR.

The RGR had been leased by the SER from 15 March 1850 and the SER tried whatever it could to increase traffic - even investigating the possibility of running omnibuses from Dorking to Leatherhead. A powerful group of SER shareholders felt that the lease, which guaranteed a payment to the RGRR of 5.5% on its capital, was an unacceptable drain on the SER's resources and took legal action to have it set aside. Although the *Railway Times* commented accurately that the lease "guarantees (the RGR) a dividend much higher than the line is worth at present," the case was lost in September 1850.

Not until mid- September 1850 was the line even ready for goods traffic, since there had been so little haste in providing facilities such as a goods shed at Shalford. The SER clung to the hope that a Bill for a "narrow gauge" line from Reading to Oxford would succeed, though it didn't help matters by refusing to let the few willing passengers actually use the line - in October 1850 a man sued the SER for 16s 6d, being the cost of a carriage from Reigate to Betchworth after a train had failed to deposit him at his desired destination. Nor was the LSWR happy, complaining in December 1850 that SER men ignored its signals on the shared lines.

Some minor attempts were made to boost traffic. Towards the end of 1850 the SER decided to provide an engine shed at Reading and cattle pens at Reading, Farnborough, Blackwater and Wokingham. The idea of running omnibuses to Leatherhead gave rise to a more useful child when, in about September 1850, work began on a new station to the north east of Dorking. The station seems to have opened about 1 February 1851 and on 13 February the SER decided to provide it with a "passenger shed". At first it was called Box Hill & Leatherhead Road, but became plain Box Hill in March 1851.

On 6 March 1851 the SER decided to spend £300 on a stationmaster's house and refreshment rooms at Reading, together with goods sheds for Gomshall and Betchworth. Perhaps the money came from savings on the RGRR directors' fees, which were cut from £1,000 to £500. In an attempt to boost excursion traffic, the SER decided in May to introduce cheap fares between Reading and Hastings.

The Kennet & Avon Canal passed close to the SER station at Reading and the two concerns had talks about exchanging goods traffic. The SER was annoyed to learn in May 1851 that the GWR had made an offer to the Canal, and considered leasing the Kennet & Avon itself. Fortunately no more came of this bizarre idea, and in October 1852 the SER refused an offer to take over the Basingstoke Canal but it did decide to put in a siding to it at Ash in November.

The SER was meant to pay the LSWR a share of the traffic it took through Guildford, but on 16 October 1851 it was informed that the LSWR had been making its own count of the passengers and disputed the SER figures. In fact the SER had been trying to avoid paying so much to the LSWR by using omnibuses to carry its Guildford passengers to Shalford since September. The LSWR retaliated by holding back money due to the SER during 1852, but the SER took legal action and won the case in 1853. In April 1853 it demanded its own clerks and porters at Guildford.

In October 1851 the SER introduced a Bill to formally take over the RGRR. There was much opposition to this within the body of SER shareholders, one of whom complained in January 1852 that the current agreement was "ruinous" and unauthorised by Parliament. There were bitter criticisms of the "reckless losses" run up by futile attempts to compete with the LSWR for Guildford traffic; it was stated that during the 1851 Great Exhibition, LSWR trains from Guildford had averaged over 200 passengers per train while the SER could barely manage five. Eleven SER trains had carried a total of eleven passengers at a mere 2s each. Goods rates were a ridiculous 4s a ton to London.

A Mr Wilson alleged that the line was losing the SER £32,000 per annum, but a meeting of shareholders approved of the amalgamation by 47-39 votes. The Act was passed on 17 June 1852, backdating the effects to 15 March 1852 so as to run consecutively from the previous two year lease. However the issue did not disappear, but remained a cause of rancour between the SER Board and prominent shareholders. Things seemed to go from bad to worse - according to the *Railway Times* in November 1852, the SER was charging only 3s 6d a ton for goods from Reading to London and was prepared to send a van to Newbury to get it. The following year John Hamilton, often the scourge of the SER Board, alleged that 1st class fares from Reading to London were only 3/4d a mile and that RGR dividends had been paid out of capital. In 1855 the SER admitted that it was losing £15,377 per year on the line, this admission coming only after MacGregor had lost the Chair - he being blamed by many for the whole fiasco. In 1856 the *Railway Times* advised that the RGR line was "redundant" as it had "no traffic" and in February 1858 estimated its losses at £30,000 per annum.

The situation at Reading was still unsatisfactory, for the RGR had been meant to provide a junction there within five years or would lose its power to charge certain tolls. By September 1851 the GWR had pledged to provide a standard gauge line between Reading and Oxford, but major works would be needed by the RGR to take advantage of this since its line had been left at a lower level. The SER hoped to use low Reading fares to force the GWR into agreement, but the *Railway Times* despaired of the whole situation:

"We despair of a successful and profitable peace being established where the war is or has been carried on at a loss so positive and severe as that which accompanies SER invasion of the west[9]*."*

In October 1852 the SER brought forward a Bill to extend their line to the GWR at Reading, spend £10,000 on a new station, and to lay a standard gauge track alongside the Great Western to Oxford.

The need to improve the situation at Reading was made more acute by the progress of a Bill for the Staines, Wokingham & Woking Junction Railway, which secured an Act on 8 July 1853 with running powers over the SER from Wokingham into Reading. The SER was authorised to build its extension at Reading (but not to Oxford) on 4 August 1853 but it was not until March 1854 that agreement could be reached with the GWR about plans for a junction. With the SER charging only 4s6d between Reading and London, the GWR was in no great haste to help it, but the SER paid the GWR £1,000 for the land at the new station and in September advertised the contract. An Act of 31 July 1854 forced the GWR to provide a standard gauge line between Oxford and Basingstoke but it did this while avoiding Reading station, and this prompted the Staines, Woking & Wokingham to seek its own extension through Reading. This was rejected in 1855.

Despite a rumour in February 1855 that the GWR was paying the SER to run down the RGR line[10], the single track extension to the new Reading station was opened on 30 August 1855. The Board of Trade insisted on strict regulations for the single track section between the "Junction" and the new station: it was to be worked on the "one engine in steam principle" with all down trains stopping at the ticket platform where the engine was to run round and push the train into the station.

Although the SER had reached its new station - an extension of about 300 yards - interchange with the GWR was still impossible because there was a gap in the connecting embankment with the GWR dragging its heels about completing the connection.

The poor state of SER facilities at Reading on 12 September 1855 were partly to blame for one of the most infamous accidents in the Company's history, but poor standards among the staff were also significant. A down London Bridge to Reading train was running late and a message was sent to Reading to send a locomotive to assist it at Guildford. This engine was despatched without proper authority from the engine shed at Reading, along the single line section and, as the points were set wrongly for it, onto the down line in the direction of Guildford. The driver, Crossley, was accompanied by a cleaner acting as stoker; the former started oiling the engine as it ran along, while the latter was told to trim the lamps since none had been lit[11]. About 1.5 miles from Reading, in the dark, the light engine collided with the 4.40pm down London Bridge to Reading at about 40 mph. Much of the first passenger carriage was destroyed and the *Railway Times* reporter found a grim scene:

"The splintered pieces of the carriage were horrible to look at, being completely saturated with blood, and pieces of human flesh and hair hanging about in all directions."

Eight people, including Crossley - who was found at the foot of the bank, were killed or died later. Initial reports tried to blame the driver of the engine from Reading, Crossley, for being "in a state of mental aberration"; Crossley's father had been an engine-driver and had also been killed in an accident - at New Cross in about 1840. The Reading Coroner interviewed the badly-injured stoker, Ferguson, in his hospital bed, then blamed the accident on Crossley. However, it soon emerged that the SER's staffing arrangements were at fault after a series of extremely angry letters had appeared in *The Times*. SER economies meant that the points were in the charge of the station porters, who had to walk 600 yards to reach them; they had not been prepared for the precipitate departure of the light engine and two of the station staff had gone out with an excursion train. The porter in charge of the points that day was working from 6am to 10pm. The whole running of the Reading station revealed "a wretched attempt at economy and...a laxity of discipline and inattention," a correspondent calling himself "Daily in Danger" wrote. The SER Board hoped to hush up the Board of Trade report but could not; Captain Barlow, in charge of running the line, was sacked.

In June 1856 the SER returned to the question of a connection at Reading; they assessed that it would cost £30,000 to build a line to join the standard gauge Oxford and Basingstoke line to the west of Reading. SER determination was increased in November when it learnt that the GWR was cutting its Reading fares and it decided to bring its own Bill. The SW&WJ also wanted a line to join the GWR at Tilehurst, potentially a great threat to the SER.

The SER's plan was similar to earlier SW&WJ ideas, passing beneath the entrance to the GWR station, rising to a level with the GW main line, then dipping beneath its Hungerford branch to join a new fork line from the north. The SW&WJ's new plan involved a line leaving the SER and going beneath the GWR main line before running along the north side.

In January 1857 the SER began to seek agreement with the LSWR (sponsors of the SW&WJ) and the GWR, hoping for a one third share in the Reading traffic. The SW&WJ Bill was passed on 27 July 1857, the GWR having accepted its inevitability; the Reading Junction line was built with 9 chains belonging to the SW&WJ (LSWR) and 62 chains to the GWR. The SER Bill was rejected but it took part in talks at Waterloo in November and agreement about the division of traffic was effective from 14 June 1858. The Reading Junction line opened to goods on 1 December 1858 and to passengers from 17 January 1859, though its use for the latter was irregular.

Despite all the controversy and excitement at Reading, the rest of the RGR line slumbered peacefully with no rapid development of traffic. In 1853 Thomas Cubitt paid for the provision of a siding near Dorking and four cottages were built at Shalford. During December 1853 there was a dispute between the Portsmouth Railway, which was planning to extend from the LSWR at Godalming, and the LSWR itself. The Portsmouth Company therefore prepared plans to build a connecting line onto the SER at Shalford so as to have an alternative route to London; this was opposed by the SER on the grounds that its line had enough traffic already, though it also said that it could not work the line as it was bound by the 1848 territorial agreement. However the Portsmouth got an Act on 24 July 1854 to extend north from Godalming to join the SER; this line was never needed since relations with the LSWR were improved, though a short spur was built at Shalford without ever being used regularly - if at all.

Further east the SER had potential rivals to deal with at Dorking, a station which was said in 1856 to be the best on the line. An extension of the LBSCR from Epsom threatened to draw away the Leatherhead traffic after opening in 1859. Local pressure then pushed forward a scheme to link Leatherhead, Dorking and Horsham which was given powers in 1862 to build a line from Box Hill station, on the SER, to Horsham. However Acts of 1863 and 1864 empowered the LBSCR to fill in the gap between Leatherhead and Dorking and to take over the independent company; a connecting spur was built at Dorking but never saw regular traffic[12]. In December 1868 a division of traffic at Dorking was proposed, with the SER to get 55% and the LBSCR the remainder.

Many people felt that the SER's *affaire* with the RGR was criminal, but few expected that stationmaster Ancell of Blackwater would actually be arrested in 1854 for obtaining money under false pretences. As far as is known, the complainants were not long-suffering SER or GWR shareholders.

A goods shed was built at Ash in 1855-6 for £645 but the growth of traffic was not to come there, but a few miles further north. In 1854 the War Office had decided to use Aldershot as a major new Army camp and in July 1858 the SER decided to provide a siding at North Camp, together with a bridge and road for the military traffic. The opening date of the new station is uncertain, for it has been claimed as 1858, was mentioned as being "new" in January 1859, but an offer of £1,500 from the War Office for its construction was only accepted in July 1859; possibly the latter relates to a goods station, for £2,000 was set aside for a goods shed in 1860.

Another new station, Wellington College, was built nearby and the opening of this is attributed to 29 January 1859, on which date the official opening of the College was held with special trains run by the SER and LSWR to "temporary" buildings[13]. The German-style uniforms of the boys caused confusion and Lord Derby, Prime Minister 1858-9 and 1866-8, once handed in his railway ticket to the school's head boy in the belief that he was the railway's ticket collector[14].

Perhaps seeing potential success at last, the SER decided to improve a number of the stations in 1860. £534 was spent at Wokingham, £100 at Dorking and £1,500 at Wellington College. Improvements also had to be made at Betchworth to avoid prosecution for "nuisance". In 1863 £9,000 was spent providing an engine-shed at Reading for joint use with the LSWR and a further £4,360 was spent at North Camp.

Inevitably, the line was eventually used for the highly profitable but very dubious practice of running excursions to illegal prize-fights. On 17 April 1860 the SER arranged for two "monster trains" to leave London Bridge at 4.20am. The first of these was of 33 carriages, but the early departure failed to outwit the Police who were spotted at the lineside with their "cutlasses". The Police were waiting along the Dover and Brighton main-lines, but the trains turned off towards Reading. At nearly 7am the first load of sporting fans were put out into the countryside near Farnborough:

45.   Gomshall & Shere station with the typical staggered platforms and foot crossing.

"...after a pleasant journey through one of the prettiest counties of England, which, illumined by a glorious sun, and shooting forth in vernal beauty, must have inspired all with intense feelings of gratification.[(15)]*"*

By the time the second train had arrived a crowd of 1,200 had gathered. The fight had reached round 37 when the Police arrived - causing chaos. The referee attempted to move the fight to another location but became involved in a fight himself; one of the boxer's, Heenan, floored his rival's assistants, and the final round became a "wild scramble." Heenan ran off but was unable to see, and had to be led back to the train; he was lifted into his compartment for the return to Bricklayers Arms.

The new traffic from Aldershot was threatened by the LSWR's proposal in 1865 for a line from Pirbright, via Aldershot, to Farnham Junction. Powers for this line included a spur to connect it with the SER at Aldershot Junction South, with the SER having powers to run into the LSWR Aldershot station; in exchange, the LSWR had powers to run over the SER between Ash and North Camp. A GWR proposal for a line from Windsor to Aldershot, connecting with the SER at North Camp, came to nothing.

During March 1865 the SER met the GWR to discuss improvement of the passenger stations at Reading; a traffic agreement in 1869 gave the GWR a secure 2/3rds share, so the GWR was prepared to discuss a new joint station and junction so that the SER station could be closed, though Gooch of the GWR wanted to retain separate platforms. The LSWR was unconcerned, and nothing was done until correspondence appeared in *The Times*[(16)]:

"There, side by side with each other, but at different levels, and divided by a space of fifty yards, stand two stations, the one belonging to the Great Western, the other to the South Eastern, between which there cannot in the nature of things be any real antagonism...yet which obstinately remain at arm's length without even a staff of porters to carry one's luggage across, and whose trains, till of late, were curiously timed as to miss one another....the obvious results are - loss of time, of money, and of temper to the travelling public; waste of labour and of plant to the Companies..."

It took several years before the situation could be improved upon; the LSWR refused to have a joint passenger station but forced the SER into improving goods facilities. New sidings and a turntable were provided in 1874-5. The old engine shed was replaced, and converted into a bonded store. The SER hoped to have a double track line that slowly climbed up to the level of the GWR but although some improvements for the interchange of goods traffic were made in 1876 an improved line was not in fact opened until 17 December 1899.

There was a runaway train at Chilworth on 1 February 1867 and on 29 September engine No.69 suffered a boiler explosion at Shalford, with the driver being flung clear. The GWR had built a siding to the Huntley & Palmer biscuit factory at Reading but, on payment of £370, the SER was also allowed a connection in 1869. Gomshall was given longer platforms in 1871 and the same year a truck weighing machine was installed at Betchworth so that trucks did not have to be worked to Redhill and back. The lime sidings at Betchworth and at Brockham were extended in 1875. At Box Hill new steps down to the road from the down platform were provided in 1872 so that alighting passengers did not have to cross the line and Wokingham platforms were extended in July 1873. Two months later the Duke of Northumberland asked for a coal shed to help the poor of Chilworth; he offered £100, but as it would cost £290 the SER passed over this opportunity. The SER had some charitable instincts though - it employed a gateman at Chilworth in 1874 who was too deaf to hear the telegraph bells!

In October 1873 the Railway Commissioners wrote to the SER saying that they had received several complaints that the junction with the LSWR at Farnborough had been taken up. In February 1876 the LSWR also complained about this and wanted the spur, 3/4 mile east of Farnborough station, reopened. The SER refused as it was "inconvenient." Relations between the two were at a low ebb in any case, with ill-feeling over the Mid Hants Railway and the SER complaining of poor track between Ash and Guildford.

The Mid Hants[17], which ran from Alton to Winchester Junction, had had a working agreement with the LSWR but by the mid-1870s were dissatisfied by the terms the LSWR were demanding for renewing it. In February 1874 the MHR Board contacted the SER, inviting them to subscribe to the Company and brandishing the possibility of through running to Southampton. As the termination of the LSWR working agreement drew near in 1875, the MHR enquired whether the SER would lend two locomotives and some carriages, which the SER felt disposed to do. The MHR put additional pressure on the LSWR by threatening to bring in a Bill for running powers over the LSWR to Guildford, a tactic which they used from 1876 to 1878. The SER never got any further with this unexpected romance, the LSWR becoming more accommodating.

With the opening of a rival LBSCR route to Dorking in 1867, the SER had lost much of its traffic from the town to London. It tried to compensate for this by running light and fast schedules for those who worked in London; in 1877 it was running an 8.20am Dorking to Cannon Street and 4.44pm return.

A rather unusual problem surfaced at Wokingham in 1877 when a man complained about being "capsized" by a points lever. The lever fouled the crossing between the tracks and was dangerous to passengers at night. Extra signals were provided at Wokingham in 1877.

Poor Sandhurst was languishing without a station and a request for one to be opened in January 1878 met a firm refusal due to the estimated cost being £4,000. North Camp was given an extra siding that year, while Box Hill's platforms were extended.

As has been seen, when the LSWR constructed its direct line from Pirbright Junction to Aldershot a spur had been laid in for running from the SER at Ash to the LSWR's Aldershot station. In mid-1878 the SER decided that it wished to exercise the powers granted to it under the LSWR's 1865 Act of running to Aldershot. The LSWR retorted that a signalbox would be needed, costing £325. The SER wanted to run a shuttle between Ash Junction (as the station was known from 1863) and Aldershot, requiring £1,800 (later reduced to £750) to alter Ash Junction station and was prepared to go to Parliament if the LSWR did not co-operate[18]. The LSWR provided a new bay at Aldershot and the service began on 1 May 1879. In August 1882 the SER learnt that the LSWR wished to exercise its balancing right to operate a service between Aldershot and the SER's North Camp station; the LSWR had been annoyed by the SER's attempts to trick it of receipts by collecting in Aldershot-bound passengers' tickets at Ash. From 1 October 1882 the LSWR was allowed to use the Ash to Aldershot curve as well, dropping its demand for an entry to North Camp. In 1886 Sir James Allport of the Midland Railway was appointed to negotiate division of fees since SER tracks were used from Ash to Aldershot Junction, and LSWR from there to Aldershot station. As a result of the Allport judgment the LSWR demanded £10,000 - but the SER sent only £5,000.

No doubt more remunerative, a potato siding at Reading cost £120 in 1879 and a siding was provided for the Carruthers sand and lime pit between Betchworth and Reigate.

A rumour that the LBSCR was hoping to buy the line surfaced in 1880, but proved to be a false hope. More typical of the reality of the line was Gomshall's complaint about the poor state of its station in 1881.

In 1882 the SER Board reviewed the state of the RGR line. At Reigate they decided to extend the down platform and provide an "ornamental" footbridge at the level crossing. Betchworth received extensions to both up and down sidings and an extra bedroom for the stationmaster. Box Hill had its platforms raised and lengthened, a new booking office and a new up waiting room, whereas Dorking gained only an up platform extension; this reflected the comparative popularity of the former station - and in fact the same review questioned whether one station could be made to serve the whole area. Gomshall station, it was considered, might need to be replaced while there was a general policy of raising the platform levels at all stations.

46. The station was renamed Crowthorne in June 1928.

In 1883 the authorities at Reigate decided to spend £12,000 in carrying the High Road over the line by a bridge instead of a level crossing, which the SER felt was unwise, although it did agree to provide extra land to help with the crossing problem. A bridge was also required to replace the crossing at Blackwater. During 1883 General Lord Wolseley lived at Chilworth for two months and asked for the 5.12pm down from Charing Cross to stop there; there is no record of the SER's reply.

In December 1883 the Board of Trade inspected Dorking station having received complaints from the Local Board about the lack of a bridge or subway

47. The situation at Reading in about 1850, showing the first SER station in the foreground with the GWR one beyond. At this stage there was no connection between the systems, though the SER line was soon extended a short distance towards the GWR station.

for passengers. In fact the SER had considered spending £650 on one in 1882, but under the additional impetus provided a subway and other improvements costing at least £5,000 in 1884-5.

Dorking, like Wokingham, had been built with staggered platforms so the passengers could cross from one end to the other. A woman was killed at Wokingham on 24 July 1886 and the SER decided to build a bridge. Traffic had increased steadily so that in 1887 it was decided to provide a new signalbox between Dorking and Gomshall. The same year platforms were extended at most of the intermediate stations.

On 29 February 1892 the 10.40pm down goods from Redhill split on Shere Heath Bank. When the two separated portions collided with each other the guard was killed.

A resignalling plan began in December 1891 with £516 being spent at Reigate. This continued in 1892 with the resignalling of Wokingham, California Siding, Blackwater, Farnborough, Ash Junction, Chilworth, Gomshall, Box Hill, Brockham Siding and Betchworth.

In 1893 a new siding was provided at Ash Junction and Chilworth station buildings were improved. Shalford gained extra traffic for a brief while in 1884 as the Bath & West Show was held nearby. Oil depots were opened at North Camp and Shalford in 1895. In 1895 the people of Crowthorne asked for the powers to provide a junction to the LSWR at Frimley or Farnborough to be used, but this issue was dead.

On 23 November 1897 the station crossings claimed another victim with the death of G Bartlett at Blackwater; it was decided to install a footbridge and warning bells. A shunting siding was provided for Wellington College in 1898 as well as more sidings at Reigate; no doubt the Earley stationmaster was also glad of a house, even though it cost a mere £350.

The most interesting developments in the final SER years of the line developed at its Reading end. Through services between the GWR and the SER had been introduced from 1 July 1863, running from Birkenhead to Dover or Hastings. However this service ceased in October 1868 and no more happened until July 1897 when an agreement was reached between the SER and GWR to improve their connections and start running through services again. From that summer through carriages ran between Birkenhead and Folkestone Harbour; there were normally two on weekdays and four on Sundays. For the summer of 1898 the service ran from Liverpool Central, via the Mersey Tunnel, the GWR slipping the coaches at Reading. The improved connection was not brought into use until 17 December 1899, avoiding the tunnel beneath the GWR line.

These through services offered a faint hint of a future great role for the line, but it was a role that had been predicted in the 1840s without real result - perhaps as much due to inter-railway politics as to any geographical factors. Sadly, it was not until the First World War that the line showed its true value to the nation.

It retained a fairly pathetic image throughout SER days. Even the famous railway author E. L. Ahrons found it an easy target for amusement:

"The fastest trains appear to average 4 mph, with occasional spurts to 5...I once tried the line for myself and decided to walk if ever I had to go that way again."

1. RGR Minutes, 4 September 1845.
2. RGR Minutes, 29 December 1845.
3. **Railway Times,** 14 August 1847.
4. RGR Minutes, 29 April 1847. Though a great engineer, Stephenson was clearly no master of railway strategy - unless he simply said what his employers wanted to hear.
5. Or so it was intended - RGR Minutes, August 1847.
6. **Illustrated London News,** 28 August 1847.
7. RGR Minutes, 29 November 1847.
8. **Railway Times,** 12 January 1850.
9. **Railway Times,** 20 September 1851.
10. Letter to the **Railway Times,** 3 February 1855.
11. **The Times,** 13 September 1855.
12. R.W.Kidner, **The Reading to Tonbridge Line,** gives opening date as 1 May 1867. It was taken out of use in 1900, though had been used only intermittently.
13. **The Times,** 31 January 1859.
14. J.Richards & J.Mackenzie, **The Railway Station,** p.98.
15. H.D.Miles, **Pugilistica.**
16. **The Times,** 14 October 1871.
17. See R.Williams, **The London & South-Western Railway,** vol.II.
18. SER Minutes, 3 October 1878.

CHAPTER 14: TUNBRIDGE WELLS AND HASTINGS

1. The Tunbridge Wells and Hastings Main Line

Tunbridge Wells, a thriving and fashionable spa, was one of the largest towns in Kent during the 1830s and the various concerns that competed to build the London to Dover railway sought the support of its inhabitants. Its geographical position, though, made it unlikely that the main-line could ever pass through the town for it stood on ground over 300 feet above sea-level but within a few miles of Tonbridge itself. On 9 October 1835 David Salomons chaired a public meeting in the town in support of the South Eastern Railway, but the town had little direct impact on plans. The only town of any significance to the south of Tunbridge Wells was Hastings, a small resort and fishing town on the East Sussex coast, but the intervening countryside was hilly and unfavourable for railway building.

In November 1835 the *Maidstone Journal* reported that the SER intended to include a branch from Tonbridge to Tunbridge Wells in its plans. The following July the SER Board discussed the issue and decided that a branch to the town should be given a high priority; they presumably hoped to obtain some extra first-class traffic from the town's wealthy visitors. They got as far as a draft proposal for a line serving Rye and Hastings with a branch to Tunbridge Wells. In November 1836 the General Meeting learnt that there was an independent scheme for a branch and that the SER was considering a line from Headcorn to Rye.

In the winter of 1839-40 Cubitt surveyed a line from Smarden to Hastings. The SER then seems to have felt that Tunbridge Wells could be accomodated with an arrangement for coaches to run from the station yard at Tonbridge, with one firm getting the exclusive contract. Plans for a line to Rye became well known in April 1840, with a proposed route from Smarden to Tenterden, Rye and Hastings. There were no harbour dues at Rye, so great statements were

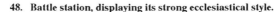

48. Battle station, displaying its strong ecclesiastical style.

made about its potential as a port to handle hops, oilcake and old rags. In November 1840 there was a flurry of interest with a "South Eastern & Hastings" Bill being proposed. The SER was also worried that a "London, Lewes, St. Leonards & Hastings" Bill would give the rival London & Brighton access into East Sussex and even Kent.

It was suggested a single track line to both Rye and Hastings could be built for £250,000 in April 1841[1].

A coach service was proposed in April 1842 from the SER at Tonbridge through to Hastings. The SER already had problems with its own coach operator on the short run to Tunbridge Wells, since the firm refused to stop the coaches at the influential Mount Ephraim Hotel. In June 1842 the SER decided to allow any firm access to the Tonbridge station yard instead of just the one. In May 1843 a Hastings innkeeper approached the SER with a plan to run coaches to Staplehurst.

During 1843 more serious plans for providing a route to either Tunbridge Wells or Hastings began to be discussed. It was felt by some that the hilly land between Tunbridge Wells and Hastings meant that a more easterly route was preferable, and this was supported by the small Wealden towns. In March 1843 a branch to Hastings from Headcorn was being proposed by a Committee led by C. Frewen, with the suggestion that it could have a branch of its own from Icklesham to Rye; the estimated cost of this was £307,000, later reduced to £250,000 after criticisms. This would have gone via Tenterden, so within a few months the people of Hawkhurst were agitating for an alternative route from Staplehurst via their own town.

The Company became known as the Tenterden, Rye & Hastings Branch Railway and began negotiations with the SER for terms. It opened in June 1843 by suggesting that the SER might like to rent it for £30,000 per annum and by January 1844 the SER was taking steps to acquire a lease of the concern by preparing a Bill and paying the Parliamentary deposit of £30,000. However by February 1844 the SER had decided that Headcorn and Tenterden was a poor route and withdrew.

There were various problems with the line including a lack of intermediate traffic if Tunbridge Wells was to be avoided. On 2 April 1844 the SER considered a route from Penshurst to Hastings and on 12 April received a deputation which argued strongly for a line to Hastings via Tunbridge Wells. The SER then acted remarkably quickly, for Barlow was sent to prepare a report on building a branch to Tunbridge Wells, on 28 May the SER decided to go ahead with it, and on 25 June they awarded a contract for its construction to Messrs Hoof. On 23 July Barlow was directed to make a detailed survey and by August the SER was buying land between Tunbridge Wells and Robertsbridge in advance of any Parliamentary authorisation.

The reason for this haste becomes obvious when one considers what had been happening farther south. In June 1844 the Parliamentary Select Committee had reported its feelings about the various proposals for railways to Hastings: it supported the Brighton, Lewes & Hastings scheme, which was associated with the London & Brighton Railway, but thought there was too little traffic to justify a Headcorn, Rye and Hastings line - though it felt both were "in the national interest." The BLH got its Act and almost immediately the London & Brighton showed interest in pushing on from Hastings to Rye and Ashford so that the whole SER heartland could be invaded by an unwelcome intruder.

The SER immediately began its own survey from Ashford to Hastings in August 1844 and by September was considering a separate scheme from Hastings to join the Tunbridge Wells branch. In October the SER decided to deposit plans for a Headcorn to Rye line but abandoned the idea the following January.

At this point the SER began to see that the Tunbridge Wells-Hastings problem was different from the Hastings-Rye-Ashford one, though the Board of Trade elected to make a single study of the lines to Hastings. By August 1844 the SER had decided to build a line from Tonbridge, via Tunbridge Wells, at least as far as Robertsbridge; beyond there it was uncertain as to whether to proceed via Battle or via the Bude Valley and Ore[2]. On 20 August it opted for the Mountfield and Battle route with the intention of forming a junction with the BL&H line already authorised. Perhaps due to this, the SER decided in November 1844 that the branch to Tunbridge Wells should be double track.

The 1844-5 Parliamentary session resulted in some complicated decisions regarding the Hastings line, the most simple of which was the authorisation of the Tunbridge Wells branch. The Board of Trade disliked the SER's plan for a direct line to Hastings and approved powers for an extension of the BLH from Hastings to Ashford. In the summer of 1845 the SER therefore began taking steps to have the powers for the Ashford extension transferred to itself, which was made possible by improved relations with the L&BR following the settling of disputes over Redhill. It was decided to extend the South Eastern from Tunbridge Wells to St. Leonards and in the meantime the L&BR would build the Bulverhythe (which the Brighton's line reached on 27 June 1846) to St. Leonards section of the coastal line.

The SER had pressed ahead with considerable rapidity on the Tunbridge Wells branch. In order to open it as soon as possible, the SER decided in May 1845 that a temporary station should be set up at Jackwood's Spring to the north of the tunnel by which the railway planned to enter the town. £350 was invested in a temporary station and in August 1845 trial trips were run for the press using one of Hoof's wagons and the locomotive *Oberon*. On 28 August *Apparition* caused a shock when it ran off the branch line and appeared unexpectedly on the main line due to its crew having been drinking. The line is usually recorded as having opened on 20 September, suggesting that construction work must have started the previous year before an Act had been obtained. In fact it was first opened on 15 September when free Maidstone to Tunbridge Wells excursions were run and then a normal service started on 16 September, only to be cancelled until four days later. The station at Tonbridge had been laid out without consideration for a branch to Tunbridge Wells, and trains for the branch had to negotiate a complicated reversal onto their line. £450 was spent adapting Tonbridge station for its new role as a junction.

The Medway Navigation Company soon intimated its desire to establish its own coal siding at Tunbridge Wells and meanwhile Hoof pressed ahead with the Tunbridge Wells tunnel in the winter of 1845-6, for which the estimated cost was £50,000. Normal practice would have been for the spoil to be taken up the shafts, but this would have meant carting it through the genteel town and so it was taken out via the tunnel portals instead. Hoof was also allowed two months to excavate the site for the permanent station.

At least some trains were now running south of Tonbridge, and the SER turned its attention to resolving the link to Hastings. In December 1845 it was estimating that a direct line to Hastings, for which it had deposited a Bill, would cost £640,000. Robert Stephenson favoured the route via Battle and this was empowered by the Tunbridge Wells and Hastings Act of 18 June 1846. This would have left the SER in possession of two routes to Hastings of which one, the Tunbridge Wells line, was commercially more attractive. The Government was concerned that a network of railways should be completed around the coast and therefore insisted that the SER must complete the Ashford and Hastings line, for which it had taken over the powers, before it could open the direct line.

Hastings was to become a major cause of bad temper between the SER and the LBSCR, and sensitivity soon became apparent. In November 1846 the LBSCR offered to share its Hastings receipts with the SER if it would abandon the direct line but it was the LBSCR that gained the advantage by being the first

49. **Hastings station is on the right of this view from its famous castle, drawn to commerate the opening of the line. The station was positioned at the edge of the town, which later grew to meet it.**

company to St. Leonards in Autumn 1846, causing a substantial drop in the SER's traffic at Staplehurst. The SER became interested in a Brighton, Lewes & Tunbridge Wells scheme.

The SER opened its extension to the permanent Tunbridge Wells station on 25 November 1846.

The first contract for the Tunbridge Wells and Hastings line, worth £202,000, was awarded to Warton & Warden in February 1847. Costs for Tunbridge Wells to Robertsbridge were estimated at £17,000 a mile. A few months later a row broke out over who held the engineering responsibility for the line, with Peter Barlow claiming to be "Engineer in Chief" to the annoyance of George Bidder and Robert Stephenson. The dispute caused Stephenson to sever his links with the line.

The most difficult part of the various Hastings lines was the coastal section between St. Leonards, Hastings and Ore. The SER already had powers for a branch-line from Lidham Hill, on the Ashford line, to Whatlington - just north of Battle on the direct line. In July 1847 it therefore considered abandoning the Lidham Hill to Hastings section altogether though in November 1847 it assured the LBSCR that it had abandoned the Lidham Hill to Whatlington idea. Work on the section through St.Leonards was advancing rapidly under the watchful eye of the LBSCR, with shafts for the tunnel being sunk by September 1847.

The SER was still anxious to economise and on 14 December 1847 considered making the Hastings direct line as a single track only. In fact the following month it was formally decided to do this, but to buy enough land for a double track. At this time the SER was still agonising over the various routes into Hastings. Perhaps a secret factor was that completion of a Hastings to Ashford line via Ore would be more useful to the SER's rivals than having to make a detour via Whatlington.

Elsewhere work was progressing rapidly. The Grove Hill Tunnel at Tunbridge Wells was completed in March 1848 at a cost of £35 per yard, the Strawberry Hill Tunnel a few months later, and the headings of Wadhurst Tunnel met in August. Yet not until September did the SER award the contracts to build the St. Leonards to Hastings (Henry Clarke: £98,143) and Robertsbridge to Whatlington (Wythes: £51,264) sections. The choice of the terminal point of the latter contract shows that the SER was still dithering about routes into Hastings, for it could have dropped the Whatlington to St. Leonards section and taken all traffic via Lidham Hill. Not until June 1850 do the SER Minutes record that Wythes was to build the section through Battle to St. Leonards, where the two lines met at Bopeep Junction. In August 1850 it was alleged that the LBSCR had offered the SER £12,000 to drop its direct Hastings line[3].

The South Eastern Board were still unsure about whether to have one track or two. Having decided on one in January 1848, the *Railway Times* reported in September 1849 that they had altered their minds and both Hastings lines were to be double. However in May 1850 they were still debating the issue, but decided on double on 17 June. Then on 3 July they thought they might open it as a single line first!

There were a number of problems with the works. Firstly, the labourers complained that they could not get their wages, and then in June 1850 the contractors were told to stop work on Sundays. In July 1850 the Railway Commissioners wrote to the LBSCR to complain about "the levels of the Hastings tunnels." The SER complained that the LBSCR had been interfering with the works, but it was also reported in the local press that Barlow had altered the tunnels by lengthening them to avoid deep cuttings. Public notice of the deviation of levels was issued in August 1850.

The old station site at Tunbridge Wells formed an ideal place for a goods station and traffic soon developed. In March 1850 a goods train ran away on the branch and ran out onto the main-line at Tonbridge, fortunately without injury. Two months later the SER decided to build a proper goods shed at Tunbridge Wells. The route had also begun to attract some local proposals for new branches by 1850, including Mayfield to Witherenden Bridge.

On 13 February 1851 the SER line from Ashford to Bopeep Junction, via Ore and Hastings, was opened. That it would be the cause of battle had already been clear in January, when the SER had written to the Railway Commissioners to enquire whether the LBSCR would have the right to appoint its own staff at Hastings station. It was advised that the stationmaster should be SER but that the LBSCR could have its own clerks.

Once the line was opened, of course, the LBSCR wanted to run its trains through from Bopeep Junction to Hastings, and this became mysteriously difficult. At first this was claimed to be because the SER signalmen had not been provided with a LBSCR timetable, but after this problem had been resolved a few LBSCR trains ran through to Hastings on 15 and 16 February. On 17 February an obstruction appeared in the shape of a relentlessly non-moving SER train full of soil, which the LBSCR tried to by-pass by using buses between St. Leonards and Hastings. The SER commenced a legal action against certain LBSCR officers for trespass and claimed that a number of important legal titles and deeds had not been produced by the LBSCR.

The issues began to clarify in early March. The SER felt aggrieved that the LBSCR had been passing on rumours that its Hastings direct line was "dangerous" and claimed to have blocked the line to force the LBSCR to establish legal title. The SER wanted the LBSCR to agree to an equal division of the Hastings receipts, but the LBSCR had a shorter route; therefore the SER threatened a fares war, with a 1st class at 10s. to London. Agreement to divide the receipts equally was eventually reached and arranged to be operative from 1 February 1852.

Work on the SER's own line was progressing steadily. On 6 March 1851 the Board decided to spend £10,000 on building six stations along it but on 3 April decided to have only five stations. The people of Burwash made it clear that they expected to have a station. Work also continued in Hastings itself, with the decision to build a goods warehouse and locomotive shed there in May 1851. In July this was revised in favour of SER locomotive and carriage sheds, and joint warehouses with the LBSCR.

In May 1851 the Mayfield Railway Bill was again being discussed and the line as far south as Robertsbridge was nearing completion. It was opened on 1 September 1851, with a special train being run to the Great Exhibition. Intermediate stations were opened at Frant, Wadhurst, Witherenden (renamed Ticehurst Road in December 1851) and Etchingham. Almost immediately the line opened Mr Hyland requested his own siding between Ticehurst and Etchingham.

During November 1851 the SER decided to cover the platforms at Tunbridge Wells and received a request from Whatlington for a station, which was rejected. The line from Robertsbridge to Battle was inspected by the Board of Trade on 20 December 1851 and opened on 1 January 1852; there were no intermediate stations on this section.

The section between Battle and Hastings was delayed through earth slips, for the SER had originally intended to open the whole Robertsbridge to Bopeep section in one and had had it all inspected by the Board of Trade. In fact it opened on 1 February 1852, thus the agreement with the LBSCR became effective from that date, and the railway policemen were instructed to watch for further slips during February. However on 5 February the SER decided to reduce speeds on the line altogether, blaming the bad workmanship of Warton & Warden in particular. There were two serious slips on the line the following winter as well.

Having opened the line as cheaply as possible, the SER then began to review its facilities. They decided to build eight cottages for railwaymen in St. Leonards, near the tunnelmouth at the junction, and ten more in Hastings. In April 1852 they decided to erect £350 goods sheds at Battle, Robertsbridge and Etchingham. In June the provision of a "siding and branch" for B. Smith at Robertsbridge was discussed. The station buildings on the line were among the most attractive built by the SER and were the work of a London architect, William Trees, employing local stone with Caen stone dressings.

On 3 June the Board decided to alter their Hastings fares to the same rate per mile as the LBSCR - 2.75d 1st class and 1.23d 3rd class. Since the LBSCR route via Lewes and Keymer was shorter than the SER via Tonbridge and Redhill, this would have meant the SER fares were more expensive to London - but the SER was protected by the Traffic Agreement.

It continued to concern itself with goods provision, being annoyed that Battle goods shed was being delayed in June 1852 but deciding the following month that Wadhurst should get a goods shed too. The SER had also changed its mind about goods provision in Hastings, for it now wanted its own separate goods shed. This sporadic construction of goods sheds reveals the SER's understanding of each district's traffic potential.

One type of traffic it was not well disposed towards was paupers from Battle. In July 1852 the Poor Law Guardians asked for a free pass for fourteen of them, who were being sent to London so they could emigrate. The SER refused any concession since it already paid two guineas poor rates in Battle.

Frant station was equipped with a carriage dock only as a result of a decision in September, but Ticehurst Road was judged worthy of a goods shed. In the same month a plan for an engine shed at Hastings was considered and in December it was decided to equip the signals at Bopeep Junction with gas lighting. Bopeep Junction was obviously an important point on the line, for from there to Hastings the LBSCR paid for the use of the SER's line. During 1853 the LBSCR paid £642 tolls. There were occasional problems such as when switchman Samson caused a collision in St. Leonard's Tunnel on 19 March 1853 and when the SER accused the LBSCR of using St. Leonard's as a goods station instead of Hastings in 1852-3, thereby depriving the SER of some toll revenue.

Initial estimates of traffic were not always accurate. The SER had expected Robertsbridge to be the principal station between Tunbridge Wells and the coast but from 1 January 1853 it was replaced as an express station by Etchingham.

By the end of 1852 the SER had invested £293,071 in the Tunbridge Wells branch and £724,507 in the line onward from there to Hastings. This did not cover all that was needed as works were still going on early in 1853. Hoof was contracted to build the Tunbridge Wells goods station for £1,916 but in March the SER refused to pay for a hop warehouse that a local company wanted at Robertsbridge station. However in May they decided to put in a siding at Frant and in December accepted £200 from Sir Augustus Webster for the installation of a siding near Battle; this was done by March 1854. In May 1855 it was reported that Frant, too, needed a goods shed.

The Hastings line was built cheaply, though with very attractive stations especially at Battle, but it was also built badly. It took Ashcroft four years to resolve disputes over the contract with Warton & Warden (also sometimes spelt Wardin). Then in March 1855 twelve feet of bricks collapsed in Mountfield Tunnel due to bad bricks being affected by frost and wet. SER traffic was stopped at Robertsbridge for several months during the Summer Season, and the LBSCR demanded that its share of the receipts be increased by 30%. The SER issued a writ for defective work on 8 November, but soon found itself having to carry out remedial measures elsewhere on the line.

50. Bo Peep Junction with the SER's West St. Leonards station.

51. An 1893 view of the awkward arrangement of Hastings station, the terminal platforms being on the right. (Lens of Sutton)

52. Hastings in about 1889, with a Class 1 0-6-0. (R.Thomas Collection)

Having been called in to investigate the Mountfield Tunnel during mid-1855, Ashcroft had decided to look at the other tunnels built by the same firm on their Tunbridge Wells to Robertsbridge contract. What he had found had led to the issuing of the writ. At the Grove Tunnel near Tunbridge Wells he had tested the work by breaking holes through the crown of the brickwork, and found that in places the brickwork was only a half brick thick instead of four bricks. He also discovered a gap between the brickwork and the earth above. He took immediate steps to support the crown of the tunnel but found that the Strawberry Hill Tunnel, though poor, was not as bad.

In February 1856 the SER was repairing the two tunnels south of Tunbridge Wells, which were relined with brick and cement at a cost of £4,700, then in November 1860 spent £250 on St. Leonards Tunnel. The case against the contractors did not reach court until 1861, with the contractors arguing that the works had been certified as satisfactory by the SER engineer at the time, Thomas Drane, in 1852, though in fact both tunnels had been built by sub-contractors. Barlow argued against this by alleging that Drane had been deceived by the sub-contractors into looking at the only parts of the tunnels that had been built properly. The Judge felt that it was partly Drane's fault and awarded the SER only £8,500[4], which was less than the cost of the repairs.

In April 1862 Wadhurst Tunnel was found to be in a poor condition because there was only one ring of cemented brickwork in places instead of the four rings that were necessary for safety. Therefore in September 1862 the SER decided that Wadhurst Tunnel had to be relined and work began on 23 October. Interestingly, Board Minutes of 9 April 1863 record that 1,218 yards of the tunnel were relined and 157 yards left unrepaired though the tunnel is usually credited with being 1,205 yards long.

Relations with the contractors, Warton & Warden, were clearly bad, for in November 1862 they had issued a claim for £86,097 against the SER for unpaid dues. The long term effect of the problems with the Hastings line tunnels was that the gauge of stock that could be used on the line became restricted since the tunnels had to be relined and therefore became narrower than was customary.

As has been seen, the junction at Tonbridge (renamed Tunbridge Junction in 1852 to avoid confusion with Tunbridge Wells) had been laid out in such a way that a reversal was necessary to get onto the Hastings line. In August 1855 the SER decided that this needed to be changed and by November was buying the land to lay in a new curve on a steep gradient. Byng told the shareholders that the original line had been "formed in the wrong direction" and it cost the SER £5,700 to correct it. The new curve opened on 1 May 1857 for goods and 15 May for passengers, but the old line remained in use as well although it had been singled by the 1890s.

All this excitement should not distract us from the normal life of the Hastings line. On 8 May 1855 there was a derailment when locomotive no.33 fractured an axle near the Colebrook Viaduct when working the 7am Tonbridge to Hastings train; it overturned and the driver was killed. The people of Hastings hoped to increase the popularity of their resort by the running of Saturday excursions during the Summer of 1855 and the SER annoyed the LBSCR by charging lower rates for its Hastings season tickets than had been agreed; perhaps this was an attempt to get the traffic back after the problems with Mountfield Tunnel.

In August 1855 the SER decided that it wanted to improve the station at St. Leonards, firstly by spending £270 though in August 1861 it decided that it wanted to make a substantial rebuild, including spending £680 extending the up side. By 1862 £1,000 had been spent improving the station. A further £525 was spent in 1864.

Not everywhere was as well looked after. An October 1856 scheme for a station at Five Ashes near Wadhurst was ignored. However in 1859 it was decided to grace Tunbridge Wells with a clock.

Little had been heard about branches off the Hastings line since the Mayfield idea, but in 1862 there was a flurry of activity. One proposal was for a branch from a point called Forwood, south of Battle, to Bexhill. A Hastings Pier & Harbour Company was also being formed, and they wanted a branch from the SER.

Something more dramatic did occur in the late 1850s and early 1860s when the SER got involved in running excursion trains to prize-fights. It had first done this to Edenbridge in 1850, for fights involving "Spider" Hailes v. Jem Madden and Wade v. Jones. On 20 September 1859 it ran a special on the main-line and again on 17 April 1860 it ran one on the Hastings line to Etchingham. This was meant to be a good site for a fight as it was in a fairly remote area but close to the boundary between two Counties. On 8 December 1863 the SER ran another special excursion to Wadhurst for an illegal prize-fight between King and Heenan. A train of 30 coaches, hauled by two locomotives, left London Bridge at 5.45am. However the Police discovered that the fight was taking place, and turned up at Etchingham station to send a telegraph message for reinforcements. The stationmaster told the Police that they would have to wait their turn, since there was a large number of other messages to send first. However, there was time enough to telegraph the result of the fight to London, though the name of the wrong boxer was sent[5]. This resulted in a summons to the SER to appear at the Sussex Eastern Sessions, where the SER announced that they had changed their rules to allow the Police to take priority in the sending of urgent messages. Although the fight was illegal, the running of a train to a remote spot where it could take place in peace was not, though in January 1864 the SER received a stern letter from the Home Secretary.

In 1865-6 the SER made a review of the state of the Hastings line, perhaps inspired by fears that the LBSCR would get powers for its own direct line to the town. In September 1865 it decided that Hastings station was rather unsatisfactory and considered whether a station should be built at Bopeep Junction. The following month it also received a request for a station to serve the northern part of Tunbridge Wells, the site of the old temporary station being suggested.

The SER Act of 1866 included powers to straighten some of the curves on the Hastings line, but the same year also brought competition to Tunbridge Wells with the opening of a LBSCR line from Groombridge on 1 October. The LBSCR cut the fares to Tunbridge Wells by 18% but the SER was not unduly worried, reckoning that it only lost 227 passengers to its rival in the first month. In April 1868 the SER decided to improve the Hastings line by removing Barlow's iron sleepers.

With the LBSCR now present at Tunbridge Wells and Hastings there was clearly the possibility that "war" could break out again. A rental agreement for the use of the St. Leonards station (later Warrior Square) was discussed during

1866 and in December 1868 an arbitrator reported on the division of traffic receipts at the various towns. Hastings and St. Leonards receipts were to be pooled with the SER getting 75%, while at Tunbridge Wells the LBSCR was limited to a mere 20%. The Hastings receipts appear to give the SER an unfounded improvement in its position, but it should be remembered that the SER had opened its direct line to Tonbridge during 1868 and therefore was in a much stronger position than before.

Early in 1869 the SER decided to install a new siding and turntable at Hastings and a footbridge at St. Leonards. They returned to the apparently vexed question of St. Leonards station in April. The SER wanted to improve it by using one platform, on the up side, for both up and down trains. The up platform could then be further extended to fit the entire distance between the Bopeep and Hastings tunnels. Captain Tyler of the Board of Trade advised against this, so Eborall devised a plan to lengthen both platforms and construct an overbridge for £500. From 5 December 1870 the LBSCR renamed its own St. Leonards station as "St. Leonards (West Marina)" and began to use the SER station which became known as St. Leonards (Warrior Square) from the same date. By the agreement of 11 June 1866 this was to become a joint station and on 23 November 1870 agreement was reached between the two companies to split its annual costs between the SER (£700) and the LBSCR (£350). However it was 1874 before the down platform at Warrior Square was finally extended to the tunnel.

In August 1869 the SER decided to spend £432 providing check rails on the curves of the Hastings line and in October to buy more land for Hastings station. On 12 January 1870 the SER and LBSCR concluded an agreement about their respective train services to Hastings and St. Leonards that reduced the total number of trains from 28 to 26. Both towns expressed annoyance at this. In April 1870 the SER discussed how the Hastings express service could be speeded up; Brady recommended putting in water troughs at Tonbridge.

Minor improvements continued as traffic grew steadily. In late 1870 an extra shelter was provided at Tunbridge Wells, an extra ladies waiting-room and toilets at Hastings, and £40 was spent on an up platform shelter for Frant. Catch points for Papillon's Siding, between Battle and Bopeep, were provided in 1871.

In 1872 £2,590 was spent on roofing over the platforms at Tunbridge Wells, but the station at Hastings was causing problems as it was too cramped to handle excursion passengers without a crush. The only changes that the SER made, however, were a new parcels office (£120, 1873) and a new goods station (£4,800 in 1875-6). Limited space at Hastings was blamed for an accident there on 29 July 1876.

In October 1875 the Sub-Wealden Gypsum Company paid the SER £1,200 to provide a siding at Mountfield.

The SER then turned its attention to Tunbridge Wells. In June 1875 it had accepted that its interests in opening up a route to Eastbourne would necessitate improvements to the station there and in April 1877 the Tunbridge Wells Local Board complained of poor facilities on the down side, including the lack of a footbridge. The SER promised to provide this immediately. It also took immediate steps to reduce fares from 1 May, the first class single to London being cut from 14s 6d to 13s. The Local Board also wanted season tickets reduced, since Tunbridge Wells fares were the same as Hastings! Also requested were better 3rd class services and better connections for Redhill.

On 3 May the SER decided on extensive works at the station in Tunbridge Wells. This included a glazed roof over the down side, the conversion of the old carriage shed into a waiting room, a lift, an extension to the covered way on the up side and an overbridge. The cost was estimated at £1,800. Nothing was done about improving station accommodation to the north of the town, where a station for Southborough had been requested in 1876.

In June 1877 the SER refused to install a brick siding between Battle and Bopeep Junction as the line was too steeply graded. On 17 August a LBSCR guard was injured in Bopeep Tunnel and it was decided that the walls needed alterations.

Neither Hastings nor Tunbridge Wells were satisfied with what had been done about their stations. In September 1877 Hastings Corporation complained to the Railway Commissioners about the stations at Hastings and Warrior Square. The platforms at Hastings were used by both up and down trains and there was too little accomodation. St. Leonards (Warrior Square) had a dangerous approach road. Improvements authorised in September 1875 had not materialised. Hastings took legal action and forced the SER to make improvements at both stations.

The row at Tunbridge Wells in 1878 was such that Byng was sent to study the question. He agreed to extend the station roof and accepted that there was a need for the booking office to be level with the road. Extra goods sidings were also required.

In May 1878 it was decided to provide a goods siding at Ticehurst Road and in July the Tunbridge Wells Gas Company agreed to pay for its own siding near the site of the old temporary terminus. The following month it was decided to install new signalboxes between Tonbridge and Tunbridge Wells.

The SER had now had enough time to formulate a response to the Railway Commissioners over the Hastings question. It planned to open new stations at Hollington, one mile up the line from Bopeep, and at Ore to the east. It also considered improving the curves on the line and agreed to build a better access road and a covered bridge at Warrior Square. Traffic to Hastings during the first two months of 1879 fell by £1,000. As if to confirm the problems, on 14 April 1879 a Hastings to London Bridge excursion was derailed near Grove Junction after heavy rain. One of the problems with Hastings was that the station was in a restricted site and could not be improved without affecting the Cornwallis Road bridge; this caused further troubles with the Corporation until the SER agreed to widen it.

Sometimes the SER did react quickly to local complaints. When the accomodation at Etchingham caused ill feeling in 1879, it agreed to spend £800 almost immediately. In 1881-2 it provided a footbridge and more platform accommodation.

By 1879 the SER was buying up some houses in Tunbridge Wells to allow the improvement of the station and in June decided to build a signalbox near the goods yard. In July Watkin suggested that a small station be opened on the north side of the goods yard, which should also be extended. The proposed passenger station would have interfered with the siding to the Medway Navigation Coal Wharf so this was taken over by the SER in 1881. In 1881 sidings at High Brooms were extended. The same year £760 was spent on sidings in Tunbridge Wells for an agricultural show.

**53. Tunbridge Wells Station c.1870, viewed from the south.
(R.W.Kidner Collection)**

In January 1880 the Railway Commissioners again directed the SER to make improvements at both St. Leonards and Hastings, including the widening of bridges. At the time Hastings station was handling 700,000 passengers a year and Warrior Square 210,000.

During 1880 the SER began a programme of improving the whole line by replacing old rails with heavier new ones and strengthening the bridges. This was expected to cost £27,000 over five years. The same year work at last got started on improving the Hastings area stations and in October the SER proposed building a new station at Hollington and a curve from there to the west end of St. Leonards. The LBSCR objected to this, though it said it would be happy to have a station at Bopeep Junction. Nonetheless the SER went ahead with a Bill for the spur, but in March 1881 it decided to withdraw it. It then considered having a new station at Mount Pleasant in Hastings.

1883 began with a slip on the line at the aptly-named Boggy Brook Bank near Battle, and the decision to spend £800 on a GPO sorting office at Hastings. Later in the year the SER raised the issue of a station at Bopeep again, but the LBSCR felt that it was no better than Warrior Square. However on 8 November 1884 the SER signed an agreement with the Misses Briscoe for land at Bopeep and the following month proposed a joint station there for £4,800. The rent that the LBSCR paid for the use of Warrior Square station under the agreement of June 1866 went up on 1 January 1885 and the LBSCR suggested that the whole line from Bopeep to Hastings should be joint; the LBSCR had free use of Hastings station, to the annoyance of the SER. Unable to interest the LBSCR, the SER went ahead with its agreement with the Briscoe family for a station at West St. Leonards which opened 1 October 1887.

Progress at Tunbridge Wells was even less satisfactory. In January 1884 the SER decided to buy the Grove recreation ground so that it could open up Grove Tunnel to provide more space for a station, but this was frustrated because of its effect on the town. The Company looked at other ways of improving facilities, included the possible construction of a new spur onto the line at Tonbridge. In

May 1887 plans for a station north of the town at Southborough were considered and in July it became clear that a number of local people wanted a station at Grosvenor Road which would serve Southborough. A High Brooms landowner had plans for a station near High Brooms siding in 1889, but was prepared to consider a station at Grosvenor Road instead. For the time being, no further steps were taken.

Further south, the platforms at Frant, Robertsbridge and Wadhurst were extended in 1887 and in 1888 the SER lent £7,000 to the St. Leonards Pier Company and subscribed a further £70,000. Battle received a new urinal and roof in 1890, costing £720, and Etchingham got a new footbridge in 1891.

The relationship with the LBSCR had deteriorated. In 1888 the SER refused to let its supposed partner put up posters at Hastings and St. Leonards stations although in 1889 Henry Oakley was called in to arbitrate on the various causes of dispute. This then introduced the possibility that Hastings Corporation would take legal action to nullify any agreement, so the two companies decided to seek Parliamentary approval for their arrangement. For Easter 1890 the SER ran some especially cheap excursions to Hastings on Mondays, costing only 4s. return. A return excursion from Hastings to London for the Kensington Exhibitions cost 3s. The normal "cheap" 3rd class return was 6s. and 1st class 15s.

In 1891 the SER at last decided to buy land for a station north of Tunbridge Wells, and bought land from the Gas Company at High Brooms. It decided to spend £2,747 and the station opened as Southborough on 1 March 1893[6]. Signals for it cost £478. In 1894 the SER refused a request to have it renamed "Tunbridge Wells North." An extra siding and a goods shed were provided in 1896.

During the last years of the SER's independence, some minor improvements were made elsewhere. A new goods office was provided at Hastings in 1891 for £300 and the station was resignalled the same year for £906. The following year a new down platform shelter was provided at Etchingham but a local request for a station at Crowhurst was refused. On 22 March 1892 nine people were injured when a Brighton to Hastings train overshot signals and ran into a SER locomotive at Hastings. In July 1896 a Charing Cross to Hastings train hit a traction engine on a farm crossing near Etchingham.

During 1892-3 resignalling work took place at Robertsbridge and Smith's Siding, Etchingham, Ticehurst Road, Frant, Ruckinge Siding, Wadhurst and Crowhurst Siding. Robertsbridge got a footbridge in 1893 and Battle a footbridge and ladies waiting room costing £550. Wadhurst did not get a footbridge until 1898. The Forest Brick Company agreed to pay for its own siding between Frant and Tunbridge Wells in 1897.

2. The Bexhill Branch

The Bexhill branch was not in fact opened until after the formation of the SE&CR, but it comes within the scope of this book since it was promoted while the SER was still a separate company.

Bexhill was served by the coastal line of the LBSCR and felt that this left it at a disadvantage compared to Hastings and St. Leonards. There were a number of proposals made to give it a direct link to the SER, including the Bexhill Direct scheme of 1884. In 1885 a new Bill was prepared for a line from Battle to Bexhill, with access to Eastbourne. In 1889 the contractors Lucas & Aird supported a scheme for a branch.

A Bill for a Crowhurst, Sidley & Bexhill Railway was promoted in 1896 and passed by Parliament in 1897 with capital of £180,000. Its engineer was A. J. Barry, but the Board included several men linked with the SER including the Chairman, Sir George Russell, Cosmo Bonsor and Gathorne Hardy. Russell died in 1898 and Bonsor became Chairman with Colonel J. Mellor becoming a director.

At the start of October 1897 the Company noted that it had received a loan of £10,000 from the SER and in December it appointed J. Price as contractor. The major engineering feature on the line was the Coombe Haven Viaduct, which he was working on by June 1898.

Early in 1898 the Company decided to alter the proposed site of its terminus to Braggs Wood and a new Bill was prepared. However the land was discovered to be unsuitable and so Bells Hill was considered as an alternative. The owner of land at Collingwood, three-quarters of a mile from Braggs Wood, suggested a deviation to there. The Act of 1 July 1898 authorised £48,000 extra capital and the deviations. The Company expected to pay £20,540 for twenty acres at Braggs Wood.

In 1899 the CSBR decided to build a hotel at Crowhurst and on 1 March Earl de la Warr became Chairman. The Earl lived at the Manor House in Bexhill and had written in asking to join the Board; Bonsor resigned to make way for him.

The Company decided to recommend that the junction, station and hotel at Crowhurst should be paid for by the SECR, but that they would pay for a hotel at Sidley. The SECR agreed to contribute £4,184 for the Crowhurst Hotel in 1901.

In 1900 it was decided to build an approach road to Crowhurst station for £4,000 and that the refreshment rooms at Bexhill should be licensed. Price was

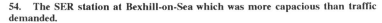

54. The SER station at Bexhill-on-Sea which was more capacious than traffic demanded.

to build Bexhill station and he laid in pipes from Coombe Haven to Bexhill to supply the locomotives with water there.

By 1902 the line was nearing completion and some of the details were being considered. An initial estimate of £792 for a stationmaster's house at Sidley frightened the Company off, so that the line was opened with little or no staff accommodation. The Bexhill station was designed by Barry & Mercer and its refreshment rooms let to Spiers & Pond; the lavishness of the architecture was in contrast to the normally prudent practices of the SER at this time.

The SECR held a private ceremony on 31 May 1902 and the line opened to the public on 1 June with Crowhurst station opening the same day. Only after the opening was it decided to create two loco pits at Bexhill for £70 and provide electric lighting for £102. At the end of July the Company decided to build stationmasters' houses within tight financial limits - Bexhill was to cost £650 at most and Sidley £560. Staff cottages at Bexhill were to be £300 each. In fact the Company did better than this, for the Bexhill contract was for £653 and Sidley only £490.

An agreement was signed with the Anglo-American Oil Company for tanks and sidings at Bexhill in 1902.

The Company was absorbed into the SE&CR in 1906.

1.   **Railway Times,** 3 April 1841.
2.   SER Minutes, 13 August 1844.
3.   **Railway Times,** 29 August 1850.
4.   The **Railway Times,** 2 March 1861, gives £3,500 whereas **The Times,** 27 February 1861, gives £8,500.
5.   H.D.Miles, **Pugilistica.**
6.   SER Signalling Notices. The author is grateful to D.Cullum for this confirmation.

CHAPTER 15: THE RYE LINE

As has been seen in the previous chapter, many of the early proposals for lines to Rye were in fact part of schemes to link the SER main-line with Hastings. After a period of proposal and counter-proposal, it was the L&BR supported Brighton, Lewes & Hastings Railway that had first been authorised to extend to Hastings in 1844.

The SER was then worried that the BLHR would seek a further extension to Rye and Ashford, and so continued to propose its own lines into the district. In August 1844 it was surveying from Ashford to Hastings and in September Cubitt was directed to survey two possible routes, going via Ore or via Whatlington and the Brede valley. In October the SER decided to apply for a Bill for a line from Headcorn to Rye with an extension from there to Ashford, but in January 1845 it decided to abandon the Headcorn to Rye line and concentrate on Ashford to Hastings, for which a route via Whatlington to avoid the difficult ground around Ore remained a possibility. What emerged from this was a compromise by which the BLHR got the powers to build the line from Hastings to Ashford, which was deemed of great national importance by the military, and the SER was authorised to take over these powers should it wish to do so - but on the condition that the Ashford to Hastings line was completed before the Tunbridge Wells to Hastings route.

The line from Hastings to Ashford that the BLHR acquired powers for passed through sparsely populated country with only one intermediate place of any significant size, Rye. The SER therefore had little difficulty in acquiring it from its erstwhile rival.

The South Eastern clearly believed that Rye Harbour had considerable potential, partly because of the Harbour dues issue. As early as 18 September 1845 it decided to give £10,000 to help in harbour improvements which was paid to the Admiralty by March 1846. By then Robert Stephenson had recommended the idea of a 1.75 mile branch to Rye Harbour and this was authorised in an Act of Parliament of 18 June 1846.

The relationship between the SER and the LBSCR over the Rye and Ashford line was not entirely a smooth one. SER Minutes in December 1846 suggest that the LBSCR was not pleased by the SER's lack of progress on the project, which also affected the Brighton Company's access into Hastings itself since the line from Bopeep to Hastings was included in it. When warning hints about the matter reached the SER Board, they decided to adopt the cheapest course, by contracting King & Spivey to build the Ashford to Rye section in January 1847 for £122,956. This section posed few physical problems and was also the most remote from the rival Company's tracks. A decision on Rye to Hastings was "postponed" on the grounds that the Board wanted to build it as a single track.

On 16 February the SER Board decided to award another contract to Wythes, which was for £131,000 and was for the Rye Harbour branch and work on the Ashford to Hastings line. The real problem for the SER was that the line from Lidham Hill, via Ore and Hastings, to the LBSCR at Bopeep threatened to be hideously expensive to build; they wished to divert the line to join the other

55. The unique and attractive swing bridge at Rye, drawn in about 1850.

Hastings route at Whatlington instead and in July 1847 began to prepare a Deviation Bill. Not surprisingly, the LBSCR objected to such a longer route and in November 1847 the SER agreed to drop the idea, possibly because they expected Government opposition to it. The route was meant to be completed by 21 August 1848, yet in January 1848 the SER had barely decided on a route. It returned to Parliament to argue for a two year time extension.

On the simpler parts of the line some progress was being made. The Board of Ordnance approved G. R. Stephenson's plans for a bridge across the Royal Military Canal near Warehorne in July 1847 and in January 1848 the Board decided that the line should be single. Decisions of the SER were made to be broken though, so in June 1848 they decided that Appledore to Rye at least should be double track. On 23 June the people of Warehorne petitioned for a station, which eventually opened at Ham Street.

On 10 August the Board learnt that the Admiralty had approved Barlow's design for a bridge over the Rother at Rye which was designed as a swing-bridge and the contract for it offered to Ransome & May. Yet in September 1848 there was still uncertainty about the route between Hastings and Lidham Hill, with Wythes actually offering to build the line from Rye to Whatlington for £55,524. It seems that only in October did the Board finally abandon the Whatlington idea and it is perhaps significant that some SER shareholders demanded that the Rye line should be abandoned altogether.

In the context of shareholder opposition, the following Board statement is of interest:

"The Directors do not hesitate to state that their principal reason in undertaking the formation of this line is to discharge the duty which we conceived would devolve

upon this Company - of carrying out the wishes of the Government in the construction of a complete chain of coast lines."

It was upon the satisfaction of this Government wish that the authorisation for the direct Hastings line rested, so that in effect the Rye line was a price the SER was forced to pay.

In fact work on the Ashford to Rye section had progressed rapidly and in September 1848 the hop-planters of Appledore had requested the early opening of the line for their harvest. However Board of Trade permission was not forthcoming. By March 1849 the SER was preparing to let the contracts for Lidham Hill to Hastings and St. Leonards.

Incredibly, they were still in two (or more) minds as to whether to open the first section as single or double track. Having decided on single in 1848, they felt in June 1850 that ballast should be provided for a double line and in July considered that it could be opened as a single line first. In September it was decided to build stations at Ham Street, Appledore, Rye and Winchelsea. In October the site for a station near Lidham Hill was also discussed, an indication as to how far west the works had progressed.

The opening of the line is almost as complicated as its genesis and is further confused by the fact that the Lord Mayor of London for part of 1850 was a man from Hastings. Sadly for the Lord Mayor his term of office was rapidly expiring, but the SER and the Mayor himself felt that he was the ideal person to open the line - providing he was still Mayor, of course. He was therefore invited to open the line on 28 October 1850, even though it was far from complete. He had also travelled by train over part of the line before this occasion in connection with some celebrations in which he had taken part. The plan was for a special to leave London Bridge at 9.30am to take the Mayor to Rye for assorted celebrations, following which there would be an inspection of the tunnels at Hastings. In fact torrential rain and the incomplete state of the line made the whole operation rather hazardous and the special train's progress was precarious:

56. **Viewed from the up platform, a train from Hastings passes the main buildings at Rye.**

"In many cases workmen were employed with hand spikes to keep the rails from sinking in the semi-liquid mud as the engine and carriages passed over them.[1]*"*

There were numerous other problems. The rain had caused a massive slip at the north end of the "Mount Pleasant Tunnel" in Hastings and the rest of the line was hardly more stable. As the train crossed the edge of Romney Marsh it showed a "tendency every now and then to heel over like a skip in a gale of wind or a cart in a miry road." Its progress was watched by "bands of navvies besmeared with mud and bearing about them the marks of recent and severe labour."

After a pause for speeches at Rye the train inched forwards to Guestling, where it had to stop for an hour as the track ahead had not yet been completed. Then it moved ahead to the Ore tunnel, which had been lit with a row of candles and in the middle of which a stage had been erected to help the Mayor insert the last brick. The efforts of men, horses and steam power were then required to force the reluctant train back into motion and Hastings was reached three hours late.

The Mayor still managed to see much of the line and inserted the last brick in the two tunnels either side of Hastings, but the ceremonial opening was no more than a ceremony. Two months after his train had passed the SER was still bemoaning the lack of ballast on the line, of which little was available locally except the Dungeness shingle.

The LBSCR had considered opposing the opening of the line before the Railway Commissioners, but in November 1850 withdrew its opposition - perhaps they knew there was no cause to worry! The SER hoped to open the line on 1 January 1851 but Wynne inspected it at the end of December and delayed the opening for a month due to inadequate signalling. At the end of January he delayed the opening for another few weeks. On 28 February Board of Trade approval was gained for the use of the second track which had been completed at last.

The second attempt to open the line, on 13 February, was more successful than the first. It is perhaps worth noting that, at a time of great financial difficulty, the capital cost of the Ashford to Hastings line by March 1853 was £789,396, making it a considerable drain on SER resources.

Following the opening of the line there was a chorus of protests about a lack of facilities. The people of Rye complained that nothing had been done about the harbour branch, so in March 1851 Wythes was directed to complete the branch with space for three vessels at the quayside. There was then a request for a proper goods station at Ham Street and a station at Three Oaks Bridge.

A second Act had to be obtained for the Harbour branch and this was acquired in 1851 with powers for a "tramroad" at the Strand. The SER had been pursuing this question in a very dilatory fashion, and even a second Act hardly spurred it into great activity. In both February and April 1852 it received complaints that the line was still not finished. It was reported to be "nearly complete" in March 1853, but reported to be in exactly the same condition again a year later. However in March 1854 the SER seems to have become interested in the possibility of using Rye Harbour for ferry services to Normandy and it seems to have opened shortly after this, probably in March 1854[2].

A request for a more direct line to Rye from off the Hastings main-line, in July 1851, must have felt like an insult to the already suffering directors of the SER.

Traffic on the line was clearly disappointing for the SER actually closed Winchelsea station from 1 September 1851. One of the reasons that the station closed was related to the effects of a tollgate nearby, the only other access to the station being across private land. The Mayor of poor Winchelsea began an immediate campaign for a reopening, or at least an opening of it as a "flag station," but his success depended on negotiations with the landowner involved[3]. On 4 December the SER agreed to reopen the station, though from what date is uncertain; perhaps 1 January 1852 would have been most likely.

On 30 April 1852 a locomotive belonging to the contractor, Wythes, was hauling a train near Ham Street when its driver, John Hadley, stopped it to examine the boiler. As he did so the boiler exploded and he was killed when part of it hit his head.

In September 1852 to March 1853 the issue of building a line from Lidham Hill to Whatlington resurfaced. Some of the land for this had been purchased but was still tenanted. Little was done though, and the reason for this probably lies in a *Railway Times* report in 1854 that the Rye line paid about a 1% return on the cost of constructing it.

The SER found other ways of boosting traffic on the line, especially since it crossed the wide open and remote spaces of Romney Marsh. Such a place was ideal for a prize-fight, and on 29 January 1856 a special train of two engines and thirty carriages was run from London Bridge for the fight between Tom Sayers and Harry Poulson. The train left at 6am and Sayers nearly missed it. The fight took place near Appledore and was won by Sayers, perhaps jointly with the SER, since Sayers struck the final blow and the SER is reputed to have made £1,000 out of the excursion. A Kent magistrate complained that "The Company is openly aiding and abetting a breach of the peace", but the SER could always claim that it had no knowledge of the purpose for which an excursion had been arranged[4].

Under these circumstances, changes and improvements were few and far between. A coal stage was built at Rye in 1854 and in 1859 £3,500 was spent rebuilding the viaduct at Ham Street. A goods shed was built at Ham Street in 1861. In 1868 the SER decided that Barlow's sleepers should be removed from the line and fishplates installed; this suggests that no relaying of track had taken place since the line opened.

In December 1870 the SER decided to spend £200 putting up a cottage at the level crossing "on the curve" between Winchelsea and Hastings. This was to break up a seven mile section and to give the platelayers somewhere to live. Some minor improvements for goods traffic were also made, with catch points being installed at the goods sidings between Ham Street and Ashford in 1871 and new sidings being installed at Rye and possibly Rye Harbour in 1874. An agreement was reached with Messrs Kelly for a siding at Rye in 1876. A boy was killed at Rye station in May 1873. By 1879 there was a gas siding at Hastings, which was near to the Rye line ticket platform.

The one part of the line where any great population growth seemed likely was at the Hastings end where the eastern side of the town was badly served. In March 1872 consideration was given to opening a new station at Ore, and in July the SER assessed the idea of a new station to break up the gap between Hastings and Winchelsea. The issue then lay dormant, though the engineer objected to the idea of a station at the Ore tunnelmouth in December 1877. There was a new scheme for an Ore station in October 1878 and SER Minutes of May 1880 record that the Company had started buying land there. Yet once more no real progress was made until in July 1886 the Board finally decided to invest £2,800 for a "small" goods and passenger station at Ore; a local landowner agreed to give £1,000 towards the cost of the Ore station, so it seems that the stations to both the east and west of Hastings were connected with property development. But things never happened smoothly on the Rye line and the opening of the station was deliberately delayed by the SER as the promised £1,000 had failed to arrive, though an agreement was finally reached on 17 November. Ore station opened on 1 January 1888.

In September 1880 the town of Rye requested that the swing bridge over the Rother should be replaced by a fixed bridge. During February 1881 the SER learnt that Rye hoped to have a road beside the railway on any new bridge. The SER hesitated, then in late 1881 presented a Bill to repeal its legal requirement to maintain an opening span across the Rother though in fact a fixed bridge was not built until 1903.

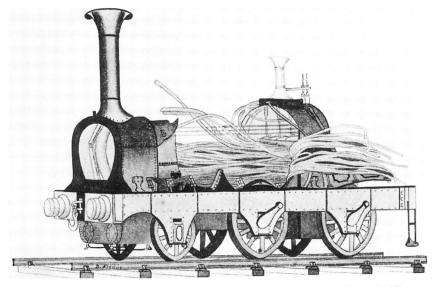

57. The contractor's locomotive that exploded near Ham Street on 30 April 1852, killing its driver. (Wakeman Collection, Ashford Library)

New signals were installed at Appledore in 1881 in preparation for the opening of the branch to Lydd, because of which Appledore attained the glorious distinction of being a junction from 7 December 1881. In October 1883 the SER Board refused to consider a station at Guestling but in June 1884 they agreed to construct a goods siding at Ruckinge, between Ham Street and Ashford. Some modest signs of expansion were apparent in June 1887 when the SER decided to lengthen the platforms at Appledore, Ham Street and Winchelsea stations. The following year the girders on the bridge at Ham Street had to be replaced.

During the early 1890s a modest resignalling programme was carried out at Ham Street, Winchelsea and Rye. In 1894 £170 was spent on building a waiting room at Appledore. A goods shed was built at the same station in 1896 for £830 and a stationmaster's house was added in 1897-8 for £450.

A number of modest improvements were carried out elsewhere, including extra platforms shelters at Rye in 1895 and plans to improve Ore station were drawn up in 1896. An 1895 plan to enlarge Rye Harbour and build a "double loop line" to give improved access to it was wisely dropped. But poor Guestling was refused a station yet again in 1898..

It has often been Sir Edward Watkin who has been criticised for saddling the SER with uneconomic lines, yet two of its poorest routes were lengthy cross-country lines promoted in the 1840s - the Ashford to Hastings and the Reading lines. The former was always a poor earner, though in 1895 the SER did announce - almost proudly - that it was at last paying its way. But it seems likely that the line owed its existence to both SER and Government concepts of strategy, and would not have been built on the eventual route otherwise. Perhaps this makes the line's survival into the 1990s all the more remarkable.

1.   **Railway Times,** 2 November 1850.
2.   J.Hilton, p.68.
3.   J.Hilton, p.68-9.
4.   G.Turner, **Ashford - The Coming of the Railway,** p.107-9.

CHAPTER 16: SURREY & SUSSEX

As has been seen, the South Eastern had an early ambition to build a line to Brighton but was thwarted in this by the scheme that eventually grew into the LBSCR. Nonetheless, SER ambitions continued to be influenced by the fact that its main-line took it southwards to Redhill before turning east to Tonbridge; the Redhill to Tonbridge section seemed to offer a perfect starting point for extensions into East Sussex. This situation was further emphasised by the successful construction of the SER's line to Hastings via Tunbridge Wells, for this offered more opportunities still for expansion in the void between there and the LBSCR main-line.

During the Railway Mania, there were several suggestions for this area. A Brighton, Lewes & Tunbridge Wells line, via Uckfield, was being discussed in September 1845 but the SER itself was more interested in a line from Godstone to East Grinstead. Barlow was sent out to survey this in November 1845 and, on the basis of an estimated cost of £110,000, a Bill was prepared. The Brighton, Lewes & Tunbridge Wells secured an Act, but it was a victim of the collapse of the Railway Mania and its powers were abandoned in 1849.

The Brighton Company obtained powers in 1846 to construct its own branch to East Grinstead only, and later that year the SER was worried by a proposed East Grinstead & Tunbridge Wells scheme to extend the tentacles of the Brighton to the select Kent spa town. Both schemes faded away in the harsher economic reality of the later 1840s.

In 1852 discussions revived. That September, the SER discussed a Godstone to East Grinstead branch once more and was worried by an East Grinstead Railway scheme to link the town to the LBSCR at Three Bridges. To complicate matters further, the Lewes, Uckfield & Tunbridge Wells Railway was threatening to invade SER territory from the south. SER actions were limited by the territorial agreement it had signed with the LBSCR on 10 July 1848, which defined all territory south of its Redhill to Tonbridge line, and west of the Tunbridge Wells and Hastings branch, as "belonging" to the LBSCR. This was very convenient for the latter, since it protected Brighton itself from invasion, but it allowed the LBSCR to gain access to the profitable Tunbridge Wells traffic if it so wished. Thus the SER could do little more than mutter about the East Grinstead branch, which was authorised in 1853 and opened on 9 July 1855.

The issue of a line connecting Lewes and Tunbridge Wells arose again in 1856. At first the SER heard only of a short branch from Lewes to Uckfield which was authorised in 1857 and opened on 18 October 1858; however in November 1858 the SER learnt that there was a scheme to extend this called the Tunbridge Wells, Brighton & South Coast Railway whose promoters were keen that their line should be worked by the LBSCR. The SER raised the issue at the meeting of the LBSCR & SER Joint Committee, but the LBSCR denied any knowledge of it; the SER were then furious to discover that the plans for it had been drawn up in the LBSCR offices[1].

The SER kept to the agreement of 1848; when a Mr Sheridan wrote to it in January 1860 about a line from off the SER Hastings route to Eastbourne, it sent a copy of the letter to the LBSCR. Later the same year a further scheme appeared to complete the gap between Uckfield and Tunbridge Wells; the SER suggested to the LBSCR in October 1860 that this might be built as a joint line, but the Brighton, Uckfield & Tunbridge Wells Act of 1861 did not allow for this since it was to terminate on the edge of Tunbridge Wells. The LBSCR denied having any formal links with the concern [2]. The SER still kept to the terms of the agreement, in March 1861 refusing to help promote a Battle to Hailsham proposal.

A second prong to the attack then appeared in the shape of an East Grinstead, Groombridge & Tunbridge Wells scheme. This was authorised in 1862 for a line from East Grinstead to join the Uckfield & Tunbridge Wells at Groombridge. The Act included powers for the line to be worked by either the SER or the LBSCR, though the former was clearly disadvantaged and may have helped to inspire a rival scheme for a line to Groombridge and Tunbridge Wells from Edenbridge[3].

However a new factor then emerged to change the pattern of developments. Just as the SER had a weakness in that the resort town of Tunbridge Wells attracted predators, so too did the LBSCR - for the poor service it offered to Eastbourne encouraged promoters of new lines to that town. In November 1862 there was talk of a line to connect the Mid-Kent Railway to Eastbourne, while the following month the LCDR threatened to invade the inner sanctuary itself with a scheme for a line from Beckenham to Lewes and Brighton. A completely separate Bill for a Tunbridge Wells & Eastbourne Railway was deposited in November 1862, but lost on Standing Orders in March 1863; significantly, legal expenses for it were paid by the SER, showing that the SER itself was attempting to get round the restrictive territorial agreement.

Now it was the turn of the LBSCR to panic. At least one report has suggested that the LCDR itself tried to buy up control of the Uckfield & Tunbridge Wells and East Grinstead & Groombridge lines as part of the BLB scheme[4]. Faced with such a horrifying threat, Schuster of the LBSCR suggested to the SER in December 1862 that both companies should take a joint lease on these lines. However the 1862-3 Parliamentary session ended with the rejection of the BLB Bill so that, for a time at least, the LBSCR was safe.

By the summer of 1863 the LBSCR was taking steps to lease both the new lines being built, but the SER was showing interest in Sir Charles Blount's scheme for a line from Hailsham to Tunbridge Wells, giving a through route to Eastbourne. However, it decided to deposit its own Bill for a £230,000 line from Battle direct to Eastbourne while the BLB also brought in another Bill. The Beckenham Bill was rejected again in February 1864.

What could have become a costly struggle was averted by a new agreement of 2 March 1864; this was crucial for the SER since it was already engaged in a fierce struggle with the LCDR and could not afford another bitter enemy. However it was also important for the LBSCR, who had been forced to reduce fares on their main-line to pacify opposition. Under the new agreement, the SER first withdrew its own Battle to Eastbourne Bill. It agreed not to promote any new lines in the territory bounded by Three Bridges, Groombridge, Heathfield, Hailsham and Bexhill. The link between Hailsham and Eridge, on the Uckfield to Tunbridge Wells line, was to be built by the LBSCR with a connection to the SER at Tunbridge Wells; over it there were to be at least six through trains to Eastbourne each day from the SER, with receipts divided on a mileage basis. The LBSCR was to have running powers into the SER station at Tunbridge Wells. The LBSCR was to withdraw the Bills for a branch from Hellingly to Bexhill and for the Surrey & Sussex Junction Railway, which was to run from Croydon via Oxted to Groombridge; the latter was to cause much further trouble.

As a result of this agreement the Tunbridge Wells & Eastbourne Act was passed on 14 July 1864 for the line to Hailsham and enabling the connection to be made to Grove Junction, Tunbridge Wells.

What should have been an effective solution to a fraught situation proved to be no more than a brief pause in a frenetic burst of rival promotional campaigns. Firstly, in October 1864, a private scheme for a line from Dungeness to Frant and to Groombridge caused confusion, then the LBSCR's promotion of a new line from Hailsham to St Leonards threatened a town where the SER already felt the keen edge of competition. But the anger really became apparent when the LBSCR's Surrey & Sussex Junction Railway was authorised on 6 July 1865 for a line from Croydon, via Oxted, to Groombridge - giving a better route to Tunbridge Wells than that controlled by the SER. The SER declared that the LBSCR should have opposed the scheme, especially since the SER had used its influence against a Caterham to Eastbourne line, and that the territorial agreement must be considered void; in private, though, the SER Board blamed the evidence given by their own member, Thomson[5].

This action of the LBSCR's produced a remarkable response - the joining together of the SER and the LCDR in promoting a new line to Brighton via Lewes. The Beckenham scheme reappeared once more, with a report that "It is no great secret...that the proposed new line is fostered by the LCD Company and the SER..."[6]. The London, Lewes & Brighton was to run from Beckenham and Penge, via West Wickham, Lingfield, East Grinstead, West Hoathly, and Lewes to Kemp Town. There were to be branches from Godstone to Edenbridge and from Titsey to Westerham. Much of this scheme was authorised on 6 August 1866, but its links with Newhaven and two branches in the London and Bromley areas were rejected. The costs of promoting the line came to £54,800 but it was to prove in vain for the LCDR became bankrupt in July 1866 and, in a severe financial crisis, railway promotion came to a sudden halt.

In the aftermath of the financial crisis there were discussions of an amalgamation of the LBSCR and SER, the former using the opportunity to drop the powers for the Tunbridge Wells to Hailsham link. The East Grinstead to Groombridge and Tunbridge Wells line opened on 1 October 1866, but the Groombridge to Uckfield line had to wait until 3 August 1868. The SER/LCDR route to Brighton was abandoned as was the new LBSCR route to St Leonards, but work on the Surrey & Sussex line progressed slowly.

The SER and LBSCR reached a new agreement on 1 February 1869. This covered the division of receipts for traffic to Hastings and to Tunbridge Wells, the SER getting 75% and 80% respectively. The LBSCR opened its own large station at Tunbridge Wells but the link to Grove Junction remained in use for goods only, since the through line to Eastbourne which would have justified its use by SER trains was not opened until 1880.

The LBSCR's hopes that the Eastbourne issue would go away were dashed as soon as the financial climate improved. In September 1871 the Duke of Devonshire, the major landowner at the Sussex resort, began pressing for a new line - preferably from Battle on the SER. Within two months other schemes were put forward for lines to Eastbourne from Wadhurst and from Ticehurst, but the SER refused to help any of them due to its agreement with the LBSCR.

The SER itself was worried about the situation with the Surrey & Sussex line. This company had been taken over by the LBSCR in 1869, but it had abandoned it although a good deal of work had already been done. This included the driving of a 2,161 yard tunnel at Oxted and a viaduct at Woldingham[7]. Although the scheme appeared to be dormant, the SER was concerned that it could be revived and used for a new direct line to Hastings; there was talk of a proposed line from Rotherfield, north of Uckfield, to Hailsham. The SER itself supported a scheme known as the Brighton, Eastbourne & London, later the Metropolitan & Brighton, which was a revival of the old idea for a line from Beckenham.

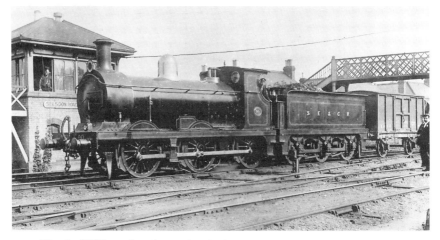

58. An SECR goods train passing the junction at Selsdon Road in about 1901. (Wakeman Collection)

Eastbourne interests continued to press for a line that would connect with the SER at Frant, whereas Laing of the LBSCR hoped to secure the alliance of the SER by offering a joint station at Tunbridge Wells and a through service between Eastbourne and Charing Cross after the completion of the Hailsham to Groombridge section. By July 1875 the two companies seem to have agreed on the latter procedure and the Tunbridge Wells & Eastbourne scheme, authorised on 5 August 1873 for a line from Red Gate Mill to Hailsham, was vested in the LBSCR by an Act of 1876. The new spirit of harmony was disrupted later in 1875 by a private scheme for a line to Eastbourne from Etchingham, on the SER Hastings line, and by revived proposals for the Beckenham to Brighton line. In 1877 the SER objected to LBSCR involvement with a scheme for a line from Barcombe, north of Lewes, to East Grinstead.

In the summer of 1875 a case was brought to the Railway Commissioners by the town of Uckfield, which objected to the lack of a through passenger service between the LBSCR and SER stations at Tunbridge Wells. The LBSCR claimed that this could not be run due to the need for improvements at the SER station, but the SER said it would have no difficulty handling the traffic[8]. In September Colonel Hutchinson, for the Board of Trade, refused to sanction the use of the connection to Grove Junction for through trains due largely to the inadequate facilities at the SER Tunbridge Wells station. For a few weeks, from the beginning of October 1875, it would seem that a few local trains were provided between the LBSCR station and Tonbridge[9] but by 21 October a local service between the two Tunbridge Wells stations appears to have been established. Following the improvements at Grove Junction and Tunbridge Wells (SER), the through service began on 1 February 1877[10]. However, the Uckfield people did not think that a through service to Tunbridge Wells SER was enough and from 1 March LBSCR services operated through to Tonbridge instead[11]. The LBSCR gave up operating the service from 1 September as it was unpunctual and the SER began a service from Tonbridge to Tunbridge Wells (LBSCR) instead.

Interest had been renewed in the partially-completed Surrey & Sussex Junction line. Both the SER and the LBSCR looked covetously at the territory left vacant between Croydon or Caterham and Edenbridge. Thus in 1875, for example, the SER hoped to persuade the LBSCR to leave the S&S alone so that it could extend from Caterham to Edenbridge; soon it began to consider a line from Caterham, via Oxted, to serve Westerham and Godstone as well.

This was not easy country to build railways through and the SER decided that a better option would be to join the LBSCR in completing the Surrey & Sussex. In February 1877 it suggested the completion of the Croydon to Oxted section, with an extension from there to Godstone and East Grinstead. The result was an Act of June 1878 for the Croydon, Oxted & East Grinstead Railway. Under an agreement authorised by Parliament on 6 July 1879, this was to be the joint property of the SER and LBSCR as far south as Crowhurst Junction North, where it was to have a connection to the SER's old main-line; southwards to East Grinstead was to be wholly controlled by the LBSCR.

The same agreement revised the earlier arrangement for the division of traffic to towns such as Eastbourne; this worked very well for the SER at first, since by February 1879 they had received a £6,000 share in the Eastbourne traffic even though the route via Hailsham had not yet opened. For 1880 the SER received £9,000. The new route to Eastbourne finally opened on 3 October 1881, after which the SER had to actually earn its share of the receipts. The SER tried to stimulate the service from 1 March 1884 by running fast trains to Eastbourne calling only at Tunbridge Wells.

Joseph Firbank, who was already the contractor for the LBSCR's line to connect East Grinstead and Lewes, was given the task of completing the rest of the route; one of the first things he did was to examine the state of the old tunnel at Oxted. His contract for completing the line between Croydon and Crowhurst was £185,000.

The Oxted line was to become the central part of a growing system of lines in the Surrey, Sussex and Kent border country. The Woodside & South Croydon, authorised in 1880 and jointly acquired by the SER and LBSCR in 1882, provided a link onto it from the SER's Mid-Kent line to the north; the Oxted & Groombridge, authorised in 1881 for a line from Hurst Green Junction to Ashurst Junction near Groombridge, was absorbed into the LBSCR by Act of 1884. The LCDR attempted to exploit the situation by promoting a London & Eastbourne Railway of its own in 1883, hoping to form a link from Dulwich onto the Oxted & Groombridge; it would have been a conspicuous waste of capital.

To look after the line, the LBSCR & SER (Croydon, Oxted & East Grinstead Railways) Joint Committee was set up in January 1884. Samuel Laing of the LBSCR was chairman, with each company having three representatives. The line opened to East Grinstead on 10 March 1884 with intermediate stations on the joint section at Sanderstead, Upper Warlingham and Oxted. Profits on the joint section were to be divided between the SER and LBSCR; for example, the SER's share for six months in 1890 was £2,196.

Clearly the line was opened before the provision of stations had been fully settled. On 12 March 1884 the Joint Committee discussed the preparation of plans for a station at "Whiteleaf", between Upper Warlingham and Oxted; in May Sir George Balfour MP suggested to Watkin that the Upper Warlingham station should be renamed "Whyteleafe" - in fact it was renamed Upper Warlingham & Whyteleafe on 1 January 1894. On 21 May 1884 the Committee decided to delay building any new station for Whyteleafe, opting later for Marden Park instead.

At the northern end of the line, the opening of the station at Selsdon Road seems to have been delayed until the Woodside line itself opened; when inspected in November 1884 it was criticised for its platform provision, and probably opened on 10 August 1885. A station at Selsdon had to be provided under an 1880 agreement with the Wigsel Trustees, but delays were caused as the SER had wanted it sited nearer the junction with the main-line[12].

An additional station was added at Marden Park (renamed Woldingham 1 January 1894) on 1 July 1885 after the landowner had given the site and £500 towards the £3,750 cost. A station at Crowhurst was discussed several times, but never provided.

The spur onto the SER at Crowhurst was inspected by the Board of Trade on 6 June 1884, although it had been used for freight since 10 March. It opened for passenger traffic on 1 August 1884 when the SER extended some of its four services that had previously terminated at Oxted; two ran through to Edenbridge and one to Tunbridge Junction[13].

Between Croydon and Hurst Green the line passed through country that included several lime works; indeed, in March 1884 a lime kiln had to be removed from under Riddlesdown Viaduct. The line quickly developed a number of sidings associated with the lime trade and other industries; as early as June 1884 the Oxted & Limpsfield Gas Company requested a siding south of Oxted station to serve their new works planned on the east side of the line. On 30 July 1884 the Joint Committee agreed for a siding to serve Hall & Co.'s sand quarry at Oxted and another one to serve the lime works 700 yards south of Oxted tunnel. The Oxted Lime siding was inspected by the Board of Trade in June 1885 and permitted to open, subject to minor signal alterations and the key to the signalling frame being kept at Marden Park station[14]. The Oxted Lime Company tried to get out of paying a share of the costs. A siding was opened at Hurst Green in December 1885.

A siding was provided at Upper Warlingham for a Mr Nicholls in 1885; there was much building work taking place in the district. There were no goods facilities at Marden Park, so that deliveries had to be handled via the passenger station. Even less commodious was staff accomodation - there was no station master's house at Oxted until late 1885, when £57 was spent "making habitable" an old cottage.

During 1886 and 1887 a number of questions about the passenger service were raised. In April 1886 the property developer at Marden Park complained that there was no up passenger service that reached London before 9am, and that sales were being damaged by this. At Oxted, people complained that there was no train back from London later than 8.25pm. Oxted people also complained about their station's lack of lighting, but had to wait until late 1891 for the installation of gas lights. Marden Park was also the destination for a number of school excursions, but these had to work forward empty to Oxted to turn; it was decided to install crossovers at Marden Park, and this was done by October 1887. In December 1888 the Committee considered changing the name of Marden Park to Birchwood, but rejected the idea.

By 1887 the Oxted & Groombridge line of the LBSCR was nearing completion. The points at Hurst Green Junction were laid in on 14 November 1887 and the line opened to passengers on 2 January 1888. A station at the junction was rejected in 1888 and again in 1889.

In 1889 a number of minor improvements were made. At Oxted a down side waiting room and extra sidings were provided, an up side waiting room was added at Marden Park, and further sidings for Upper Warlingham and Sanderstead. A siding had been provided at Upper Warlingham under an agreement between Colonel Wigsel and the S&SJ of 1865 - it had not been used up to this time due to there being no agreed goods rates to it. A siding and dock for horse and carriage traffic was added at Upper Warlingham in 1892.

Stationmasters' houses were added at Marden Park and Sanderstead in 1891; the Marden Park stationmaster had 4s a week deducted from his wages to pay for it. Further sidings were added there in 1892. Upper Warlingham did not get a stationmaster's house until 1893.

The key to property development was the provision of a station close at hand. Passing through very attractive countryside yet within easy reach of London, the Oxted line spurred local landowners into developing their property. In February 1892 the Committee received a request for a station south of Riddlesdown tunnel, which was ignored, as was a similar request for a new station "near Oxted" in 1893. However the Committee did respond to local pressure in agreeing to rename Marden Park as Woldingham and Upper Warlingham as Upper Warlingham & Whyteleafe from 1 January 1894. Not everything about Upper Warlingham was appreciated locally however, for in September 1894 there were complaints about "noxious odours coming from foul matter in the trucks" in the sidings there; the Committee ruled this to be a LBSCR affair. The matter was solved by moving the manure siding in 1900.

Oxted was the largest place on the joint section of the line, and attracted most attention. New sidings for the gas company were completed in 1892 and seem to have been part of an arrangement to light the station. In 1894-5 substantial additions began at Oxted, including a new signalbox (1896), goods warehouses and passenger toilets.

With traffic growing steadily, it was decided to improve the signalling arrangements. In May 1898 the Committee decided that the signalboxes at Riddlesdown Viaduct and Oxted Lime Siding should be staffed permanently rather than occasionally, and employed four extra signalmen at £1 per week; a new elevated signalbox had to be provided at Riddlesdown in 1898-9.

Competition between the SER and LBSCR probably resulted in more lines being constructed through the territory between the LBSCR main-line and the

Hastings line of the SER than was necessary, and this is shown in the high proportion of closures that have since taken place. However, the solution eventually found to the problem over the Oxted route was a sensible one and filled a gap that had been bereft of railways since the decision, fifty years before, to reroute the SER main-line via Redhill.

1.   Minutes of LBSCR & SER Joint Committee, 15 December 1858.
2.   Course, vol.II, p.74.
3.   **Railway Times,** 7 June 1862.
4.   **Ibid,** February 1863.
5.   SER Minutes, 10 August 1865.
6.   **Brighton Guardian,** 26 October 1865.
7.   R.W.Kidner, **The Oxted Line,** p.6-7.
8.   SER Minutes, 26 August 1875.
9.   Minutes of LBSCR & SER Joint Committee, 3 November 1875; SER Minutes, 7 and 21 October 1875.
10.   It is not always possible to say, with certainty, when a railway service began. The link between the companies at Tunbridge Wells was forced upon them by the Railway Commissioners, as at Strood with the SER and LCDR. There is the possibility, therefore, that a purely local service was begun as soon as possible to avoid further trouble, but the opening of the line not advertised until it was ready for full use.
11.   SER Minutes 22 February 1877 give this date; LBSCR & SER Joint Committee Minutes, 13 June 1877, give 16 April as date for this service.
12.   SER Minutes, 16 February 1882.
13.   R.W.Kidner, **The Oxted Line,** p.10.
14.   LBSCR & SER (CO&EGR) Joint Committee Minutes, 17 June 1885.

CHAPTER 17: BRANCH LINES IN CENTRAL KENT

1. The Tenterden and Hawkhurst Area

The central area of Kent, south of the main-line, contained several small towns but none that was a major attraction for railway promoters. Small market towns like Goudhurst, Cranbrook and Tenterden also tended to be situated on high ground, making access to them difficult for railway engineers. As has been seen, towns like Tenterden did feature in early proposals for lines to Rye but in the event Tunbridge Wells proved to be a more convenient starting point for a line to the Sussex coast.

Thus the Railway Mania passed the towns of the southern Weald by, and their people decided to take action. A local committee in Tenterden was especially active, pressing for a branch from Headcorn in October 1851. The SER took a mild interest in the subject, but concluded in 1852 that such a line could never be profitable[1]. Not to be put off, the committee was still active in 1854 but the SER would offer only to work the line, not to finance it.

Tenterden alone, it seemed, would not be able to develop a line. Thus in 1856 a new local plan emerged, for a line from Tenterden to Cranbrook, Headcorn and direct to Maidstone. The Maidstone part of the line seems to have been soon dropped, but in December 1857 the SER was still refusing to even guarantee the capital of a Tenterden and Cranbrook to Headcorn branch. The same year there was a proposal for a branch from Marden to Goudhurst and Cranbrook[2].

Undeterred, local pressure continued. In June 1859 the SER learnt of another scheme for a branch to Cranbrook and Hawkhurst. Three years later an independent proposal was made for a line from Paddock Wood to Rye. In fact 1862 threatened to be a year of railway mania in the Wealden towns, for apart from the Rye scheme there was a proposed branch from Paddock Wood to Hawkhurst via Cranbrook, and a Headcorn to Tenterden line which the SER disliked as it was "not laid out in the proper direction[3]." This latter remark reveals the SER concern that any line in the area should be capable of being extended to Rye or the coast.

In 1864 the Weald of Kent Railway emerged as a strong contender to fill the gap, with the blessing of the SER; it planned a line from Paddock Wood to Hartley, near Cranbrook, then on to Tenterden and Appledore with a possible extension to Hythe and Sandgate. The SER was also keen to promote a line from Paddock Wood to Cranbrook and on 23 June 1864 was authorised to build a line to Hartley, near Cranbrook. The Weald of Kent gained its Act on 25 July 1864 for a line as far as Tenterden and discussions were held with the SER to prevent any conflict of interest. It was agreed that the Weald of Kent should construct the section between Cranbrook and Tenterden and that the SER should prepare a Bill for Hartley into Cranbrook. By August 1864 the legal costs of the Weald of Kent scheme were £15,433.

If all these lines had been built, central Kent would have been densely served by railways. There were yet more proposals to come, for in October 1864 a private plan for a line from Dungeness to Groombridge via New Romney, Rolvenden, Hartley, Lamberhurst and Frant was discussed.

It was clear that the Weald of Kent line could be extended to meet the SER's Rye line, especially as there were a number of schemes to build further branches to New Romney and Dungeness. After a suggestion that a line should be built from Tenterden to Kenardington, near Ham Street, an Act was obtained on 16 July 1866 to extend the SER from the Weald of Kent at Tenterden to Appledore.

1866 was a fateful year for new railway schemes and neither the SER or the Weald of Kent proceeded further with the various lines. In February 1867 it was decided not to start work on the Cranbrook line[4] and in September 1869 the SER felt it would be best to abandon the powers for both its own line and the WoK. This provoked reaction from local landowners, notably Mr Gathorne-Hardy MP, of Hemsted Park at Staplehurst. In October Watkin pointed out that it would cost £180,000 to serve Cranbrook by the lines already authorised, whereas the job could be done for £70,000 if a different plan were adopted. He suggested dropping the Paddock Wood to Cranbrook line, and the line from the WoK to Appledore, in favour of a branch to Cranbrook from Staplehurst[5] which could be constructed for about £50,000.

Some of the Cranbrook residents saw the wisdom of this, but Hardy wrote to say that, "I cannot say that personally I take much interest in what would practically be a mere tramway." One can feel the wounded pride in Gathorne Hardy's letter. The SER gained authorisation to abandon the various schemes on 2 August 1870.

Thus the towns of the southern Weald were still bereft of railway communication and for a time the SER turned its attention north of the main-line, where Lord Romney of Mote Park was leading a scheme to build a line from Maidstone to Ashford. This had been authorised on 10 August 1866 to extend from the terminus of the LCDR-backed Sevenoaks, Maidstone & Tunbridge Railway to Ashford, with a spur to the SER station in Maidstone. Its Act included powers for James Stoddart of Sandway to stop one train in each direction per day at the station nearest his home. With the SM&T moribund after financial collapse, in 1870-1 there were discussions as to whether this should join the SER main-line at Chart or Pluckley, the latter being selected eventually. The SER showed a much more supportive approach to this scheme than to the Wealden branches, being prepared to lend it £100,000 in 1870 and counselling it against a "contractor arrangement"; "Such things never end well," Watkin advised, no doubt thinking of the infamous LCDR arrangements. It was agreed that the line should alter its Act to run from the SER in Maidstone to Pluckley, but without the SM&T the line had little purpose and proceeded no further.

In March 1871 the SER learnt of a scheme to close the gap between Maidstone and the Weald towns - by a tramway. This was to run from Maidstone to Headcorn and Tenterden; the idea was quickly followed by proposals for lines from Maidstone to Pluckley and from Maidstone to Headcorn. Again nothing solid resulted, nor did anything result from renewed interest in the Maidstone & Ashford question in 1874.

One would have thought that despair was the only appropriate emotion for local people, whose 30 year campaign for a railway had produced no result.

However, in September 1876 two further ideas emerged - a "light railway" from Paddock Wood to Cranbrook and a SER plan for a line from Maidstone to Chilham. In November 1876 the SER met the promoters of the Cranbrook & Paddock Wood Light, which proposed to limit its trains to 25mph. The SER was asked if it would subscribe £25,000 and run the line; it declared that it was prepared to guarantee a return of £4,500 per annum. In January 1877 the SER altered its view, deciding to subscribe up to £50,000 providing the line was not a "light" railway. On 10 January the Cranbrook company accepted this, and progress at last seemed possible.

The Cranbrook & Paddock Wood Railway gained its Act on 8 August 1877 but by July 1878 it was clear that the scheme was having difficulty raising the required capital. By October the SER was arguing that money could be saved by altering the position of Cranbrook station. Work on the line started in February 1879[6] but was stopped due to the shortage of money.

With this unhappy situation, Cranbrook once more emerged as a pawn in a larger game. By late 1879 relations between the SER and LCDR were again unsatisfactory and the SER was keen to defend itself against further invasions of its territory. Fearing an attempt by the LCDR to secure a new Maidstone & Ashford line, the SER first considered a short branch from Ashford to Charing as a blocking move and then an extension of the Loose Valley goods branch (which terminated at Tovil) to Harrietsham. Despite these ideas, the LCDR's Maidstone & Ashford line was authorised in August 1880 though it was to have connections with the SER at both ends and SER running powers over it.

This contest resulted in a modest victory, though hardly a profitable one, for the LCDR. Watkin was determined to win the struggle for the continental traffic, however, and by 1880 was enraptured by the idea of a new harbour at Dungeness - which was approached by a branch from Appledore to Lydd. What was needed to make a success of the Dungeness idea was a more direct route from Appledore to London, so by May 1881 the idea of a line from Headcorn to Appledore was revived.

The Cranbrook line was to be extended to Hawkhurst, and indeed powers were obtained for this on 12 July 1882. The Lydd line was to be extended from Appledore to Headcorn (also authorised 1882) and a Tenterden Railway was to join the SER at Headcorn or Staplehurst. What emerged from this excitement was a scheme to extend the Lydd Railway across the Weald, connecting with a Tenterden branch, to Headcorn, and from there to join the Loose Valley Railway into Maidstone. The Loose Valley was authorised to extend from Tovil to Headcorn in 1883.

1884 thus became a year of much excitement. A time extension had to be obtained for the Paddock Wood to Cranbrook line and the SER wrote to the LCDR advising that it intended to exercise its running powers over the Maidstone & Ashford until its own line from Maidstone to Headcorn had been completed. In March 1885 the SER was buying land at Headcorn station ready for its important new role and later that year the Loose Valley line was transferred from the SER[7] to the Lydd Railway by the Lydd Railway Act of 16 July[8], its capital value being recorded at £31,730. Also transferred to the Lydd were the powers to build the line from Tovil to Headcorn. The Loose Valley powers were transferred back to the SER by Act of 12 August 1889.

Thus the Lydd came to be in possession of two totally disconnected lines, one of which had actually been removed from the SER's direct control. The

Lydd, however, concentrated on its activities in the Dungeness area and the line across the Weald was forgotten. The SER, meanwhile, took a closer look at the Cranbrook branch and decided that it wanted a deviation between Yew Tree Farm and Hope Mill, near Goudhurst. A further SER Act for the line was therefore passed on 12 July 1887.

But there was no work being done on it. Lord Cranbrook wrote to the SER in November 1887, expressing elegantly feelings that must have been typical among local people; "I address you with an almost despairing feeling about the Cranbrook Railway which personally I can hardly expect to see completed."

By April 1888 the SER had got as far as assessing the land requirements of the Cranbrook line and in February 1890 offered to guarantee 3% per annum to its shareholders. In March 1890 it was decided that Joseph Firbank could do the construction for £6,000 per mile and the following months the terms for the shareholders were raised to 3.5%. In March 1891 it was decided to divert the line to a terminus near Hartley at an additional cost of £11,500; this would not be helpful for the people of Cranbrook, but would allow future extensions to Etchingham or Rye.

It must have been with feelings of considerable relief that local people saw the commencement of services between Paddock Wood and Goudhurst on 1 October 1892; the terminus was known as Hope Mill for Goudhurst & Lamberhurst, being renamed Goudhurst when the extension to Hawkhurst was opened on 4 September 1893. The SER Directors Report of February 1893 reported that traffic on the line was of a "remunerative and encouraging character." At Paddock Wood it was necessary to install new signalling, sidings and a footbridge.

It was a highly unsatisfactory line in many ways. There were steep gradients, none of the main towns in the district was served by a convenient station, and the prospect of a through line with better services seemed within grasp. Thus the imminent opening of the branch did nothing to diminish local pressure: on 16 January 1892 a meeting at Rolvenden, led by Mr Pomfret Pomfret MP, asked for an extension from Hawkhurst to Appledore since the Lydd Railway scheme had not materialised.

The discussion of a Hawkhurst to Appledore line alarmed the people of Tenterden, who would be missed by 2.5 miles, so they revived the idea of a Headcorn, Tenterden and Appledore line. Thus a new factor emerged - an intense rivalry between Rolvenden and Tenterden. In July 1892 the SER suggested its support for Rolvenden by agreeing to invest £30,000 in an extension of the Cranbrook line.

In October 1893 the SER reviewed the whole area. There were three options. Firstly, there was the already authorised line from Headcorn to Appledore via Biddenden and Tenterden; secondly, the branch to Hawkhurst could be extended to Appledore via Benenden, Rolvenden and Newenden; thirdly, a new line could be built from Hartley, via Sissinghurst and Tenterden, to Appledore. After a good deal of discussion locally, it was discovered that the SER had decided not to proceed at all. In 1895 an Act was obtained by local people under the name of the Tenterden Railway for a line from Headcorn to Appledore, but finance was lacking.

In May 1896 there was a request from Hastings for an extension from Hawkhurst. In March 1897 the SER offered to assist, but not contribute to, the Rother Valley Railway which had gained an Act for a line to Tenterden from

Robertsbridge on the Hastings line on 2 July 1896. This joined the Tenterden Railway at Rolvenden, and indeed the section from there to Tenterden Town was eventually built as part of its plan. The SER then decided to deposit a Bill to extend their branch themselves and to double it, and agreement was reached with the Tenterden Railway promoters to pay their legal expenses from the 1895 session. However, the SER Bill was withdrawn in July 1898.

The Cranbrook & Paddock Wood company was absorbed into the SER in 1900.

The end of the SER's independent existence left the Tenterden area still in a highly confused state after many years of railway promotion. It would be tempting to see this lack of success as reflecting the area's restricted traffic potential, and indeed this view seems to be supported by subsequent events. The Rother Valley Railway, subsequently Kent & East Sussex, opened progressively between Robertsbridge, Tenterden and Headcorn in 1900-1905, but lost regular passenger services in 1954. The Hawkhurst branch, opened after so many delays, closed in 1961.

2. The Lydd and Dungeness Area

South of the SER's Ashford to Rye line lay a large area comprised mostly of marshland or barren shingle banks. It had few centres of population and attracted little attention from railway promoters until it began to become a factor in railway politics. The area barely figures in the history of the SER until 1859, when the Town Clerk of New Romney wrote to suggest a line from Folkestone to Rye via Dymchurch and Lydd. The SER was not interested, preferring to look more closely at the question of access to Folkestone from off its main-line via Hythe. In October 1864 a scheme for a line from Dungeness and New Romney to Groombridge also met little response.

In 1865 to 1866 there was a brief outburst of enthusiasm for new railway schemes, one of which included a new harbour at Dungeness. A Bill for a New Romney Railway, leaving the SER at Appledore, was viewed favourably by the SER and an Act was obtained on 30 July 1866. It included a branch to Denge Beach, near Dungeness[9].

The 1866 financial crisis delayed any progress on the New Romney line, but in 1869 its directors decided to extend their line to a point 760 yards from the Dungeness lighthouse, and to build a jetty there at a cost of £85,000. Eborall, reporting on the matter for the SER, felt there would be too little traffic. In September 1869 the SER discussed provision of a train service with the NRR, suggesting four trains a day with the SER being paid £5,000 per year; these terms were rejected and the NRR faded from view.

SER interest in the possibilities of Dungeness were rekindled by rival proposals for cross-channel traffic, such as Fowler's scheme that would have affected the balance of power at Dover. In 1872 the SER decided to support a Bill for the Rye & Dunge-ness Railway & Pier. This was passed on 5 August 1873, authorising a line from Rye to Dungeness with a 100 yard pier and a landing stage, and running powers over the SER into Rye station; however, it proceeded no further. In October 1874 Watkin pointed out the dangers of the scheme being taken over by a rival and suggested the SER should obtain powers to take it over, providing the Government could be persuaded to set up a

Harbour of Refuge at Dungeness. Having deposited the required Bill and gained the powers in 1875, the SER lost interest once more.

It was eventually the rivalry with the LCDR that brought about construction of a line in the area. In June 1880 a proposed railway to Dungeness and harbour there were discussed by the SER. Suggestions that this was to be another example of Watkin's profligate expenditure may be unfair, for in October 1880 the SER decided that the line could be built cheaply using the old track from the Hastings line.

A Bill was deposited by the Lydd Railway for a branch from Appledore to Lydd. There was the prospect of a healthy level of traffic, for discussions had started to develop the artillery range at Lydd and by November 1880 the Lydd company was selling 300 acres of shingle to the SER. The size of the War Office operation at Lydd can be judged by the fact that a tramway already existed there in January 1881[10], while the SER hoped to develop a trade in taking shingle to London - perhaps a precursor of the subsequent development of aggregates traffic in southern England. The Lydd Railway was also very cheap to construct - the *Railway Times* thought that it cost less than £2,000 a mile.

The line was authorised by Act of 8 April 1881 and, incredibly, ready for inspection by Major-General Hutchinson on 3 October 1881. The line was built by Thomas Walker, using an 0-4-0ST appropriately named *Dungeness*[11]. However Hutchinson refused to sanction the opening of the line until the old rails that had been used were replaced with new ones. The line opened to Lydd on 7 December 1881[12] for all traffic and to Dungeness for freight only. Its chairman was Alfred Watkin. The line was hardly an immediate success - receipts up to 28 February 1882 amounted to £569-5-11d, but this was only what had been taken at the stations. However, it should be noted that the directors were each being paid £300 per year, while Edward Watkin had claimed £1,000 for "professional services[13]".

On 24 July 1882 a further Act was obtained to extend the line to New Romney, and also northwards to Headcorn. Walker was again contracted to do the New Romney extension and 1,000 acres at £5 an acre[14] was obtained at Dungeness for digging out shingle and for possible development as a harbour. Powers for a 350 foot jetty at Dungeness were never acted upon. The contract for the New Romney extension was for £10,700.

The section from Lydd to Dungeness was opened to passengers on 1 April 1883; the New Romney branch had a private opening on 18 June 1884, with public services commencing the next day. The cheap construction of the line can be gathered from the fact that the Board of Trade questioned the lack of gates at the level crossings.

In 1893 a new standard gauge railway system was opened for the Royal Engineers at Lydd, using materials salvaged from the Suakin & Berber railway[15]. This was an 18 mile railway built for the Army but lifted on Government orders before completion; some of its stock was kept at Marsh Siding, Plumstead, which became known as "Berber Siding" for a number of years.

When the dream of the Dungeness harbour began to fade, there was little apart from the shingle and military traffic to bring excitement to the branch. There were brief talks with the Admiralty in 1891 about extending the line from Dungeness lighthouse to a new pier. As discussed above, plans to extend it to

Tenterden and Maidstone never reached fruition. Eventually, by Act of 20 June 1895, the Lydd Railway was absorbed into the SER.

In April 1895 £1,000 was spent improving Lydd station and a jetty at Dungeness was discussed once more.

The Dungeness branch is often held out as an example of Watkin's wasteful obsession with beating the LCDR, yet its cost was very small in comparison to the sums spent closer to London. It was, perhaps, a tactical move, but it generated some useful goods traffic and provided the SER with much of its ballast.

1. SER Minutes, 23 September 1852.
2. P.A.Harding, **The Hawkhurst Branch Line,** p.5.
3. SER Minutes, 6 November 1862.
4. **Railway Times,** 23 February 1867.
5. **Ibid,** 30 October 1869.
6. Harding, p.5.
7. The LVR had been absorbed into the SER by Act of 1881.
8. This Act also authorised a deviation between Loose and Sutton Valence.
9. **Bradshaw's Railway Manual,** 1869.
10. **Railway Times,** 22 January 1881. This refers to there being 20 miles of tramway - perhaps an exaggerated estimate.
11. P.A.Harding, **The New Romney Branch Line,** p.5.
12. Lydd Railway Minutes, 23 March 1882.
13. **Ibid,** 16 February 1882.
14. **Railway Times,** 18 July 1891.
15. R.M.Lyne, in **Journal of the Railway & Canal Historical Society,** July 1982, p.112.

CHAPTER 18: THE HYTHE AND ELHAM BRANCHES

1. The Hythe & Sandgate Branch

The ancient town of Hythe was avoided by the original main-line of the SER and served only by a distant station, opened as Westenhanger & Hythe, on 7 February 1844. The provision of a branch to the town was not high on the SER's own agenda, and the issue was first raised by local interests in November 1851[1]. In April 1852, Colonel Sandilands, the Mayor of Hythe, wrote to the SER suggesting a branch to serve Hythe and nearby Sandgate. Drane, the SER engineer, prepared a report on the proposed line but the SER directors felt that Hythe was best served with a new carriage road between the town and a proposed station at Sandling Park bridge on the main-line.

The issue was raised again in January 1853 when the owner of Sandling Park requested a station at Bargrave, at the point where the road from Hythe to Elham crossed the SER main-line; the SER rejected this due to the need for an improved road, but six months later reconsidered the matter.

Another local attempt was made in 1856, with a deputation from Sandgate visiting the SER board in August. The SER made no positive move and, though a local scheme was again considered in October, nothing resulted.

No doubt some considered the SER to be lacking in public spiritedness, but its policy was wholly compatible with the good husbandry of its shareholders' investments. If the SER paid for a Hythe branch itself, it would be unlikely to make a substantial profit - if any at all, since Hythe people already used the main-line station; if the sole purpose of such a branch was public convenience, and if no rival was in the field, why should it not be the public who paid for it? Thus it was only when the interests of the people of Hythe coincided with those of the SER that progress was made.

The threat posed by the East Kent Railway's extension to Dover caused the SER to examine its own continental facilities. One of the problems was the poor access it had to Folkestone Harbour, and on 15 July 1858 the Board therefore discussed building a new route from Saltwood to the Harbour via Hythe. The idea was embraced enthusiastically and the planning process was begun, until Captain Warren, one of the SER directors, suggested a loop instead from Cheriton to Folkestone Harbour. A comparison of the two routes revealed that the Cheriton line would cost £55,000 whereas the line from Sandling Park via Hythe would be £120,000[2]. Fearing that Hythe would still not get a station, the Mayor of Hythe requested the removal of Westenhanger station to a point between Sandling Park and Saltwood Tunnel in January 1861.

The scheme for which the SER presented the Folkestone Harbour Communications Bill in the 1861 session was the cheaper one, avoiding Hythe, though it was still estimated in March 1861 to cost £30,000 for land and £78,000 for works. Leaving the main-line at Cheriton, it was to pass just to the east of Sandgate and then along the seafront to Folkestone Harbour; it included stations at Cheriton and Sandgate. The Bill was opposed by the major local landowner, Lord Radnor, for its effect on The Leas, while local gentry such as Sir John Bligh and General Hankey were also set against it. The Bill was rejected.

59. 4-4-0 no.189 at Sandgate. (Wakeman Collection)

On 15 August 1861 one of the SER directors, Thomson, urged the adoption of a branch serving both Hythe and Folkestone. John Hawkshaw was sent to investigate the matter and reported that a line to Folkestone Harbour via Hythe would damage much valuable property at Sandgate[3]. He advised that the scheme would again be opposed by Bligh and Hankey, but that it could take a route further east than that proposed the previous year - and use tunnel. A week later Hawkshaw estimated that a branch to Hythe only would cost £50,000 and £100,000 if extended to Folkestone.

The 1862 Bill was again frustrated by landowners, yet as early as 11 September the SER had decided to try again the next year, though also considering a branch to Hythe only for £25,000. No doubt they were worried by discussions of a LCDR supported branch from Canterbury to Hythe via the Elham Valley.

The third attempt to win an Act for the line made little progress either, despite a promise to Bligh that the bridge over his carriage road would be "ornamental". Folkestone Corporation opposed it again, demanding that much of the line should be in tunnel. Lord Radnor was consistent in his distaste for the matter; he wrote to his son, "The SER people are behaving very unhandsomely. They are, I believe, a blackguard set of directors."[4] In October 1863 the SER changed tactics, opting instead for a three mile branch to Sandgate only, at a cost of about £70,000 for works and land. This avoided the main centre of opposition and so was authorised on 23 June 1864.

The SER then did nothing - until September 1866, when it discussed applying for an extension of its powers to acquire land for the branch. On 18 October the SER Board discussed a proposal from the Elham Valley Railway, which wanted its own line from Canterbury to Hythe and was anxious that the SER's Hythe plan should be dropped to facilitate their own scheme. However 1866 was not a good year for railway schemes and the EVR collapsed.

In February 1868 the SER considered dropping the whole line altogether, but in August discovered that there were two separate local schemes to fill the void. Action would therefore be necessary, for any independent scheme could fall into the grasp of the LCDR; thus, when George Smith organised a local group with the intention of taking over the SER's own powers for a branch, the South Eastern acted favourably. On 29 April 1868 it offered to lease and work the line for 4.5% of the £65,000 capital; it was later agreed that profit beyond this should be shared.

A Hythe & Sandgate Railway was formed including George Smith as a director, but also SER men such as Beattie, Byng and James Whatman. At first it was intended to obtain a a new Bill transferring the SER powers to the H&SR, but in the event an Act was obtained on 2 August 1870 to merely extend the time limit.

500 acres of the estate of Sir Courtenay Honeywood was bought and the Seabrook Estate Company formed to develop it as residential property. Shareholders in the SER were given first chance to buy shares in the new company, which was ready to begin building late in 1873. It is a rare example of a railway company setting out to develop and profit from property itself.

Later in 1870 the SER became interested in a suggestion that the north bank of the Royal Military Canal could be used for a new railway, to be constructed by the SER or jointly with the War Office. Thinking that it could be used for a tramway from Ham Street to Shorncliffe, close to the military camp, Watkin offered what he called "a very low price" - £40 an acre. The War Office hoped for rather more, so discussions dragged out through most of 1871. In January 1872 the SER was still discussing Ham Street to Shorncliffe but the War Office was not prepared to sell or lease the section through Hythe to Shorncliffe and the plan collapsed.

Work on the actual branch was slow to commence, having been held up by disputes over the cost of land when demands reached as high as £350 an acre. Land for Hythe station cost £2,500. In March 1872 the contract to construct the line was awarded to Philip Stiff for £43,769; interestingly, the highly successful firm of Aird & Sons tendered for £84,406[5].

The formal opening of the works was held on 11 April 1872, with Prince Arthur wielding the ceremonial spade - which promptly snapped in two[6]. In April 1873 William Griffey died after an accident on the works, leaving six children. The following month the use of soldiers from Shorncliffe Camp to help build the line was discussed but there were, apparently, too few then available.

There were to be two stations on the line, at Hythe and Sandgate, though neither was especially convenient - the latter was closer to Seabrook than Sandgate. Francis Brady estimated the cost of the station buildings at £2,100 for Hythe and £2,900 for Sandgate. However hopes that the line would open on 1 May 1874 were dashed by the slow work of the contractor and a slip at Saltwood in March; eventually, Philip Stiff was paid £6,500 to give up the contract and the SER itself took on the task. The line was opened on 9 October 1874, with the first train leaving Sandgate for Ashford at 10am. The formal opening was conducted by the Duke of Teck. It was a double celebration for Watkin, since in February he had been elected M.P. for Hythe, a constituency which included Folkestone.

Little provision had been made for goods traffic. From February 1875 goods at Sandgate was handled on the down platform while passengers used the up;

Hythe did not get a wooden goods shed until 1875. There were also early problems with slips of the various banks and on 23 November 1875 one damaged the Hythe stationmaster's house.

The SER was still keen to extend the line into Folkestone. In September 1874 they had discussed extending the line and also building a new road from Shorncliffe station into eastern Folkestone, neither of which met with Lord Radnor's approval. Early in 1875 the SER Board considered a very short extension from the terminus, which was really at Seabrook, to The Broadway in Sandgate, but by September had decided to seek the full extension into Folkestone instead. Clearly something was needed to bring more traffic to the line, for it was being reviled by the *Railway Times*, which described "the sight of empty passenger trains (travelling as seldom as possible)" and "the constant recurrence of minor accidents" such as the breaking of couplings. It was also pointed out that the double-track line had only one track in use[7]. Nonetheless, Lord Radnor still opposed any extension, and spared no quarter in his struggle with the SER; "I have learnt by experience it is no good dealing liberally with a public company in the hopes that it will do the same by you," he wrote[8].

The extension plans of 1876 included keeping much of the line in tunnel to pacify Radnor and other opponents, but there was vociferous opposition to the scheme and a poster campaign was waged against it[9]. Watkin and other supporters of the scheme were not afraid to portray the property owners as being self-interested, whereas they cared only for the common good; ironically, Watkin's son, Alfred, later became just such a property owner when he took over Dunedin Lodge in Folkestone. However, Radnor accepted that a line in tunnel would cause less damage and an Act was finally obtained.

The 1876 plan was delayed by problems over Shorncliffe Camp, which the line passed near to in tunnel, and Sandgate Castle - which the SER eventually bought. In May 1877 the SER felt itself nearer to an agreement with Lord Radnor, considering improvements to Shorncliffe station and new roads a small price to pay for his approval. The estimated cost of building a line largely in tunnel was £327,825, too much even for the optimistic Watkin to consider; although the short extension to Sandgate only was considered again in November 1877, the matter was allowed to lie dormant.

Elsewhere, the SER had been trying to develop the line by other means. On 21 July 1880 it opened its Seabrook Hotel, which had been built at a cost of £22,998. There were complaints among the SER shareholders that this hotel existed purely to provide Watkin with accomodation when he visited his constituency: "While Sir Edward enjoyed the music, the South Eastern paid the piper," it was alleged[10]. However the hotel was successful enough to need enlarging in 1881.

One impediment to the extension of the branch from Sandgate was solved when, on 6 January 1881, the SER decided to buy Sandgate Castle for £20,000. Other extensions also seemed possible that year: the SER considered buying up the tramway used in the construction of the Hythe seawall while it also looked at the possibility of a line from Hythe to Dymchurch. In May 1881 Watkin reported that the traffic potential of the latter was "very limited" but Thomas Walker, who was building the Lydd Railway, was invited to give a tender. He estimated a line from Hythe to Dymchurch could be done for £37,181 and to Lydd for £31,590. Wondering if some profit could be made out of a link between the Hythe School of Musketry and the Lydd artillery ranges, the SER

60. Sandgate in 1891, with a train from Sandling Junction.

approached the War Office with a suggestion of a jointly-financed line for which the War Office would have "toll-free" use; it was not interested.

SER interest in the extension to Folkestone continued in that it bought any available land in 1882, but the lack of progress led to a rift with the Seabrook Estate Company. In July 1884 Watkin studied the area due to his fears of a LCDR attempt to gain entry to Folkestone; he recommended a new line to New Romney from Hythe, an extension from Sandgate to the main-line at Shorncliffe and a new route to Folkestone Harbour by branching off the main-line to the north, then curving under the Foord Viaduct. This clearly shows that the SER had accepted that an extension of the Hythe line direct to the Harbour would never be possible and, in fact, an Act for the spur off the main-line was passed in 1885[11] though the line was never built - perhaps because the threat from the LCDR faded away.

To have extended the Hythe & Sandgate line would have cost £73,915, and it was not proceeded with. Instead, the SER looked west and in August 1885 wondered whether the materials from the Suakin & Berber Railway in the Sudan, in store at Lydd, could be used for a line from New Romney to Hythe. The War Office, though, preferred a line along the Canal from Sandgate to Appledore; this would have cost £30,147. Attempts to get the War Office to subsidise the line failed.

In January 1886 Hythe Town Council approached the SER and requested some improvements. They asked for one through train to London each day, lower fares, and the provision of a station at Sandling Junction. The latter was opened on 1 January 1888, though only after the SER had been frustrated in its attempt to close the station at Westenhanger. Goods traffic was also slow to grow, though by 1883 there were sidings on the down side to Hythe waterworks, north of Hythe, and a Hythe stone siding between that town and Sandgate.

The weather continued to be among the branch's worst enemies. In 1891 a passenger train was trapped overnight in a snowdrift near Saltwood Castle and reached Sandgate eleven hours late[12] and there was a "disastrous" landslide at Sandgate on 4 March 1893, which swept away the home of a railway employee; Watkin gave £100 to the local relief fund. Nature did have a more benevolent side, though; in 1898 the water from Saltwood Tunnel was diverted to serve the locomotive needs at Hythe and Sandgate.

2. The Hythe & Sandgate Tramway

The Hythe and Sandgate branch never made its way into Folkestone, but the SER eventually managed to extend its activities in the area by the setting up of a tramway instead. Neither Hythe nor Sandgate stations served their communities particularly well, and in 1880 powers for the setting up of tramways at Sandgate had been granted. However the first actual tramway was the one used in the construction of the Hythe seawall and in April 1881 the SER had considered whether they should buy this. Both the local plan, and the SER one, failed to produce effects, though in 1882 the SER did try to get Folkestone Corporation to take over the old tramway.

In 1883 the Folkestone, Sandgate & Hythe Tramway Company was launched with plans for a 2ft 4¼in. tramway from Shorncliffe station and Folkestone to Hythe and New Romney, using the bank of the Canal from Sandgate to Hythe. The SER hoped to persuade the company to use standard gauge, and offered to lay down "trial" rails between Shorncliffe station and Folkestone. The Act was passed on 28 July 1884, but only allowed for horse power and nothing was done.

On 27 August 1885 the SER decided to get estimates for a tramway from Seabrook to Hythe beach while the following month the Mayor of Hythe asked for a tramway from the Quay to Hythe station.

Thus encouraged, the SER acquired powers in 1886 and began work on constructing a tramway from Hythe station to the seafront, and from the Seabrook Hotel, along the front, to a point near Sandgate station. The SER had great ideas for this project and by July 1886 was planning to extend it via Lower Sandgate Road to Folkestone Harbour, using electric power. In March 1888 Dick, Kerr & Co. were given the task of supplying track for the extensions and work began on laying the line between Seabrook Police Station and Sandgate National School. An extension to Sandling Junction was also considered.

By July 1889 the tramway had been completed as far as the Coastguard Station at Sandgate, but then it hit the traditional problems: Lord Radnor objected to any extension into Sandgate although the section had been authorised in 1884 as tramway no. 3 and no. 4. With the opening also held up by the Board of Trade, the tramway was used only to help with repairs to the seawall - for which an engine from the Suakin & Berber Railway was employed.

Radnor objected to the tramway on several counts, citing his agreement with the company of 16 June 1886. He objected to its gauge being more than 3ft 6ins, he disliked the use of steam power, and he did not want any tramway along Lower Sandgate Road.

Radnor would only agree to the line being extended from the Coastguard Station to the National School at the foot of Sandgate Hill, but this depended on it being narrow gauge; to try and pacify Radnor, the SER hoped to persuade the tramway to drop its 1890 Bill for an extension up Sandgate Hill to Folkestone, which the latter's Corporation supported. However Radnor commenced legal action in June 1890 when he found that work was continuing in Sandgate while the SER recommended to the tramway company that it should pull up the rails in the disputed section.

Despite the uncertainty, the SER ordered two tramcars to be built for £165, yet on 11 December Watkin gave the order to remove one rail on the tramway no.3 through Sandgate so that the company could not be prosecuted for having a gauge wider than 3ft 6ins. On 18 May 1891 services began between the Seabrook Hotel and the outskirts of Sandgate while negotiations with Radnor continued.

In July 1891 a draft agreement was drawn up for the extension of the tramway through Sandgate at a gauge of 3ft 6ins and with a third rail being laid down on the rest of the system. The westward extension from Seabrook Hotel to Red Lion Square, Hythe, which opened on 1 June 1892, was nonetheless constructed as standard gauge.

Radnor seems to have changed his mind, so that when a formal agreement was signed in July 1892 the tramway into Sandgate was permitted to be standard gauge. At Sandgate it linked up with the Sandgate Hill Lift, built on land leased from Radnor himself, and in which he had a financial interest. The extension to Sandgate Hill therefore opened as a standard gauge tramway on 1 August 1892.

In August 1892 the SER decided that up to £2,000 should be spent acquiring premises for the tramway; these were built in Hythe in 1894, to which a turret clock was added in 1898. In the meantime, the SER Act of 29 June 1893 allowed it to formally take over the tramway.

The Hythe & Sandgate Tramway never reached Folkestone, but in April 1898 the SER decided to buy two "char-a-bancs" to operate connections between Sandgate and Folkestone. In the end, one bus was ordered[13] and in use by the end of the year.

3. The Elham Valley Line

Between Canterbury and Dover the Kent landscape is formed of rolling chalk downland rising, in places, to nearly 600 feet. It was an area largely avoided by the promoters of early railways, until the East Kent built a direct route between Canterbury and Dover - but only at the cost of a tunnel at Lydden. No railway was built to connect Canterbury with Folkestone, though the valley of the Nail Bourne offered a reasonable route at least as far as Lyminge.

Thus the Railway Mania passed the villages of Barham, Elham and Lyminge by. As in the case of Hythe, if anything was to be done there clearly had to be pressure from the local interests and so, in 1865, an Elham Valley Railway was formed. The line was planned to run from the seafront at Hythe, heading eastwards to Sandgate and then north, via a 660 yard tunnel at Etchinghill, to Canterbury, where there would be connections to both the SER and LCDR[14].

The EVR received its Act on 6 August 1866, with capital set at £300,000. Prominent among its directors were William Mackinnon, of Acrise Park, and Major Alexander Dickson, of Waldershaw Park - both local landowners. Another leading "shareholder" was the contractor, Mr.Shrimpton.

The SER's attitude to the line was cautious, perhaps because the financial embarrassment of the LCDR meant that the SER no longer needed to welcome new concerns. The EVR's attempt to get the SER to drop its own plans for a Hythe branch met with no response.

The EVR was a classic victim of the financial problems of the times. It had few investors, and funds were depleted further when its secretary eloped with some of them in October 1867. The company gained permission to abandon its powers in 1873, when its assets stood at a mere £43[15].

There was then a lengthy lull in the fortunes of the Elham Valley scheme until 1879, when a revived financial market and the interest of the SER in any scheme that would thwart LCDR ambitions (it had proposed its own line to Folkestone in 1878), placed the plan in a more favourable light. A number of local men, with support from outside interests such as the contractor George Furness, formed a company to build a single track Light Railway. A Bill was presented for the 1880 session but withdrawn due to objections to the company's plan for level crossings and to the opposition of the owner of Bourne Park, Bishopsbourne.

A renewed attempt, with a few modifications, was made the following year and the Act for the EVLR was passed on 28 July 1881 despite opposition from the LCDR. The line was to start from a junction with the SER at Cheriton and join it again at Canterbury.

Nothing was done to complete the line for nearly three years until, on 3 March 1884, a SER Board Minute notes that company's anxiety that no progress had been made. This was not, of course, an expression of altruistic concern for the isolated residents of the Elham Valley, but a sign of self-interest. The LCDR had presented a Bill for its own line to Folkestone via the Alkham Valley, and a bitter campaign had been launched; clearly the SER, unable to provide anything but a very indirect service between Folkestone and Canterbury, would be in a stronger position if the Elham Valley line seemed to be in progress. The SER responded by offering to provide materials so that the EVLR could be built to main-line standard and through its Act, passed on 28 July 1884, obtained authority to take over the Elham company. The LCDR abandoned its highly expensive plan to enter Folkestone from Alkham, but later adopted the tactic of seeking running powers from Ashford.

Such was the SER's haste to complete the line that in July 1884 it was already discussing the need to improve the junction station at Shorncliffe by extending the down platform. Thomas Walker was engaged to do the work, including the tunnel of 102 yards at Etchinghill; work at the tunnel had started several weeks before the official cutting of the first sod, which took place at Peane on 28 August 1884. To make the line more suitable for "main-line" running, the

61. F Class no. 203 at Shorncliffe, for the opening of the Elham Valley Railway. (Wakeman Collection)

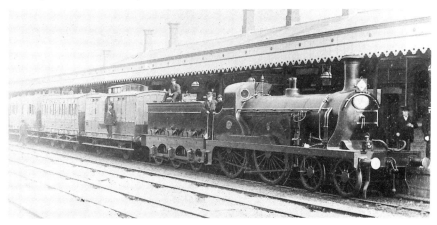

gradients on the approach to the tunnel were eased under powers obtained on 25 June 1885, authorising the raising of an extra £15,000. However the greatest problem faced in the construction of the line was the opposition of some of the landowners, notably Matthew Bell of Bourne Park; Bell eventually won a protracted legal dispute, so that a covered way of 329 yards kept the railway hidden from his bedroom window.

By April 1886 progress had reached the stage of designing stations for Lyminge, Elham and Barham. A single line was laid in from Cheriton Junction to Shorncliffe station, for the use of the Elham Valley trains; this was used by both up and down services until the extension of the line to Canterbury opened, when a double junction was provided, the original single track becoming the Elham down line[16].

Watkin saw the Folkestone Art Treasures Exhibition as a source of potential profit, and on 8 April 1886 decided to extend the Elham Valley line from Shorncliffe to the Exhibition site at Trinity Gardens; General Hutchinson inspected the single track line and it seems to have entered use about 1 July 1886, though the Exhibition closed within three months. The SER's income from it was £10,952.

Technically, the Art Treasures Exhibition branch was therefore the first part of the Elham Valley line to open, but the actual line opened from Cheriton Junction to Barham on 4 July 1887; there were intermediate stations at Lyminge and Elham.

North of Barham work had been delayed by the argument with Matthew Bell, and Walker's men could not start work until 18 September 1887 on the Bourne Park section. The remainder of the line opened on 1 July 1889. There were intermediate stations at South Canterbury, Bridge and Bishopsbourne. At Elham, sidings served the brickworks, while elsewhere on the line there were sidings at Ottinge and Wingmore, opened on 6 June 1888.

From 1 July 1891 the EVR was vested in the South Eastern but improvements between 1889 and 1898 were few, though the extending of all trains to run to and from Dover in 1890 was an obvious step forward and helped to answer the critics of SER local services in the Folkestone area. The SER provided a footbridge at Nackington in 1890 and in 1896 spent £205 on a stationmaster's house at South Canterbury.

1. Brian Hart, **The Hythe & Sandgate Railway**, p.1
2. SER Minutes, 8 November 1860. The Hythe route involved substantial engineering works.
3. SER Minutes, 7 October 1861.
4. See article in **Bygone Kent,** June 1981, p.358.
5. SER Minutes, 14 March 1872; Aird & Sons later became part of Lucas & Aird.
6. Hart, p.9.
7. **Railway Times,** 4 December 1875.
8. Letter from Lord Radnor to his agent, 1875, quoted in J.Simmons, **The Railway in Town and Country,** p.262.
9. See O.S.Nock, **SE&CR,** p.82-4 for a detailed description of the poster campaign.
10. **Railway Times,** 24 July 1880.
11. 48-49 Vic. c.137, 31 July 1885, authorised 1.25 miles of new line from Cheriton Arch to Folkestone Harbour.
12. Hart, p.35.   13. Hart, p.141.   14. M.Forwood, **The Elham Valley Railway,** p.9.
15. **Ibid,** p.15.   16. **Ibid,** p.44.

CHAPTER 19: EAST KENT AND THANET

1. The Canterbury & Whitstable Railway

The Canterbury & Whitstable Railway has achieved considerable fame for a relatively short local line(), and it has on occasions been ranked with other lines such as the Stockton & Darlington. To claim for it great historical significance could possibly be misguided however, for in its early years it made only very unsatisfactory use of locomotives and had to be largely rebuilt within a few years by the SER. Though the C&WR was undoubtedly an interesting line, its long-term significance in the history of railways in the South-East is minor when compared to, say, the London & Greenwich[1].

Where the Canterbury & Whitstable can claim fame is in being the first railway in Kent. Its origins can be traced to the pioneer of railways, William James, who in the early 1820s had surveyed a number of railway proposals including one across the South-East from Rochester to Shoreham in Sussex. In April 1823 James visited Canterbury, where there was dissatisfaction with transport facilities, and began work on surveying a route to Whitstable. The latter was a growing port, though separated from Canterbury by a low ridge.

James surveyed three possible routes and by November 1824 a company to build a railway was being formed, with capital set at £25,000. This was increased to £31,000 when the Act was obtained on 10 June 1825.

James, however, was pushed aside when George Stephenson became engineer to the line after visiting Canterbury in August 1825. Stephenson disliked James' approach to Canterbury, preferring to extend the line to a terminus at North Lane rather than adopt James' sharp curve to end in Whitstable Road. This deviation was authorised in an Act of 2 April 1827. Although Joseph Locke also helped with the surveying, John Dixon from Darlington was appointed as resident engineer.

Work on the Tyler Hill Tunnel began in October 1825 and Dixon pressed ahead until the workings met in May 1827. The tunnel was constructed with a clearance of only 11 feet, so that in later years engines on the line had to operate with cut-down boiler fittings. However, within a few months work had to stop due to financial difficulties and Dixon left the company. It was revived by new financial arrangements based on an Act of 9 May 1828 and an arrangement to lease the line to Lister Ellis for 14 years.

The line was constructed in several sections involving trains being moved by stationary engines along inclined planes, but also with sections intended for locomotive working. The locomotive, *Invicta*, was brought by sea to Whitstable and tested on the line by Robert Stephenson on 2 May 1830. However the bulk of the traffic movement was to depend on two stationary engines operating at Tyler Hill and Clowes Wood, hauling trains up the inclines of about 1 in 50.

The official opening was held on 3 May 1830 with the Board and guests travelling in a special train up the incline out of Canterbury. Most of the journey depended on the winding engines, but between the foot of Clowes Wood Incline and Whitstable it was hauled by *Invicta*. Ordinary services began the following day. Sunday services were run for a month in 1832 only but reintroduced in 1843. Whitstable Harbour was formally opened on 19 March 1832.

Joshua Richardson, who had replaced Dixon as resident engineer, was appointed manager of the line and £1,200 was spent in purchasing Westgate Vicarage in Canterbury for him to use.

The use of a steam locomotive soon proved a disappointment. *Invicta* was unable to haul a train up the Church Street Incline out of Whitstable and for a while horses did the job; in the summer of 1832 a third stationary engine was installed at Bogshole to cover this task. The C&WR tried to sell *Invicta* in 1839 but failed to find any takers.

Although the railway helped Canterbury by keeping the price of coal down, it was not profitable since the road services were very competitive. In 1838 it was decided to lease the line to Nicholson & Bayliss; in 1840 these gentlemen were providing a service of five passenger trains a day, but in 1841 they went bankrupt.

There then followed a sad period as the C&WR Board tried to let the railway and the harbour for seven years at an annual rental of £3,500, but could interest no-one.

The C&WR was saved by the promotion of the SER's line from Ashford to Canterbury and Ramsgate. The SER decided to proceed with this in January 1841 and examined the prospects of the Canterbury & Whitstable carefully. The *Railway Times* reported that, by the end of 1841, the position was uncertain; fares had been reduced from 9d to 6d on 1 February 1841, resulting in a startling increase in traffic - from £9,388 in 1840 to £23,719 in 1841. However passengers in August were 1,873 less than the same month the previous year.

In August 1842 the *Railway Times* told its readers that the accounts of the C&WR were "of so complicated a nature that it was next to impossible to understand them." It reckoned that the line had made a net loss of £704 in 1841 and criticised the fact that it had two managers, each earning £150 per annum. However one of these, the Whitstable Harbour Master, resigned.

Desperate to increase its traffic, the C&WR began running cheap excursions in July 1843 - even on Sundays. Over 500 people made use of the first Sunday trains and the Canterbury station was improved. The *Railway Times* estimated that, by mid-1843, the line was making an annual profit of at least £2,850.

In March 1844 a deputation from the C&W visited the SER to request a junction between the two companies. Three days later, on 23 March, the SER discussed whether it should lease the line and an Act of 23 May 1844 allowed the SER to do so for 14 years from 29 September. The SER agreed to pay the interest on various debts, amounting to £44,221. It also agreed to pay a rental of £1,200 in the first year, rising to a maximum of £3,000 in subsequent years.

The C&WR continued to show signs of improving fortunes during its last few independent months. During the summer of 1844 it was getting over 300 passengers on Sundays. According to SER Minutes, the SER took possession of the line on 30 September 1844.

Selling out to the SER seemed the best option for the C&WR, but the SER shareholders must have wondered what they were to do with this new property. Already, by 1844, a rope-worked railway must have seemed archaic and hardly the sort of thing that a dynamic railway company would wish to tarnish its image

62. The opening train on the Canterbury & Whitstable line, climbing away from Whitstable Harbour. (R.W.Kidner Collection)

with. But there were advantages, and as early as February 1845 Peter Barlow was directed to clear the mud out of Whitstable Harbour so that it could be used for ships[2]; this cost £1,200. In May Barlow even examined the cost of converting the line to the then-fashionable atmospheric system; there was a contemporary proposal for an atmospheric line from Chilham to Faversham and several other schemes affecting Kent.

Yet the problem remained that the line had a very low level of traffic in terms of receipts, for it was a short line with high handling costs. In the first week of March 1845 it took £146-5s-3d, but the SER felt confident enough in October 1845 to increase the salaries of the line's staff. On 18 December they considered the cost of converting it to "a locomotive line"; five days later it was agreed to pay Grissell & Peto £16,000 to relay the track with heavier rails and replace rotting sleepers.

It was decided to provide a new station at Whitstable, and locomotives took over the traffic from 6 April 1846. They soon proved too heavy for the works and one of them was derailed near Bogshole due to subsidence. At the Canterbury end the trains were diverted to run into the new SER station, though the old station remained in use for coal traffic. It became possible to make the full journey in 20 minutes. In 1847 an Act was obtained by local promoters for a branch from Whitstable to Herne Bay; it was not built[3].

As far as the SER was concerned, it was the harbour at Whitstable that had the most potential. In April 1846 they discussed building a coal pier there and decided to expand the facilities to relieve pressure on Folkestone. A plan for an outer pier, deeper channel, coke works and staff housing was devised, estimated to cost £12,450. One of the old stationary engines was moved to Whitstable and used to drive pumps and a crane. £1,766 was then spent on coke ovens, for at the time locomotives could not run on coal.

Not surprisingly, the citizens of Whitstable did not take kindly to the sudden arrival of belching industrial plant like a coke works, and there was already tension by December 1846 followed by complaints of "smoke nuisance" in 1850. A Harbour Master was appointed in May 1845 on £150 per annum.

In January 1852 the SER discussed whether they should buy the line or continue to lease it. They offered £60,000 plus about £40,000 to settle the liabilities and an Act of 4 August 1853 authorised the absorbing which was completed in December.

The SER continued a policy of minor improvements - in April 1852 it had even splashed out on new horses for the Herne Bay omnibus. The electric telegraph was extended over the line in 1852 as well.

This was a time when the SER was prone to scandal, and even such a backwater as the C&W was prone to injudicious activity. In September 1853 the Board was disturbed by reports that the Harbour Master, Clay, had refused permission for two ships to unload and there were suggestions of "favouritism". The SER decided to ask "if any of the nautical men in the service of the Company would wish a berth ashore." One did - Chief Mate John Robinson, but he was rejected.

The Whitstable branch came under serious threat when a branch line off the East Kent Railway at Faversham to Herne Bay was promoted in 1856-7. The *Railway Times* had reported in September 1855 that the line was losing £3,089 a year and the loss of the Herne Bay traffic and also that of Whitstable itself could have been a mortal blow. In June 1857 the SER discussed promoting its own line from Whitstable to Herne Bay to keep out the intruder, but this was the time of considerable tension between factions on the SER Board and the idea was opposed bitterly by Kay and Child. A discussion on whether to oppose the intrusive Herne Bay & Faversham Bill was deadlocked at 5-5 and a suggestion that the SER should build a line from Herne Bay through to Margate was rejected as "altogether unnecessary." The Herne Bay & Faversham Railway got its Act on 17 August 1857 and eventually extended to Margate and Ramsgate.

This episode is worthy of comment, for it shows how division on the SER Board, and a drastic lack of understanding of railway politics, allowed a rival a foothold. Through blind adherence to a policy of non-expansion, the SER lost its complete control of the gateway to the Thanet resorts.

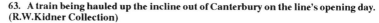

63. A train being hauled up the incline out of Canterbury on the line's opening day. (R.W.Kidner Collection)

When the work on the new line began the SER soon found reason to object to the means by which it crossed over the Whitstable branch. In January 1859 a temporary timber viaduct was proposed to keep the SER trains running, but the matter was eventually referred to the Board of Trade who awarded £36-11s-5d to the SER.

Subsequent efforts were made by private individuals to provide a direct link from Herne Bay to Canterbury. Talks were held with the Herne Bay & Canterbury Junction Railway in December 1862, but the SER refused to support it. The idea was revived in 1869, again in 1871-2 and in 1874-5.

With such steep inclines, there were some dangers in working the Whitstable line. Therefore, in February 1871, catch points were authorised at Sand Hole and Clowes Bank sidings.

Whitstable station received a new booking office in 1875 but local demands the following year for a link between the SER and LCDR lines there went unheeded.

Further schemes to connect Canterbury and Herne Bay emerged in 1884-5 and in 1887; the latter proposal was for a Lartigue monorail from Herne Bay to Sturry.

Whitstable was resignalled in 1892 and the SER also listened to local requests for a new station. In 1893 it considered providing a new one but only in February 1894 was a new station was opened slightly further south   with new buildings and roofing over the platforms. Whitstable's unique traffic was in oysters, and the SER provided a shellfish shed in 1895.

2. The Canterbury & Thanet Line

A number of early schemes for railways into Kent were attracted by the possibility of building a line along the natural routeway of the Stour valley through Canterbury and on to Ramsgate. Both the latter and nearby Margate were then enjoying a period of rapid development as holiday resorts, based largely on steamers from London, while Canterbury itself was a busy market town.

The New Kent Railroad, promoted in April 1834, included a branch to Canterbury from Ashford while in November 1835 the London & Dover Railway proposed the same. Colonel Landmann, the engineer of this line which actually was to run from Northfleet to Dover, proposed a route through the North Kent towns and Canterbury as being much more useful to the County than the SER's route.

Canterbury people generally opposed the SER for the simple reason that their town was not central to its ambitions. Some saw Canterbury's stance as "perfectly absurd[4]." Nonetheless, the SER gained its Act in June 1836 and the wishes of Canterbury were ignored.

The dissatisfaction of Canterbury and the Thanet towns was bound to breed other schemes, and indeed it seems that the SER's rivals never died but simply recast themselves in different guises. By August 1836, when the printer's ink on the SER Act was barely dry, the London & Dover Railway had reorganised itself to promote a line to serve Ramsgate and Margate; the SER's promise of a branch from Ashford to Canterbury proving insufficient to quell local discord.

By October 1836 the Kent Railway was also in the field, suggesting a line along the coast from the Thanet towns to Dover via Sandwich, Deal and Walmer. There was also a London & Sandwich proposal.

The SER therefore proposed its own scheme for a line from Ashford to Ramsgate and Sandwich in January 1837. The shareholders were told that this was a "local scheme", though it seems to have been largely a SER project for which they sought local representatives. It was not proceeded with.

Interest then died down for a while, though there were still occasional schemes. The Central Kentish Railway of 1838 attempted to revive the fortunes of Sandwich as a seaport by making it the terminus of a line via Maidstone.

During the latter months of 1840 the SER became concerned that rival schemes were stirring once more, and determined to promote their own line once again. On 5 January 1841 the Board agreed to promote a line from Ashford to Canterbury, Ramsgate and Margate. Robert Stephenson was directed to survey the line as far as Ramsgate, which he did by May, but once more the SER decided not to continue.

Matters lay dormant until 3 October 1843, when Joseph Cubitt was directed to tread in the steps of Stephenson by surveying to Margate. Two weeks later Grissell & Peto applied for appointment as contractors for the line and the preparation of a Bill began; in fact the contract went to Miller & Blackie of Liverpool in September 1844.

The SER were unsure of the value of the line and in January 1844 decided to lay only one track but to acquire enough land for two; bridges were also to be for a double-track. The plans had to be altered since the proposed line infringed Chartham Green between Ashford and Canterbury[5].

The Act for the line was passed in 1844 and allowed for a diversion of the River Stour at Grove Ferry; this was never made, and so the line curved sharply there to avoid the river. There was to be a "main-line" from Ashford direct to Ramsgate, from where a branch ran across Thanet to a seaside terminus at Margate; reversal was to be necessary at Ramsgate; costs were estimated at £385,339. The line from Ashford to Ramsgate was to include a number of level crossings, which the Parliamentary committee sanctioned on the grounds that "Trains on the Railway would not probably be very frequent." However crossings at Canterbury and Wye were restricted by the threat of a fine if the road traffic was kept waiting for more than five minutes; trains were expected to halt at the crossings and wait for them to be cleared before proceeding across. To take advantage of the compulsory delay for down trains at the level crossing west of the Canterbury station, the SER erected a ticket platform there; this remained in use until at least 1852.

As soon as it was clear that the SER really intended to proceed with the line, other local schemes came forward; in particular, Faversham interests like C.J.Hilton proposed a branch from Chilham to their town. The issue was discussed in September 1844 and the SER Board visited Faversham to meet Hilton and other prominent interests, but generally the SER's policy with such suggestions was to leave as much to local interests as possible. This was to prove fatal, for Faversham became highly influential in the promotion of the East Kent Railway - latterly the London, Chatham & Dover.

Meanwhile Cubitt was at work on the detailed planning of the new line. By September he had chosen a site near Margate harbour for its terminus, but the Ramsgate station was in a less advantageous position away from the town. Work had begun by January 1845 with over 300 men reported to be at work; a particular factor in the construction of the line cited in press reports was the need for six bridges between Ramsgate and Margate. Navvies on the line caused problems in July 1845 when they helped a man escape from Police custody; the SER's own Police stood by and did nothing.

64. The opening of the Ashford-Canterbury line, 1845, showing one of the level crossings which were legally protected by the Railway's Act. This is St. Dunstan's Street.

During February 1845 the SER considered prospects for its new line and decided that it should be double track as far as Canterbury, single thereafter. Stations were to be built at Chilham, Canterbury, Minster, Ramsgate and Margate only; Sturry, Wye and Grove Ferry would have to wait.

The line was inspected by General Pasley on 5 February 1846 and opened the following day as far as Canterbury. On the opening day a special was run from London but was delayed by mechanical failure near Tonbridge. The Canterbury Brass Band was ferried over the line as part of the celebrations. Canterbury station was in an incomplete state and did not open for goods until about six weeks later. The extension to Ramsgate opened on 13 April with stations at Grove Ferry, Minster and Ramsgate. The SER hoped to develop Ramsgate as a Channel port with a daily steamer to Ostend.

There is some doubt about the precise date of opening of some of these intermediate stations. As late as January 1846 the people of Wye were petitioning for a station, so if one was provided on the opening day it can only have been the most rudimentary of structures. A temporary platform there was certainly in use by April 1846, for there were reports that it needed altering[6]. At the same time it was decided not to provide a station at Godmersham. Canterbury station, rather more permanent, had cost £5,000 by 8 May 1846, and two months later it was decided to add an extra goods siding. On 17 July the Board discussed the intermediate stations again; it was reported that stations were being built at Wye and Grove Ferry, but that "mixed trains" already stopped there. Clearly both were instances of the SER policy of opening very basic stations at first. In September 1846 the SER received a request to replace the ferry at Grove Ferry with a bridge, but this was refused.

The people of Margate were not entirely impressed by the route, especially since a reversal was needed at Ramsgate. Instead they first proposed a new line from Chislet, close to Grove Ferry, to their town and in February 1846 requested a branch from Sarre. Opposition from landowners seems to have prevented either, but it is doubtful that the SER would have been over-concerned. The Chislet scheme was mentioned at the General Meeting in September 1846, then disappeared from view.

The SER hoped that the Margate branch would be open by 21 October 1846, but it was delayed until 1 December 1846. The station there was, in keeping with SER frugality, a typical semi-permanent wooden structure. Although the single-track section between the two resort towns was less than four miles long, it was plainly an inconvenience; in December 1846 Barlow suggested that a passing loop should be provided on it.

At the end of 1846 there were a number of active schemes for lines affecting the Thanet branch. Some of these, such as the line to Deal and Dover, are dealt with below, but there was also continued support for a line from Chilham to Faversham which was supported by Hon. Stephen Lushington and by C.Hilton; it was surveyed by Robert Stephenson in late 1846 and estimated to cost £19,550, but its promoters fell out with the SER over the issue of land costs. By December 1846 there were also Bills for a line from Strood to Chilham (estimated £871,033, promoted by the SER) and Maidstone to Chartham (£415,000).

The problem for the SER was that it offered no real service to the North Kent towns like Faversham and Sittingbourne, together with only a devious route to Canterbury. In the Parliamentary contest of 1846-7 it therefore sought to defend itself against outsiders seeking this traffic by proposing an extension from the Gravesend & Rochester Railway at Strood to Chilham. This was to include a bridge across the Medway at Rochester with a "lateral cut" so that the masts of vessels could pass through easily. The SER also pledged to extend the line from Canterbury to Dover, hoping to win the support of the Duke of Wellington. But there were rivals in the field, hoping to feed off local discontent; these included a LBSCR-backed scheme for a line from New Cross to Canterbury. There was a third scheme planning to link London and Canterbury via Maidstone. Worried by a bad press and the appearance of "erroneous statements", the SER spent £3,000 on an advertising campaign in early 1847. However the collapse of the two rival schemes soon revealed that the SER plans were merely defensive, for it withdrew its own Bill perhaps in the fear of being compelled to make the extension from Canterbury to Dover. No doubt the SER directors saw this as prudent housekeeping, but by withdrawing the Bill they showed bad faith to local people and provided moral ammunition for their enemies in later debates. Feelings were not helped by what local people saw as exploitation of a monopoly - fares to Canterbury were increased in August 1847 and train services - especially of 3rd class - cut back from 1 February 1848.

On 22 April 1847 the SER decided to provide a new intermediate station at Sturry, to open by 1 June. This indicates, as usual, the policy of putting up a very basic station which could be used to assess the extent of potential traffic before building a proper facility. Something more permanent duly evolved, for in

October 1848 it was decided to equip both Sturry and Wye with platform awnings. Sturry gained a booking office in 1851.

On 6 July 1848 the Board agreed to allow Mr Divers to put up a platform to serve the Tivoli Gardens at Margate and in September it was decided to provide a verandah for the Margate station. The Tivoli station was about a mile south of Margate station, and was used until at least the 1850s for excursion traffic; it was close to the present Tivoli Park. On 27 December 1848 a Mr Chandler was run over and killed at Minster.

The collapse of rival schemes proved only temporary, and by the later stages of 1848 the SER was again facing rivalry in the district. In October the prospectus for a Dover & Rochester Independent Railway was issued, while by December the Faversham interests were again active in calling for a line from Strood to Chilham, with possible extensions to Dover or Deal. The SER took the view that it had "no funds available" to assist. On 20 July 1849 the SER discussed the issue of extending the North Kent line from Strood to Canterbury, but left the issue without making a positive stance.

The independent scheme for an extension eastwards from Strood, surveyed by Mr G.Taylor, deposited a Bill at the end of 1849. It drew a lot of support on the grounds that the SER line to Dover could be cut by an enemy fleet but it was rejected in April 1850 largely because of its demands for running powers over the SER west of Strood.

As the time drew near for depositing Bills for the 1850-1 session, rivals reappeared once again. Prominent among them was the Mid-Kent & Dover, which included a principal route from Bromley to Canterbury and Dover. A rival, the Strood & Dover Direct, was rumoured to be a stooge of the SER but both Bills were again failures.

In August 1851 the SER met two prominent landowners, Lords Sondes and Harris, to discuss a line from Strood to Canterbury. This developed into the East Kent & Maidstone, which initially aimed at a line from Strood to Canterbury and was promoted largely by persons from the Faversham district. By December the SER had determined to oppose it, though the promoters still held out hopes of an agreement; the SER was rumoured to be behind a branch from Chilham to Faversham Creek as yet another defensive scheme. The scheme was, however, abandoned in January 1852 due to insufficient support within Kent.

Later that year attention became focussed on the East Kent Railway, which proposed a line from Strood to Chilham with access on to Canterbury; a further extension to Dover was likely, but abandoned to pacify the SER. In fact the SER steadfastly refused to support it and warned:

"Your profits will be nil; it is a line that by no possibility can pay; the South Eastern Company would not take it at any price; and if you, the gentry, embark on it, you will all be ruined."

Although the East Kent was promoted by Faversham men, the SER failed to recognise the significance of it having substantial backing from London, including that of the engineer Sir Charles Fox. The SER rejected an offer by the EKR to lease itself to the SER for a mere 3% and, after a bitter Parliamentary contest, the East Kent gained an Act for a line from Strood to Canterbury. The EKR had powers to build their own line into Canterbury or to use the tracks of the SER; the SER tried to get the EKR to abandon its own approach in March 1855, but - unsurprisingly perhaps - the EKR refused this invitation to thrust itself further into the embrace of an unreliable partner. An Act for a Dover extension was passed in 1855; the SER was restricted in its opposition to this since its own Strood to Maidstone line had been authorised in 1853 on a condition of not opposing the EKR's Dover extension, so it opposed the line on the grounds of the site of its terminus and the effect that its branches would have on the *Lord Warden Hotel*. Various financial problems delayed construction of the EKR Dover extension and by June 1858 the Duke of Devonshire was expressing concern that a work "of great national importance" was incomplete. On the SER, Rich and Teulon argued for their company to take over the line and to seek amalgamation with the EKR, but by 28 June it was clear that the EKR had rejected this prospect. Some materials for the new line were delivered via the SER to Chilham and in January 1859 the EKR had to threaten legal action since it felt some rails were being "detained" there. The line opened to Canterbury on 9 July 1860 and to Dover on 22 July 1861.

The significance of all this was considerable, for the SER had pursued a policy of trying to block other lines being built in an area that - by the standards of the 1850s - was badly served by railways. Having built its initial line to Canterbury and Thanet, it had failed to extend its services to other towns like Faversham. It had also acted in bad faith, promoting lines like one from Canterbury to Dover in 1847, only to drop them when the threat of an intruder had passed. Lack of vision and a greedy desire to hold onto "territory" without a genuine desire to serve the public, eventually cost the SER its monopoly control of eastern Kent.

During all the Parliamentary debates, the SER continued its slow policy of making minor improvements to the rudimentary station facilities on the line. In line with this policy seems to have been a decision in September 1850 to spend

65. The SER's terminus at Ramsgate.

£60 on a platform and waiting room for a station at Chartham; the opening of this station has usually been given as 1859. Also in 1850, a footbridge was provided for Canterbury station. In 1852 extra waiting rooms were provided at Minster and a crane at Wye.

Passengers in the 1850s were often nervous about railway travel, for one could be enclosed in a compartment with unknown - and possibly dangerous - strangers. In October 1852 Mary Hayward, an Ashford clockmaker's wife, was robbed of eight sovereigns between Ashford and Canterbury.

By the beginning of 1853 the Canterbury and Thanet line formed one of the SER's most substantial investments, with a capital value of £881,797. Improvements, though, came in a very desultory fashion - with five staff cottages being built at Minster late in 1853 and the siding at Grove Ferry lengthened in 1854.

In January 1856 a deal was agreed with the Commercial Steam Boat Company to operate steamers from London Bridge or Gravesend to Margate and Ramsgate, excursionists returning to London by train. Later that year the platforms at Margate were extended to cater for growing traffic, to handle which the timber bridges on the line had all been replaced by brick structures. A permanent Margate station was built in 1859 at a cost of £3,900. Canterbury station was enlarged in time for an agricultural show in July 1860.

On 30 June 1858 there was an accident at Chilham when the "crank axle tree" of a locomotive broke as the 3.30pm train from London Bridge approached the station. The locomotive and first three coaches reached the station, but the remaining six coaches were derailed; three carriages ended up in a field of wheat. An electric telegraph message was sent and a special train brought several surgeons from Canterbury, apparently within half an hour, and took away the injured. Two people died on the day of the accident and a third two days later. It was reported that the track on the line had not been replaced since 1846. Two months later there were injuries at Ramsgate station when a guard failed to brake a train properly. In December 1860 a passenger train collided with a light engine at Grove Ferry; one of the passengers, a damask salesman named Charles Ayling, was awarded £2,000 damages for internal injuries. The SER objected to the severity of the damages and employed an "agent" to keep watch on him.

In the latter stages of 1858 it became clear to the SER that the EKR acolyte, the Herne Bay & Faversham Railway, was planning an extension to Margate and possibly Ramsgate. On 1 October 1858 the SER therefore considered a new spur to provide through running from Minster to Margate without reversal at Ramsgate. In November the Board ordered a survey to be made of a branch from Ramsgate to Broadstairs, since this was the one town in the district without a SER service. This branch was estimated to cost £20,000, but the Ramsgate stationmaster reported that Broadstairs only contained 1,400 people and could accomodate a mere 1,100 visitors in a four month season; the idea was dropped.

Opposition in Parliament failed to prevent the HB&F scheme for an extension to Margate being authorised in 1859, so in August 1860 the SER again considered the question of a spur to Margate which, it was estimated, would save 40 minutes journey time.

In August 1861 an Act was obtained for a further extension of the rival line from Margate to Ramsgate Harbour. In May 1861 the Kent Coast Railway, the SER's rival in the district after the HB&F had outgrown its original title, reached agreement to use Ramsgate Harbour and the SER feared that a takeover of the Harbour by the LCDR was likely, so that it made objections to the Board of Trade early that month. Ramsgate people offered to oppose the

LCDR's use of the Harbour if the SER would build a branch to it. In the event, the Kent Coast dropped the idea.

In October 1862 the SER Board reviewed their position in Thanet very carefully. They decided to build a short spur at Ramsgate to allow direct running between Minster and Margate and to double the line to Margate. The new works were conducted during the first part of 1863 at a cost of £13,707, but the SER refused to extend its Ramsgate line further into the town. A light engine and twelve horses were employed in doubling the Margate line.

In August 1864 there was an accident at Margate station when an arriving train collided with one already at the platform; a first class carriage was forced up to the roof of the station, forming "a complete pyramid" with two others. One woman died, reports commenting that "She was literally scalped, a great portion of her hair being found with her head-dress among the debris."

In October 1864 the SER Traffic Committee recommended that the line should be extended further into Ramsgate to King Street and a new direct link built to Deal across Pegwell Bay. No doubt this was inspired by fears that the LCDR would try to reach Deal.

The main stations on the line all had refreshment rooms. Those at Ramsgate and Minster were rented out for £50 a year while one was built at Margate in 1873. The footbridge at Canterbury was replaced in 1869.

During the mid-1860s competition for Thanet coastal traffic had been lessened by the LCDR's financial problems, and in April 1869 the two companies met to discuss the division of traffic receipts. The SER was annoyed to learn in May that the LCDR was planning to restart its cheap excursions from London at 3s or 3s6d.

In 1871 a number of local interests began to promote a direct line from Canterbury to Herne Bay (a revival of an 1863 scheme) and in June 1872 the promoters approached the SR with a proposal to form a junction into the SER station at Canterbury. Agreement was reached in June 1873, but a branch off the Whitstable line, costing only £45,000, seemed more attractive. The SER never reached Herne Bay, but there were revivals of the idea in 1884, in 1887 when a Lartigue monorail link to Sturry was in vogue, and 1902. In the period 1882-3 there was also call for a link from Minster to Westgate-on-Sea.

On 28 December 1874 there was an accident due to the poor behaviour of two young men at Canterbury station. They fell off the platform in front of a train; one was killed and the other had to have a leg amputated. On 23 November 1875 a guard was trapped between the buffers whilst on shunting duties at Canterbury and also killed; his widow was awarded £125. Other staff who left the SER's employment unwillingly included the Ramsgate stationmaster, who was pensioned off in 1877 at the grand age of 75.

Canterbury was resignalled in 1874 for £1,350 and in 1876 the Chilham stationmaster was provided with a new house; Chilham had gas installed in 1877. On 1 January 1877 much of Kent was struck by gales; at Canterbury the station roof was damaged and a timber bridge across the line blown down. This bridge may actually have been the station footbridge, since three months later it was decided to replace the footbridge with a subway for £400.

In October 1878 the SER considered making substantial changes to Canterbury, and debated whether an approach should be made to the LCDR for a joint station. In 1879 a subway was considered for St Dunstan's Crossing in the city, and a siding was provided for Mr Howard in 1883 for £170 as well as extra goods sheds for private use in the station yard. Less well-planned were the changes to the buildings caused when there was a gas explosion at Canterbury station on 26 July 1884; there were several injuries.

An extra siding was provided at Chartham in 1883 and extensions to the platforms at Chartham, Grove Ferry and Sturry in 1887.

Resignalling continued in the 1890s, with interlocking being installed at Ramsgate in 1890-1 for £1,389 and in 1892 Chilham, Wye, Sturry and Grove Ferry were resignalled. Margate gained a cattle siding in 1893. The Board of Trade complained about the state of Ramsgate station in 1894.

The worst accident to occur on the line took place in the early morning of 9 October 1894. A one-horse waggon was taking 21 hop-pickers from Canterbury to the hop gardens at Corrie's Farm; at 6.45am it was struck by the 4.15am Ashford to Canterbury goods train at a farm crossing near Horton Chapel Farm. Five of the hoppers and the horse were killed immediately, with two more hoppers dying later. The SER was not to blame for the accident in any way for the fault lay with the waggon driver, Finch, who had not bothered to check if a train was approaching.

Facilities for goods and cattle at Ramsgate were extended in 1895 and in 1898 an extra horse dock siding was added at Wye for the race traffic.

3. The Deal Branch

With the discussion of railway projects in East Kent and Thanet, it was inevitable that the towns of Sandwich and Deal should require a service too. One unlikely starter in 1836 was for a London to Sandwich line, but prominent among the proposals of 1836-7 was the Kent Railway which was to include an extension along the coast via Sandwich, Deal and Walmer to Dover.

When the Canterbury and Thanet line was authorised in 1844 there was no provision for Deal or Sandwich. In June 1844 the Mayor of Deal made a formal

66. Deal Station c.1860. (R.Thomas Collection)

request for a branch but the SER was only spurred into action when a meeting at Deal in October proposed an independent line to London. The SER therefore deposited a Bill for its own branch from Minster, but the site of the Deal station was not popular. The line was authorised in 1845.

The SER decided in September 1845 that the new branch should be built as double-track, indicating a more long-term view than had been shown in the construction of the Margate line as a single track. Peto won the contract to do the whole line for £133,000, including a swing-bridge across the Stour near Minster for £3,000. To help with the work a locomotive was brought by road from Dover to Deal that winter, using a "lorry" and 16 horses; considerable difficulty was experienced with it at the hill near Oxney Bottom[7]. However it was reported in March 1847 that the opening of the line was being delayed by the double swing-bridge, with each track having its own span.

The SER hoped to open the line on 12 June 1846 but this was delayed by the incomplete state of the junction station at Minster. Although this station's opening has been given as 13 April, from timetable evidence, it is possible that trains did not actually begin to call until 1 July when the Deal branch opened. To celebrate, a large dinner was held at Deal Town Hall at which Charles Dickens spoke having been summoned down by electric telegraph. On the day, "the town had the appearance of a swarm of bees, fully on the wing, all under one impulse...the Directors of the Company generously supplied the wines without stint or measure.[8]"

Later the same month the SER showed its goodwill towards the district by giving 50 guineas to a fund for a new church in Deal, while the Deal Pier Company even had hopes of selling out to the SER. Clearly Minster Junction was built in the usual frugal style for unproven stations, for waiting rooms had to be added in 1851-2.

The Deal branch, however, was always the poor relation of the Ramsgate line so in July 1852 the SER received a number of complaints from Deal about its service. A famous passenger on the line was the Duke of Wellington, who for a time lived at Walmer Castle. The steps at Deal station had to be altered to allow the Royal carriage to pass through and when the Duke died in the autumn of that year the SER charged £90 for the "removal of his remains."

The town of Sandwich, once a prominent port, had experienced a long decline. In 1853 the Sandwich Improvement Association hoped to halt this by developing a better port at the Haven, with a branch from the SER. Its requests fell on deaf ears.

The service over this short line was fairly meagre, amounting to no more than about seven trains each way per day, and in July 1854 Captain Barlow suggested that economies could be made by removing the up line except for a loop at Sandwich. Despite the protests of Deal and Walmer, who no doubt saw this as some sort of unkind comment on the prospects of their towns, the work was done by May 1855. However the Board of Trade was not pleased and inserted a clause into the SER (Capital) Act of 1855 that it could compel the restoration of a second track or fine the SER £500 per day. The second track was restored in 1864-5 at a cost of £16,000[9].

A number of the trains using the line ran from Deal to Ramsgate with a reversal at Minster; a few went as far as Margate. This was a difficult service to operate and, in the face of fears of hostile lines in the district, the SER considered installing a new spur at Minster in October 1858. By 1860 the SER was planning to install loops at both Minster and Ramsgate so that a service could be operated between Deal and Margate with a journey time reduced by 40 minutes. This was in response to fears of a LCDR invasion from Ramsgate, although in 1862 the LCDR actually secured authority for a line to Deal from Dover. However, when the Board made their inspection of lines in the district in October 1862 (described above), both the plan for a loop at Minster and a suggestion to restore the double track - estimated to cost £15,850 - were left aside.

67.   Deal's original station is on the right, the other platform dating from the opening of the joint line from Dover.

In October 1864 the doubling of the Deal branch was agreed on and it was also suggested that a new line should be built across Pegwell Bay avoiding Minster altogether; the SER's problem was that it would have liked to run a frequent service between Deal and Margate, but as its lines were arranged it was impossible to do this without missing out Ramsgate or making a reversal there.

A rare moment of excitement occurred at Deal on 3 June 1865. The crew of locomotive No.72 built up its fire and then went off to the public house for an hour; pressure in the locomotive built up until its boiler exploded.

Resentment about the inferior service continued to simmer in Deal and Walmer. In June 1870 they complained that they had no service comparable to the cheap fasts offered to Ramsgate and Margate, some feeling this was because they had no rival LCDR line to stimulate the SER. In 1872 the SER did invest £1,600 in improving the branch; this included a new up bay for the Deal train at Minster, plus a new signalbox and refreshment room at Deal.

Nonetheless canny local people knew that improvements were most rapidly acquired by encouraging the LCDR. In October 1872 the SER was concerned to hear about an Adisham to Sandwich scheme, which soon became a Bill for a Walmer, Deal & Adisham line, but this failed to secure the necessary LCDR backing. A subsequent scheme was rejected by Parliament. The issue was finally settled by an Act for a Dover to Deal line to be built by both the SER and LCDR; this was acquired in 1874 and is described in the next section.

All trains arriving at Deal stopped at a ticket platform before pulling into the station. This ticket platform was only ten feet from the place where blood and fish manures were loaded in the goods yard, so in 1873 the SER decided to improve the situation - encouraged by the need to prepare for the Dover extension. A number of cottages were bought up and demolished to create more space.

In 1875 a siding was provided at Ash Road near Sandwich for the use of a brewery; it could handle 14 trucks and a further siding was added in 1889. An extra siding was provided at Deal in 1876.

The opening of the extension to Dover would increase traffic on the original Deal branch, so the SER made a number of preparations. The swing-bridge near Minster was strengthened and in September 1879 land was bought at Minster for the long-discussed curve, which opened with the Joint line on 15 June 1881. For a brief while it seemed that Minster might become a veritable Clapham Junction of Thanet, for there was a proposal in 1882 to build a branch from there to Westgate as well. However, the Minster spur only remained in use for a few months; it apparently closed in October 1881 although the track was not removed until 1905 and the signalboxes survived until 1907[10].

The opening of the Joint line did not end LCDR hostilities in the Deal district. In 1884 details emerged of a LCDR plan to create a new harbour, coaling station and marine workshops between Sandwich and Deal, to be connected to the rest of the system by a proposed Canterbury & Kent Coast line.

Sandwich station was resignalled in 1892 but two years later the Board of Trade recommended that the entire station should be rebuilt. This was done for £4,500. In 1895 the SER subscribed £10,000 to the South Eastern (Deal) Hotel Company. Designed by James Brooks, it was "fitted throughout in the latest modern style" and provided with "every convenience that would possibly add to the comfort of visitors[11]." The hotel was typical of the way in which the SER encouraged Deal; perhaps it was no coincidence that E.Knatchbull-Hugessen, a SER director, was also the town's MP until he became Lord Brabourne.

In 1898 a siding was opened at Richborough, to handle the sand and gravel traffic to Martin Mill in connection with the Dover Harbour works.

4. The Deal & Dover Joint Line

As has been seen, once the SER began to construct a branch from Minster to Deal it was natural that other parties should seek to extend it on to Dover. There were active local proposals for this in November 1846. A similar scheme failed in March 1854 with legal costs of £2,700. In 1862 the LCDR actually secured an Act for such a line but it allowed the powers to lapse in 1865. The Dover, Deal & Sandwich Railway, promoted in 1864-5, found favour with neither the SER nor the LCDR.

Deal and Walmer were definately disadvantaged by their position on the railway system, for they were the slowest growing Kent resorts in the 1860s. However the financial crisis of 1866 dampened enthusiasm for most new railway projects, and it was not until January 1872 that a SER shareholder again raised the issue of a line from Deal to Dover. The SER was worried about new lines direct from the LCDR at Adisham and by September 1873 was discussing a joint project with the LCDR.

The SER prepared a Bill for the line, though it faced opposition from the Deal, Walmer & Dover and the Ramsgate, Deal & Dover. A "truce" was agreed with the LCDR and as part of this the Deal to Dover line was to be constructed as a joint project. Rival schemes were withdrawn by May 1874 and the Joint Bill was authorised. A Dover & Deal Joint Committee was formed of which James Staats Forbes of the LCDR was chairman; Brady of the SER and Mills of the LCDR were joint-engineers.

There were a number of delays before work actually began, these being blamed on landowners and the problem of access to Walmer, though it is interesting that the initial setting out of the line was delayed by the harvest. There was also a dispute over the effect the line would have on fox-hunting. T.A.Walker was awarded the contract for works, at £147,644-2-8d. Land costs were also substantial, especially at Deal and on the new curve in Dover, with a number of houses needing to be demolished. According to SER Minutes, the first sod of the line was to be cut at Deal on 29 May 1878 but a special ceremony was held on 29 June, so one hopes no-one arrived too early. A special train was run from Charing Cross to Deal via Ashford, hauled by two locomotives. At Deal, "the usually quiet town was...in a fever of enthusiasm. Flags decorated every house, triumphal arches were erected, and a salute fired by the local Volunteers greeted the advent of the train[12]." Watkin presented a spade and barrow to Earl Granville, who was to perform the ceremony. Granville, "with some little difficulty extricated the already partly cut sod." Granville was given the barrow and spade, though relations between him and the Joint Committee were strained by his demands for a bridge rather than a level crossing on his land; he was bought off with £300.

The line was to join the LCDR at Buckland Junction, running into Dover over LCDR tracks and with a new curve from Hawkesbury Street Junction to Archcliffe Junction in Dover. Access to the SER's own Dover station was impossible without reversal, so by October 1878 discussions were being held about a new joint station in Dover. The engineers investigated the possibility of building a station on the new curve at Dover, but the Joint Committee had no powers and insufficient land, while the engineers felt that it was a poor and cramped site anyway. Though the issue was again raised in 1882, no new station was built; instead, the LCDR's Priory station took on the role.

The works on the line were considerable and included a 1,412 yard tunnel at Guston. In 1879 a further Act had to be obtained to extend the time limit on powers for construction. The SER planned to use the new line to increase through running from Dover to Deal and Ramsgate or Margate. It spent an estimated £12,000 in rebuilding Deal station, including new down side buildings, a turntable, water tank, goods and locomotive sheds; this station remained the sole property of the SER but was open for joint use. The double-track loop provided at Minster cost £6,500 and had signalboxes at each end, though the Board of Trade was initially unhappy with its signalling and catch points.

In February 1879 the Joint Committee received requests for stations at Martin, East and West Langdon, Guston and to serve St Margaret's Bay. It decided to provide stations at Walmer and "St Martin's Mill"; the former was to cost £14,000 and the latter £7,400. Both stations were provided with signalboxes and three-bedroom stationmasters' houses.

A short but very important part of the Joint scheme was the spur in Dover from Archcliffe Junction to Hawkesbury Street Junction. This included level crossings across some important streets and £581 was spent on interlocking signals and crossing gates. Nonetheless the opening of the whole line was delayed when the Board of Trade inspector objected to the safety of the crossings.

The ceremonial opening of the new line took place on 14 June 1881 with a special Dover to Deal train drawn by a locomotive of each company passing beneath a triumphal arch on its arrival. As far as Dover was concerned this was the wrong way round - their Town Clerk had asked for celebrations to be held at the opposite end of the line. Public traffic began the following day but goods traffic did not begin for at least three months. The day the line opened an injunction was served on it for obstructing Elizabeth Street in Dover[13].

The LCDR gained more direct access onto the line from 1 July 1882 by opening a short spur from Kearsney Loop Junction to Deal Junction, making the running of through expresses from London to Deal more practicable.

In the first two months traffic receipts came to £1,629 of which the SER share was £1,035. Letters arrived from people in Margate and Dover complaining about the lack of goods services and through booking facilities for passengers. The Railway Clearing House sorted out the latter question in 1883.

However, the Joint Committee was sufficiently encouraged to order minor improvements in December 1881; these included paving the platforms at Walmer and Martin Mill, installing gas lights at Walmer and providing a gatehouse at Cold Blow Crossing in Walmer.

As has been seen, the level crossings on the Dover spur soon produced legal action. In December 1881 the Joint Committee decided to seek powers to stop up the level crossings. In April 1882 the Committee learnt that the use of the spur was causing severe delays to road traffic and much opposition, and it decided to try a six month experiment of working trains by reversing at Admiralty Pier. The Board of Trade required strict regulations for this, including the employment of signalmen on the Pier and two gatekeepers. In addition, the Joint Committee had to pay an additional £25 towards the Pier Master's salary and a rental of £300 per year for using the Pier.

The Board of Trade sanctioned the use of this curious route for some trains from 25 August 1883, but opening was prevented when the LCDR objected to there being a SER man in the Pier signalbox. At this point the two factions on the Joint Committee began to revert to their normal enmity; Watkin, for the SER, wanted the question referred to the Board of Trade but the LCDR representatives voted against this. At the following meeting Forbes, of the LCDR, physically altered the Minutes with his own hand.

One of the problems was that the line onto the Pier from both directions was only single track and caused problems with movements to the LCDR goods sidings. Hutchinson, for the Board of Trade, had a second look at the facilities and, apart from recommending some extra signals, found nothing to object to that matched the violent protests of the LCDR. In November 1883 Forbes suggested that they revert to using the spur line again.

Use of the Admiralty Pier route for a "trial" six months finally began on 1 April 1884 and was then extended for a further period. Dover Corporation was not impressed with the service and there was a good deal of pressure for a better service between Folkestone, Dover, Deal and Ramsgate. When the Corporation requested that bridges be built on the spur line, the Joint Committee replied that it had no powers.

However, from 1 October 1885 the Joint Committee opened a new platform on the spur line close to the SER's station and reverted to using this route instead of reversing at the Pier. Almost immediately there were protests that trains waiting between the LCDR's Harbour station and Archcliffe Junction blocked the level crossings. The Joint Committee agreed to install a crossover beside the Council House Street signalbox to ease shunting problems.

The whole issue gradually developed into a remarkably long-running saga. The Joint Committee committed itself to building bridges but then, in August 1887, paid Dover Corporation £4,000 to be released from this obligation. In July 1888 Dover Corporation said it would put up three footbridges, but within a few months reduced this to two. Map evidence suggests that a footbridge was only built at the Elizabeth Street crossing. In November 1892 the Corporation requested "swing gates" at Council House Street Crossing, but was refused. On 15 March 1895 a child, the daughter of a guard, was injured in an accident at Great Street Crossing. Fortunately, Joint Committee objections to a Corporation Tramway being built across one of the crossings in 1896 proved successful. The LCDR's Bill of 1897-8 included clauses to stop up the level crossings.

In October 1886 Major Lownes offered land for a station to be built at Kearsney Loop Junction, where the LCDR's Kearsney Loop from Deal Junction joined the joint line. The station was to be known as Crabbe but the LCDR objected to it and votes on the Joint Committee were tied. Watkin said that the SER would go ahead and build the station itself - but it never did.

Trouble then blew up over Deal station, which was wholly owned by the SER. Terms for the use of the station by the LCDR had not been agreed, and on 23 March 1887 the SER gave notice that it would prevent the LCDR running into the station unless accounts were settled by 1 May. Henry Oakley of the Great Northern Railway was appointed arbitrator before this action proved necessary. It took Oakley until November 1896 to reach his decision - hopefully not an indication of the speed with which things were done on the GNR. He ruled that Deal station should remain SER property and that the LCDR should pay £866 per year for the use of it up to 31 December 1895. Platforms at Deal station were extended in 1898.

An omnibus service was provided from Martin Mill station to St Margaret's Bay, which the Joint Committee subsidised at £2 per week from at least 1887. However, after an accident in August 1890 the Joint Committee refused to give the operator, Philpott, any more money. Philpott took exception to this since he felt he was not to blame for the accident, and the dispute ended with him £300 to the good. He resumed the service on 16 April 1894, getting two guineas a week from the Joint Committee.

In October 1895 the Joint Committee discussed moving Dover Corporation refuse to a new siding at Martin Mill, but deferred the decision. However in August 1898 the Committee did agree to provide new sidings at Martin Mill for the Harbour extension works traffic.

A station in Lower Walmer at Cornwall Road was requested in 1898 but refused.

On 6 July 1898 some SER vehicles were allowed to run away from Walmer station and down the incline to Deal, where they collided with the empty stock of the LCDR's 4.55pm Deal to Kearsney train. The LCDR guard, Clarke, had to be sent home with shock and damage amounted to £269.

The Dover & Deal Joint Committee continued as a separate entity after the creation of the SE&CR Managing Committee. Sir Edward Watkin remained on the Joint Committee until 1899, when he was replaced by his son Alfred.

1.   For a detailed account see R.B.Fellows, **The Canterbury & Whitstable Railway.**
2.   SER Minutes, 20 February 1845. It seems likely that the harbour was silted up so that only barges could use it easily.
3.   These promoters included the Burge family, a notable contracting firm.
4.   **Herapath's Railway Magazine,** quoted in **Maidstone Journal,** 12 April 1836.
5.   **Maidstone Journal,** 16 January 1844.
6.   See SER Minutes, 24 April and 1 May 1846. R.H.Clark gives its opening as contemporary with the rest of the line.
7.   J.Laker, **History of Deal,** p.379. A contemporary description is given in **Bygone Kent,** June 1984, p.353.
8.   S.Pritchard, **History of Deal,** 1864.
9.   SER Minutes, 6 October 1864.
10. **Southern Railway Magazine,** March 1930.
11. **Deal & Sandwich Gazette,** 1896.
12. **Railway Times,** 13 June 1878.
13. For details of the level crossing issue, see Dover & Deal Joint Committee Minutes.

CHAPTER 20: ACROSS THE CHANNEL

1. Folkestone Harbour and its Branch

The position of Folkestone did not readily allow for its development as a rail-served port. The landscape was amongst the most hilly in Kent, with the chalk downs meeting the coast and the Foord valley posed a problem for railway builders that could only be solved by one of the largest viaducts on the SER. To provide a main-line that passed close enough to the harbour[1], for the convenience of cross-Channel passengers proved impossible, despite calls in November 1836 for a route that required no branch[2]. At the early stages of the line's promotion it was, in any case, envisaged that Dover would be the principal port and in 1838 Cubitt estimated that 52,000 passengers per year were handled at that place.

Folkestone harbour was in a poor state, blocked up by drifting shingle and mortgaged. All this was changed by the possibility of the SER itself acquiring control of Folkestone Harbour after the terms demanded by the Dover Harbour Commissioners had proved excessive[3]. In August 1842 it was decided that the SER Chairman, Tyndale, should actively pursue the question of acquiring Folkestone Harbour from the Exchequer Loan Commissioners although a contractor, Morris, may have acted as intermediary[4]. This plan was successfully completed in April 1843 when a cheque for £18,000 was paid over; it was to prove one of the best SER investments of the 1840s. At the General Meeting in August 1843, shareholders were told that the Harbour was "an acquisition of the utmost importance to the ultimate prosperity of the company."

Almost immediately the SER began planning a branch-line to the Harbour. Discussions about it were reported in the *Railway Times* of 22 April and work seems to have begun almost immediately. The "Folkestone Branch Railway" was discussed by the Board on 30 May 1843 and on 10 June the *Railway Times* reported that it would be open by July. Reports a fortnight later that it would open on 28 June, the date that the line from Ashford to the western part of Folkestone actually opened, were unfounded since there was much work still to do.

In August 1843 it was reported that the branch was being built along the "natural channel formed by a hollow between the Hills", but despite this assistance from Nature a gradient of 1 in 32 was required. At least 20 houses were actually demolished[5]. At the foot of the gradient the line was to run 150 feet on to the wooden pier which separated the Inner and Outer harbours; the pier was widened and provided with gas lighting. Depth of water was sufficient for ferries to lie alongside the pier for three hours either side of high tide. In September it was noted that Lewis Cubitt was working on plans for the Harbour station.

Not everyone was impressed by the prospect of Folkestone as England's continental gateway. In September 1843 a *Railway Times* reporter found it "a most wretched place", complaining that there were "one or two miserable hotels, where the accomodation supplied and the charges made are in inverse ratio."

68.   One of the earliest known views of the Folkestone Harbour branch, drawn c.1849-50.   The viaduct across the Inner Harbour has been completed and rails installed on the swing-bridge, but they do not yet run across on to the South Quay. The position of the train indicates the approximate place in which passengers, initially, detrained.

The town was in a moribund state, perhaps explaining why a local composer, W.Tolputt, dedicated his *South Eastern Railway Quadrilles* to the daughter of the SER's chairman, Baxendale.

To improve the facilities of the town, the construction of the Royal Pavilion *Hotel* out of a converted boat builder's shed, intended to accomodate 100 diners, was begun on land reclaimed from the Inner Harbour. According to the *Maidstone Journal* of 8 August 1843, it was built in three weeks; the contractors were Grissell & Peto. It seems to have opened in December 1843 but can hardly have deserved a prediction that it would be a "stupendous hotel." When Dickens visited it, he found it "a strange building which had just left off being a barn."

The *Railway Times* 2 December 1843 reported that the Harbour "tramway" was finished and expected to open to a permanent station at any time, but a local press report three days later only felt that it was nearing completion[6]. The same report gave space to rumours that the SER wanted to demolish 500 houses in the town.

No conclusive opening date of the branch has been found and it was, plainly, inadequate for the continental passenger traffic so that by January 1844 the SER had a Bill "to make or complete" the branch in passage through Parliament. In the meantime it was decided that the line should be used for goods traffic; the most likely opening date is therefore 18 December 1843[7], when the main-line was extended into Folkestone, or possibly 7 February 1844, when it was extended from Folkestone to Dover. It was certainly in use by 19 March, for on that date a platelayer was killed on the incline by a coal wagon and the Board decided that it needed to fit brakes to them for use on the branch. However in September the Board expressed doubts about the working of traffic on the branch; it may have been that, despite the passage of their Act to authorise the use of the line for passengers, that the original practice of using buses between the south pier and Folkestone station seemed more reliable than a steeply-graded railway. At first a boat-builder's shed was converted to cater for the passengers at the Harbour.

A new Harbour House was provided on the south side of the Harbour; the ground floor was for use as a Customs Hall and the upper floors by the Harbour Master. A more commodious Customs House was built in 1846.

As originally opened as a freight line, the branch ran down to the north side of the Harbour and out on to a short pier. This left it remote from the south side of the Harbour where, at South Pier, there was sufficient depth of water for small boats to call at most states of the tide. The idea of providing a swing bridge to connect the railway jetty with the south side of the Harbour was first discussed in February 1846, an idea strongly favoured by Barlow. In December it was agreed to spend £5,844 on a 138 feet long[8] "swivel bridge", which it was hoped would be ready by May 1847. However, the bridge was a considerable step forward for the technology of the time and was delayed by problems with the contractor; it was still having problems in March 1848, nine months after it should have opened. As part of the improvement, a lighthouse and flag station were provided at the Harbour entrance in 1847.

While it waited for the completion of the bridge, the SER looked at the type of station that should be provided. In July 1847 it considered that a passenger shed and platform could be provided for £1,611 and work seems to have begun early in 1848. This may have referred to the facilities actually provided on the Pier, where - at first - passengers got out of the carriages. This was an inauspicious year to be engaged on developing the cross-Channel traffic, for France - and several other European states - was plunged into sudden revolution. The branch finally opened to passengers on 1 January 1849. Passengers got off the trains on the viaduct or Pier at the Harbour, and walked across the swing-bridge to the quays. Rails were extended across the swing-bridge in 1850. The improvement of the South Pier into The Horn allowed use of the Harbour at all stages of the tide, but this was not the case at Boulogne so services still followed a tidal pattern.

The steeply graded branch demanded special locomotive provision. In January 1851 it was reported to the shareholders that Robert Stephenson & Co. were building five locomotives at £1,500 each[9] to work the traffic at Folkestone and Whitstable harbours. The first two engines were delivered to the branch in July and replaced Bury 0-4-0s. The steep gradients also forced the provision of extra coaching stock, with the SER deciding in August 1851 to build more brake carriages for use on the line. However there was an accident at Folkestone Harbour on 20 December 1854 due to a locomotive descending the incline too rapidly.

A Customs House and Baggage room for the Harbour station was suggested in January 1853 for £5,000, but by May 1854 the cost had actually worked out at £7,650. This was provided at the south side of the Harbour, just to the east of the swing bridge; new goods sidings and a warehouse were then opened still further to the east in 1855. In November 1855 *The Times* criticised the SER facilities at Folkestone Harbour. The SER therefore decided to replace the old - and, as usual, "temporary" - passenger station with a new one further along the southern quay.

The SER acquired some unusual properties when it bought the Harbour. One of them was an old gun known as *Mary Rose*; it was sent to the Tower of London in 1851.

Further extensions to the railway facilities were linked with attempts to improve the actual ferry service by providing deeper water berths. Thus in August 1856 the expenditure of £10,000 on extending the South Pier had been discussed and in 1858 the need for a low-water landing stage was also aired. By extending the "Horn" or South Pier, money could be saved on the boats; this was a time when the SER was increasingly aware of the danger of competition from the East Kent Railway, and had taken steps at Dover to run its trains directly onto the Admiralty Pier.

On 21 June 1860 it was estimated that an extended pier would cost £6,638 for about a further 50 feet, but one of the directors, Captain Warren, was worried about "the working expenses and risks on the present Harbour branch." It was also decided to lay in some temporary rails along the Stade, at the north side of the Harbour. It was increasingly common for lightly laid sidings and tramways to be installed in port areas to reduce the problem of transhipment; in July 1861 the Dover Town Clerk authorised a tramway there to the Inner Harbour for the convenience of the Post Office vans.

However, if Folkestone was really to be competitive with the LCDR's Dover route, the method of obtaining rail access to the Harbour station clearly had to be improved. Few real improvements could be made to the branch and substantial progress was made in 1860-1 to make the maritime facilities non-tidal. An entirely new Folkestone Pier, 600 feet long and costing £20,000, was opened on 16 August 1861; although rail tracks reached this, they were used only for wagons with passengers walking from the Harbour station. The best solution for the trains seemed to be an entirely new route and in November 1860 a branch to the Harbour from Cheriton, just to the west of Folkestone, was discussed. This idea was nearly dropped in November 1861, but a Bill was presented for a line from Cheriton, curving under the Foord Viaduct, then descending to the Harbour but it would have ruined the seafront views at The Leas and incurred the hostility of many local gentry and landowners. This was to be the perennial problem that prevented better rail access to the port, for

69. **Folkestone Harbour in 1882, showing the inner harbour, cut off by the SER's viaduct. The Customs House and Station building can also be seen.** (Folkestone Library)

Folkestone had become both a Channel ferry port and a fashionable residential town, and the two functions did not combine comfortably. The key figure was Lord Radnor, the leading local landowner, who commented that the despoiling of the seafront was "too high a price for Folkestone to pay for improved communication with Paris[10]." Another Bill was deposited for the 1863 session; this was thrown out by the House of Commons in February[11].

The development of the Admiralty Pier at Dover, discussed in Chapter Ten, had put the facilities at that port considerably ahead of those at Folkestone though the latter had an advantage in times of bad weather when SER services to the Admiralty Pier were liable to be disrupted. In November 1869 Watkin's attention was attracted to the poverty of covered accomodation at Folkestone, and he advised that something, however small, should be done; "We must show our desire to do something even if we actually do little at present," he wrote to the Board[12]. This was the time when Fowler's International Communication Company scheme for train ferries and a large new dock at Dover was threatening the SER and LCDR duopoly of Channel services.

In May 1870 Hawkshaw was sent to Folkestone to study how facilities could be improved to defeat the Fowler threat. It was a rare example of SER improvements in Kent being motivated by the threat of something other than the LCDR, for Fowler's scheme was a prodigious and prophetic plan. He hoped for "huge floating railway stations, which would traverse at high speed the distance between the English and French coasts." These train ferries were to be 450 feet long and 57 feet wide, with trains loaded onto them by hydraulic hoists[13]. Hawkshaw thought that the train ferries were "undesirable and would be productive of inconvenience", but that they might be useful for goods traffic; he favoured loading them by hoists rather than "inclined plane."

Hawkshaw's solution to the threat of the train ferries was to recommend a new deep water pier at Folkestone on to which the trains could run; it was to be at 90 degrees to the shore, extend 220 feet further than the existing pier, and the tracks would be extended from the Harbour station to a new Quay station alongside the boats.

Fowler's International Communication Bill was withdrawn in July 1870 following the failure of French Government guarantees to materialise; its prospects were then dashed further by the outbreak of the Franco-Prussian War. The SER did not abandon its own improvement plans, but sought financial help from Folkestone Corporation, which refused to assist when the SER refused to open the Harbour to general traffic.

Fowler made a new attempt to win approval for his scheme in 1872 but was opposed by the SER as being "experimental and doubtful." The ICC Bill was rejected by the House of Lords in July 1872.

Hawkshaw's scheme for improvements to the rail facilities was gradually put into effect. A new siding on the Pier for baggage traffic was installed in 1875 and it was decided to enlarge the Harbour station and extend the line on to the new low-water pier at a cost of £8,500. The work included the rebuilding of the viaduct across the Harbour, but it was badly damaged in a storm on 14 November 1875. The new facilities opened on 4 March 1876; rails were extended through the Harbour station to a new platform at the Pier, making a longtitudinal extension of the Harbour station. Perhaps because of this, early references to the new facility as "Folkestone Pier" station failed to gain support and the whole area remained known as Folkestone Harbour.

The new facilities were badly damaged in a gale of 1 January 1877; three piers of the new viaduct were damaged and a number of signals blown down.

Within four years the SER had outgrown its new facilities. On 6 January 1881 the Board discussed the need to enlarge the Harbour; the following month a storm caused £20,000 damage to the Pier. Various options were available, including spending £43,000 on a further extension to the Pier and £150,000 on enlarging the Harbour itself by 130 acres. On 12 October 1881[14] the Prince of Wales laid the first stone for the new works using an ivory mallet. The Pier extension was completed towards the end of 1883 at a cost of about £60,000[15]. From this time, the South Pier lost its importance for passenger traffic.

70. **The swing-bridge and branch line at Folkestone Harbour, showing the point at which trains originally terminated.** (Folkestone Library)

During the time it was improving its property at Folkestone, the SER was also having to fight off attempts by the LCDR to gain access to the town. An attempt was made to gain authorisation for a line from Kearsney to Folkestone via Alkham in 1878 and again in 1884; the defeat of the latter cost the SER £4,000 in legal fees.

In response to these pressures, and also to cope with growing traffic, the SER revived plans to form a new line to the Harbour in January 1883. The SER's Bill for 1884-5 included powers for better access to the Harbour from Cheriton Arch and extension of the Harbour, the latter being opposed as usual by Lord Radnor. Nonetheless, the SER secured an Act for the Cheriton Arch route on 31 July 1885 but then did nothing about it; Watkin seemed to have expended his energies in seeking to extend the Hythe branch into Folkestone or, perhaps, saw no need for the new Harbour branch once LCDR attempts to enter Folkestone had been defeated. Perhaps he was also distracted by his periodic dreams of completely new ports, such as Dungeness and Littlestone-on-Sea. A "Direct Harbour branch" was still being considered in 1889.

In 1890 the SER considered whether Folkestone Harbour should be extended to allow its use as a torpedo station. More mundanely, £176 was spent on a crossing keeper's cottage at Folly Crossing on the Harbour branch in 1891.

In 1892-3[16] the swing-bridge at the Harbour was rebuilt due to the substantial quantity of traffic it was carrying, both freight and passenger.

Powers for the SER to buy land on the Cheriton Arch to Folkestone Harbour route were due to expire on 31 July 1894; on 28 June the SER decided to allow them to lapse. This did not help the confidence of Folkestone in its future prosperity, for there were already fears that a new deep-water harbour at Dover and possible amalgamation of the SER and LCDR could lead to the loss of the ferry traffic. However, early in 1897 the SER decided to extend and widen the Pier. This work was not completed until 1905.

2. The Development of the Channel Services

As early as 1840 the SER directors became aware that it was in their interest to foster rail links on the other side of the Channel. In July 1840 they listened sympathetically to a deputation from the Calais Chamber of Commerce about railways in France and Belgium then, in July 1841, the SER agreed to give £2,000 to help survey an Amiens to Calais line to connect with a Paris and Lille railway.

The agent the SER employed to watch over continental railways was Robert Stephenson, who was active at various stages in 1842. France was lagging behind Belgium, where the port of Ostend had been connected to Brussels in 1838 and by 1843 offered a service through to Cologne.

As soon as the SER had bought Folkestone Harbour it began discussions with a Mr Hayward, a Dover shipowner, about the provision of a steamer service to Boulogne. On 24 June the Board made a trip to Boulogne on board *Water Witch*, hired from Hayward. On 4 July 1843 the Board decided to advertise for steamers to operate a service from Folkestone to Boulogne, Calais and Ostend, spurred on by an offer from the Post Office of £6-10s for each journey made with the Mails.

During July the SER made an agreement with the Commercial Steam Packet Company to operate a service from 1 August using two boats, the *Sir William Wallace* and the *Emerald*. The SER would guarantee £30 per day on a Folkestone to Boulogne service. Special celebrations were held at Folkestone to inaugurate the new service, with *Sir William Wallace* steaming into the Harbour amidst the firing of cannon. Later the same day the *City of Boulogne* also arrived to help with the service, increasing the number of boats to three. A Mr Faulkner was appointed Harbour Master and was responsible for the ships; he was paid £200 per year.

The new service did not run smoothly. There were problems with loading and unloading at the Harbour; in August a Mr Prior won 1,093 francs damages from the SER "for damage to his carriage etcetera by immersion in the water at Folkestone Harbour." The *Sir William Wallace* soon proved inadequate and *Ramsgate Packet* was chartered as a replacement, but the SER disliked it as it was too small; *City of Boulogne* soon damaged a paddle while *Emerald* was damaged in gales. However, the SER was interested in using Mr Hayward's new iron steamers for services to Ostend.

Rail connections at the French side were making only slow progress due to rivalry between Calais and Boulogne. Cubitt was involved with a Boulogne to Amiens line and Stephenson with one serving Calais.

In December 1843 the SER began to form links with the Belgian Government which from the start pursued a very thorough and organised transport policy. With such direct offers being made, the SER became increasingly dissatisfied with the feeble efforts of the CSP Company to maintain a service; things were not helped when the *Sir William Wallace* broke down mid-Channel in January 1844 while carrying Princess Alice. Therefore, on 30 January 1844, the SER decided to order two iron steamers from Ditchburn & Mare. However it could not remove the CSP Company from the service since the SER was contracted to provide a Mail service using down trains from London at 1.30am and 8.30pm. It therefore hired *Water Witch* and the *Royal George* from Hayward and the CSP Company withdrew from 23 February; Hayward carried on operating a service from Folkestone, to the annoyance of Dover tradesmen, who arranged for the General Steam Navigation Company to begin a Dover-Boulogne service from May 1844. Hayward's vessels were hardly up to the task demanded of them; "the diminutive size of the *Royal George* has caused a considerable deal of mirth," the *Maidstone Journal* recorded[17].

Thus the SER had learnt that reliance on others weakened its control over the quality of the service and in August 1844 it decided to form the South Eastern & Continental Steam Packet Company. To help with services while the two Ditchburn & Mare steamers, *Princess Maude* (1844, 177 tons) and *Princess Mary* (1844, 294 tons), were being constructed, the *Orion* was hired for six months at £52-10s a week; it soon proved unsatisfactory too. In October it was decided to buy a third boat from Ditchburn & Mare at £12,572; this became the *Queen of the Belgians* (1844, 207 tons).

The Boulogne & Amiens Railway was becoming a continental branch of the SER; by July 1844 it shared a secretary and three directors, as well as an engineer, with the SER. During that month the SER agreed a Mails contract with the Belgian Government and on 28 July the *Orion* made the first run from Dover to Ostend; the French Mails were carried from Dover to Calais by the Admiralty and then, from 1854, by the firm of Jenkins & Churchward, but both sets of Mails were carried by SER trains. The Belgian Mails boat sailed at night and took five hours.

The SER's service was designed to reflect seasonal variations in traffic; night boats were provided on the Folkestone to Boulogne route for the summer of 1844 but were withdrawn from 30 September.

The first of the SER's own steamers, the *Princess Mary*, was delivered in September 1844. Since she was to be used for the Belgium Mails, the SER objected to her having to pay the Harbour dues at Dover. This is one indication of why the SER preferred Folkestone - since it owned the port, it had no dues to pay. Control of the Steam Packet Company was protected by a clause that limited its shareholders to those who held shares in the SER itself.

The success of Folkestone was rapid. Of 75,790 passengers who embarked at Boulogne in 1844, 33,088 travelled via Folkestone and only 15,780 via Dover; 1,189 used Ramsgate and the remainder went directly to London[18].

By September 1845 the Steam Packet Company had five boats in operation, having that year added the *Queen of the French* (207 tons) and the *Prince Ernest* (272 tons); the latter was used on the Dover to Boulogne service for the winter months. During the summer, *Water Witch* had been hired to help with peak traffic.

An attempt to start a service from Ramsgate to Ostend after the SER had opened to the former in 1846 did not prove a success. The winter service in particular lost money and it was stopped in October 1847, with all Ostend services concentrating on Dover. The fleet was expanded by the addition that year of *Princess Helena* (267 tons) and *Princess Clementine* (307 tons); *Lord Warden* (307 tons) was added the following year to bring the total to eight. *Herapath's Railway Magazine* put the cost of the fleet at £99,406.

The SER made early attempts to develop continental excursion traffic. On 26 June 1845 it decided to run a half fare excursion to Boulogne, outward on 12 July and returning two days later. For Whitsun 1847 it offered London to Boulogne excursions at £1-11-6d first class and 16s-3d third class; Ostend excursions were £2-2-0d first class.

71. The Mary Beatrice leaving Folkestone Harbour. (R.W.Kidner Collection)

The SER Board was disappointed by the slow progress of railways in France. The Amiens & Boulogne Railway opened only as far as Abbeville on March 1847 and did not open to Boulogne until 17 April 1848[19]. The opening of the Nord's route to Calais via Lille was expected by the *Railway Times* in August 1848 but did not occur until 2 September; the first Calais station was remote from the port, but a Marine station opened in 1849. Some of the SER Board felt that the Boulogne & Amiens may have been influenced by the London & South Western Railway, who were operating a rival cross-Channel service via Le Havre; there was a row when some of the SER directors who also sat on the B&A Board were accused of failing to keep a proper watch over events, and Captain Tyndale resigned from the SER in September 1847.

The opening of the railway to Calais may have encouraged the SER to begin using Dover as a port again from 1 November 1848. Prior to that, it had run trains in connection with the ferries and mail sailings operated by others, but had used Folkestone for all its own sailings. This created a feeling of mistrust towards the SER amidst the Dover tradesmen - a contributory factor in the rise of the LCDR.

At both Dover and Folkestone large hotels existed to serve the passengers; the Dover hotel, The Lord Warden, was often used for famous travellers such as the King of France, Louis Philippe, in 1844. Not everyone appreciated it however; a letter to the *Evening Mail* in July 1848 complained that passengers were not allowed on to the boats at Dover when their trains arrived so that they were forced to spend money at the hotel.

The Boulogne route began to achieve superiority over the Calais one. From 1 April to 31 July 1846 14,991 used it, but in the same period the following year the traffic rose to 18,103. By this time the SE&CSP Company was operating two services each day even in winter, with the fastest taking about 1hr 45mins. In January 1849 it was agreed to put on a daily Folkestone to Calais service to connect with the trains of the Nord; the SER guaranteed a "reasonable" return to its own offspring company, with the Nord contributing £8 a day. From August 1850 the SER contributed £10 and the Nord £5 a day for a twice daily service to Calais all year round.

In June 1850 the Belgian Government renewed its interest in a service from Ostend to Ramsgate. The SER offered to run a 6.30am train in connection with this if there were two sailings a week. From 1 October the Belgian steamers were replaced by SE&CSP ones to Ramsgate and Margate; there were four steamers a week on this route, but one every night from Dover at the same time.

There was thus a good deal of fluctuation in the level of services offered across the Channel and even in the ports used. Both the two French and two main English ports were very comparable in their facilities, and the level of service often depended on the subsidy from railway companies - the SER paying for all routes, with contributions from the two French companies for Calais or Boulogne. The situation was simplified from 1 July 1851 when the Boulogne & Amiens was absorbed by the Nord, after which it increasingly favoured Boulogne as offering a shorter London to Paris transit time; this was to the detriment of Dover as well.

In 1853 the SER absorbed the SE&CSP Company, paying £99,406 for its eight steamers. An Act for this was passed on 4 August after opposition by the Steamship Owners' Association, though the Belgian Government approached the SER with an offer to sell its own ships. The number of passengers at this time averaged 473 per day[20].

During December 1854 the SER considered using its new fleet to operate a cross-Channel service from Rye to Normandy. More realistic was the need to handle the growing goods traffic across the Channel; a boat to carry 120 tons on the Folkestone to Boulogne run was chartered in April 1855 and three months later two goods boats were ordered at £14,000 each.

Following criticism in *The Times* during November 1855 of arrangements at Folkestone, the SER decided to sack the Harbour Master, Captain Hathorn, and appointed Captain Boxer as Harbour Master and Superintendent of the Fleet on an annual salary of £300 and a house. The Harbour facilities were plainly inadequate for the heavy traffic generated by the Crimean War, which was forwarded via Marseilles, and the Paris Exhibition of 1856. In addition, *The Times* publicised the evils of "touting" by baggage agents at Folkestone. It was also unsatisfactory that the principal boat expresses ran according to the state of the tide and not to the needs of the market. All these factors contributed to a desire to provide deep water and commodious facilities at Folkestone.

But the SER was not free to do as it pleased, as was clear when the Nord pointed out that it would prefer the Dover & Continental Steam Packet Company to replace the SER on the Dover to Calais run. Boulogne harbour was also inadequate for a fixed timetable service, whatever the SER did at Folkestone.

In 1857 discussions began of a link between the old Boulogne & Amiens Railway at Boulogne and the Nord line at Calais. At first the Nord planned this to pass four miles to the east of Boulogne, but the SER argued in November 1857 for a line passing right through Boulogne itself. This route was eventually adopted, but it took until 1 January 1867 for the line to open.

Problems were encountered with Captain Jenkins of the *Prince Ernest*. In July 1857 he was reported as having been drunk on duty, but the Board voted 6-4 not to sack him. A year later he was in command of the *Princess Helena* when it collided with the harbour entrance at Folkestone and lost its figurehead. Yet still Jenkins retained his position. *Prince Ernest* was involved in a collision with the cutter *Cloud* off the South Foreland in December 1859; the SER had to pay £50 compensation to its owners.

In October 1860 it was decided to operate the tidal service, which would have been an additional summer-only train when the Folkestone works had been completed, as an all year service. It was decided to support this growth with two new steamers ordered from Samuda and Samuelson. However in December 1860 the unprofitability of the Dover to Calais service was discussed; this led to a Boardroom row when the Chairman ordered the removal of the service without the permission of the Board.

A new Folkestone-Boulogne night service began in May 1861 and in July negotiations with the Nord produced a solution to the Dover-Calais problem: there was to be a fixed evening service in place of the second tidal service via Folkestone and Boulogne. It would take parcels too, and would leave London at 4.30pm.

The new deep water pier at Folkestone opened on 16 August, before the new and larger vessels which it was planned to accomodate were ready. *Victoria* arrived in September, and soon recorded a Folkestone to Boulogne time of 1hr 34mins; she came close to disaster in September 1864 when she struck part of a wreck in heavy seas, limping into Dover. *Eugenie*, named after the French empress, was tested on the River Humber on 21 November; she failed to achieve the specified 16 knots, had a draught greater than was intended and the boiler pressure was considered to be too high by the SER. After modifications she arrived on station for the Folkestone to Boulogne run on 12 March and was formally accepted in April 1862, allowing *Princess Maude* to be hired to the Belgian Government at £250 per month. A third new ship, *Albert Edward*, was bought from Samuda on an improved version of the *Victoria* design; in August 1862 it achieved 16.7 knots and was claimed to be the fastest vessel afloat.

Eugenie became controversial. She was returned to Samuelson in December 1862 for enlarged boilers and in March 1863 was sold to Saul Isaac of Cunards for £18,233 although she had only cost the SER £16,600. The reason for this was that the American Civil War had put a premium on any ship capable of running a blockade and Cunards had acted as intermediaries for the Confederate Government in acquiring *Eugenie* for such a purpose. The *Railway Times* later published an allegation by John Hamilton, a rebellious SER shareholder, that there was"an ugly looking discrepancy" in the SER accounts over the sale of the ship, forcing Samuel Smiles to sue; Hamilton argued that the actual sale had been for £23,500 and that Smiles and Eborall had profited from the affair.

In November 1863 the SER decided to replace the *Eugenie* with another Samuda product for £21,500. She was delivered in 1864 and named *Alexandra*, with the *Queen of the French* being sold to the Belgians for £9,500 and the *Princess Clementine* being converted into a cargo boat.

This period of hectic activity, spurred on by competition from the LCDR, continued into April 1865 when increasing traffic via Folkestone and Boulogne encouraged the restoration of the *Lord Warden* to service although *Princess Maude* was also converted to goods service. In June it was agreed that another vessel should be ordered from Samuda for £19,500; this was the *Napoleon III*.

The LCDR began operating its own cross-Channel service on 1 July 1862, having bought up the fleet of Jenkins & Churchward who had taken over the Mails operation from the Admiralty. Talks between the SER and LCDR to prevent "undue competition" began in January 1863. Heads of Agreement were drawn up to cover the pooling of receipts from 1 February; the receipts were to be divided on a sliding scale, with the SER getting 68% and the LCDR 32% in 1863, with parity being achieved in 1872. The Agreement was to cover all traffic originating within six miles of Charing Cross and using Channel ports between Margate and Hastings. Discussions included the proposed working of a LCDR continental service from Ramsgate as a joint venture. The Continental Agreement was not formally agreed until 7 September 1865, with effect from 22 September, but it affected relationships earlier than that. For example, in June 1863 it was agreed to operate the Calais Mails contract jointly and this began on 20 June.

Perhaps the SER would not have been so keen to conclude the Agreement had it known that the LCDR would go bankrupt in 1866. It was a year in which the Government announced major improvements at Dover, including a 7,150 foot eastern arm to the harbour and an extension to the Admiralty Pier on to which both SER and LCDR trains ran. Plans were announced by other bodies for improvements to the harbour at Calais and for a new harbour in France at Ambleteuse; Captain Boxer was unimpressed with the latter. During the summer of 1866 traffic was hit badly by a cholera scare and the Austro-Prussian War, but the SER directors felt confident enough to hire one of their own vessels for the Spithead Naval Review - at a cost of £5 each.

The visit of the Sultan of Turkey in 1868 brought extra traffic worth £1,000 and the Paris Exhibition generated an estimated 33,563 extra passengers via Folkestone. However the Boulogne to Calais railway gradually produced a reduction in Folkestone's popularity after its opening for continental traffic on 2 April 1867.

One of the problems for the SER was that at Boulogne, the natural partner of Folkestone, the trains did not run onto the quays alongside the ships as they did at Calais. In May 1869 it made clear its position - it wanted the ferry berths on the west side of the harbour, not the east, and if the accomodation was not improved it would transfer all services to Calais. The new Quai Bonaparte would have direct rail links and would get rid of the hated buses, but the SER was impatient for improvement and the Nord supported it. Time passed by though, and only in March 1870 did the Nord agree to build the rail extension

72. Crossing the Channel on a SER steamer in the 1880s with ferries attempting to enter the Harbour at Boulogne. This picture shows graphically why the SER sought to provide larger vessels on what was a short but often stormy passage.

to the Quai. However, within two months the Nord and the SER had fallen out over the former's talks with Fowler's train ferry company and a stern letter was sent to the Nord's chairman, Baron de Rothschild.

The SER was also interested in improving the ships. The *Albert Edward* had been a great success, although on 11 June 1869 it hit the rocks off The Horn at Folkestone, when approaching the new Pier "at an unusual speed"; Captain Goodburn was suspended for 12 days, damage being "only a graze." The shipbuilding partnership of Samuda & Penn suggested the fitting of a "hurricane deck" on the SER's ships like *Albert Edward* and *Victoria*; new ships, they said, should have a bow and rudder at each end to avoid turning. Captain Boxer, though, disliked these ideas.

However all thoughts of improvements were thrown into chaos when war broke out between France and Prussia in 1870. By August the SER was taking medical supplies and nurses free to Boulogne, but then there were sensational accusations that the SER was transporting "contraband of war". Suspicious cases were opened by Home Office officials and found to contain...Bibles! However, one man was fined £65 for sending cartridges and revolvers to France without declaring them. Altogether the SER carried 6,959 free packages, but the passenger traffic was badly hit as the Siege of Paris continued into 1871 - to be followed by the bloody scenes as Thiers' government suppressed the Paris

Commune. The tenant of the Pavilion Hotel complained of heavy losses due to the War. Continental traffic on the SER in 1870 was down £19,632.

At the time of the collapse of Napoleon III's government in 1870, many members of his family were forced to seek exile in England. Whilst landing at Dover, they passed members of the Orleanist royal family returning to France after their own period of exile. The Lord Warden Hotel became the scene of many such poignant encounters.

The tidal passenger service did not restart until 15 July 1871 and it was found that the Nord had lost a third of its passenger stock, so the SER lent 20 carriages. The Nord lost some carriages through the fighting, but much of its stock was "conveyed away to quiet nooks in Germany, from which their French friends feared it would be difficult to find it[21]." An unusual result of the War was that it created a new trade in vegetables, for the farmers of northern France sent their produce to London instead of Paris which was first besieged by the Prussians and then affected by the events of the Commune.

The SER was concerned that it did poorly out of the cross-Channel traffic in bonded goods due to a lack of its own bonded warehouse at Folkestone or in the City. Bonded goods forwarded from Boulogne or Calais direct to London by sea included £24,693 of wine from Calais and £38,152 from Boulogne. Tea, coffee, chocolate, dried fruit and a very substantial amount of sugar went this way, leaving the SER with only 47,406 cases of alcohol. Sadly it concluded that a bonded warehouse in the City would be too expensive.

Rumours circulated about new Channel ports, including the use of a route from Hastings to Le Treport in December 1870. There was also talk of a new port at Andresselles in France, which the Nord gave in 1872 as one of its excuses for failing to complete the line to the Quai Bonaparte promised in 1869. But the

73. A plan of the train ferry scheme of 1872, showing the SER facilities at Dover in the early 1870s, with the Archcliffe Fort dominating the station.

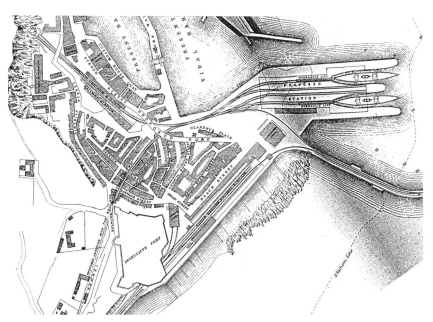

SER's aim was a London to Paris service in only eight hours, which needed quick connections at both ports but should prevent rival schemes like Fowler's achieving success. By August 1872 the SER was pleased to learn that rails were at last being laid on the Quai.

With improvements being made at Folkestone and Boulogne, the SER looked at its ships again. In July 1872 covered decks were fitted to *Albert Edward* for £2,000 and the following month Captain Dicey showed Boxer his novel model of a ferry. It was:

"A raft supported by two halves of a ship connected together by iron girders and an arched tunnel, in which the two propelling wheels are placed."

It was, in fact, a catamaran; there was a brief fashion for such ships in the 1870s, but the SER complained that no dock was big enough for Dicer's version.

The SER and LCDR learnt the perils of falling out with each other in September 1872 when they each tried to bid for the French Mails contract; the result was that a third party, Delahaute, won it. They agreed to make a joint bid in future.

On 1 April 1873 the cargo boat, *Queen of the Belgians*, ran aground off New Romney in fog. There was a fierce dispute over whether the compass had been defective, with the crew alleging it was and the coastguard denying this after an inspection. It would seem that the compass was in fact deflected by iron in the cargo. The Captain, Mortlemann, resigned but was reinstated; the chief mate and second mate were sacked. Boxer was warned about discipline and told that ships should be inspected before each voyage.

The saga of Boulogne continued. So impatient were both the SER and LCDR that in October 1872 they suggested their own £300,000 scheme to improve the harbour there but by May 1873 the Nord had still not provided for passenger trains to run onto the Quai, suggesting instead that as a temporary solution the luggage vans alone should run up to the ships on the rails. Concern over the rival route of Newhaven and Dieppe, together with the interest of the French Government, eventually encouraged a £500,000 scheme for major improvements including a rail connection between the Quai and the Nord. Growth of Dieppe seems to have been at the expense of Boulogne:

Passengers Embarking at French Ports

	Calais	Boulogne	Dieppe
1869	157,360	114,423	50,992
1873	181,970	103,996	52,551
1874	199,356	105,517	56,265

This dilatory saga continued until 15 October 1875, when passenger trains began to use the Quai - but the Nord promptly withdrew the tidal service from using it on 1 November since with only one track it could not handle a complete service. After all the trouble, the buildings there burnt down in January 1876. During this period the SER was not entirely committed to Boulogne, for in October 1874 it examined the possibility of using Le Treport as a ferry port.

The 1870s were not a good time for the SER's continental services. When the Shah of Persia came to England in July 1873 his train had to be stopped due to a hot axle box on the royal saloon. The following month *Princess Maude*, *Albert Edward* and *Victoria* all suffered mishaps. Perhaps fearing the worst, *Princess Mary* escaped by being sold off for £750 that August. Worse did come, in the shape of a strike at Folkestone on 26 August which started on the *Princess Maude*. Boxer reported that its crew had been "severely worked", but the crew were all given two weeks' notice, including an old shipmate of Boxer's. The Harbour Master lamented that "...it is hard, very hard, to deal with him, but example must be made..."

During 1874 two more of the SER's fleet ran into problems. The *Queen of the Belgians* collided with an Italian barque at Dover in March and on 25 May the goods boat, *Clementine*, ran into even more severe problems. During foggy weather it ran aground on rocks off Lydden Point and heeled over at a point very close to the cliff. Fortunately it was refloated and struggled into harbour with 13 passengers on board. *Clementine* was the fastest of the goods boats and its captain was not used to the speed. On 24 August *Queen of the Belgians* was involved in another collision, this time at Boulogne; Captain Robinson was reported as sacked in the Minutes, but two weeks later seems to have been reinstated. In November *Clementine* returned to harbour with an unusual trophy; it was struck in mid-Channel by a foreign brig, which promptly disappeared into the mist leaving its figurehead on board the SER vessel.

The Continental Agreement with the LCDR had survived its initial stages but the SER was horrified to learn, by reading about it in a newspaper, that the LCDR was to start an entirely new service from Sheerness to Flushing on 26 July 1875. John Shaw, the SER secretary, was sent to test it out on the first day and reported that the route offered a far cheaper journey to Cologne than via Ostend. This service was in fact suspended from 14 November to 15 May 1876, and then restarted from Queenborough. It caused considerable fury in SER circles for the LCDR did not have to pay receipts from it into the pool for the other continental traffic. SER research in September 1876 suggested an average of 53 passengers used each voyage, on the basis of which a claim was made for a share of the revenues in July 1877.

By September 1879 the SER calculated that it had lost £20,727 through the Queenborough to Flushing service, but the LCDR was unrepentant. Forbes argued, quite correctly, that Queenborough had not been included in the Continental Agreement drafted by Eborall. SER claims had risen to £99,400 by August 1884, during which period it had tried to avoid the restrictions of the Continental Agreement by using Shorncliffe as a station for Folkestone ferry passengers. In December 1884 the LCDR began an action to have the receipts from Shorncliffe paid into the continental pool, and this culminated in a Judgment of 16 November 1887 - Shorncliffe and Radnor Park receipts were to be paid into the fund, Queenborough was excluded. This was a bitter blow for the SER, since it was also forced to pay £45,000 to the LCDR as the reputed earnings of Shorncliffe and Radnor Park from continental traffic. When interest was added, the award came to £51,735; the SER disputed the amount of interest, but lost the case again in 1890.

From 1 April 1877 the SER made a few improvements in its own boat train services, in addition to the opening of the new Folkestone Harbour station a few weeks earlier. A new Marine station also opened at Boulogne that year but there was still insufficient depth of water there to operate a reliable non-tidal service. From 1 April the SER's Ostend boat train joined its Calais train in running onto the Admiralty Pier at Dover, for which the SER paid an extra £77 per year. The Admiralty installed a refreshment room on the Pier in 1878. The tidal trains were accelerated from the same date by omitting the Tonbridge stop.

In 1878 a new cargo ship, the *Folkestone*, was delivered from Earle for £12,500; it was a screw steamer of 420 tons and a sister ship, the *Boulogne*, was launched later the same year. These new deliveries enabled the *Princess Maude* to be sold for £1,100. During 1879 and 1880 it was decided to order three new passenger ships: two from Samuda & Penn were estimated to cost a total of £77,500 while a third, from Thomson, was costed at £35,500. The two Samuda vessels became *Albert Victor* and *Louise Dagmar*, the Thomson one was named *Duchess of Edinburgh*. *Albert Victor* soon damaged some cylinders, while the *Duchess* was returned to Thomson after a number of minor accidents and problems.

The *Duchess of Edinburgh* then became embroiled in a legal battle. Its draught was six inches more than stipulated, it was difficult to navigate in bad weather, and its speed had to be reduced to 15.5 knots due to problems with the paddles. The SER wanted to reject it altogether, but Thomson, a Deptford shipbuilder, fought the case in the courts. It ended in October 1884 with the SER having to pay £4,300 - it reckoned its losses from the affair at £10,269 altogether. The errant vessel was renamed *Manx Queen*, bought by the Midland Railway in 1905 and was scrapped in 1908.

On 1 October 1881 the Nord took over the branch railway from Abbancourt to Le Treport. This raised the possibility of using Le Treport as a rival for the Dieppe route, but the idea attracted little long-term support.

On 18 April 1882 there were many rumours that the *Albert Edward* had been lost at sea with 144 passengers. It had failed to arrive at Folkestone after breaking down in mid-Channel. However it eventually reached the safety of Dover.

On 15 June 1882 the *Mary Beatrice* was launched as a replacement for the disgraced *Duchess of Edinburgh* and a new cargo boat, the *C.W.Eborall*, was launched the same year. In 1884 the last of the eight ships acquired in 1853 were disposed of - *Clementine* and *Prince Ernest* for £800, and *Queen of the Belgians* for £500. In May 1885 the SER asked the Admiralty if it wished to arm the three fastest SER steamers, but the Admiralty declined the offer. Other additions to the fleet included a new cargo boat in 1886 named *Achille Adam*, after an official of the Nord; this cost £11,200 from Samuda and after an unspectacular career was a victim of hostilities in 1917. The *Jubilee*, a powered lifeboat for Folkestone, was built in 1887.

The SER was unable to offer the same fixed time services as the LCDR until the deep water berths at Boulogne opened in 1885. Following these various harbour improvements and the building of new ships, a new fixed service began operating on 15 April 1885. This left Charing Cross at 9.45am, with a Paris arrival at 6.25pm. For the summer, three fixed services were offered, the first of which ran from Charing Cross at 8am to Paris for 5.41pm via Dover and Calais. The 9.40am service via Folkestone and Boulogne was appreciably faster, reaching Paris at 5.57pm. The 11am from Charing Cross also ran via Dover, reaching Paris at 7.45pm. In October 1886 the SER was alarmed to find that the LCDR was promoting a twice weekly service to the French Riviera and thus capturing some lucrative traffic; it was a sign of changing leisure habits among the wealthy.

In 1886 the Belgian Government brought pressure to bear for three services a day on the Ostend route. This led to tension with the LCDR, made more complex when two of the Belgian steamers broke down and the Belgian Government asked to hire *Albert Edward* and *Victoria* from the SER. According to the *Railway Times*, the SER had been afraid that the Belgian service would be lost to the Great Eastern at Harwich, but that the situation was saved by a meeting between Fenton and the Belgian King.

Although the 1880s were not the heyday of smuggling, there was still quite a bit of it on a small scale. In October 1886 brandy was found hidden among the coal on locomotive no.152 and it was chained to the rails by the Customs until the situation could be resolved[22]. In April 1889 the notorious French "revolutionary", General Boulanger, travelled from Ostend to London and was given a special train by the SER - probably as a result of Watkin's influence, but to the annoyance of many shareholders. Boulanger, however, lacked the commitment to be a real revolutionary and ended his life by committing suicide on the grave of his mistress.

On 29 March 1889 the Belgian ferry, *Comtesse de Flandre*, collided with *Princess Henriette* which was on a Dover to Ostend run. In dense fog off Dunkirk, the two ships both attempted to avoid collision with a fishing smack with the result that the *Comtesse de Flandre* struck the *Princess Henriette* in the middle of the starboard side. The latter was cut almost in two, and the inrush of water caused its boilers to explode with the consequent loss of 15 lives. Prince Jerome Bonaparte, one of the passengers, survived but his valet died; the Prince himself died in the Zulu Wars a few years later. The Captain of the *Princess Henriette* was among the dead.

Alexandra and *Napoleon III* were sold for scrap in 1890 and two small boats for the Sheerness-Port Victoria service, the *Myleta* and *Edward William*, added in 1891. By 1892 the SER fleet contained twelve vessels, including the lifeboat *Jubilee*, but this number was reduced on 7 March 1893 when *Albert Edward* ran aground off Cape Gris Nez and was "a total wreck." It was replaced by the *Duchess of York*, built in 1895, which suffered a boiler explosion on 4 November 1897 but continued in service until it was scrapped in 1904. The *Princess of Wales* was built by Laird and began trials in October 1898; at 1,366 tons, it was by far the largest of the SER ships at the time, and was sold to the Argentine in 1910[23].

Another major Paris Exhibition in 1889 coincided with the improvement of Calais Harbour, but the SER felt that its attempts to capture the Exhibition traffic by running premium services were a disaster - it made a net loss on the operation. Both the SER and the LCDR ran *Club Trains*, which competed for the wealthier travellers. The LCDR wanted to abandon the service in 1893 when it found that passengers were between 6 and 43 on outward services, and 2 and 23 coming back; in comparison, SER figures were 5-51 and 3-27.

With fares 16s above normal first class, not even luxurious *Wagons Lits* carriages on the French run could tempt many to use the service but the French Government was anxious for it to continue. However, the *Club Trains* ceased running at the end of September 1893 since the Nord refused to share in the loss made on the services.

Relations between the English companies and the Nord were not good at this time. The Nord felt that the profits on the maritime service were being made by the English companies only, and in April 1893 declared that it wanted a joint fleet. Certainly the French were in an inferior position to the Belgians, who had their own ships for the Ostend run including the *Leopold II*, said to be the fastest paddle-steamer in the world at 22 knots. By July 1893 the Nord was even suggesting that it might set up its own fleet, causing joint discussions between the SER and LCDR with the lateness of current services being blamed on the

Nord. The *Railway Times* viewed the whole issue calmly, reckoning that the operation of boats was always "a dead loss"[24]. From 1896 the French Mails were carried by the Nord using ships chartered from the LCDR until their own two vessels were put into service in 1898.

While these discussions were continuing, the SER was looking at ways of getting around the restrictions of the Continental Agreement after its defeat in the Shorncliffe Judgment. In January 1892 Watkin had visited Littlestone-on-Sea in his special train and in October 1893 there were rumours of an agreement with the Nord to operate a Dungeness to Le Treport service. Fortunately these follies were eclipsed by the improved relations between the SER and LCDR in the mid-1890s.

The improved relationship did not please everyone. Folkestone was worried that the fusion of the two companies would lead to all daytime shipping services being transferred to Dover; on 26 January 1895 the *Railway Times* reported the fears that Folkestone would be left with only a single night boat in competition with the LBSCR's Newhaven service. The Newhaven service had improved with more regular services being introduced in 1889 and an express service via Newhaven and Caen in 1894. Folkestone was further worried by the SER's use of the Dover and Calais route for its 9am Charing Cross to Paris service from 1 July 1895. From the same date it also provided a thrice weekly service to Carlsbad for the summer season. Fears in Folkestone were partially eased when it was announced that a new afternoon Paris service would commence on 1 June 1897 via Folkestone, with the GWR providing a connection from Birmingham.

In October 1898, with the start of the South Eastern & Chatham Railways Managing Committee approaching, the two companies met to discuss their shipping stock. Of the SER boats, it was decided to keep the *Princess of Wales*, the *Duchess of York*, the *C.W.Eborall*, the *Folkestone* and the *Achille Adam*. Other vessels were sold off or scrapped. At the time the *Mabel Grace* was under construction; launched in 1899 at 1,215 tons, this was the last paddle steamer for the route and was sold in 1909.

It is clear that the SER built up the position of Folkestone as a Channel port because of its ownership, but by the 1880s Dover had better facilities in most ways. The town of Folkestone was probably right to fear the arrival of a joint SE&CR, though eventually it was the continued growth of traffic that ensured that both ports survived as ferry terminals.

Channel Traffic By Routes:

	Dov-Ost	Dov-Cal	Folk-Boul	Newhaven-Dieppe
1850		54,036	82,016	
1860	5,449	76,318	96,652	36,899
1869	18,125	157,360	114,423	50,992
1879	25,566	181,015	117,069	66,824
1887	43,079	235,695	116,657	72,591

3. The Channel Tunnel

A tunnel across the English Channel was first proposed seriously in 1802 by a French engineer, Albert Mathieu, during the temporary peace established at Amiens that year. Mathieu intended two tunnels, one each from England and

74. Hector Horeau's plan for a Channel Tunnel, from an illustration of 1851.

France, meeting at an artificial island on the Varne Bank. Mathieu found few supporters, but the idea had caught on and the following year Tessier de Mottray suggested a steel tube be laid across the sea-bed.

Thome de Gamond, a French engineer, began a hydrographic study of the Channel in 1833 and was captivated by the idea of a permanent crossing. In 1834 he suggested a tunnel, but in 1836 decided that a bridge would be better. The cost was a barrier to both.

In October 1850 SER director Martin Pritchard told the rest of the Board of his interest in a Dover to Calais bridge. In November 1851 the SER heard of a plan for a "submarine railway". Presumably this fanciful effort was the work of Prosper Payerne, a developer of diving bells. In 1852 he proposed using his diving bells to enable workmen to build a tunnel of prefabricated sections on the sea-bed. This was estimated to cost £87.4m and promised "to do away with the pleasures of a sea voyage by a fearful mode of transit[25]." De Gamond re-emerged in 1856 and managed to interest the Emperor, Napoleon III, in his new tunnel scheme. This included a plan for a new international port at Varne Bank and rail connections at the Dover end and at Marquise in France. After a period of enthusiasm, the scheme was killed by one of the periodic frosts that affected Anglo-French relations.

The late 1850s saw a positive "Mania" of Channel schemes, including James Wylson's tube of 1855, a £30million "Marine viaduct" planned by James Boyd in 1858 and Hector Horeau's submerged tube of 1860 - the latter described as having enchanting turrets and tents festooned across the Channel.

William Low, a mining engineer, developed his own plan in 1865 before teaming up with de Gamond and the designer of the Mersey tunnel, Brunlees. The scheme now made rapid progress and, by 1869, was winning useful political support until the outbreak of the Franco-Prussian War in 1870.

In all of this the SER played only a low-key role, rarely even discussing the issue at Board meetings. On 13 May 1869 it noted the receipt of a letter from the Submarine Tunnel Railway, reflecting the gathering interest of John Hawkshaw, the engineer responsible for much SER work and who had been interested in the Channel since at least 1865, in the idea. Hawkshaw favoured a double-track railway tunnel on a slightly different route to the Low one. Significantly, when the SER looked at the question of introducing train ferries in April 1870, Hawkshaw advised that they would be "undesirable and... productive of inconvenience"[26]. The issue was also studied that year by Thomas Brassey and an engineer from the French Ouest company, Blount; they concluded that a tunnel would take between seven and ten years to construct and would yield a return of only 2%. The de Gamond scheme got as far as a Bill but it was withdrawn in July 1870 due to the lack of assurances about finance from the French Government.

A new Channel Tunnel Company was formed in 1872. The force behind it was Hawkshaw, who said that it could be built in ten years at a cost of £10million. The contractor, Wythes, was also interested as well as Lord Richard Grosvenor and the SER became closely involved. In February 1872 it offered a £250 contribution towards the cost of trial drillings and a drift mine providing Byng and Eborall were added to its Board. At the same time the SER opposed a scheme by Fowler and Boxer to start running train ferries across the Channel. On 31 December 1873 the SER Board discussed an invitation for Watkin to join the Board of the Channel Tunnel concern. Hawkshaw planned to start from St Margaret's Bay and to use a single-bore tunnel of 21 feet diameter.

By April 1874 the SER and the LCDR were both making contributions to the construction of an experimental driftway. Watkin felt that the scheme was practicable but needed the respective Governments to guarantee the capital; he promised to use his political influence to raise the matter with Gladstone[27], but the Liberals lost the subsequent election. On 10 September the SER Board voted 4-3 not to pursue an interest in the Tunnel but about £100,000 was needed to support trial workings and that autumn a Bill was deposited to acquire land at St Margaret's Bay in preparation for the work.

A French Channel Tunnel company was formed on 1 February 1875 under the guidance of Michel Chevalier. The SER had heard, in February, that the French company had received a subsidy of £80,000 and on 11 March it discussed its views on the issue once again. Queen Victoria was less enamoured of the idea, writing to Disraeli in February that she found the Tunnel "very objectionable." Again there was some division, but it was decided to recommend to the shareholders that £20,000 should be disbursed to the Channel Tunnel company according to powers in the SER's 1874 Act. On 15 July the SER took note of a rumour that the Midland Railway was interested in the Tunnel and on 12 August lent its steamer, *Princess Maude,* to the Channel Tunnel company to help with soundings.

Acts authorising works by both the French and British companies were passed on 2 August 1875; the British end allowed acquisition of land and the start of trial works at St Margaret's Bay. Hawkshaw hoped to be able to build his tunnel between there and Sangatte, where trials had already begun. Then however, the company encountered the greatest problem of all - it could not raise sufficient capital to begin its works.

With the failure of Hawkshaw's scheme his rival, Low (de Gamond died in 1876), saw a possibility to revive his own plan. He approached Watkin with the scheme; this was a wise move, for though Watkin did not always excel at day-to-day management, it was the sort of epic scheme to which he would devote enormous energy. In June 1880 the SER considered constructing an experimental tunnel, seven feet in diameter, under the sea near Folkestone; they expected to bore a tunnel one mile long for about £3 per yard. Watkin secured powers in the SER's 1881 Act to acquire land at Abbotts Cliff and Shakespeare Cliff, between Dover and Folkestone, for trial works. By June 1881 a gallery 900 yards long had already been constructed at Abbotts Cliff but debate about the military wisdom of it had already begun[28].

To support the new project, Watkin created the Submarine Continental Railway Company, with a capital of £250,000 authorised in 1881. Both Watkin and Mellor had 1,000 shares in it. He feared that the St Margaret's Bay scheme might become too close to the LCDR under Grosvenor's leadership. By 1 September there was a 153 feet deep shaft at Shakespeare Cliff and Watkin said of the Tunnel that, "There is no reason why this great work should not be completed in three or five years." The works were supervised by Francis Brady, the SER's own engineer.

In October 1881 much of the machinery was transferred from the Abbotts Cliff to the Shakespeare Cliff workings. Drilling was authorised to extend another mile, but only 30 men were reported to be at work. On a number of occasions, visitors were allowed to inspect the works which were lit for their convenience by electric lights. In February 1882 a special press visit included the opportunity to drink champagne when 500 yards out beneath the sea, bathed in the glow of Swann's electric lamps. The chalk through which the tunnel was being driven was described as "not harder than tolerably hard cheese, and the steam-driven boring knives work in it like cheese-tasters in an uncut Stilton[29]."

In January 1882 a new Bill for a rail link to the works was being discussed but in April 1882 the Board of Trade ordered that no more borings should be made until Sir Archibald Alison had studied the whole question.

Speaking in January 1882, Watkin attacked those who said the Channel Tunnel would weaken national security:

"The Military authorities might take the option of blowing up the Tunnel by touching a button in the War Office, that would light an electric spark, letting in the sea, or of burning to death the people in the Tunnel by a small stream of petroleum, or any other way their humanitarian feelings might permit."

The issue was, of course, politics. One newspaper claimed that:

"The silver streak is a greater bar to the movements of Nihilists, Internationalists and Bradlaughites than is generally believed, but with several trains a day between Paris and London, we should have an amount of fraternising between the discontented denizens of the great cities of both countries, which would yield very unsatisfactory results on this side of the Channel."[30]

Aside from fears of rampant atheism (and blissfully ignorant of the fact, it would seem, that Karl Marx had spent his most productive years in Britain), there were more personal attacks on Watkin. Much was made of the suspension of his "boring operations." The greatest venom concentrated on the issue of the Tunnel as a threat to British military security, with Colonel Beaumont suggesting that it should be capable of being flooded.

The Submarine Continental Railway Company abandoned its operations on 1 July, but deposited a Bill for the construction of the Tunnel itself. Also deposited was a Bill for the Channel Tunnel company, supported by the LCDR. A committee of both Houses of Parliament studied the Bills, but Alison had advised against them and they had little chance; the committee advised the Government, by seven votes to three, to oppose both Bills.

The French despaired of the perfidious British and, lacking anyone to meet halfway, abandoned their own works at Sangatte on 18 March 1883.

In 1886 Watkin's Submarine Continental Railway took over the Channel Tunnel Company; in 1887 he renamed it the Channel Tunnel Company Limited.

A revived scheme for a Channel bridge, designed by Schneider and Hersent, was aired in 1889 but was opposed as it caused a danger to shipping even though it included a mid-Channel harbour. John Fowler and Benjamin Baker were also involved with the project[31].

Watkin was still hoping for success with the Channel Tunnel, though the Bill was rejected in July 1889; ever hopeful, a new Bill was prepared for the ensuing session. Clearly some work was already proceeding in advance of Parliamentary approval, for coal was discovered 1,180 feet down in borings at Shakespeare Cliff in February 1890[32]. On 25 March an inspection of the works was made by the Board of Trade, who found a tunnel 2,020 yards long and mostly dry. The new Bill was debated in the House, where Watkin sat as a MP of course, on 5 June 1890. Watkin suggested a novel reason for supporting the Tunnel, that it would "extend the British Empire some 11 or 12 miles in the direction of France." Despite the support of Gladstone, the Bill was lost on its second reading by 234 to 153 votes. The defeat of the Bill was blamed on the jingoistic sentiments of Joseph Chamberlain by the *Railway Times*[33].

There the issue should have died, except for the unceasing efforts of Watkin to promote what must have seemed dangerously like an obsession. It is curious that a man of his abilities, despite being something of a maverick, never developed his political career; one of the reasons for this may have been that, at times, his political interests seemed to focus exclusively on the Tunnel. In 1893 he was accused of having interfered in the election at Grimsby in support of a pro-Tunnel candidate against a Unionist; Grimsby was a seat influenced by the Manchester, Sheffield & Lincolnshire Railway.

1.   The harbour was authorised by an Act of 1807, with capital of £22,000.
2.   SER General Meeting Minutes, 10 November 1836
3.   **Railway Times,** 1 April 1843.
4.   R Bucknall, **Boat Trains & Channel Packets,** says that Morris paid £10,000 for the harbour, then sold it to the SER at £18,000; p.2.
5.   **Maidstone Journal,** 12 September 1843.
6.   **Maidstone Journal,** 5 December 1843.
7.   **Railway Times,** 2 December 1843, reported the branch as ready for use.
8.   **Railway Times,** 19 June 1847.

9.   SER Minutes, 23 January 1851. Bradley gives an order date of a week later and a price of £1,400, so some negotiation may have taken place.
10.   Quoted in B.Hart, **The Hythe & Sandgate Railway.**
11.   **Railway Times,** 21 February 1863.
12.   SER Minutes, 11 November 1869.
13.   Slater & Barnett, **The Channel Tunnel,** p.79.
14.   SER Minutes, 10 November 1881; Hart, **Hythe & Sandgate Railway,** p.25, gives the date as 15 October.
15.   SER Minutes, 13 March 1884.
16.   SER Minutes, 25 August 1892.
17.   Given in A.Hasenson, **The History of Dover Harbour,** p.154.
18.   **Railway Times,** 18 January 1845.
19.   SER Minutes, 24 April 1848. See also A.Hasenson, **The Golden Arrow.**
20.   **Railway Times,** 19 March 1853.
21.   **Railway Times,** 22 July 1871.
22.   D.L.Bradley, **The Locomotive History of the SER.**
23.   For this and other ship details, see RAIL1005/393.
24.   **Railway Times,** 22 July 1893.
25.   **Railway Times,** 25 November 1851.
26.   SER Minutes, 28 April 1870.
27.   According to Slater & Barnett, p.54, Watkin's "kindliness and courtesy" towards Gladstone "extended to providing....a private branch line to his country home, and to arranging Gladstone's continental holidays for him."
28.   **Railway Times,** 18 June 1881. This reports the gallery as already being 900 yards, but SER Minutes of 18 August give 880 yards and a rate of construction of 11-14 yards per day.
29.   F.S.Williams, **Our Iron Roads,** 2nd edition 1882.
30.   **The Sunday Times,** 16 April 1882.
31.   **Railway Times,** 3 October 1889.
32.   **Railway Times,** 1 March 1890; SER Minutes 6 March.
33.   **Railway Times,** 18 July 1891.

CHAPTER 21: THE TRAFFIC

1. The Passengers

One might have thought, from the early attitude of the SER, that its main purpose was to discourage passengers altogether, for the rules it introduced in April 1842 seemed to ban all that made the Englishman's life pleasurable - the SER trains were to carry no dogs, no drunks and no smokers. This repressive attitude seemed even more comprehensive when, on 23 May 1842, the Board decided they would ban Sunday travellers as well by taking off the two Sunday trains then running each way. Like the Brighton line, which sought to keep the lower orders off its railway altogether, the SER soon found that ideals tended to wither in the harsh climate of economic reality - on 25 July 1842 it was decided that a Sunday "mid-day" train should reappear, due to "public necessity"[1]. Sunday trains were provided on the Greenwich line, but not between 10.45am and 1.15pm.

The SER was primarily a passenger railway and its early receipts grew slowly as the people became more used to the idea of railway travel; weekly receipts increased from £555 to £846 in the early months of 1842. It also was an early discoverer of the practice of reducing fares in order to boost income: a "low fare experiment" was inaugurated on 31 August 1842 in order to win traffic away from the stage coaches which ran to places such as East Grinstead. Fares were reduced by about 25%, and receipts increased by about £200 per month. In July 1845 fares were reduced again, with a 1st class to Dover falling from 18s 6d to 15s, and a 3rd class from 7s4d to 6s; again a "great increase" of traffic resulted, especially of passengers taking advantage of "day tickets."

At this stage the main-line was still incomplete. The first service, in May 1842, involved four trains each way to Tonbridge, taking two hours. When the line was extended, the SER ran six trains a day to the new terminus at Headcorn, in a fastest time of 2hrs 15mins; after the line reached Folkestone it increased the service to seven per day, the fastest in 3hrs 5mins.

After initial reluctance, the SER allowed 3rd class passengers on some trains. Accomodation, though, was hardly welcoming since it was not until April 1844 that the directors agreed to have roofs on the 3rd class stock; the lack of roofs could cause problems - in April 1843 a family sued the SER after red hot cinders burnt their clothes during a 3rd class journey. In April 1845 the SER considered running entirely separate 3rd class trains, but this policy never became popular though the idea of "cheap" trains evolved into the excursion.

The SER encouraged the poorer travellers by taking up the running of cheap excursions, though it should be noted that the very poorest of people would not have been able to afford any railway journey. On 27 August 1844 it was decided to run cheap excursions on Saturdays and Sundays during September. The following Spring the directors stuck to their Sabbatarian principles by allowing no excursion on Easter Sunday, but they did run early excursions on the Monday and Tuesday. At Whitsun, they ran excursions on the Saturday, and Monday to Wednesday, but again not on Sunday. During June to September 1845, cheap excursions were run from Bricklayers Arms to Dover on Saturdays and Mondays.

Maidstone's status as County Town of Kent generated some unusual traffic. In October 1844 the SER agreed to convey prisoners to Maidstone for 50s a van and on 25 April 1845 an extra train was run to the town for the West Kent election. After the opening of the direct line to Tonbridge, the SER gained a steady income by transporting convicts from Chislehurst to Maidstone, until the LCDR won the traffic by offering cheaper fares in 1874.

The speed of trains increased gradually. In September 1843 SER trains averaged just over 24mph for "fast" trains and 21mph for "slow"; by March 1846 this had risen to 35mph and 21mph respectively.

The Select Committee of the House of Commons on Railways, 1846, gathered a large quantity of information which reveals much about early passenger traffic on the SER[2]. In 1845 the SER carried 840,465 passengers, of whom 41% were 1st class, 43% 2nd and only 16% 3rd - reflecting the way in which lower class travel was not encouraged. The destination of travellers to or from London was as follows:

Croydon: 1,979	Merstham: 6,895	Reigate: 27,014
Godstone: 17,186	Edenbri.: 16,365	Penshurst: 8,456
Tonbridge: 74,972	Tun. W.: 17,359	Pdk Wood: 8,749
Yalding: 2,671	Marden: 4,796	Waterb'y: 6,940
E Farl.: 2,136	Stapleh.: 29,282	Maidstone: 32,760
Headcorn: 6,268	Pluckley: 3,114	Ashford: 32,193
Westenh'r: 4,889	Folkest.: 46,419	Dover: 88,949

Figures were collected for traffic between all stations; it is notable that there were 84,280 local journeys between Dover and Folkestone only. In comparison, there was one traveller between Merstham and Pluckley and no-one at all from Merstham to East Farleigh.

The Duke of Wellington was a regular passenger on the line, travelling to his residence at Walmer Castle. In October 1844 he complained that the 11.25am up train was over an hour late. He was generally treated as a privileged passenger, with his own carriage attached to express trains. After the Duke died, the line's best-known traveller was generally Charles Dickens who used it for journeys to his home near Higham, to Broadstairs, and to France. Being famous had its advantages, as he noted in 1854:

"Leaving Calais on the evening of Sunday, the 10th of December; fact of distinguished author's being abroad was telegraphed to Dover; thereupon authorities of Dover Railway detained train to London for distinguished author's arrival, rather to the exasperation of the British public."[3]

What the SER could never completely control was the behaviour of its passengers. In 1845 there were persistent problems with people smoking on the Greenwich line. On 15 July 1845 a passenger tried to leap onto a down Brighton train at Reigate and fell between the carriages; he was killed. On 13 August a fisherman died while travelling in a SER carriage; the coroner recorded a verdict of "death by the visitation of God." In January 1847 the company had to ban the dangerous practice of passengers taking lighted candles into the carriages, though in November 1845 it had been agreed that roof lamps should be provided even in the Parliamentary trains[4]; however there were still no lamps in the 3rd class covered carriages in 1852 and the problem of candles continued - one director suggesting that the 3rd class should be made to do

75. One of the "midnight" hop-picker trains from London Bridge. Note the large
quantities of luggage in ths picture, drawn in the 1880s.

without the roofs on their carriages. In December 1852 it was finally agreed that
lamps should be provided in all 2nd and 3rd class stock. First class travellers in
1845 had the luxury of a SER rug in winter months. What, though, could be done
about a shareholder named Allmann, who sent his "fancy pig" by passenger
train?

The company tinkered endlessly with its services and fare levels, trying to
find the most profitable policy. Towns like Edenbridge could petition for better
services, as they did in December 1847 - with the result that the fast trains at
4.30pm down and 8am up began to call there. Excursions continued to be run
in the late 1840s, such as the 8.30am down provided on Whit Monday and
Tuesday 1848, and by May 1850 the SER was encouraging the growth of
Ramsgate and Margate with an extra cheap summer train in competition with
the steamboats. By 1848 though it had decided to charge 1.25d a mile for 3rd
class, wherever legal. Yet the company was not entirely mercenary - in
November 1848 it provided free 3rd class travel to 160 German emigrants who
had survived the wreck of the *Burgundy*.

Another slow-growing, but ultimately rewarding, traffic was commuting,
though the term was not then in use[5]. By the middle of 1849 the SER was
offering low-priced 1st class annual tickets - one from Gravesend cost £26-5s.
This led one journalist to conclude that the North Kent line was "...one of the
most valuable possessions of the South Eastern Company."[6] In fact the SER
was an early example of a railway that took positive steps to encourage
residential development, and clearly realised that profits would be higher if
season-ticket travel was from stations further out of London. On 2 November
1854 it prepared a list of stations where special terms would be offered to
builders. Any builder erecting more than six houses within two miles of the

station would be offered one free season ticket per house and a 25% reduction on goods rates for his materials. The concession applied to the country stations between Redhill and Tonbridge, to Betchworth, Gomshall and Chilworth on the Guildford line, to Frant and Wadhurst on the Hastings route, and in North Kent to stations between, but exclusive of, Woolwich and Gravesend. Revenue from the season tickets rose steadily: it was £14,460 in 1852, £26,816 in 1858, £31,010 in 1861, £47,508 in 1867, £68,000 in 1871 and £130,140 in 1877[7].

For the summer season of 1850 3rd class passengers could make a return trip to Margate on the 4.55am train for the price of a single ticket and the same offer was available on several Sunday trains. The Margate offer was stopped when the SER found that Ashford people were abusing it to get to their own town cheaply. There was also a Sunday train that offered a 1st class excursion fare to Margate. On 26 August 1852 the Board decided to start running a Sunday excursion to Ramsgate and Margate again; they were immediately put under pressure by Sabbatarians, but after examining the traffic returns refused to withdraw their decision. The train was a clear success, for it continued to run even in the winter. In October 1857 Charles Gilpin, a SER director, tried to get all Sunday excursions stopped.

The overall level of normal services had not increased greatly - trains tending to become heavier and, gradually, faster, but not more frequent. By July 1850 there were still only eight through trains, the best of which, the 8.30pm down Mail, reached Dover at 11pm. The following year the service was reduced to seven, though there was an additional train to Maidstone. The running of local services between Maidstone and Tonbridge ceased in 1850.

The 1851 Great Exhibition brought additional traffic to the line, much of which was handled by special trains (such as the one from Robertsbridge on 1 September) rather than normal services. The SER prepared for the event by ordering new stock - 20 "break" vans, 20 1st class and 20 2nd class carriages.

This was also the time at which the SER got into trouble with various authorities for running excursions to prize fights, such as one held near Edenbridge on 24 September 1850. Another was run to Appledore on 29 January 1856 and also to the Aldershot area on 25 January 1859.

The practice continued, and there was a notable fight at Etchingham on 20 September 1859 for which the SER ran an excursion from London Bridge, leading to a letter of protest from the Home Secretary. SER staff were very unco-operative, refusing to allow the police to send urgent telegraph messages, leading to legal proceedings in both Kent and East Sussex. Three fights took place in a field between Headcorn and Pluckley in December 1859, again served by a SER train. On 17 April 1860 two trains were run to the Aldershot area for the Sayers v. Heenan fight; the SER collected over £3,000 in fares[8]. Another excursion was run in December 1863 to Wadhurst, with a further complaint from the Home Secretary, and the last one seems to have been run by the SER on 23 April 1867 though one of the "pugilists" failed to turn up. The practice of running trains to these fights was made illegal in 1868 by the Regulation of Railways Act.[9]

One of the main problem areas seems to have been the North Kent line. In February 1851 a passenger indecently assaulted another, while in April two men were ejected from the train at Blackheath for smoking. North Kent season-ticket holders persistently flouted the anti-smoking rule, and in January 1853 one of them, Mr. Edmonds, was fined 10s with 12s costs. There were also a number of instances of drinking on this line. This line also caused problems through occasional "surges" of traffic - such as when the *Royal George* was launched at Woolwich in 1854.

Passenger carriages improved only slowly - witness the length of time taken to provide proper lighting. New 2nd class carriages in 1854 were described as "light and cheerful", featuring stuffed leather cushions[10]. Beattie, though, thought the 1st class carriages to be in a "disreputable state" in September 1858, by which time the SER was conscious of comparisons with the East Kent. In March 1859, 25 new 1st class carriages were ordered.

With the threat of the EKR, the SER had to consider how to retain the loyalty of its passengers. In November 1858 the maximum speed reached by trains was meant to be 50mph, but this was apparently exceeded quite frequently. However the SER opted to fight its rival by reducing fares in August 1861 - with the result that, over eleven weeks, its income fell by £14,000. However agreement over fares was reached with the LCDR in 1863, so they were promptly increased again - thereby giving ammunition to those who opposed railway amalgamation in southern England. Traffic levels, though, were healthy, so the SER had to order 100 new 3rd class carriages from Gloucester in 1863, costing nearly £200 each.

The use of slip coaches on the SER began about 1860, with carriages on the 2.30pm down express being slipped at Sturry and Minster from July[11]. A Reading and Maidstone train, which divided into portions at Redhill, slipped a carriage at Caterham Junction in 1861. In July 1878 it was decided to alter some six-wheel carriages for use as slip coaches.

One issue that came to exercise SER minds a great deal was the means of communicating between the driver and the guard on passenger trains. The issue was first discussed in December 1864; by the following May it had been decided that the Mail and Tidal trains should be provided with such devices. Later in 1865 Cudworth prepared a trial apparatus and by July 1866 it was in use on these trains, allowing the passengers to communicate with the driver and guard

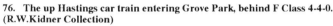

76. **The up Hastings car train entering Grove Park, behind F Class 4-4-0.**
(R.W.Kidner Collection)

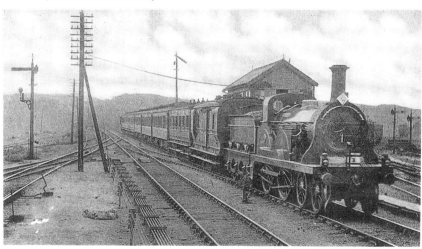

too. An electrical apparatus rang a bell in the guard's van and showed a disc outside the compartment window where a problem had arisen.

A review of the timetable in January 1869 shows that the SER was progressing towards providing more frequent services. The Reading line had five through trains from Charing Cross on weekdays, the best of which was the 9.45am arriving at 12.30pm; ten other trains ran only as far as Dorking[12] while one terminated at Guildford. Between Redhill and Tonbridge there were still ten services, despite the opening of the Sevenoaks route. On the Hastings line there were six through trains and also a portion off the 7.25am down Mail, running via Ashford; three other trains ran only as far as Wadhurst. On the Ashford to Hastings route there were six weekday trains, with a market train between Appledore and Ashford on Tuesdays. The Margate line had seven weekday services, with another train terminating at Sturry; Deal was served by a similar timetable. The best train on the system was the 7.25am Mail from Charing Cross, which reached Dover Town at 9.25am and Admiralty Pier at 9.30am; seven weekday trains ran down to Folkestone Harbour station, which was used by local people as much as by continental travellers. Most of the main routes had a highly restricted service on Sundays, generally as few as two trains in each direction.

The electrical communication became a favourite source of jokes for Watkin when he needed some humour to lighten the SER General Meetings. In February 1868 he told the shareholders that the device had been fitted to 12 engines and 170 carriages, and had been used 13 times since 5 April 1867. There had been a number of false alarms, including a boy who had lost his cap, but on one occasion the train had actually been off the line. In August 1869 it was decided to fit the communication system to all main-line trains, with the result that Watkin had a large fund of good stories for the shareholders in July 1872. The system had been set off by a passenger annoyed by some card-sharpers in the compartment, by the staff of the Burmese Embassy "for curiosity", and by Captain Tyler of the Board of Trade who was testing it - whether officially or not, Watkin failed to explain. In 1877 a man pulled the communication cord in Blackheath Tunnel, claiming that two ladies had "pinched him".

Though the communication cord was a novelty at first, it was a great advance. Similar advances were made by the SER in beginning experimental use of continuous brakes in January 1873; by October 1877 all expresses were fitted with the vacuum brake, making the company one of the national leaders in this respect.

Passengers did not always appreciate the SER's cares for them. On 10 January 1869 two men wrecked a compartment of a London to Dover train. They were discovered when the ticket collector at Dover found they had thrown nearly everything they could out of the window of their 1st class carriage. The two men tried to escape prosecution on the grounds of their high social status, but the SER brought them to court where, unfortunately, they escaped punishment due to a legal technicality.

The year 1866 was a poor one for railway companies. The SER tried to boost its position by increasing fares from 1 November, so that a 1st class single to Canterbury increased from 13s to 15s. Watkin had other ingenious ideas for improving traffic, though, for in May 1869 he suggested that ladies should be able to travel at half fare when accompanied by a gentlemen. One wonders if he would have allowed this to apply to the disreputable traffic between Charing

Cross and Cannon Street. Passengers generated income indirectly too; W.H.Smiths' had a bookstall monopoly at SER stations, for which they were paying £6,000 a year in 1868. The SER also owned 24 public houses and ten station bars by 1872.

The idea of running special luxury trains occurred to the SER in 1873, when George Mortimer Pullman visited Britain. Little was done at the time, but the gradual improvement of coaching stock continued. By June 1874 only 42 four-wheel carriages were still in use, which Mansell wanted to convert to six-wheel. In January 1876 it was agreed that toilets should be provided in all main-line carriages; there seems to have been an inconvenient delay, since Wainwright was instructed to provide toilets for the Mail and Continental trains in 1888. Some improvements were also necessary for the safety of passengers - a carrier named Duval was killed in Shakespeare Cliff Tunnel on 22 May 1878, following which a metal bar was fitted across some carriage windows.

In the early 1880s the issue of 3rd class travel came to the fore. On 26 May 1881 the SER made the decision to include 3rd class facilities on all trains except the Mail and Tidal expresses. In July 1884, another major step forward, it was decided to issue 3rd class season tickets at Dartford for an experimental period. Conditions in the 3rd class carriages were not especially wonderful - in July 1884 the SER was sent a packet of dry rot which a passenger had collected in carriage no.462. Early the next year, *Truth* magazine commented that, "Third class passengers on the South Eastern are still treated as if they were habitual drunkards, felons or pigs."

For the SER there were dangers in improving the 3rd class trains. By 1892 the company was alarmed at the gradual decline of 1st class, especially in the London area. An accident near London Bridge revealed a 3rd class carriage full of "respectable people who might and ought to have paid first-class fare," Watkin complained[13]. Later that year Watkin himself said that he always travelled 3rd class between Waterloo and Cannon Street as "he met well-dressed and highly intellectual people" - the inference being that such people ought to pay for 1st class. Lord Brabourne thought that the 3rd class carriages were "so comfortable, nobody wanted anythi..g else."

The pressure for cheap travel came also from the other end of the line. In 1888 the people of Folkestone asked for a cheap excursion to their town, wanting fares as low as 5s so that they could compete for visitors against Brighton. The excursions trade was a highly volatile one - in 1889 the SER lost an estimated £5,000 when a Bank Holiday was very wet. In November 1892 Folkestone interests requested that 3rd class carriages be attached to the Dover boat trains for their own use.

The June 1893 timetable gives a good idea of SER services at this stage. There were regular Monday excursion trains, offering a return trip for only 4s; the 8.05am called at stations on the Dover and Margate lines, while the 9.05am served the Hastings route. One of the best services to Hastings was the 11am via Ashford, giving an arrival in Hastings at 2.03pm. On the Oxted route most SER trains terminated at Oxted, but two ran through to Edenbridge and one to Tonbridge, the 10.37am, which arrived at 12.13pm. In connection with this, 11 weekday trains ran on the Woodside & South Croydon line. On the Lydd branch, there were nine trains to New Romney and three between Lydd and Dungeness. Bromley was served by 21 trains while the Mid-Kent service was mostly hourly. Three trains ran between Strood and Rochester Bridge only, taking one minute, and nine over the Blackfriars spur, generally via York Road to Woolwich. The 3pm Club Train from Charing Cross reached Dover in a creditable 1hr 45mins.

The SER's solution to the declining use of 1st class was to invest in a new generation of luxury carriages. Six Pullman-type cars were ordered from Gilbert Car Manufacturing Company of America, and shipped to the SER in sections for assembly. In early March 1892 the cars were used for a special run to Hastings, after which they were employed singly and in pairs on the Dover and Hastings lines, with a run to Canterbury being added later that summer. These cars created a new class, more expensive than first class, so the SER now had four tiers of travel. They were rebuilt with vestibules in 1896 and from 1 December formed the Hastings Car Train.

On 26 November 1896 the SER ordered eight Pullman carriages from the Metropolitan Carriage & Wagon Company. On 22 September 1897 these were used for a trial run from Charing Cross to Dover Town. Then, from 1 October, they were employed on the 8.55am up from Folkestone and 4.35pm return. At first this train was called the *Folkestone Vestibuled Limited* but later became the *Folkestone Car Express*. However an attempt to start a similar service to Tunbridge Wells, from 2 September 1897, was a failure.

The SER worked hard to develop its suburban and main-line traffic, but annual passenger figures often depended more on the weather than on its own efforts. A high proportion of its revenue came from leisure traffic, and much of this was the most fickle of all - excursion and day-trip journeys. It was a problem that Watkin acknowledged in 1876, when he told the SER shareholders that the difference between a fine and a wet week often amounted to £3,000: "A year with more than the average of sunshine, and a year with less than the average of sunshine, makes a difference to you of £100,000." Such a variation could represent 10% of the SER's annual income - a very significant proportion.

2. Premium Traffic - The Mails and Gold Bullion

The first Mail traffic to be carried on what became the SER system was on the London & Greenwich line, where there was a contract to carry the traffic from the start of 1837. This increased gradually so that, for example, the Royal Mail paid £10 a year to have an extra mail bag carried between Deptford and London from March 1847.

The Admiralty had begun running the Mails service across the Channel from Dover in 1837, and it was therefore inevitable that the service should make use of the SER between there and London[14]. An early service that attracted a great deal of attention was the Indian Mails service. The Mails were delivered at Folkestone after a long voyage by sea and land, then taken to London by a special SER train with its distinctive headcode of three white lamps. The news from the sub-continent was awaited eagerly by newspapers and during times of special interest the newspapers could hire their own train to take the latest news to London; such trains were charged at 5s a mile, or at £2-10s a day to keep a locomotive and its crew waiting[15]. The interest in these services obviously declined with the advent of the electric telegraph.

As early as July 1843 the SER had agreed a contract to carry the mails between London and Dover at £6-10s per journey and in February 1844 the celebrated Mail trains began running, at 1.30am down and 8.30pm up. By early 1847 the SER was running the special Mail trains, the premium expresses of the line. In March 1847 the General Post Office requested that the trains should be accelerated; the SER offered to run the 8.30pm from London to Dover in two and a half hours, an hour less than before, for an extra £3-5s-4d per trip. In December 1847 the GPO enquired whether travelling sorting vans could be run on the SER as they were on the London & North Western Railway. From 1 November 1848 the Mails always ran to Dover rather than Folkestone, using Admiralty Pier from late 1860; the "Tidal" boat trains, though, used Folkestone..

From 1 November 1858 the Mail train was retimed to leave London at 9pm instead of 8.30pm, and to reach Dover in two hours, no longer stopping at Redhill and Tonbridge. The GPO agreed to pay £1,000 a year for this advantage, of which the SER estimated it would cost £700 a year to provide an extra 8.30pm train to Tonbridge.

In February 1860 the GPO complained about the up Mail trains. It wanted the 5.20am train retimed to leave at 9.15am and to be accelerated. The SER agreed to this, providing the 2am up Mail was discontinued. From 20 June 1863 the Mails service was operated jointly by the SER and LCDR, with the former operating the trains and the latter the ships. Problems were later encountered with the marine leg of the arrangement after the two companies encountered one of the periodic rifts in their relationship, but the Mail expresses retained their prime position on the SER - though they gradually became as important for their passenger traffic as for the mail carried. By the 1870s they were regularly attaining speeds of 60mph and over, though helped by the relatively limited loads.

The other "premium" traffic for which the SER became well-known, perhaps too well-known, was in gold. In March 1845 the order was given to build two bullion vans and the traffic seems to have begun about January 1848. The fee was based on the value of the gold - to transport £100 worth of gold between London and Paris earnt the SER 6s, and 5s was earnt on each £100 of silver. The precious cargo was insured during its rail journey but could not be insured for the sea passage, apparently.

The traffic ceased very abruptly when the 1848 French revolution broke out, since the bullion could not be insured against "civil commotion" or "the Queen's enemies."

Regular movements of bullion were bound to attract the criminal fraternity, and so one of the most famous incidents in the history of the SER occurred in 1855[16]. Its central figure was Edward Agar, a skilled locksmith and habitual criminal. He was said to have made £45,000 from a raid on Rogers' Bank in London and lived in comfortable style with Fanny Kay.

Agar's accomplice was William Pierce, who had a grievance against the SER after being sacked from its printing office after printing tickets there for another concern. It is interesting in the light of this that in June 1852 the SER had sacked a ticket printer for "having a connection with a Westminster Bridge betting house"; could this have been Pierce, printing betting slips when he should have been producing third class singles to Gravesend?

These two men needed inside help in their bid to raid the SER bullion vans. They ingratiated themselves with Burgess, a SER guard and the son of a senior officer in the company, and with Tester - a clerk in the superintendent's office at London Bridge whose duties including arranging the guards' rosters.

Agar and Pierce went to London Bridge several times to watch the departure of the 8.30pm for Dover, but realised there was no set pattern for the gold shipments. Sometimes there was some, sometimes there was not.

Tester's job was to ensure Burgess was the guard when the robbery took place, but the gold shipments were so irregular that he had to be kept on duty for three months. Tester also provided an impression of the keys that opened the iron chest in which the gold was kept. Agar and Pierce, meanwhile, spent some time in Folkestone before concluding that the gold could only be stolen during the course of the train journey.

Agar had to make at least seven trips down the line in Burgess' van before the key he had made would fit the iron chest. For nearly two weeks, therefore, Pierce and Agar had to go to London Bridge each evening, carrying lead shot in carpet bags, with more strapped around their bodies. This was to replace the weight of the gold.

One evening in May 1855 they at last got the signal - Burgess raised his hat and wiped his face to indicate gold was on the train. The two thieves bought tickets for Ostend via Dover right in front of stationmaster Weatherhead - who later became governor of Newgate Gaol.

A porter took their bags to the guard's van and the two men sat down in separate carriages. When Weatherhead was not looking, Agar slipped into the guard's van. As soon as the train pulled out he started work; at Redhill, one bag of gold was handed out to Pierce, who was waiting on the platform, while Tester joined the train. By Folkestone the safe had been loaded with lead shot and the carpet bags with gold; the criminals watched as it was unloaded. At Dover the criminals collected their bags from the guard's van.

Pierce was disguised in a black wig, whiskers and broad-brimmed hat, no doubt making him a strange apparition on Dover Town station in the middle of the night. A porter, Winterden, asked them if he could take their bags and was suspicious when they asked for the London train since he knew both had Ostend tickets; he had to be tipped to allay his curiosity, but a year later was able to identify Agar.

The two men returned to London with the gold which was kept in the wash-house behind Agar's home. He whitened the windows so that Fanny Kay did not know what was happening, then melted down the gold bars and sold them to James Saward of Walworth for about £15,000. Burgess and Tester only got £700 each.

When the crime was discovered, there was great consternation. Rees, the SER law clerk, began an investigation. It was not known at first where the gold had been stolen, and the SER was quick to protest that it was more likely to have disappeared in France than England. However suspicion centred on Burgess, who was questioned and admitted to allowing men to ride in the brake van, but not on the night in question; he was watched by detectives for weeks - but to no avail. Also under suspicion was the Folkestone stationmaster[17] since the cases of "gold" had been left unattended in his office all night. Tester left the SER for a railway management position on the Royal Swedish Railway, but no-one had connected him with the crime, and Samuel Smiles had written his "certificate of character."[18].

The crime might not have been solved except that Agar and Pierce attempted to pass a forged cheque at a Lombard Street bank in August 1855. A chase took place and Agar was caught, but Pierce got away. Agar was sentenced to life imprisonment but had arranged for Pierce to receive £7,000 to help look after Fanny Kay and Agar's child by her; but Fanny drank heavily, so Pierce threw her out and kept the money.

Agar had nothing to lose so when he heard of Pierce's behaviour, he turned "approver". He confessed to the bullion robbery and named his accomplices. Several witnesses could testify to having seen the men at London Bridge, Folkestone and Dover, and all were captured, though Tester returned from Sweden voluntarily. Pierce spent two years in prison, while Burgess and Tester were sentenced to 14 years, the difference being due to the more severe punishments prescribed for railway officials. Later in 1856 Fanny Kay actually visited the SER offices and told her version of the story to Samuel Smiles and Rees.

Following the robbery, some changes were made in the working of the gold traffic. An iron strong room was installed at Folkestone and the vans carrying the gold were sealed in transit. In 1867 the SER complained that the gold traffic had declined sharply, but in April 1877 another attempt was made to rob a gold van at Folkestone, following which it was decided to install electric alarms. Gold traffic continued to run at a level of at least £4,000,000 a year.

3. Goods Traffic

The SER lacked the industrial base in its region to guarantee high levels of goods traffic. The principal industries in its district were paper-making, brewing and the cement or lime industries, but all made great use of cheap water transport. The SER therefore had to rely on agriculture and what it could bring into the region from other areas.

In the early 1840s there was still a considerable trade in coal by sea. In May 1843 the SER started to make arrangements to distribute coal from Dover; it later did so from Whitstable, Strood and Folkestone as well. Coal, it thought, could be sent to the various stations at 3d a ton mile.

In the later months of 1843 it made arrangements for other types of goods traffic. "Garden produce" it thought was potentially profitable. Fullers Earth was to be transported from Reigate to New Cross at 3d a ton mile. Much more profitable was the fish trade - in October 1843 it decided that fish from Folkestone could be sent to London by passenger train at 60s a ton. From March 1851 fish was even allowed on the up Mail express.

Yet agriculture was to offer the most potential for development - but at a risk, for Kent agriculture depended largely on fruit and hops, notoriously subject to weather conditions. In September 1843 it was decided that hops would be taken as far as New Cross or Cold Blow, but not into London Bridge. A novel idea, and a good one, was to take chalk from the cutting at Merstham and sell it to farmers at the wayside stations.

In August 1844 an extra goods train was put on from Staplehurst in the fruit season, but the SER had less success with fruit-farmers closer to London. These people would take cartloads of fruit into London, and return with a cartload of manure for their farms.

Rick cloths were issued to all relevant stations in 1845 so that the hops could be protected while waiting for forwarding. In 1846 sidings for hops and fruit

77.   Down goods at Grove Park, probably in late 1890s.   (R.W.Kidner Collection)

78.   Staplehurst in 1887, with fruit baskets in profusion.

79.   Open 10-ton wagon built by Birmingham Railway Carriage & Wagon Co. for the SER.   (R.W.Kidner Collection)

were put in at Bricklayers Arms and henceforth that station became the centre of the trade, though from the SER point of view it was highly seasonal traffic.

As has been seen in Chapter Three, the SER was not a "carrier" and this allowed firms like Pickfords' to profit at its expense. On 7 January 1845 Pickfords' were directed to vacate their premises at various SER stations, and the SER became a carrier itself from 1 February. This allowed it to collect parcels and deliver them, charging its own rates in competition with other firms. It took the question of developing the traffic seriously, in 1850 offering stationmasters a 2.5% "gratuity" on increases of goods traffic at their stations. A Goods Superintendent was also appointed, named Fothergill, the Board resolving rather threateningly that "he had better cultivate the long traffic."[19] In fact he was sacked in 1851 for being dishonest about money, and replaced by J.C.Shaw on £600 a year. However in 1859 carrier companies were still complaining that the SER gave Pickfords' preferential treatment.

Coal traffic grew steadily, amounting to 26,420 tons in 1845; it increased sharply in 1856 when supplies began to reach the SER via the LNWR and GWR to Reading. By 1846 the cattle trade was bringing in about £103 a week and other goods £982. In March 1847 parcels of clothes for the Irish poor were carried free.

The fruit and vegetable traffic was charged "per sieve" and farmers had to be careful to deliver it by set times to the various stations. The cost per sieve from Maidstone to London was 4.5d, 5d from Ashford. Hops were charged per pocket; from stations between Godstone and Paddock Wood or Maidstone, it cost 1s 6d; from Headcorn 1s 7d; from Canterbury 2s. Some fruit traffic did come from stations nearer to London - in April 1851 the need to accomodate "garden produce" at Abbey Wood and Northfleet stations was noted.

From 1 May 1848 the SER divided goods into six classes. First class goods included bricks, chalk and cinders while second class goods featured such delights as ale, coffee, wine and currants. The SER was somewhat annoyed to discover in 1850 that companies had been packing cases full of parcels for various continental destinations, to avoid paying the SER a number of separate fees; when the railway company sought legal redress, it lost the case.

With goods traffic growing healthily in 1851, a large amount of new stock was ordered. This included 72 coal trucks, 60 cattle, 30 for sheep, and eight "combustibles".

Some revision of the fish trade was made in 1852. Fish was divided into "prime" and "offal", the latter including plaice, prawns and cod. Prime fish included turbot, sole and crab. Fish from Hastings to London was charged at 30s a ton, including collection and delivery. From Deal, costs varied between 53s 6d a ton if sent by passenger train, down to 15s for a ton of salted herrings.

A number of instances show the variability of the SER goods traffic. In June 1859 there were complaints that accidents had been caused by packages falling off trains, but the following year there was a serious failure of the hop harvest with the SER losing an estimated £13,480; in 1869 a bad hop season led to an estimated loss of £7,518. The hop traffic each year in the period 1860-70 varied between £6,000 and £24,000. In comparison, fruit and vegetable traffic in the second half of 1873 was worth £16,400. Less serious, the cattle trade dropped by £405 in 1865 due to disease. However, by 1867 the SER was so encouraged by the Irish cattle trade via Reading that it decided an extra goods locomotive was needed on that line.

For some, the temptations of working with the goods were too much. On 20 March 1869 the guard on a Chislehurst to Tonbridge goods was found drunk in his van by a stationmaster, having consumed half a bottle of brandy. A complaint had been received by a customer in Hastings that a hamper had been delivered minus the brandy that had earlier been in it, and the guard had been caught out by a deliberate repeat of the process. He was fined £2.

Some other types of traffic are worthy of mention. Sandwich brewery was typical of many small lineside industries, providing steady traffic worth about £500 a year in the 1870s. Due to a fashion for seawater bathing, a truck was built to convey seawater to the Charing Cross Hotel in 1888. In April 1894 oil traffic for the Anglo-American Oil Company began to run from Angerstein Wharf to the LBSCR; later, sidings were added at a number of SER stations. There was always, of course, the manure traffic; never popular with ordinary people, it caused occasional rows - such as that over the "nuisance" it was causing at Marden in 1893. During the agricultural depression of the 1890s the SER agreed to reduce the charge for carrying manure by 25%. By 1898 the SER was also preparing for the new harbour works at Dover - shingle was to be brought from Dungeness and sand from Sandwich, to Martin Mill. New sidings were needed for the traffic at Richborough, Martin Mill and Dover.

The fish traffic, though never vast, was always remunerative and was handled at a surprising number of stations. During 1881 3,423 tons were collected by the SER[20].

1. SER Directors' Report, 21 December 1842.
2. See PRO ref. RAIL 1124/35, pps.535-545.
3. From Dickens' **Reprinted Pieces.**
4. The cheap trains for the working classes introduced by order of the 1844 Railway Act.
5. The term was used in America in the 1840s, but not in Britain until the 1960s. See J.Simmons, **The Railway in Town and Country,** p.60.
6. **Railway Times,** 4 August 1849.
7. **Ibid,** 23 February 1861 and 23 February 1867; also various General Reports of the SER.
8. J.Hilton, vol.III, p.118.
9. For a full account of the various fights, see H.D.Miles, **Pugilistica,** published 1880-1.
10. **Herapath,** 4 March 1854.
11. **Bradshaw,** July 1860.
12. Reduced to seven in the June 1869 timetable.
13. Speech reported in the Railway Times, 23 January 1892.
14. The marine leg of the mails journey was taken over by Jenkins & Churchward in 1854 and by the LCDR in 1861.
15. See Hilton, volume II, p.79.
16. The following account is based on SER records, **The Times** and on the **Railway Times.** The gold robbery has been written about many times, not always accurately, and made into a rather imaginative film.
17. Samuel Smiles, Autobiography. Not clear which Folkestone station Smiles is referring to.
18. Samuel Smiles, Autobiography.
19. SER Minutes, 7 October 1850.
20. SER Minutes, 28 September 1882, give the following tonnages: Hastings 558, Ramsgate 303, Folkestone 913, Deal 205, Whitstable 799, Dover 127, Rye 101, Appledore for Lydd 112, Margate 170, Gravesend 84, Strood 17, Sandgate 18, Hythe 3, Ham Street for New Romney 0, Lydd 13.

CHAPTER 22: WORKING FOR THE SOUTH EASTERN

1. The Staff

Although the SER Minutes tell us a number of things about early managerial appointments, little else was recorded about staff on the line at the time of its opening, except for the employment of policemen. Although a few engine-drivers were brought in from elsewhere, most of the SER's first employees can have had little practical railway experience; the first stationmaster at Tonbridge was only 27 years old[1].

Early wage levels seem to have been quite generous, for the Tonbridge carriage examiner was employed at 30s a week in May 1842, and switchmen at 25s, though these were responsible jobs and often with very long hours. The ticket collector at Tonbridge, John Jordan, was paid 25s and had to find £40 security. Police inspectors were paid 25s-30s, constables 20s.

The SER, and other railways, offered a career structure at a time when this was fairly unusual for working-class people, especially in rural areas. Thus William Parker was promoted to Head Guard in July 1842 - but after the previous one had been sacked. The SER had a system whereby "meritorious servants may be rewarded for faithful and honest services", but in August 1842 complained about the lack of educated men. They re-stated their view in 1845:

"The Directors desire to record their intention in the management of the Company to be, to reward merit and encourage those of the Company's officers who faithfully do their duty by promoting to such vacancies as occur in superior offices Gentlemen already in the Company's employ who are believed to be competent and worthy[2]*."*

The expenses of staff were matched to the value of the station. Thus in 1842 the annual expenses at Penshurst were £208 while at Tonbridge they were £1,349. P.C.Smith was appointed in charge of Bletchingley, presumably to signal trains at the tunnel, while Penshurst was left in the care of a clerk on 35s a week due to its lack of importance. Among the lowest paid workers were porters, earning 20s a week; the more important, like a clerk at Ashford, received annual salaries - in his case, £75.

The SER was one of the first railways to introduce a sick fund of its own. From February 1843, 1s a week was deducted from weekly salaries and 10s a week was paid to employees who were ill. Staff had to work long hours but were given occasional respites - in 1851 all staff were allowed three days off and cheap fares to attend the Great Exhibition. It was noted in 1851 that London Bridge clerks rarely had a whole day off a week, and the Board decided to try and ensure this. That September it was resolved that staff should have alternate Sundays off. There was still pressure at this time against Sunday work; in July 1852 the SER received a suggestion that stationmasters should read prayers to their staff on Sundays.

It was also the general policy to make payments where staff had been killed at work through no fault of their own, and sometimes even when they died through negligence. Thus in December 1852 the SER paid the funeral expenses of a policeman, and then allowed his widow 10s a week for three months. This was more than many employers would have done. By 1853 a pension scheme was also in operation, allowing a pension of 7s 6d a week.

The Board did not hesitate to sack unsatisfactory staff - a severe punishment in the days of the workhouse; Benjamin Waghorn, the Ashford watchman, was sacked in April 1843 for being drunk. Cases of drunkeness were generally punished with dismissal - in June 1843 two guards who were drunk on duty were also given two months hard labour by Reigate magistrates. Perhaps it was due to a shortage of staff that both men were later re-employed as porters. Dishonesty was another serious offence - the "clerk-in-charge" at Headcorn was sacked for "interfering with the safe". He was replaced by a stationmaster paid £70 per year, but the Ashford one earned £100 and the Folkestone official £180. Stationmaster Sutherland at Tonbridge was sacked in 1844 for the "ill manner" in which he ran his station while driver Bennett was dismissed after a "slight collision" at Folkestone on 17 June 1845.

80. SER platform staff in 1885. (Wakeman Collection)

By May 1843 wages were showing a slight increase and reflecting the system of promotion: a night watchman earned 15s, a porter 18s, a switchman 21s and guards could earn 25s or 30s. Policeman J.Cook was promoted to ticket collector at the Cheriton ticket platform. Uniform gradually became normal for most station staff, beginning with the policemen; in April 1846 it was decided that clerks should wear uniform.

Perhaps the most interesting part of the promotion structure was the way station staff could progress through the grades to become a stationmaster, and

81. Stationmaster C.Spurgeon, signals a train away in 1885.
(Wakeman Collection)

then increase their salary by moving to more important stations. Thus in March 1847 an employee could have advanced from stationmaster at Pluckley, on 25s a week, to Tonbridge booking clerk on 27s, or to stationmaster at Grove Ferry or Marden on 35s. Coxhead, the Reigate stationmaster in 1846, was paid £120 a year, but his colleagues at Ashford and Tonbridge were on £100. This was reflected in the staff changes of May 1848 when the SER sacked the stationmasters at Strood, Wateringbury and Penshurst. The Wye stationmaster was then appointed to Strood and a head guard made Penshurst stationmaster; the Margate ticket collector became Grove Ferry stationmaster. Most senior of all, the London Bridge stationmaster was earning £300 a year by 1853. All staff were expected to work long hours; at the time of the Lewisham accident it was a cause of much comment that one of the guards often worked a 16 hour day, while the Blackheath stationmaster was "much wearied and fatigued."

The SER Staff Book of 1851 gives a good general picture of employment at stations[3]. Sandhurst had one employee, though this was probably just a switchman, but stations were operated with very low numbers - Frant, Ticehurst Road and Grove Ferry had only two men. Many "roadside" stations had a staff of between three and seven. Larger stations were usually junctions, like Paddock Wood with 12, bigger towns (eg Maidstone, 25) or termini (eg Ramsgate, 41). The staff at Wadhurst included an Inspector of Gates while of the five at Sturry two were horsekeepers. At Merstham there were only two platform staff, but one cutting watchman and four tunnelmen.

The SER's attitude to unions was generally hostile. In February 1852 they were angry to hear of "combinations" among the men in the various workshops. In May 1866 signalman Brown was sacked for organising a trade union; he alleged in return that the traffic superintendent, Knight, was profiting from a personal interest in the signalling firm of Saxby & Farmer.

During the 1850s a system of punishments replaced the old style of immediate dismissals. Thus in August 1852 the driver of a Tunbridge Wells excursion was fined 42s for neglecting the signals at Redhill, while the Hastings stationmaster was transferred to another station after unjustly suspending a porter after an argument about the election. The Wokingham stationmaster was told to learn how to operate the telegraph or be sacked.

Captain Barlow completed a major review of staff arrangements in October 1853. He criticised the way station staff were all paid different rates and advised that stations should be classified in eight grades with the stationmasters paid accordingly. Class one included London Bridge alone, at £300. Class two included stations like Dover and Ashford but also, perhaps surprisingly, Whitstable (where the stationmaster was also harbourmaster), at £175. Class eight, for example Wadhurst, was rated at £78. Barlow also created scales for all the other staff, ranging from Head Clerk (£120 p.a.) down to telegraph boy (5s a week). Porters in London were paid 2s a week more than elsewhere, while some gatemen had 1s 6d a week deducted as they were provided with a cottage. There were few female employees, but a "waiting room woman" was paid 10s a week. Seamen's wages had to be increased from 18s to 23s in 1854 as the best were leaving the company.

Scrupulous standards of personal honesty were always expected. A SER rule said that goods guards were personally responsible for losses of goods in transit. In 1855 the Marden stationmaster was threatened with the sack if he did not make good losses from hops at his station. White collar crime was always the hardest to detect - a clerk in the legal department managed to embezzle £526 from land sales in 1862. In 1864 a storekeeper was deprived of his pension after the SER had discovered that he had bought oil at inflated prices from his son's employer.

82. 2-4-0 no. 21a, Class E1, fitted with a Stirling boiler in 1892. Note the lack of protection for the driver. (R.W.Kidner Collection)

By September 1859 the SER employed 4,155 men on a weekly wage. It was decided to make a few increases, so that the Godstone stationmaster's pay rose from £71-10s to £80. The Board even considered linking pay increases to the annual dividend if it was over 4%. Three weeks later it was decided to issue all stationmasters with "superfine cloth coats braided." The stationmaster was an important figure in any community; when Wedderburn, the Ashford stationmaster, retired in 1860 he was presented with 100 sovereigns, a silver teapot and a milk jug by 200 subscribers.

Some of the rules applied to the staff by the SER Board caused public interest:

"Some consternation has been occasioned among the porters and others employed at the different stations of the SER, in consequence of an order having been received requiring those who had adopted moustaches to have them at once shaved off. Shortly after having been communicated with by the Stationmasters a general denuding of the upper lip was commenced, rather than adopting the alternative which disobedience of the order would have required of them."[4]

An interesting postscript to this tale is that in 1877 the staff petitioned for the right to have moustaches - and the Board allowed it.

Although the SER Board attempted to hold back pressure from its workers, it could not always afford to do so, especially when skilled staff were involved. On 29 November 1866 a deputation of drivers and firemen actually met the Board to ask for a ten hour day and regular hours. In return the Board offered a package of measures including reduced Sunday work, a 72 hour week, and better rest facilities with the provision of newspapers. They would be given a new greatcoat each year, lodging allowances would be increased from 1s to 2s6d and there would be good conduct premiums. In 1876 the Board even arranged that drivers and firemen should be given coffee at station refreshment rooms in bad weather.

There was not a general softening, however, for in 1867 the Board considered the reduction of wages at the Ashford works as one of its first steps in making economies. In 1871 the Ashford staff asked to have their hours reduced from 58 per week to 54hrs 30mins. Their daily hours were reduced from 10 to 9 in 1873, without a reduction of pay.

Pension arrangements were improved in 1868. Staff would be provided with a pension if they had spent 20 years with the SER, and were to contribute 0.5% of their salary. In 1874 a 77 year old carriage washer at Bricklayers Arms, who had worked for the SER for "38 years"[5], was awarded a 10s pension. A nightwatchman at St. Johns, who worked for the SER from September 1840 until 1875, was also given a 10s pension.

In 1869 the stationmasters at Charing Cross and Cannon Street were each paid £175. More pay increases were awarded in 1873, with goods guards calling for a pay increase from their present 30s; the SER agreed to only 2s6d a week lodging money, since they commonly spent three nights away each week. It is interesting, however, that the railway staff seemed to campaign for pay increases by their different grades, rather than combining together.

With the growth of the railway traffic, the role of stationmaster was increasingly important. To match this, the SER set new wage levels in 1874 - Charing Cross and Cannon Street at £250; London Bridge, Redhill and Ashford at £225; Folkestone at £190.

In May 1884 the SER had 8,896 employees. All employees received an extra day's pay in recognition of Queen Victoria's Jubilee in 1887. Lucky ones with 33 or more years service with the SER were given a medal - with the Queen on one side and Watkin on the other.

The ten hour day, almost the holy grail of the Victorian labour movement, was granted to SER drivers in 1890. Working a six day week, they could then expect to earn 8s a day after ten years experience, with 2s 6d lodging money.

The tradition of making payments when staff were killed continued, though not always generously. Signalman Bartlett of Blackheath was killed on 9 August 1890 when he tried to save a woman from being run over by a goods train. He left a widow and nine children, one of whom was an "imbecile"; his widow was given £50 but the coroner's jury recommended that the SER should provide a footbridge at the spot, indicating where it felt blame lay.

By January 1891 the SER employed about 12,000 people. Shareholders were told that the movement for shorter working hours and higher wages was having an adverse effect on profits. Later that year, though, a rumour alleged that porters at London Bridge made such a good living from tips that they paid the SER £1 a week for the privilege of wearing its uniform[6].

2. The Senior Staff

Few of the first South Eastern directors had any practical experience of railways, so in December 1841 they appointed J.S.Yeats as their Superintendent of the Line[7]. He was paid £700 a year, but had to provide security of £2,000 in case he absconded; he resigned in November 1842.

To bolster the company's management, Captain O'Brien RE was appointed Manager, on a salary of £1,000, in October 1844, although he then replaced Whitehead as Secretary in February 1845. Captain Charlewood RN, who had been Line Superintendent since April 1843 at £500, took over some of the management.

The rewards could be considerable for the senior officers, but the SER expected full attention from them. For much of the 1840s it relied on engineers who were really acting as a consultant rather than giving their full attention to the SER - Joseph Cubitt, and then Robert Stephenson. In August 1847 the SER decided to appoint Peter Barlow as their "engineer in chief"; he had gained much experience working with Henry Palmer and Sir William Cubitt. After a hiatus in January 1848, when he resigned, he was re-engaged on a salary of £1,500. His salary was increased to £2,000 in 1849, but his attention continued to be occupied by the Barlow Patent Track, and he was sacked in 1851, to be replaced by Thomas Drane (1851-4). Perhaps railway engineers were in short supply in the 1850s, for when Francis Brady was appointed engineer in 1870, succeeding Peter Ashcroft who had died, the salary was then only £1,000. Brady was a good example of promotion within the ranks, having been with the SER since 1848; indeed he remained engineer until 1896, working on many associated lines, until finally being replaced by Percy Tempest. Described on at least one occasion as "pig-headed", Brady was as much part of the SER as Watkin.

A consulting engineer was also retained. John Hawkshaw held the post for much of the Watkin era, having taken over in September 1861 although he was already heavily involved with various projects like the Charing Cross line. He was knighted in 1873. He ceased working for the SER in 1881, but was involved with the Channel Tunnel until 1886.

As has been seen with Barlow's patent, outside business interests caused problems. In July 1870 Brady was warned by the Board after he had taken out a patent on an interlocking apparatus, leading to the SER being sued by its former foreman of smiths over the same apparatus. Brady was told not to take out any patent without the Board's permission. He was allowed, however, to act as engineer for a number of concerns with links to the SER, such as the Hundred of Hoo Railway. He also helped with the Channel Tunnel, and is credited with having found coal 1,180 feet down at Shakespeare Cliff[8].

During the early 1850s James MacGregor acted as the SER General Manager, having taken over from O'Brien in 1845; he paid himself £2,000 and was actually a banker, not a railway manager. The day-to-day management of the traffic remained the responsibility of the Line Superintendent. Captain R.H.Barlow was appointed to this post in February 1851, at £500 a year; Finnigan was "passed over", but awarded 100 guineas compensation. Barlow took over as Manager in April 1854 (being opposed by MacGregor) but was sacked in October 1855 after the Reading accident; his replacement as Line Superintendent was G.W.Brown.

83. The inside of Charing Cross signal box in about 1890, showing two vital types of employment on the SER - the signalman and the clerk. It was the latter's task to log details of all train movements.

1854 saw a number of senior management alterations. G.Herbert retired after nine years as Secretary, being awarded £1,400, and was replaced by Samuel Smiles until 1866. Thomas Drane also resigned as engineer (rewarded with £1,166), to be replaced by Peter Ashcroft, who was paid £200 less at £800 than his predecessor. G.W.Brown, the new superintendent, was paid £500. The following year the folly of having both a General Manager and a Line Superintendent of comparable seniority was revealed by the Reading accident. Thus Eborall took over as General Manager and Superintendent on £1,000 a year, £1,500 by 1861, a post which he developed most successfully until his death in 1873.

When Eborall's health forced him to go abroad in 1862, the SER gave him £100. His salary was increased in keeping with the traffic - to £1,800 in May 1863, to £1,900 when Charing Cross opened and £2,000 after the opening of Cannon Street. Beneath him were a range of more specialised officials, such as the goods manager on £900 and Knight, the traffic superintendent, on £550. In May 1866 it was agreed that Eborall should be paid £2,250, with an increase of £250 each year for five years; no doubt this allowed him to return to his home at Lee Park, Blackheath, satisfied of his worth - for it is clear the SER Board took all care to keep him with them. Although he was allowed six months off from May 1873 due to illness, he never fully recovered and died on 19 December.

Eborall's replacement as Manager (the title General Manager was abolished) was John Shaw, who since 1868 had been Secretary and until 1879 managed to combine the posts, though Watkin took over some of the duties - perhaps he had some spare time after being defeated in the Exeter election. Shaw had risen since being appointed goods manager in 1851 and remained Secretary until his death in 1887.

In April 1869 Knight was promoted to Traffic Superintendent of the LBSCR and his place on the SER taken by William Cockburn. It is noticeable that Watkin became more involved with the practical questions of running the SER during the 1870s; we find him doing this on a number of occasions in the Board Minutes - such as in September 1878, recommending alterations in the Greenwich line junctions. Such matters were not really his field, for he was above all a grand strategist and a figurehead, and needed a skilled railway administrator to complement his talents. It is notable that the period 1877-9, before the appointment of a new General Manager, was the time when Watkin had the greatest difficulty in carrying his Board with him.

Under Eborall and Shaw the post of Line Superintendent became secondary; it was held by J.P.Knight until 1869 and then by William Cockburn until 1877 under the title of Outdoor Superintendent.

Myles Fenton became the General Manager in 1879 (with Shaw reverting to Secretary alone), holding the post until 1895; Fenton took care of the daily administration of a large railway company, allowing Watkin to be the visionary. Watkin always liked to be visible to - such as when he insisted on accompanying all Royal trains from July 1885. Fenton took on a number of worthy tasks, such as chairing the Charing Cross Hotel Company. He was knighted in 1888.

It would, however, be unfair to characterise Watkin as entirely responsible for the SER's more ambitious projects. He has been vilified for his desire to turn Dungeness into a port, but the SER were still considering that very question in October 1895, after he had retired from the Chair, and indeed they were also planning to extend facilities at Port Victoria.

The ebullient Watkin did find it easy to make enemies, and he often deserved the bad press he got. To push aside the complaints of season-ticket holders by saying that most of them were "fools" was hardly diplomatic, and got a deserved riposte from the *Railway Times*:

"The perversion of intellect which it seems is required to manage the undertaking [the SER] is once more seen to disadvantage in the arguments put forward at the meeting to account for the notorious shortcomings of the past year." [9]

Fenton, after whom the steamer *Myleta* had been named, retired in 1895. Management was reorganised to allow for the departure of both Watkin and Fenton; separate passenger and goods departments again had considerable leeway. The Chairman ceased to have a managerial role, especially since Watkin's replacement was, remarkably, Byng; born in 1818, he died at Tunbridge Wells on 21 May 1897. His successor, Sir George Russell MP, died on 7 March 1898. This left the way clear for Cosmo Bonsor, who was paid an allowance of £1,200.

The death of Byng really brought the SER era to an end, for Bonsor was to become the dominant figure in the SE&CR. Alfred Willis, the SER's passenger manager in 1895, became the General Manager of both the SER and LCDR from January 1899.

3. The Locomotive Department

The SER employed large numbers of staff at its London stations, but only in the various locomotive and rolling stock departments did it employ large numbers of people outside of the capital. In comparison, the numbers employed at the SER signalling works, at Angerstein Junction, were small.

The Locomotive Department was in the care of James Cudworth, appointed in July 1845 on £500 a year. Born in 1817, Cudworth had learnt his trade with Robert Stephenson at Darlington[10]. His salary had risen to only £650 by 1863, making him rather poorly rewarded compared to others of the senior SER staff. He remained Locomotive Superintendent until January 1874, when he was redesignated Locomotive Engineer and Alfred Watkin took over his previous title. Cudworth resigned in October 1876, leaving Watkin in sole charge until his removal in 1878. James Stirling became Locomotive Superintendent in March 1878.

84. SER 2-2-2 no. 147, probably photographed in about 1877 for it has a chimney designed by A.M.Watkin. The engine was scrapped in 1879.
(R.W.Kidner Collection)

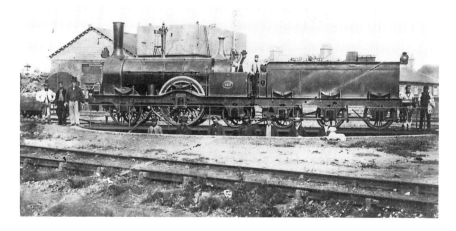

85. F Class, no. 11, built 1895 and withdrawn 1937.

During 1845 the SER had become increasingly discontented with the over-crowded locomotive works at New Cross, which it shared with the Brighton and Croydon companies. It decided to set up a new base at Ashford, the principal junction outside of London. In February 1846 £21,000 was spent on 185 acres of land and soon the company began to take a proprietorial interest in the town - in June it decided to provide £100 a year to support a clergyman, also providing money for a school and church, though the school did not open until 1852. A complete new town was planned by the SER architect, Samuel Beazley. By March 1847 houses were being built for the labourers; 48 were built in blocks of four costing £674 per block. In July the Board considered that a rent of 3s6d a house was appropriate. The first houses were ready in October, with more following soon afterwards. A Mechanics' Institute started in a room of one of the cottages on 4 October.

The growing town soon attracted attention. The *Maidstone Journal* was favourably impressed:

"The situation is most eligible and healthy and altogether this little community of industrious artisans and their families gives promise to become very flourishing, at once comfortable and cleanly in all their internal arrangements and highly picturesque in outward appearance."

The SER called its new town Alfred Town, but the name failed to achieve local popularity. Houses at Ashford reflected the rank of the employees - homes of a "better sort" were provided for clerks and foremen[11] but the public house was turned into an off-licence only.

The Locomotive Superintendent was responsible for the maintenance of the engines and the care of the staff involved. By December 1849 the costs involved were already considerable - the weekly wages bill varied from £197-15-2d at Ashford workshops, down to £8-14-6d at Canterbury. Bricklayers Arms and Deptford were the only other major depots with costs exceeding £50 a week.

The SER also set to work building the main workshops. The principal block was 396 feet long, there was a 280 feet long engine shed and a water tank capable of holding 56,700 gallons. Much of the planning was done by Robert Stephenson and the works came into active service in early 1847.

The first locomotives to be designed and built at Ashford emerged in 1853. Under Cudworth, the works at Ashford expanded massively, especially between 1859 and 1861. In the year up to 30 June 1859 six engines and tenders had been built at Ashford and 724 repaired, with the respective figures for the year to 30 June 1861 rising to 18 and 945[12]. For carriages and wagons, there were 99 new builds in the year to 30 June 1859 and 3,592 repairs, rising to 108 and 4,727 in 1861. Extension of the buildings then allowed 9,225 square yards for the construction and repair of engines and 5,420 square yards for the carriage and van department, as well as 2,434 for wagons. The locomotive running sheds increased to a capacity of 1,353 square yards. By January 1874 the SER had 243 locos in stock, of which one was "useless"; 166 were needed in the winter, and 170 in summer.

Cudworth was not responsible for carriages and wagons, which were the province of the C&W superintendent, Richard Mansell; the creation of the department at Ashford began in 1850[13].

Cudworth was censured after a fire at Ashford works on 17 July 1852; men who helped extinguish the blaze were treated to an excursion to France. However, Cudworth found that there were advantages to his job. In 1855 Napoleon III was so pleased with his journey on the SER that he gave Cudworth a gold snuff box mounted with jewels. His most famous locomotives were the *Mails*, two of which were built at Ashford in 1861 though others were ordered from outside contractors.

When Cudworth resigned in October 1876, an action largely forced on him by the commissioning of the *Ironclad* class from an outsider, the Board discussed whether Mansell or Alfred Watkin should replace him. In January 1877 both men filed a report as a result of which the whole Ashford works was placed in the charge of Mansell as "Mechanical Engineer", while Watkin became Locomotive Superintendent on £800. His dismissal later that year is discussed in Chapter Four. Mansell held the post long enough to influence the design of three small classes, including the *Gunboat* 0-4-4Ts built for suburban service after complaints from drivers about tender-first operating.

James Stirling, from the Glasgow & South-Western Railway, was appointed in Alfred Watkin's place in March 1878.

In November 1878 Mansell advised the SER that he would be resigning his post to go to Brazil, though in fact he remained with the SER until his retirement in January 1882. He was awarded a "piece of plate" selected by Lord Hothfield and a "consulting fee" of 50 guineas per annum.

In succession to Mansell, W.Wainwright was appointed Carriage & Wagon Superintendent - the SER's second choice. Stirling remained with the SER until the creation of the SE&CR, building many notable locomotives. Among the most handsome were probably the F class, which dominated the boat expresses in the later 1880s.

In 1893 Stirling requested improvements to the works at Ashford. By this stage Ashford had grown into a large and important town, though it was not a perfect site for the SER's works. In 1887 there had even been rumours that the SER would move their mechanical activities nearer to London; Paddock Wood, Sevenoaks and Grove Park were mentioned as prospective sites. Yet Ashford remained the centre of activity, perhaps because relocation costs would have been considerable, and in 1894 £7,590 was spent on new locomotive shops. Under Stirling SER employees at the works rose to 1,300 and the SER continued to act as a landowner of the old school - literally so, for it endowed the school and provided its pupils with an annual outing to Margate[14].

1. See the excellent social and economic study of the railway and Tonbridge - A.G.E.Jones, **When the Railway Came To Tonbridge.**
2. SER Minutes, 16 October 1845.
3. RAIL 635/196
4. **Maidstone Journal,** 1 January 1866.
5. Presumably this is a miscalculation, since there would have been few SER employees in 1836, although the man could have been a former L&GR employee, absorbed into SER staff in 1845.
6. **Railway Times,** 26 September 1891.
7. Titles of officials are those used at the time, including the practice of denoting the importance of some by the use of capitals.
8. SER Minutes, 6 March 1890.
9. **Railway Times,** 25 January 1890.
10. J.Marshall, **Dictionary of Railway Engineers.**
11. SER Minutes, 6 January 1853.
12. SER Minutes, 18 July 1861.
13. E & J Larkin, **The Railway Workshops of Britain,** p.94.
14. G.Turner, **Ashford - The Coming of the Railway.**

SOURCES

The following sources have been of special use in the writing of this book:
Minute Books, Reports etc. of the following railway companies:
Bexleyheath Railway
Bromley Direct Railway
Chipstead Valley Railway
Cranbrook & Paddock Wood Railway
Crowhurst, Sidley & Bexhill Railway
Dover & Deal Joint Committee
Hundred of Hoo Railway
London Bridge & Charing Cross Railway
London, Brighton & South Coast Railway
LBSCR & SER Joint Committee
LBSCR & SER (Croydon, Oxted & East Grinstead Railways) Joint Committee
London, Chatham & Dover Railway
London & Greenwich Railway
Lydd Railway
Reading, Guildford & Reigate Railway
South Eastern Railway
West Wickham & Hayes Railway
Westerham Valley Railway
Woodside & South Croydon Railway and Joint Committee

The following periodicals have been used:
Bygone Kent
Chatham Observer
The Graphic
Herapath's Railway Magazine
Illustrated London News
Journal of The Railway & Canal Historical Society
Journal of Transport History
Kentish Gazette
Maidstone Journal
Pall Mall Gazette
Railway Times
The Times

The following works have been consulted to varying degrees:
H.V.Borley: *Chronology of London Railways*
D.L.Bradley: *The Locomotive History of The South Eastern Railway*
R.Bucknall: *Boat Trains & Channel Packets*
R.H.Clark: *Southern Region Record*
C.R.Clinker: *Clinker's Register of Closed Passenger Stations*
J.Corley: *The Tunbridge Wells, Snodland & Edenbridge Suspension Railway*
E.Course: *The Bexleyheath Line* (two different editions, 1954 and 1982)

The Railways of Southern England, vols. I and II
M.Forwood: *The Elham Valley Railway*
B.Hart: *The Hythe & Sandgate Railway*
A.Hasenson: *The Golden Arrow*
       The History of Dover Harbour
J.Hilton: *History of the SE&CR*, vols I-III
J.Howard-Turner: *The London, Brighton & South Coast Railway*
A.A.Jackson: *London's Termini*
D.J.Jeremy: *Dictionary of Business Biography*
A.G.E.Jones: *When The Railway Came To Tonbridge*
R.W.Kidner: *The North Kent Line*
       The Oxted Line
       The Reading-Tonbridge Line
J.Laker: *History Of Deal*
H.D.Miles: *Pugilistica*
O.S.Nock: *The South Eastern & Chatham Railway*
N.Owen: *The Tattenham Corner Branch*
S.Smiles: *Autobiography*
R.H.G.Thomas: *The London & Greenwich Railway*
E.W.P.Veale: *Gateway To The Continent*
R.A.Williams: *The London & South Western Railway*
T.Woodman: *The Railways To Hayes*

ACKNOWLEDGMENTS:

The author is grateful to the staff of the following institutions:
Public Record Office, Ashford Library, Cambridge University Library, Kent Local Studies Library, Maidstone Borough Library, and Rochester Library.

My thanks are also due to my fellow members of the Railway & Canal Historical Society, who have spent many hours checking my manuscript for errors of fact and grammar. To Edwin Course, Alan Jackson, Roger Kidner, and Ron Thomas I am extremely grateful. My thanks also go to Lens of Sutton for the very great help they have been with illustrations. Keith and Caroline Mullins have provided hotel accomodation on many occasions. My wife, Fiona, has been a model of patience while the twins have delayed their arrival long enough for me to complete this present work. G.Boyes, E.Baldock, D.Cullum and G.Gardner have also helped in a variety of ways.

No work of railway history can ever be judged complete. The author is therefore always interested to hear of new evidence which might shed extra light on the events described in this book.

INDEX OF CHARACTERS

Abernethy, James 101
Agar, Edward 291-3
Allport, James 126, 188
Angerstein, John 9, 74, 77-8, 82
Ashcroft, Peter 29-30, 41, 79, 116, 161-2, 200, 302-3
Barlow, John 32, 38
Barlow, Peter 15, 25-6, 58, 62,, 77, 180-1, 193-6, 200, 212, 215, 241, 261, 302
Barlow, Capt. R. 28-9, 31, 145, 184, 252, 300, 303
Barne, Colonel 88-9
Barry, E.M. 116-7, 120
Baxendale, Joseph 16, 20-2, 140, 260
Beadle, Charles 87
Beattie, Alexander 29-30, 45, 49, 65, 130, 135, 167, 232
Beazley, Samuel 77, 144, 306
Betts, Edward 19, 170-1
Bibby, John 39, 45-6
Bidder, G.P. 72, 195
Bonaparte, Prince Jerome 276
Bonsor, Cosmo 50, 52, 68, 206, 305
Boulanger, General 51
Boxer, Capt. 268,270-1, 273-4
Brabourne, Lord E. (formerly Knatchbull-Hugessen) 45, 50, 64, 143, 254
Brady, Francis 41, 87, 89, 100, 148, 167, 202, 232 255, 302-3
Brogden, John, junior 23-4, 76-7, 94, 105
Brogden, John, senior 23
Brown, G.W. 28, 30-1, 303
Brunel, Isambard K. 75, 116
Buckley, Nathan 45
Burton, Decimus 7, 15, 21
Byng, Hon. James 28-30, 32, 34-5, 38-9, 45-6, 50-2, 112, 114, 200, 232, 305
Camden, Marquis of 158
Campbell, Sir J. 27-9
Charlewood, Captain 141, 302
Child, Coles 27-8, 32, 35, 37-8, 114, 131, 133, 242
Chubb, J.A. 40
Clarke, Henry 196
Cockburn, William 304
Cubitt, Joseph 157, 244, 302
Cubitt, Lewis105, 140, 171, 254
Cubitt, William 11-14, 20-1, 54, 75, 192, 259, 265
Cudworth, James 44, 305-7
Darnley, Lord 80, 173
Devonshire, Duke of 33, 217, 248
Dickens, Charles 95, 142, 147, 252, 260, 284
Dickson, Alexander 236
Dixon, John 239
Drane, Thomas 29-30, 58, 158, 200, 302-3

Eborall, Cornelius 31-2, 39, 41-2, 98, 125, 130-1, 148-9, 164, 202, 274, 304
Edwards, Capt. 132-3
Fenton, Myles 46-7, 49, 52, 68, 86, 123, 276, 304-5
Fielden, Joshua 45
Fielden, William 23-4
Firbank, Joseph 137, 219, 226
Forbes, James Staats 39, 41, 46, 50, 96-7, 125, 255
Forster, Matthew 27-30, 59
Fowler, Henry 79, 227, 263, 271
Fox, Sir Charles 90, 247
Furness, George 66, 100, 237
Gamond, Thome de 278-9
Gathorne-Hardy, A. 52, 206, 224
Gibbs, J. 13
Giles, Francis 177, 180
Gilpin, Charles 32, 286
Gladstone, Willam 55, 104, 279
Granville, Earl 255
Green, William 7-8, 72
Grenfell, P.St L. 8, 11, 15
Grissell, Peto & Betts, 19, 105, 171, 241, 244, 260
Halswell, Edmund 15
Hamilton, John 27, 32-3, 35, 38, 183, 270
Harding, Benjamin 22
Harris, Lord 247
Hawkshaw, John 42, 108, 112-5, 117, 265, 279-80, 302-3
Herapath, John 8-9
Herbert, George 29-30, 58, 303
Hilton, Charles 34, 159, 244, 246
Hoof, Messrs. 105, 171, 193-4
Horeau, Hector 279
Hutchinson, General 83, 136, 138, 218, 228, 238
Hutchinson, Lt. 20
Jackson, Thomas 87
James, William 6-7, 239
Jay, John 161-2
Joliffe, Sir William 56
Kay, J. 31, 114, 242
Kersey, Robert 87-9
Kirkland, Sir John 23
Laing, Samuel 41, 46, 48, 62, 218, 230
Landmann, Col.George 7, 9-10, 70-4, 243
Leopold, King of Belgium 49, 276
Locke, Joseph 171
Low, William 279
Lucas & Aird, Messrs. 83, 80-9, 125, 135, 150, 232
Lushington, Charles 159
Lushington, S.R. 246
MacGregor, James 22-30, 78, 128, 130, 145, 176, 179, 183, 303
McIntosh, Hugh 70-1
Mangles, Frederick 177
Mansell, Richard 307
Mathieu, Albert 277-8
Mellor, Col. John 49, 206

Mellor, Jonathan 27, 29-33, 37, 44-6, 49, 112, 280
Miller & Blackie, Messrs. 244
Mocatta, David 178
Mottray, T. de 278-9
Napoleon III 145, 163, 272, 278-9 307
Northumberland, Duke of 187
O'Brien, W. 23, 302
Oakley, Henry 49-50, 62 205, 257
Palmer, Henry 6-7, 9, 11, 72, 302
Pasley, General 19-20, 92, 245
Payerne, Prosper 278
Peto & Betts 19
Peto, Samuel Morton 19, 65, 85, 157
Pierce, William 291-2
Price, J. 206-7
Pringle, Capt.J. 7, 11
Pritchard, Martin 22, 24, 179, 278
Pullman, G. 289-90
Radnor, Lord 42, 150, 153-4, 231, 233, 235-6, 264
Ramsbottom, John 44
Rastrick, John 90
Rawson, Henry 45
Redesdale, Lord 39, 82, 113
Rennie John 6, 12
Rennie, Logan & Matthews, Messrs. 16
Renshaw, James 25, 28-30, 130
Rich, Henry 26-7, 30, 34, 39, 59, 114, 248
Richardson, Joshua 240
Rigby, William 89, 166
Romney, Lord 175
Russell, Sir George50, 52, 206, 305
Salomons, David 8, 124, 177, 179, 192
Sandilands, Col. 230
Schuster, Leo 35, 60, 132, 216
Scott, Archibald 166,7
Shaw, John 40-2, 46, 58, 295, 304
Sinclair, Peter 9
Smiles, Samuel 29-34, 38, 40, 111-3, 270, 293
Smith, G.E. 26-8, 232
Sondes, Lord 34, 247
Spens, Nathaniel 50
Stephenson, George 33
Stephenson, G.R. 209
Stephenson, Robert 29, 33, 76, 92, 94, 110, 158, 170-1, 179-80, 195, 208, 239, 244, 246, 265, 307
Stiff, Philip 232
Stirling, James 305, 307-8
Surtees, Col. Charles 45, 88
Telford, Thomas 6, 70
Tempest, Percy 302
Teulon, Seymour 28, 34, 39, 112, 248
Thompson, W.G. 24, 32, 39, 112, 160
Toomer, J. 96-7
Torrington, Viscount 24, 28
Tredwell, Messrs. 15, 76
Tyler, Captain 31, 83, 116, 122, 202, 288
Tyndale, Thomas 8,15, 259, 267
Tyrell, J. 15
Victoria, Queen 70, 107, 164, 279, 302
Vignoles, Charles 75-6, 176

Wainwright, W. 307
Walker, James 10, 57, 70
Walker, Thomas 228, 233, 237
Walter, George 7-8, 10, 70-4
Warburton, Lord 10
Warren, Capt. Daniel 27-8, 32, 121-2, 262
Warton & Warden, Messrs 197, 200
Warwick, Countess of 18, 56
Watkin, Alfred 42, 44, 46, 135, 258, 305-6
Watkin, Edward 22, 36-52, 64-5, 82, 99-100, 102, 108, 111, 119-23, 127, 144, 151, 154, 162-5, 167, 203, 224-5, 227-9, 232-3, 235, 238, 255, 257-8, 264, 277, 279-281, 288-9, 302, 304-5
Webster, Sir Augustus 198
Wellington, Duke of 55, 115, 252, 284
Whatman, James 27, 39, 45, 49, 64, 112, 232
Wigsell, Capt., and Trustees 66, 220
Willis, Alfred 52, 305
Wilson, Josiah 24-5, 183
Wynne, Colonel 58, 211
Wythes, George 30, 77, 112-4, 116, 162, 173, 188, 196, 211-2
Yeats, James 11, 16, 302
Yolland, Colonel 61, 64, 101, 108, 118, 134

INDEX OF COMPANIES ETC

Note: the SER itself is not included in this section, but sections of it can be found under the Place Names index. Companies formed independently, but later absorbed into the SER, are included here.

Beckenham, Lewes & Brighton Rly 35, 111, 216
Beckenham & Sydenham Jct Rly 132
Bexleyheath Rly 49, 87-90
Boulogne & Amiens Rly 265-6, 267
Brighton, Lewes & Hastings Rly 193-4, 208
Brighton, Lewes & Tunbridge Wells Rly 195
Brighton, Uckfield & Tunbridge Wells Rly 216
Bromley Direct Rly 42, 164, 166-7
Canterbury & Whitstable Rly 7, 239-43
Caterham Rly 30, 65-8
Caterham & Godstone Valley Rly 67
Central Kent Rly 8, 10, 158-9, 244
Channel Tunnel Co 42, 152, 277-81, 303
Charing Cross Hotel Co 115, 120. 296, 304
Charing Cross Rly 36, 112-25
Chipstead Valley Rly 68-9
Commercial Steam Packet Co. 249, 266
Cranbrook & Paddock Wood Rly 225-7

Croydon & Caterham Rly 133, 137
Croydon, Oxted & E.Grinstead Rly 137, 219-22
Crystal Palace & S.London Jct Rly 42, 121, 166
Direct London & Portsmouth Rly 29, 59, 176, 181
Direct Mid-Kent Rly 28, 158
Direct South Eastern Rly 35, 39, 150-9
Dover & Deal Joint Rly 44-5, 48, 254-8
East Kent Rly, see **London, Chatham & Dover**
East London Rly 45, 49, 63-5, 127
Elham Valley Rly 48-9, 231, 236-8
Epsom Downs Extension Rly 68-9
Gravesend & Rochester Rly 76-7, 90-5
Great Eastern Rly 63-5
Great Northern Rly 25, 49, 62, 108, 125-7
Great Western Rly 25, 37-8, 86, 117, 178-9, 182-90
Headcorn & Maidstone Jct Rly 175
Herne Bay & Faversham Rly 242-3
Hundred of Hoo Rly 48, 51, 100-2
Hythe & Sandgate Rly 152, 230-6, 264
Hythe & Sandgate Tramway 235-6
International Communication Co. 263
Kent Rly 74, 158, 244, 251
Kent & E.Sussex Rly 227
Kentish Railway (1829) 6-7, 74
London & Birmingham Rly 12
London & Blackwall Rly 75
London & Brighton Rly 11-14, 16-18, 23, 48-56, 104, 176, 193-4, 208
London, Brighton & S. Coast Rly 27, 38-69, 80, 84, 104-6, 122, 133, 137-9, 158, 185, 189, 196-8, 200-5, 215-22, 304
London Central Rly 121
London & Chatham Rly 74-5
London, Chatham & Dover Rly 22, 26, 32-52, 78, 82, 94, 96-102, 111, 114, 124, 131-3, 135, 146, 150-4, 158-60, 163, 165-7, 174-5, 219, 231, 234, 236-8, 243-4, 247-50, 253-8, 262-5, 270, 274-5, 277, 279-80
London, Chatham & N.Kent Rly 75
London & Croydon Rly 12, 14, 16, 18, 53-6, 75, 104-6, 157
London & Dover Rly, see **Northfleet & Dover**
London & Gravesend Rly 9
London & Greenwich Rly 7-11, 24, 54, 70-4, 104-6, 290
London, Lewes & Brighton Rly 39, 217
London & North-Western Rly 25, 37, 40, 112, 119, 122-3, 168
London & South-Western Rly 39, 110-1, 116-20, 123, 178-90, 267
Loose Valley Rly 174-5, 225
Lydd Rly 225-9, 233
Maidstone & Ashford Rly 44, 50, 152-4, 175, 224
Manchester, Sheffield & Lincolnshire Rly 37-8, 50, 123
Metropolitan Rly 41, 44-6, 50, 63-5, 114, 122, 125-7
Metropolitan & Brighton Rly 218

Metropolitan District Rly 64, 120
Mid Hants Railway 180-9
Mid-Kent Railway 23, 27, 33, 35, 56-8, 60, 79, 115, 128-35, 137, 159, 216
Mid-Kent (Bromley-St Mary Cray) Rly 131-2, 159, 160
Mid-Kent & South Kent Rly 66
Mid-Kent & Tunbridge Rly 159
Midland Rly 108, 125-7, 188
Nord Rly (France) 268-75
Northfleet & Dover Rly 9, 243
North Kent Extension Rly 99
North-Western & Charing Cross Rly 117
Pickford & Co. 22-3
Reading, Guildford & Reigate Rly 25-6, 39, 57, 176-90
Rye & Dunge-ness Rly & Pier Co. 227
Seabrook Estate Co. 44, 233
Sevenoaks, Maidstone & Tunbridge Rly 158, 160, 164, 173-4
South Eastern & Continental Steam Packet Co. 266-8
South London Rly 80, 111
Staines, Wokingham & Woking Jct Rly 185-6
Submarine Continental Rly Co. 280-1
Submarine Tunnel Rly 279
Surrey & Sussex Jct Rly 51, 67, 137, 217, 219
Tenterden Rly 225-7
Thames & Medway Canal 90-1
Tunbridge Wells & Eastbourne Rly 218
Tunbridge Wells, Snodland & Edenbridge Suspension Rly 6-7
Upper Medway Navigation 170-1, 194
Walmer, Deal & Adisham Rly 253
Weald of Kent Canal 6
Weald of Kent Rly 223-4
West End of London & Crystal Palace Rly 27, 29, 33, 111, 130-1, 158-9
West Kent Rly 158
Westerham Valley Rly 167-9
Westminster Terminus Rly 110
West Wickham & Hayes Rly 135-7
Woodside & S. Croydon Rly 46, 137-9

INDEX OF PLACES

Abbey Wood, 77-79, 295
Abbott's Cliff, 19, 20, 155, 280
Addiscombe, 14, 64, 133, 134, 137
Adisham, 41, 253, 255
Admiralty Pier, 145, 146, 148, 150, 256, 262, 263, 270, 274, 288, 291
Albury, 179
Aldershot, 187, 188, 286
Aldershot Junction, 187, 188
Alkham, 237, 264
Allington, 173
Alton, 177-181, 188
Ambleteuse, 270
Amiens, 265, 267
Andresselles, 272
Angerstein's Junction, 79
Angerstein's Wharf, 77, 87, 133, 296
Appledore, 41, 209-213, 223-288
Archcliffe, 14, 18, 20
Archcliffe Fort, 21, 141
Archcliffe Junction, 255, 256, 257
Archcliffe Tunnel, 141, 151
Arundel, 176
Ash, 178, 179, 181, 182, 187, 188
Ash Junction, 181, 188, 190
Ash Road, 254
Ash Vale, 180
Ashford, 8, 11, 18, 19, 42, 44, 47, 49, 50, 55, 59, 75, 96, 140-146, 149, 152-158, 165, 175, 193-195, 196, 208-214, 224, 225, 227, 237, 240, 243, 244, 249, 255, 259, 286, 288, 297-301, 306, 307
Ashurst Junction, 219
Aylesbury, 127
Aylesford, 173, 175
Baker Street, 123
Banstead, 68
Barcombe, 218
Bargrave, 143, 230
Barham, 236, 238
Barnehurst, 88, 89
Basingstoke, 184, 185
Basingstoke Canal, 180, 182
Bat & Ball, 163
Battersea, 34, 111
Battle, 195, 196, 197, 198, 202, 203, 204, 205, 216, 218
Beachborough, 9
Beadle's Siding, 83
Beckenham, 35, 111, 126, 128, 130, 131, 132, 133, 150, 216, 217, 218
Beckenham Junction, 131, 134
Beckenham Road, 134
Beltring, 171
Belvedere, 79, 81, 86
Belvedere Road, 115
Benenden, 226
Bermondsey, 71
Betchworth, 182, 186, 187, 189, 190, 286
Bexhill, 201, 205, 206, 207, 216
Bexley, 52, 79, 81, 85, 86, 88
Bexleyheath, 78, 87, 88, 89, 90
Bickley, 39, 131, 132, 161
Bingham Road, 137, 139
Birkenhead, 190
Birmingham, 277
Bishopsbourne, 237, 238
Blackfriars, 41, 65, 112, 113, 114, 120, 122
Blackfriars Junction, 62, 108, 121-127, 290
Blackfriars Road, 111, 123, 125
Blackheath, 39, 76, 77, 84-89, 286, 299, 302, 304
Blackheath Park, 88, 89
Blackheath Tunnel, 77, 79, 80, 81, 83, 86
Blackwater, 179, 181, 182, 185, 189, 190
Bletchingley, 15, 17, 18, 143, 297
Bletchingley Tunnel, 141, 148
Blue Anchor, 62, 70
Bopeep, 197, 208
Bopeep Junction, 196, 198, 201, 203, 204
Bopeep Tunnel, 202, 203
Borough Market, 124
Borough Market Junction, 121, 124
Boulogne, 41, 265-275
Bourne Park, 238
Bowbeech, 15
Box Hill, 182, 185, 187, 188, 189, 190
Brampton Park, 87
Brasted, 169
Brasted Park, 168
Brenchley, 15
Bricklayers Arms, 24, 30, 53, 55, 57, 58, 62, 63, 70, 75, 78, 80, 104-108, 110, 122, 126, 132, 165, 171, 173, 284, 294, 295, 301, 306
Bricklayers Arms Junction, 58, 106, 108, 126
Bridge, 238
Brighton, 7, 8, 11, 12, 18, 35, 39, 40, 55, 60, 111, 120, 176, 193, 195, 215, 216, 217, 218, 283, 289
Brixton, 108, 118
Broad Street, 121
Broadstairs, 34, 249, 284
Brockham, 180, 187
Brockham Siding, 190
Bromley, 27, 29, 33, 42, 44, 128, 130, 131, 132, 135, 158, 164, 166, 167, 247, 289
Brussels, 265
Buckland Junction, 255
Bulverhythe, 194
Burgh Heath, 68, 69
Burwash, 197
Caen, 277
Calais, 35, 41, 265-278, 284
California Siding, 190
Camberwell, 6
Cannon Street, 32, 36, 40, 47, 99, 108, 109, 114, 117-125, 155, 188, 289, 301, 304
Cannon Street West Junction, 120
Canterbury, 6-8, 26, 35, 43, 44, 70, 77, 141, 142, 153, 157, 171, 231, 236-251, 288, 290, 295
Capel, 176

Caterham, 30, 65, 66, 67, 68, 133, 137, 169, 217, 219
Caterham Junction, 61, 66, 67, 68, 137, 287
Catford Bridge, 134
Cator Estate, 88, 130
Channel Tunnel, 42, 46, 50, 51, 152, 277, 303
Charing, 225
Charing Cross, 32, 33, 34, 36, 38, 47, 52, 60, 88, 95, 107-125, 189, 218, 255, 270, 275, 277, 288, 290, 301, 303, 304
Charing Cross Hotel, 50, 115, 296, 304
Charlton, 75, 76, 77, 79, 82, 83, 85
Chart, 158, 224
Chartham, 244, 246, 248, 251
Chatham, 6, 26, 42, 47, 48, 75, 76, 90, 92, 94, 95, 96, 98, 101, 121
Chatham Central, 51, 98, 99
Chelsfield, 162
Cheriton, 7, 230, 237, 262, 298
Cheriton Arch, 152, 153, 264, 265
Cheriton Junction, 238
Chevening Halt, 169
Chilham, 26, 76, 77, 92, 110, 175, 241, 244-251
Chilworth, 187, 188, 189, 190, 286
Chipstead, 68, 69
Chislehurst, 79, 80, 122, 131, 159, 161, 162, 163, 164, 166, 284, 296
Chislet, 246
Church Street Incline, 240
Clapham, 108, 110, 118, 122
Clapham Junction, 122
Clayton, 11
Cliffe, 99, 101
Clock House, 134
Clowes Bank, 243
Clowes Wood, 239
Clowes Wood Incline, 240
Cobham, 75
Cockle Shell Hard, 99
Cold Blow, 293
Colebrook Viaduct, 200
Cologne, 265
Combe Farm Lane, 85
Commericial Dock, 64, 78, 81, 108
Coombe Haven Viaduct, 206
Coombe Lane, 137, 138
Corbetts Lane, 11, 53, 54, 56, 57, 62, 84, 106, 108, 109, 123
Coulsdon, 14, 62, 63, 65, 67
Crabbe, 257
Cranbrook, 223, 224, 225, 226, 227
Crayford, 6, 75, 80, 81, 82, 86
Crowhurst, 205, 206, 207, 219, 220
Crowhurst Junction North, 219
Crowhurst Siding, 155, 205
Crowthorne, 190
Croydon, 9, 11, 14, 27, 35, 40, 54, 56, 59, 60, 118, 128, 131, 133, 139, 157, 217, 219, 220
Croydon Central, 65, 133
Crystal Palace, 42, 46, 49, 59, 60, 64, 121, 123, 133, 134

Crystal Palace High Level, 81
Cuxton, 131, 171, 173
Danson Park, 87
Dartford, 6, 32, 77, 78, 79, 80, 82, 85, 86, 87, 99, 131, 160, 161
Dartmouth Arms, 14, 54
Deal, 8, 27, 42, 44, 45, 47, 48, 165, 246, 247, 250, 251, 252, 253, 254, 255, 256, 257, 288
Denton, 95
Deptford, 63, 70, 71, 74, 76, 78, 81, 83, 85, 86, 275, 290, 306
Deptford Creek, 76
Deptford Pier, 74
Deptford Royal Dockyard, 84
Dieppe, 273, 275
Ditchling, 11
Dorking, 35, 40, 60, 176-182, 185-190
Dover, 6-12, 14, 15, 18-21, 27, 35, 40-45, 48, 50, 58, 70, 72, 74, 140, 141, 145, 148, 149, 150, 154, 171, 190, 192, 227, 236, 238, 246, 247, 248, 251-270, 275-284, 288-293, 296, 300
Dover Harbour, 14, 146, 254, 259
Duncton Green, 166
Dungeness, 41, 42, 49, 211, 217, 224-229, 289, 296, 304
Dungerness, 227
Dunkirk, 276
Dunton Green, 164, 165, 166, 169, 173
Dunton Green & Riverhead, 162
Dymchurch, 227, 233
Earlswood, 13
East Croydon, 60, 66
East Farleigh, 171, 174, 175, 284
East Grinstead, 137, 138, 215-220, 283
East Peckham, 171
Eastbourne, 60, 202, 206, 215-219
Eden Park, 136, 137
Edenbridge, 6, 17, 140, 144, 145, 146, 201, 217, 219, 220, 285, 286, 289
Edgware Road, 122
Elephant & Castle, 14, 54, 124
Elham, 48, 49, 230, 231, 236, 237, 238
Elham Valley, 231
Elmers End, 133, 134, 135
Eltham, 6, 75, 77, 78, 79, 81, 83-87, 157
Eltham Park, 87, 89
Embankment, 117
Epsom, 57, 68, 176, 185
Epsom Downs, 68
Eridge, 216
Erith, 77, 79, 81, 83, 85, 86, 87, 134
Etchingham, 197, 198, 201, 203, 205, 218, 226, 286
Etchinghill, 236, 237
Euston, 121, 123
Evelyn Estate, 85
Exeter, 304
Falconwood, 89
Farnborough, 7, 130, 179, 180, 181, 182, 188, 190
Farnham, 177, 180, 181
Farnham Junction, 187
Farningham Road, 88

Farringdon, 114, 125
Faversham, 26, 46, 101, 241, 242, 244, 246, 247, 248
Faversham Creek, 247
Finsbury Park, 121
Flushing, 43, 48
Folkestone, 7, 8, 11, 12, 15, 19, 21, 35, 41-50, 140-143, 146, 152, 153, 155, 165, 227, 231-237, 241, 257, 259-275, 277, 280, 283, 284, 289, 290, 292, 293, 298, 301
Folkestone Art Treasures Exhibition, 238
Folkestone Central, 154, 155
Folkestone Harbour, 34, 144, 190, 230, 231, 235, 259, 261, 264, 265, 274, 288
Folkestone Junction, 20, 148, 149, 151, 152, 153
Folkestone Pier, 262, 263
Folkestone Warren, 15, 140, 141, 148, 152
Foord Valley, 259
Foord Viaduct, 19, 21, 234, 262
Foots Cray, 79
Forest Hill, 14, 57, 58, 62
Forest Row, 6
Forwood, 201
France, 23
Frant, 197, 198, 202, 205, 217, 218, 224, 286, 299
Frimley, 181
Frindsbury, 92
Gillingham, 98, 99
Godalming, 176, 177, 178, 185
Godmersham, 245
Godstone, 8, 11, 12, 15-17, 28, 67, 140, 143, 144, 145, 149, 154, 155, 215, 217, 219, 295, 301
Godstone Road, 65, 66
Gomshall, 177-182, 187, 189, 190, 286
Goudhurst, 15, 223, 226
Grain, 44, 101, 102
Gravesend, 6-9, 24, 31, 48, 51, 70, 72, 74, 75, 77, 78, 80, 84, 86, 90, 92, 94, 95, 99, 249, 285, 286
Great Chart, 152
Greenhithe, 7, 77, 86
Greenwich, 6, 7, 8, 10, 24, 32, 33, 54, 60, 63, 70-80, 82, 116, 128, 160, 284, 290, 304
Greenwich Park, 74, 75, 76, 78
Grimsby, 44, 281
Groombridge, 201, 216, 217, 218, 219, 224, 227
Grove Ferry, 244, 245, 246, 249, 251, 299
Grove Hill Tunnel, 196
Grove Junction, 203, 217, 218, 219
Grove Park, 153, 164, 165, 166, 167
Grove Tunnel, 200, 204
Guestling, 211, 213
Guildford, 176, 178, 181-184, 188, 288
Guston, 255
Hadlow, 165
Hailsham, 216, 217, 218, 219
Hall's Siding, 60
Halling, 173, 175
Halstead, 163, 164, 166
Ham Street, 209-213, 224, 232
Hampstead Road, 117
Harrietsham, 225
Hartley, 223, 224, 226

Hastings, 36, 40, 42, 49, 57, 58, 59, 142, 161, 182, 190-198, 200-217, 226, 228, 270, 272, 288, 289, 290, 295
Havant, 176
Hawkesbury Street Junction, 255, 256
Hawkhurst, 193, 223, 225, 226, 227
Hayes, 135, 136
Hayes Common, 135
Haywards Heath, 16
Headcorn, 15, 17, 28, 145, 153, 155, 173, 174, 175, 192, 193, 194, 208, 223-228, 286, 295, 298
Heathfield, 216
Hellingly, 217
Herne Bay, 32, 241, 242, 243, 249, 250
Herne Hill, 14, 34, 122
High Brooms, 203, 205
High Halstow, 100
Higham, 23, 90, 92, 94, 95, 284
Higham Tunnel, 90
Hildenborough, 162, 163, 164, 165, 166, 173
Hither Green, 80, 86, 109, 164, 165, 166
Hither Green Junction, 164
Holborn Viaduct, 41
Hollington, 203, 204
Hoo Junction, 94, 95, 100
Hoo Peninsula, 44
Hope Mill, 226
Horsham, 185
Horsmonden, 15
Hove, 8
Hundred of Hoo, 48, 51, 99, 100, 102
Hungerford, 105, 185
Hungerford Bridge, 32, 106, 110, 112, 114
Hungerford Market, 32, 110, 111, 112, 114
Hurst Green, 11, 220
Hurst Green Junction, 219, 221
Hythe, 20, 41, 42, 44, 50, 140, 149, 150, 152, 223, 227, 230-236, 264
Icklesham, 193
Ightham, 157, 158, 159, 165
Isle of Grain, 43, 99, 100
Jackwood's Spring, 194
Jolly Sailor, 11, 12, 13, 14, 53
Kearsney, 47, 48, 258, 264
Kearsney Loop Junction, 256, 257
Kemp Town, 217
Kenardington, 224
Kenley, 65, 66, 67
Kennett & Avon Canal, 182
Kentish Town, 121
Keymer, 198
Kidbrook, 89
King Street, 250
Kingswood, 68, 69
Knockholt, 162, 163, 164, 165, 166
Ladywell, 134, 164
Ladywell Junction, 81
Lamberhurst, 224, 226
Le Treport, 272, 273, 275, 277
Leatherhead, 35, 182, 185
Lee, 75, 81, 84, 85, 87, 88
Leigh, 155

Lewes, 11, 34, 35, 39, 40, 193, 195, 198, 215-219
Lewisham, 27, 30, 35, 40, 77, 78, 79, 84, 128, 130, 131, 158, 159, 161, 164, 165, 299
Lewisham Junction, 77, 80, 131, 132
Lewisham Road, 161
Lidham Hill, 195, 196, 208, 209, 210, 212
Lille, 265
Limpsfield, 11
Lingfield, 217
Little Wickham, 135
Littlestone, 49
Littlestone-on-Sea, 264, 277
Liverpool, 22, 24, 39
Liverpool Central, 190
Liverpool Street, 64, 127
London Bridge, 17, 18, 27, 33, 51-62, 70, 71, 72, 83, 86, 97, 98, 104, 105, 110-118, 124, 126, 132, 145, 161, 184, 210, 212, 249, 286, 289, 292, 293, 297, 299-302
Loose Valley, 174, 225
Lord Warden Hotel, 27, 144, 146, 148, 149, 150, 154, 173, 268, 272
Lower Sydenham, 134
Ludgate, 114
Ludgate Hill, 125
Lydd, 213, 225-229, 233, 234, 289
Lydden, 236
Lyminge, 236, 238
Maidstone, 6-9, 17, 23, 24, 27, 41, 42, 44, 47, 67, 77, 81, 92, 94, 128, 140, 152, 153, 154, 158, 160, 164, 165, 169-175, 194, 223, 224, 225, 229, 244, 246, 248, 286, 295, 299
Maidstone Barracks, 174
Maidstone Road, 17
Manchester, 27, 31, 37, 38, 130
Mansion House, 120
Marden, 17, 153, 155, 223, 296, 299, 300
Marden Park, 220, 221
Margate, 6, 7, 36, 43, 102, 141, 242-250, 252, 253, 255, 256, 268, 270, 285, 286, 289
Marseilles, 268
Martello Tunnel, 150, 151, 155
Martin Mill, 254, 255, 256, 257, 296
Mayfield, 196, 197, 201
Maze Hill, 79, 82, 83, 85
Meopham, 9
Merstham, 11, 13, 14, 16, 18, 25, 26, 54, 56, 58, 59, 60, 61, 63, 140, 145, 284, 293, 299
Merstham Tunnel, 56, 63
Metropolitan Junction, 124
Mid Street Siding, 149
Milton, 95
Milton Range, 95
Minster, 245, 248-255
Minster Junction, 252
Mount Pleasant, 204
Mount Pleasant Tunnel, 211
Mountfield, 202
Mountfield Tunnel, 30, 198, 200
Nackington, 238
Naval School, 77
New Beckenham, 133, 134

New Cross, 34, 41, 45, 46, 54, 55, 57-65, 77, 79, 81, 84, 104, 105, 108, 110, 111, 122, 123, 293
New Cross & Naval School, 106
New Cross (LBSCR), 80
New Eltham & Pope Street, 84
New Hythe, 7
New Road, 78
New Romney, 224, 227, 228, 234, 235, 273, 289
Newden, 226
Newhaven, 11, 217, 273, 277
North Camp, 186, 187, 188, 190
North Kent East Junction, 63, 76, 85, 106, 161
North Kent West Junction, 86, 106
Northfleet, 8, 9, 77, 86, 295
Norwood, 11, 13, 14, 59, 110, 130, 131, 132
Norwood Junction, 53
Nutfield, 149, 155
Ore, 195, 196, 203, 208, 211, 212
Orpington, 122, 161, 162, 166
Ostend, 43, 245, 265, 266, 267, 268, 275, 276, 292
Otford, 157, 159, 164, 169, 173
Ottinge, 238
Oxford, 182, 183, 184
Oxted, 8-12, 46, 67, 137, 138, 169, 217, 218, 219, 220, 221, 289
Oxted Lime siding, 220, 221
Oxted Tunnel, 220
Paddock Wood, 142, 144, 146, 149, 152, 153, 154, 157, 158, 159, 170, 171, 173, 223, 224, 225, 226, 295, 299
Papillon's Siding, 202
Paris, 265, 268, 275, 276, 277, 291
Parks Bridge Junction, 81
Pavilion Hotel, 272
Peckham, 14
Penge, 11, 14, 35, 217
Penshurst, 12, 17, 23, 140-144, 154, 155, 193, 297, 299
Pirbright, 187
Pirbright Junction, 188
Plaistow, 167
Pluckley, 19, 145, 153, 173, 175, 224, 284, 286
Plumstead, 7, 79, 86
Polhill, 161
Pope Street, 84, 87
Port Victoria, 46, 51, 95, 99, 101, 102, 276, 304
Portsmouth, 29, 54, 176
Preston, 171
Purley, 13, 68, 69
Quai Bonaparte, 270, 272
Queenborough, 46, 48, 100, 101, 102
Radnor Park, 153, 154
Ramsgate, 7, 8, 10, 34, 35, 64, 75, 141, 148, 240-255, 257, 266, 267, 268, 270, 285, 286, 299
Ravensbourne, 71
Reading, 25, 26, 30, 31, 39, 57, 58, 65, 176, 179-214, 288, 295, 304
Red Gate Mill, 218
Redhill, 13, 14, 16, 18, 40, 49, 53, 55-63, 128, 144, 148, 149, 151, 154, 157, 176, 194, 215, 286, 287, 288, 291, 292, 300, 301
Regent Circus, 110

Reigate, 18, 60, 61, 68, 176, 177, 178, 181, 189, 190, 284, 298, 299
Reigate Junction, 17, 18, 140
Reigate Town, 58
Richborough, 254, 296
Richmond, 39, 118, 179
Rickmansworth, 127
Riddlesdown, 9, 11, 12, 13, 221
Riddlesdown Tunnel, 221
Riddlesdown Viaduct, 220, 221
Riverhead, 67, 168, 169
Robertsbridge, 193, 195-198, 205, 227, 286
Rochester, 8, 9, 26, 70, 75-77, 96, 97, 99, 171, 239, 246
Rochester Bridge, 96, 98, 99, 289
Rochester Common, 98
Rolvenden, 224, 226, 227
Romney Marsh, 211, 212
Rosherville, 75, 84, 90
Rotherfield, 218
Rotherhithe, 46, 63, 78
Rotherhithe Canal, 108
Rotherhithe Road, 63, 86
Round Down, 20
Royal Pavilion Hotel, 260
Ruckinge, 213
Ruckinge Siding, 205
Rye, 23, 25, 192, 193, 194, 208, 209, 210-214, 223, 224, 227, 268
Rye Harbour, 208, 211, 212
Saltwood, 19, 34, 230, 232
Saltwood Castle, 234
Saltwood Tunnel, 230, 234
Sanderstead, 220
Sandgate, 20, 140, 146, 149, 150, 152, 155, 223, 230-236
Sandgate Castle, 233
Sandgate Hill, 235
Sandhurst, 181, 182, 188, 299
Sandhurst College, 179
Sandling Junction, 152, 153, 154, 234, 235
Sandling Park, 12, 152, 230
Sandwich, 41, 244, 251, 252, 253, 254, 296
Sangatte, 280, 281
Sarre, 246
Seabrook, 232, 234, 235
Seabrook Estate, 44, 153
Sellindge, 154
Selsdon, 137, 138
Selsdon Road, 138, 139, 220
Sevenoaks, 7, 35, 47, 158-166, 173, 288
Sevenoaks Junction, 163, 165, 166
Sevenoaks Tunnel, 164, 166
Sevenoaks Weald, 41
Shakespeare Cliff, 14, 15, 18, 20, 152, 154, 280, 281, 303
Shakespeare Cliff Tunnel, 15, 19, 21, 141, 289
Shalford, 178, 180-185, 187, 190
Shalford Junction, 180, 181
Sharnal Street, 100, 102
Sheerness, 43, 46, 75, 95, 99, 100, 101, 276
Sheerness Pier, 51

Shere, 181, 190
Shere Heath, 180, 181
Shirley, 133
Shoreham (Kent), 8, 157
Shorncliffe, 48, 49, 145, 149-155, 232-238, 277
Shorncliffe Camp, 146, 149, 151, 153, 154, 232, 233
Shortlands, 130, 131, 132, 165
Sidcup, 79, 81, 84, 85, 86
Sidley, 206, 207
Sissingshurst, 226
Sittingbourne, 8, 99, 246
Slades Green, 87
Smarden, 192
Smeeth, 20, 141, 143, 149, 151, 153
Smith's Siding, 205
Smitham Bottom, 69
Snodland, 6, 173, 175
South Canterbury, 238
South Croydon, 46, 59, 137
Southampton, 181, 188
Southborough, 203, 205
Southwark Park, 86
Spa Road, 62, 71, 76, 81, 83, 84, 111
St. Catherine's Tunnel, 181
St. George's Fields, 14, 54, 104, 110
St. Johns, 164, 165, 166, 301
St. Leonards, 193-198, 201-205, 210, 217
St. Margaret's Bay, 255, 257, 279, 280
St. Mary Cray, 33, 79, 130, 131, 159, 160
St. Pancras, 121
St. Pauls, 48
St. Thomas' Hospital, 113, 115
Staines, 183
Staplehurst, 17, 142, 144, 146, 148, 154, 155, 170, 193, 224, 225
Stoat's Nest, 14, 16, 53, 56, 58, 61, 133
Stockport, 42
Stoke, 100, 101, 102
Stone, 75
Stoney Street, 118
Stoney Street Junction, 121
Strawberry Hill Tunnel, 196, 200
Strood, 6, 8, 24, 26, 32, 33, 35, 77-81, 86, 90, 92, 94-99, 131, 150, 173, 174, 246, 247, 289, 293, 299
Stroud Green, 134
Sturry, 243, 245, 246, 251, 287, 288, 299
Sun Pier, 92
Sundridge, 169
Sundridge Park, 161, 167
Surrey Canal, 70, 158
Surrey Canal Junction, 106, 165
Sutton, 68
Sutton Valence, 174, 175
Swanley, 96, 159
Swanscombe, 85
Sydenham, 27, 130, 132, 157
Tadworth, 68
Tattenham Corner, 67, 68, 69
Tenterden, 41, 173, 192, 193, 223-227, 229
Three Bridges, 215, 216
Ticehurst, 218

Ticehurst Road, 197, 198, 203, 205, 299
Tilehurst, 185
Titsey, 217
Tivoli Gardens, 247
Tonbridge, 6-9, 12, 13, 15-18, 28, 30, 32, 34-40, 50, 54, 57, 60, 80, 128, 130, 131, 140-144, 148-173, 192-196, 198, 202, 203, 204, 215, 219, 245, 274, 283, 284, 286, 288, 289, 291, 296-299
Tonbridge Junction, 200
Tooley Street, 71
Toomer Loop, 96, 97, 98
Tovil, 174, 175, 225
Tovil Siding, 174
Tudeley, 12, 140
Tunbridge Junction, 145, 220
Tunbridge Wells, 6, 8, 40, 59, 66, 171, 192-198, 201-204, 208, 215-219, 223, 290, 300, 305
Turkey Mill, 175
Turner's Hill, 11
Tyler Hill, 239
Uckfield, 66, 215, 216, 217, 218, 219
Upnor, 95
Upper Caterham, 67
Upper Warlingham, 220, 221
Victoria, 33, 34, 42, 111
Victoria Station, 111
Villiers Street, 115, 116
Wadhurst, 197, 198, 201, 205, 218, 286, 288, 299, 300
Wadhurst Tunnel, 196, 200
Walmer, 251, 252, 253, 254, 255, 256, 258, 284
Walton Heath, 68
Walton-on-the-Hill, 69
Wandsworth, 8
Warehorne, 209
Warlingham, 66, 67
Warrior Square, 201, 202, 203, 204
Wateringbury, 171, 299
Waterloo, 84, 105, 110, 111, 113, 115, 116, 119, 124, 289
Waterloo Junction, 116, 120, 123, 124
Watford, 177
Well Hall, 88, 89
Welling, 89
Wellington College, 186, 190
Wembley Park, 42
Wembley Tower, 51
West Croydon, 11
West Hoathly, 11, 217
West St. Leonards, 204
West Street Junction, 125
West Wickham, 135, 136, 217
Westcombe Park, 82, 85
Westenhanger, 12, 20, 140, 141, 143, 149, 152, 153, 155, 230, 234
Westerham, 67, 136, 159, 165, 167, 168, 169, 217, 219
Westgate, 254
Westminster, 110, 120
Weybridge, 177
Whatlington, 195, 196, 208, 209, 212
Whistable, 243

Whitechapel, 64
Whitstable, 7, 124, 239, 240, 241, 242, 243, 250, 293, 300
Whitstable Harbour, 59, 240, 241, 261
Whyteleafe Crossing, 67
Wickham, 136
Wickham Green, 135
Willesden, 119, 122, 125
Willow Walk, 107
Wimbledon, 118
Winchelsea, 210, 212, 213
Winchester, 188
Windsor, 187
Wingmore, 238
Witherenden, 196, 197
Wokingham, 179, 181, 182, 183, 186, 187, 188, 190, 300
Woldingham, 218, 220, 221
Woodside, 46, 61, 134, 137, 138, 139, 220, 289
Woolwich, 32, 35, 70, 75, 77, 78, 80, 84, 126, 286, 287, 290
Woolwich Arsenal, 77, 78, 84, 85, 96, 126
Woolwich Dockyard, 77, 82
Wouldham, 7
Wye, 6, 244, 245, 247, 248, 251, 299
Yalding, 171, 175

Also from Middleton Press -

CHARING CROSS TO DARTFORD
via Greenwich and Woolwich and including Cannon Street

LONDON BRIDGE TO EAST CROYDON

EAST CROYDON TO THREE BRIDGES
featuring Redhill

READING TO GUILDFORD

GUILDFORD TO REDHILL

ASHFORD TO DOVER
including the Hythe & Sandgate branch

DOVER TO RAMSGATE

TONBRIDGE TO HASTINGS
including the Bexhill West branch

HASTINGS TO ASHFORD
including Rye Harbour, Dungeness and New Romney branches

BRANCH LINE TO ALLHALLOWS
featuring Port Victoria

BRANCH LINE TO HAWKHURST

Many of the former SER lines are illustrated in the popular pictorial albums compiled by Vic Mitchell and Keith Smith and produced by Middleton Press. They do not repeat the historical detail to be found elsewhere but are intended to offer a visual record of the evolution of each station. The 25" to 1 mile Ordnance Survey maps of various editions are included at each location, to show historical detail of both the track layout and the buildings. The development of the station environs is thus similarly revealed. The photographs are arranged in station order and are shown in chronological order at each location.

MP Middleton Press

Easebourne Lane, Midhurst, West Sussex. GU29 9AZ
Tel: (0730) 813169

Diagram of the
South Eastern Railway
in 1898

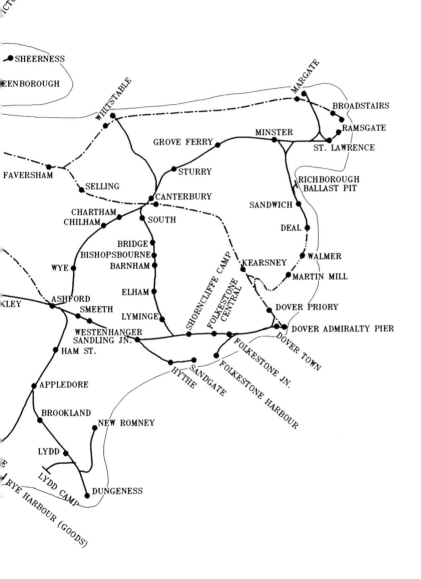

Diagram of the
South Eastern Suburban Line

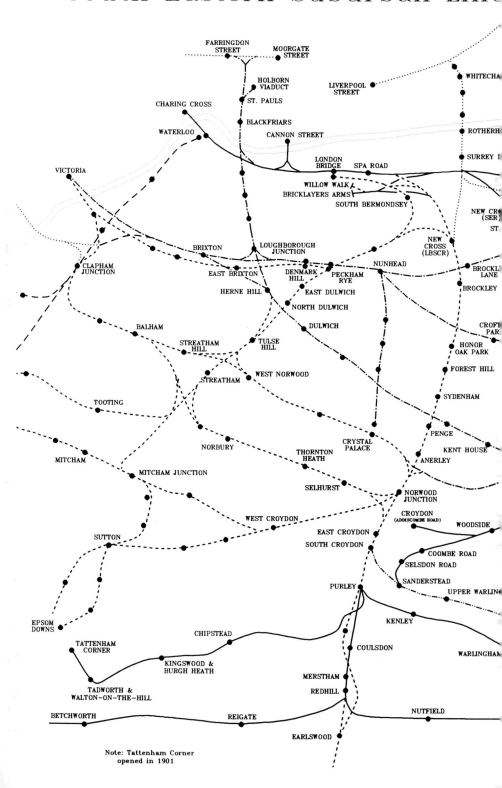

Note: Tattenham Corner
opened in 1901